Michael Bell and Eunjeong Seong

8 Minutes 20 Seconds

Housing After Banking
Encrypting the Sun

ACTAR

Table of Contents

8 Minutes 20 Seconds

1973

December 19: The US Naval Research Laboratory's spectroheliograph was in orbit aboard Skylab.

It captured a "unique electronic photograph of the sun in the extreme ultraviolet radiation from ionized helium (304 angstrom wavelength)."

"One of the most spectacular solar flares ever recorded, spanning more than 588,000 kilometers (367,000 miles) across the solar surface."

"Theoretically, if it were possible to harness the energy of this eruption, it would have provided for all of mankind's power needs for the year 1 A.D. to the present—perhaps the next 2000 years."

Text and Image Source:
Courtesy of Naval Research Labs, Naval Research Labs Solar Spectroheliograph
US Naval Research Labs (NRL) Solar Spectroheliograph imaging of the Sun was sourced from a commemorative postcard published by NRL. The author's father William D. Bell served as lead electronics engineer on the instrument. See also: Donald C. Elder, "The Human Touch: The History of the Skylab Program," National Aeronautics and Space Administration, NASA Office of Policy and Plans. NASA History Office, Washington, D.C., https://history.nasa.gov/SP-4219/Chapter9.html.

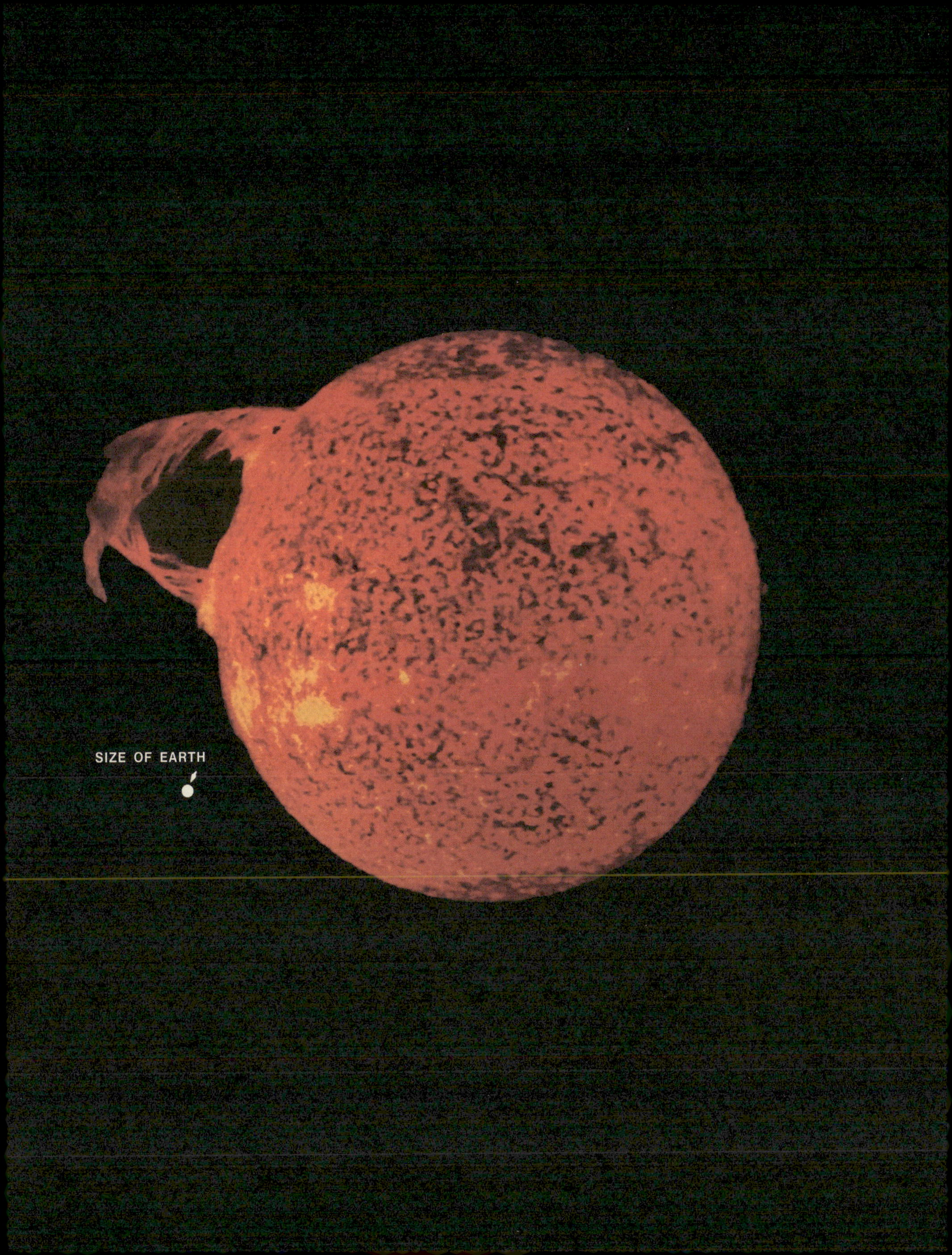
SIZE OF EARTH

2003

"This view of Earth's horizon as the Sun sets over the Pacific Ocean was taken by the Expedition 7 crew on board the International Space Station in 2003. Anvil tops of thunderclouds are also visible."

Courtesy of NASA

Climate change will couple with the advanced automation of labor (of jobs), instigating deep change in the last century's nexus of housing, mobility, and energy in settlement patterns worldwide.

Integrating renewable-energy production into advanced building components turns the past century's home—a real estate asset—into an energy asset oriented to the sky and Sun rather than land, a new photon-based agrarian dwelling.

Housing is realized as a downstream by-product of renewable energy.

Never on the grid and deployable to lower-cost land, it uses advanced manufacturing to be assembled in hours.

... The Sun: five billion years of encrypted basic income.

Model C. 2018–23
Photovoltaic cells are placed in-board of the building envelope. They are easily interchanged in the future with a new cell. In the winter, the heat gain from the cell is used for energy; in the summer, it is vented in a continual air exchange at the upper level of the glazing. Precise and controlled embodied energy: simple and complete disassembly allows recycling. Reuse or downstream deployment are at the ready.

What would it mean for housing:

. . . if energy were abundant rather than scarce?

Renewable energy is actually abundant.

. . . if property was less scribed upon the Earth?

And instead sourced and stewarded in the atmosphere and sky?

Model A. 2017–18
Model A provides 340 square feet of interior space.
It weighs 12,000 lbs.
Solar cells are laminated into the roof structure.
Laminated glass composed of interlayers provides thermal and privacy controls and is optimized for the site, combining renewable energy and precision manufacturing.
Renewable-energy production encrypted in housing can be exported and its value secured.
A distributed renewable-energy production and storage network is created by integrating advanced forms of renewable energy into every aspect of housing materials and production.

What would it take:

. . . to dramatically lower debt accumulations in the private finances of households?

In less than a century, we have spent our future. Household debt increased from 18 percent of GDP to 101 percent between 1945 and 2008. Today they are close to their historical peaks again.

. . . to remove debt and banking from housing?

Can we rely less on future income to pay for shelter? Can we design a house that lowers rather than raises debt?

. . . to remove the role of government in securitizing housing and real-estate debt.

In 2021, the United States Federal Reserve was holding assets worth as much as 35 percent of the nation's GDP, more than five times its 2007 holdings. Central banks worldwide are holding more than twice their World War II peaks.

King Post + Structural Laminated Glass Insulated Panels. 2017–18
A king post cable system holds insulated photovoltaic panels and batteries. The laminated glass is composed of ultraviolet and infra-red-filter interlayers. The system's tall height allows heat to rise. The skin is an active interlayer, or glycol heat sink. Capillary veins maintain thermal control of the interior.

What would it mean:

... to de-commoditize shelter and housing?

What if housing was freed of real-estate valuations?

Housing can instead become a downstream by-product of renewable-energy production.

... What if housing was a utility available without cost to anyone who needed it?

We can monetize what has up to now been called housing as a renewable-energy product instead of real estate, funded by the persistence of the Sun. The would-be house is untethered to an occupant's personal income. It does not know someone is home.

... What if renewable energy expanded and was a proxy for housing?

An abundant supply of solar, wind, and tidal energy offers deep cost reduction in ownership and becomes a surrogate bank and federal treasury, a financial backstop without a central bank.

Models A, B, C. 2017–23
It's not a decarbonization of the grid. It was never on the grid. It's a platform for encrypted and secure energy use and peer-to-peer trade.

… Will development follow the production of renewable energy, and if so, how?

Autonomous vehicles open new territory and land to occupation. Autonomous electric vehicles and transportation as a service promise steep reductions in mobility costs. The nexus of land value and building value is deeply altered, liberated to follow new settlement patterns, full of opportunity, abundance, and entirely new matrices of risk and reciprocity.

Model C. 2018–23
Comprised of laminated glass panels. Manufactured in 47 minutes at scale. Assembled on site in two hours. Glass allows precision; precision allows speed of manufacturing and assembly.

8 Minutes 20 Seconds

Energy generated by nuclear fusion of the Sun reaches the surface of the Earth in 8 minutes and 20 seconds.

Massless photons transmit radiation at the speed of light: 299,792,458 meters or 186,000 miles per second.

If the speed of light is difficult to imagine, it becomes unfathomable when coupled with the duration of a day or the persistence of days over weeks or years. It becomes a light year, or thousands and millions of light years.

Renewable energy in the form of solar radiation reaches Earth in quantities we can't fathom. It is not scarce.
It is non-denumerable.

8 Minutes, 20 Seconds imagines an architecture based on renewable energy, caching forms of energy that are essentially inexhaustible and persistent, and virtually non-denumerable in quantity. It anticipates a *post-scarcity* era enabled and reorganized by a new form of housing that serves as an arbiter of post-sustainability human settlements.

Fossil fuels were formed under intense pressure and heat over 250 to 350 million years ago. Excavated in immense quantities, capitalized and extrapolated into settlement patterns worldwide, their reserves have been culled and are projected to reach depletion after just 150 short years of industrial use. Renewable energy—especially solar energy—transforms our relationship not just from one energy source to another but to a completely other experience of time. The Sun becomes five billion years of encrypted basic income: a perpetual source of unrealized and untitled wealth and security. It eclipses any monetary system or form of economy in scale and unending delivery.

Up to now, architects have been imagining *sustaining* the settlement patterns of a fading economy based in structurally scarce energy, rather than embracing the inexhaustibility of renewable energy. How do we imagine an architecture as a truly new form of settlement—from the materials we employ for building to the energy that fuels production and mobility—when the economy we have built and its physical armatures have been understood as naturally and inevitably scarce? ***8 Minutes, 20 Seconds*** traces the outlines of housing markets and settlements as we know them today—the material and financial means and methods of the recent past—seeking to instigate a new level of imagination and entry into the rescaling of housing industries.

Housing, the shelter essential to all other productivity, is imagined in relation to an emerging and untitled asset: Renewable energy at scales society has never accessed, let alone valued and implemented, becomes a new untethered integer. It provides housing as a downstream by-product of that energy, made possible and conceptualized not as scarce but as a new type of asset altogether.

Job Scarcity and Renewable-Energy Abundance

It is likely, if not inevitable, that the next stages in addressing climate change will take place in an increasingly automated labor environment, a less employed and in some cases jobless society.

The science of climate change and a growing awareness of the need to act is on course to coincide with new advanced forms of automation in labor, artificial intelligence, machine learning, and ultimately, labor displacement. A steep rise in computational power along with decreases in its cost, coupled with access to large data sets, will inevitably disrupt labor markets and private income.

We know that climate migration has already instigated a shift in the last century's nexus of housing, mobility, and energy in settlements worldwide. But addressing climate change and migration is likely to occur without a vast number of the jobs that propelled the last century of development. These lost jobs will be the same ones that funded the expansion of real-estate markets through which housing and shelter emerged. Real estate and financial mechanisms constitute the nexus of development through which government tries to adjudicate social equity and security, for better or worse.

But if progress is being made in addressing sustainability through legislation to increase density and efficiency, for instance, little attention has been given to anticipating the possible character of a near-future economy. In the context of an economy that today is already deeply stressed and inadequate for housing billions of people worldwide, how will development occur, and how will housing and shelter be made possible in an even more precarious, jobless future economy?

In many cases, we have been gaining ground and making the case for the sustainable-development aspirations of 30 years ago, in particular, those defined by the 1987 United Nations *Our Common Future* study. Conceived just as pivotal shifts in the economics of globalization were taking place, the 1987 sustainable-development goals were imagined before an acceleration in internet access altered the territory and sharply reduced the cost of digital communications. Since then, digital control over immense sectors of financial markets, data, and derivatives have radically altered the value of assets. Events like the financial collapse of 2008 led to a massive wealth transfer of what were private homes to hedge funds and private equity.

A photovoltaic panel's cost per watt of electrical output in 1987, at the time of the United Nations sustainable development goals, was approximately $12 per watt. Ten years earlier it was $77 per watt. Today it is less than 50 cents per watt. While wealth inequality has surged since the 1980s and entire sectors of the housing market were traded into private equity in the aftermath of Great Recession, we have simultaneously seen a plunge in the cost of access to renewable energy. This should herald a new wave of tools to address inequity, using the emergence of an expansive new energy resource to give birth to an entirely new imagination of how we build and scale the economics of development. This is an opportunity to build something far more just, but it would be a massively capital-, research-, and development-intensive endeavor. It would require investment applied to housing technologies, something we have never seen before, except in smaller increments through components such as heating, cooling, and recently, digital controls. The 1987 United Nations mandate focused on this concern with respect to developing economies and emphasized the urgency to see sustainability as a shared mission, its success necessitating a global effort. Today this needs to be reevaluated based on indices of development that are increasingly precarious. If household debt in the form of mortgages secured by employment is no longer reliable, the economic foundations for sustainability are cast into question in every region of the world.

We believe there needs to be a dramatic shift in how we understand sustainability. Our technological capacity and the cost to harness renewable energy should not be confused with believing that renewable energy is itself scarce. The capture of renewable energy has up to now primarily been aimed at sustaining settlement patterns as we know them. Yet a near-future situation is emerging: the equation of wealth and ownership that drives housing could be upended by the potential of a new clean energy combined with lack of employment, producing an entirely new economic cartography of energy, debt, employment, where we live, how we build, and how we fund shelter. We believe this is a window of opportunity, a moment in history when entirely new assets are emerging, and their future ownership and valuations are not yet captured by existing industries. Ownership of the future is in play in ways it has not been in a century.

Decarbonizing development is a larger project than housing. The effect of automation on labor immediately calls into question housing as a nexus of settlement and the industrial era's division of home and work, bridging climate work on buildings with mobility. If our near future requires less time away from home, the entire development economy and its territorial distribution can and will change. The future could offer more stability and a more equitable access to shelter and security. But the arbitration of core facets of urbanism such as housing and shelter will be enacted on new terms. ***8 Minutes, 20 Seconds*** recounts our unpacking of some of these terms, informed by 30 years of experience working in the area of housing, including academic research, design studios, and workshops; architectural and urban planning projects commissioned by non-profits and museums; deep collaboration with colleagues in economics, geography, real estate, housing policy, and shelter; as well as volumes on climate and structural engineering, manufacturing, materials science, and energy. Much of this was enabled by our founding of Visible Weather in 2010 as a dedicated research office within our architecture studio and by relationships with those who collaborated with us over the past decade.

8 Minutes, 20 Seconds proposes a housing market securitized by its capacity to produce renewable energy. ***8 Minutes, 20 Seconds*** asks: If housing markets in the United States and the financial systems that back them have ceased to be sustainable as debt models, could housing itself fund its own existence through the production of renewable energy, replacing the role of credit and banking? To do this, the cost to produce housing would have to be amortized—paid in advance, like an investment in a series of small autonomous factories—to mirror its capacity to produce, store, and trade renewable energy. This cannot be accomplished within current methods of development, prefabrication, or construction. We believe such an investment in renewable-energy-generative housing cannot be addressed with current forms of debt and backstopping of government debt and that the way debt has been used is in fact a detriment to advancing a new, more equitable, and accessible form of housing.

8 Minutes, 20 Seconds proposes a form of housing only achievable through advanced manufacturing. What was a housing asset becomes a new form of energy asset. Would this be more appropriately called a renewable-energy asset? This geospatial hardware integrates energy production, storage, and transmission into every building component—an unimaginable goal in the current housing industry, either at the level of components, or fabrication, or construction. **Part One: Housing After Banking** traces a historical path that shows how the possibility of renewable energy-producing housing is not only reasonable but urgent if one looks closer at how few people current housing markets serve and how many owners and renters are burdened by debt and real-estate-driven risk. **Part Two: Encrypting the Sun** explores how we would create such a product, not only in terms of the design team, engineering, and materials science, but most critically, the need to aggregate capital for sophisticated research and development.

		Model C		Model B		Model S	
Roof Size	unit	sq ft	sq meters	sq ft	sq meters	sq ft	sq meters
		410	38	**800**	74	**1500**	139
Solar Panel Number	1 Panel: 17.5 sf	**23**	Panels	**46**	Panels	**86**	Panels
Power (kW/ Panel): DC power	**400W(.4kW)**	**9**	kW(DC)	**18**	kW(DC)	**34**	kW(DC)
Power (kW/ Panel): AC power	10% loss	**8**	kW(AC)	**16**	kW(AC)	**31**	kW(AC)
1 **Solar Production Electricity**							
Daily Energy (kWh)	Solar Hours = 5.5	46	kWh/ Day	91	kWh/ Day	**170**	kWh/ Day
Monthly Energy (kWh)	30 days	1,415	kWh/ Month	2,761	kWh/ Month	**5,176**	kWh/ Month
Yearly Energy (kWh)	365 days	16,932	kWh/ Year	33,038	kWh/ Year	**61,946**	kWh/ Year
2 **Consumption Electricity**							
IF U.S. Average House	0.45 kWh/ sf	**185**	kWh/ Month	**360**	kWh/ Month	**675**	kWh/ Month
IF Model C/B/S = 40% U.S. Average	0.18 kWh/ sf	**74**	kWh/ Month	**144**	kWh/ Month	**270**	kWh/ Month
Consumption Model C / B / S		**886**	kWh/ Year	**1,728**	kWh/ Year	**3,240**	kWh/ Year
3 **Sale Electricity**							
Sale after Use / Total Monthly	kWh/ Month	**1,341**	kWh/ Month	**2,617**	kWh/ Month	**4,906**	kWh/ Month
Sale after Use / Total Annual	kWh/ Year	**16,093**	kWh/ Year	**31,400**	kWh/ Year	**58,875**	kWh/ Year
Sale kWh to $ / **Annual**	$ 0.20 / kWh	**$3,219**	Dollars/ Year	**$6,280**	Dollars/ Year	**$11,775**	Dollars/ Year
Sale kWh to $ / **Month**		**$268**	Dollars/ Month	**$523**	Dollars/ Month	**$981**	Dollars/ Month
Sale kWh to $ / **15 Yrs**		**$48,278**	Dollars/ 15 Yrs	**$94,201**	Dollars/ 15 Yrs	**$176,626**	Dollars/ 15 Yrs
4 **Purchase Cost**							
Sale Price		**$80,000**	Dollars	**$152,000**	Dollars	**$250,000**	Dollars
Monthly Mortgage / 100% finance	15 YR @ 4%	**$590**	Dollars/ Month	**$1,124**	Dollars/ Month	**$1,849**	Dollars/ Month
Mortgage Interest	amortized total	**$26,515**	Dollars/ 15 Yrs	**$50,379**	Dollars/ 15 Yrs	**$82,860**	Dollars/ 15 Yrs
Mortgage Interest	if flat / monthly	**$147**	Dollars/ Month	**$280**	Dollars/ Month	**$460**	Dollars/ Month
Sale kWh to $	monthly	**$268**	Dollars/ Month	**$523**	Dollars/ Month	**$981**	Dollars/ Month
Net Mortgage after Energy Sale	monthly	**$322**	Dollars/ Month	**$601**	Dollars/ Month	**$868**	Dollars/ Month
Households that can Afford	without energy sale	84.30%		66.70%		50.50%	
	with energy sale	92%		84.30%		76.70%	

Solar Bank–Personal Energy

The United States Energy Information Administration (EIA) calculates that the US consumed 101.41 quadrillion (quads) British thermal units (BTUs) in 2022. Production was 102.91 quads.

Renewable energy accounted for 13 percent or 13.40 quads. Solar energy accounted for just 14 percent of renewables or 1.88 quads. Residential real estate accounts for 16 percent of consumption, but just eight percent of residential real-estate energy was sourced from renewables. Natural gas and utility-level electricity fueled largely by natural gas are the primary sources of residential real estate's power needs. Natural gas and utility-provided electricity each represent more than 40 percent of household energy consumption.

In the spreadsheet Solar Bank–Personal Energy, we project a benchmark cost for a new energy product as shelter. A 410-square-foot accessory dwelling unit, the Model C–ADU, is manufactured at scale with the efficiency and sophistication of automobile assembly lines, its integral solar-energy production used to offset mortgage interest, effectively creating a mortgage-free shelter. Over a fifteen-year mortgage, the building would generate approximately $48,278 of electricity (at present value) that is tradable, offsetting $26,515 of would-be interest and a large portion of the overall mortgage. This assumes 100 percent financing at a four percent interest rate over 15 years and a target price of $80,000. The monthly mortgage of $590 would be reduced by income from the sale of $268 worth of electricity. Model C would be within reach of 92 percent of households, supplemented by energy sale income.[1] A large 1,500-square-foot dwelling, Model S, sold at a target price of $250,000, would be within reach 76.7 percent, excluding land. The buildings, if amortized at longer terms, could fund their purchase if they were the primary source of energy for other services and industries.

8 Minutes, 20 Seconds, Part Two, Encrypting the Sun, explores the design and engineering of a dwelling that consumes a small fraction of the energy normally required for shelter, creating an excess salable form of energy. That energy would be moved to other local sectors of development such as commercial, industrial, and transportation.

The opportunity to diminish total electric generation and transmission losses would be a tremendous benefit provided by a local renewable-energy grid powered by the residential sector. EIA research shows that most "electrical system energy losses occur in the generation of electricity at electric power plants, which use primary energy to turn electric generators." Transmission losses are estimated at five percent, but totals including plant-based losses are as high as 24 percent. A local renewable grid could dramatically lower losses.

A disruptive product replaces power plants and an entire industry of subcomponents. ***8 Minutes, 20 Seconds*** presents research and design that would bring housing expenditure to a lower cost, not as a result of federal or state subsidies but as technologically advanced manufacturing and secured, yet-to-be-titled, renewable-energy assets for those living in the homes and sustaining their production and maintenance.

A quasi-agrarian project harvesting zero-carbon electricity localizes energy production and effectively encrypts its value on behalf of its owner-harvesters. Such renewable-energy housing would not be monetized as real estate but instead as clean energy and universal basic income for an era that is sure to be more automated and less traditionally employed.

Parallel Paths and Convergence

8 Minutes, 20 Seconds is organized in two parts that we imagine as two parallel books and media, made into one and bound together. The work presented in each book was developed along parallel paths. In concentrated ways, we focused for weeks at a time on one body of work, while creating notes and sketches that established ideas that would impact the other. We worked with each other this way and with our partners and mentors in housing, housing advocacy, and economics, as well as real estate, engineering, advanced manufacturing, and materials science.

The two books do not have a one-to-one relationship: one does not cause the other, and the impacts, while real, are not intended as overtly correspondent. Each is offered as a way into a field of work we hope to help define as much as offer paths and solutions to. Instead, each body of work sets a stage of concerns that the other might address, alter, and ideally disrupt. Equipped with enough knowledge about housing economics, can we imagine a better way to eliminate housing scarcity? With enough knowledge about the photochemistry of photovoltaics, can we invent a new version of them? As our work evolved, we were increasingly guided by an overarching question: could a future of renewable-energy assets beget housing? Instead of housing being made sustainable by the addition of renewable-energy products, could we simply design a new type of energy product itself?

We began the project with a then-nascent title that has stayed with us: **Housing After Banking**. At the outset, this indicated a hypothesis but also a concern. We asked ourselves, is housing the economic powerhouse and foundation of our economy to the extent we imagine? How does the near-century of federal support for housing since the New Deal evolve, and especially in recent decades, how do massive government and central bank interventions in housing markets shape and mask the actual instability

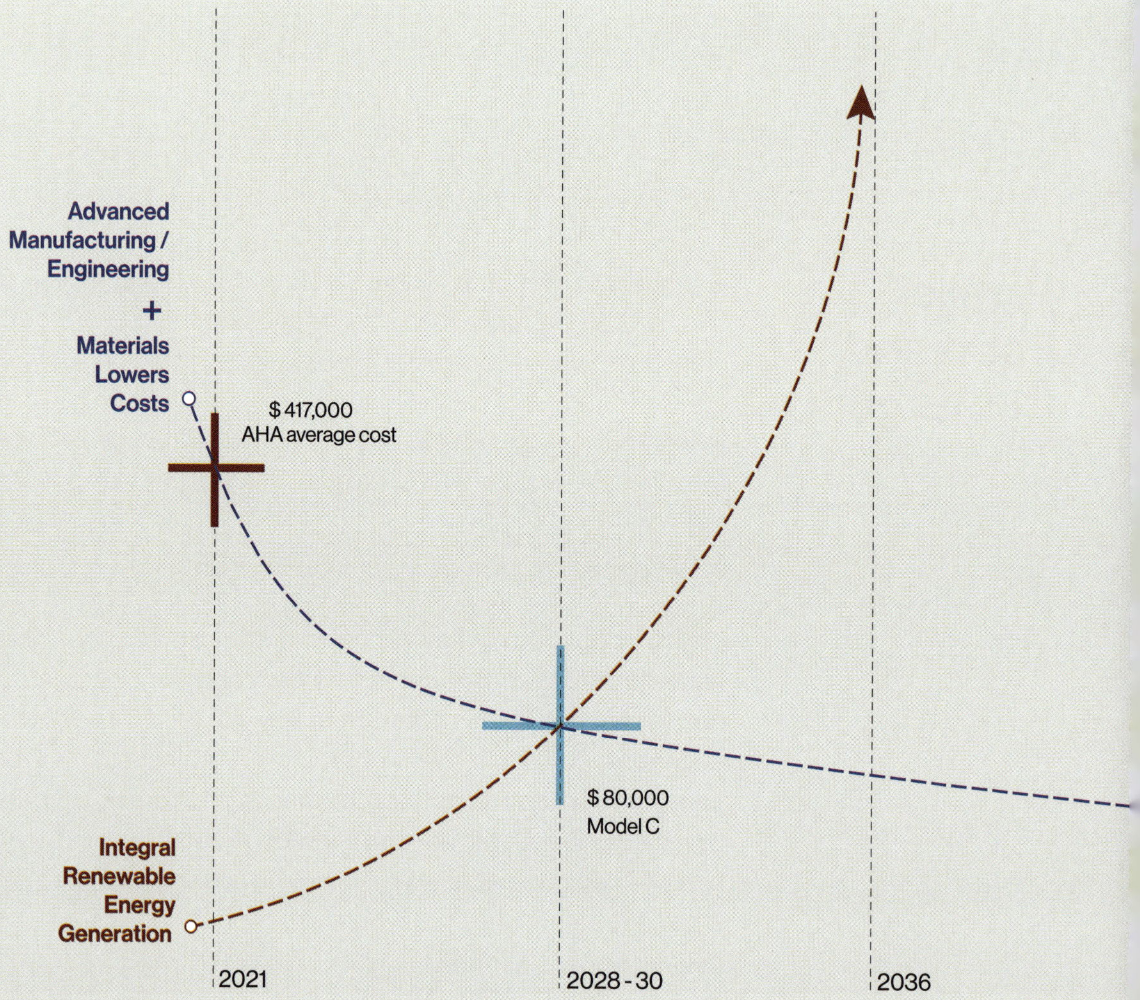
Advanced Manufacturing / Engineering
+
Materials Lowers Costs
$ 417,000
AHA average cost
$ 80,000
Model C
Integral Renewable Energy Generation
2021
2028 - 30
2036

2036 Distributed Renewable-Energy Trade to Industry with Direct Payment
Domestic excess energy yield powers industry and provides universal income

2030 Subscriptions Services (Macro) Block Chain Trade to Utility
Excess energy yield traded outside community via block chain

2028 Subscriptions Services (Local) Energy Share and Trade
Energy yield allocated to personal mobility and community trade

2026 Housing becomes an Energy Asset
Software, development, partners, community of homes

2022 Energy Value = 15 Year Finance Cost of House (Eventually covers cost of shelter)
Advanced manufacturing allows cost reduction to and from supply chain and labor advances
Manufacturing of house in less than 1 hour

Housing After Banking

By use of advanced manufacturing and logistics, such as those used in automobile supply chains, housing labor and costs could be lowered by levels that allow its production to be deeply underwritten by integrated renewable-energy production and sale. Settlement and housing become, in part, a project of developing a distributed renewable-production network. A grid with little carbon footprint or climate externalities after implementation could afford shelter and housing as a downstream by-product.

In making new use of the advanced logistics of automobile supply chains, this by-product anticipates an emerging era of electric vehicles and transportation as a service (TAAS) that increasingly decrease automobile production. There will be a need to repurpose this supply chain. Such an enterprise would rely on being capitalized as a technology company with levels of research and development to sustain the experimentation needed for a project at such a large scale.

of housing markets and the physical architecture and jobs that underlie them. Our backgrounds in housing have long made us doubt the true vitality of housing markets and the forms of punitive scarcity they presage for most people. But nearly 50 years into a receding welfare state, we doubt a meaningful scale of direct government participation in addressing the real need will exist anytime soon.

These issues take some unpacking, and the book offers this, but preliminarily, we take on this project to test not just new solutions but a new path, or more accurately, parallel paths that sustain a non-convergence toward easy answers until enough is known to imagine fully new directions. In our case, we hope to offer new ways to imagine the nexus of economic relations (jobs, government support, private-sector investment, energy production, short-term profit-making) from which housing emerges and to propose a new goal, a new asset, a new product, and a new economy from which to imagine this nexus. This would likely not be possible with traditional real-estate partners and architecture-world colleagues whose expertise meets ours, so we have developed the project with a view to potential technology, venture capital, and manufacturing partnerships, but it's also critical that everyone try to understand the parameters and potentials of each profession, type of partner, and end-user.

8 Minutes, 20 Seconds offers a body of work undertaken in design and engineering, but it also traces a nexus of factors that have shaped housing in the United States over the past 80 years to suggest that there is indeed an emerging moment for something far larger than incremental change. It also resets terms from sustainable development, suggesting that the call for a just transition to a sustainable future can be reasonably accomplished with the help of technology in collaboration with planning and design.

8 Minutes, 20 Seconds is organized to invite readers to hover over the recent past and near future, and to see connections that could yield entirely new outcomes if assimilated into design. This is a moment where change must be critically demanded, but also where former regimes of housing, housing finance, development, mobility, and energy are coming undone, revealing the level of disruption possible. We address scarcity in housing, for instance, and suggest that classical economic understandings of scarcity are in many ways misplaced in housing. Not only is the lack of access to shelter deeply real and damaging to hundreds of millions of lives, but housing markets as we know them are so fraught with complications tied to regulation, financing, access to debt, labor, and an assemblage of material sub-components and markets that it would be beneficial to distinguish the many points where housing and scarcity manifest themselves. At which sub-levels and sub-markets of the shelter industry does market failure occur? Which if any of these markets and sub-markets are even concerned to address actual need? Our research asks if the largest homebuilders in the United States are capitalized in ways that would allow them to address scarcity: Can they fund innovation that would alter delivery of housing? We think they cannot. Can they broaden their ability to address a range of incomes or a lack of incomes? Median new housing costs preclude most buyers. Can they imagine other consumers? Markets sometimes take this on as rentals or other short-term non-wealth-building mechanisms.

We do not believe housing markets as we know them will address the wider scope of need, and, as such, classical understandings of scarcity constitute a misplaced performance benchmark. Because of the way housing is built, markets cannot on the aggregate level solve this. Housing sub-components and commodity items are, however, more measurable as beneficiaries of market-driven innovation. So too are spatial denominators and measurements of housing. For example, housing on a per-square-foot basis is more than 45 percent more energy efficient today than it was in 1985. Insulation, windows, and mechanical equipment have provided this. Discrete components like these have benefitted from technical analysis and research; they diminish scarcity and simultaneously act as agents of an expanding market. This can be countered by pointing to a now fifty-year-long decline in how and where government enters housing markets. Large-scale public direct aid and expenditure by the federal government in the form of public housing was transposed into tax credits and rent vouchers, subsidizing markets that have not, themselves, performed. Housing is scarce to the unsheltered, but to solve this we must break down what we call housing and reassemble the parts that are worth keeping. Where we have tolerated the experience of scarcity, we often imagine the cruelty of markets justifies it. But we must ask, are these really markets? Why accept the cruelty?

There is a demand to forecast the near future and to ask how and whether equity and security might be produced in markets we have yet to create, even as we analyze the problems of historical and recent markets. If renewable energy is increasingly imagined as the substrate of future human settlements, in the sense that energy is a precondition of modern housing yet is limited and increasingly dangerous to life in its predominant carbon-based forms, we can ask, how does one form a market for a product that is abundant rather than scarce. Instead of repairing a flawed market-based housing model, let's focus on assuring a more equitable renewable-energy market. This is a watershed moment when there is a massive tranche of unassigned wealth before us, theoretically available to society. How are we preparing to imagine a fairer and more just world given the potential for production of new wealth of an immense scale? This is a question for anyone involved in the future of the built environment, but it also requires a team that can imagine the parallel paths of housing and energy that must converge to make such a new world.

Book Organization

The primary medium of Part One: Housing After Banking is an extended text, based on academic research focused on the past century of housing policy and legislation. Housing After Banking explores housing economics and valuations, and, more broadly, the nexus of forces that have shaped real estate's role in economic development, especially in the decades since World War II and after 1971, when the Bretton Woods Agreement that shaped post-war international monetary policy collapsed. The role of federal legislation is here examined, especially where it points to failures of housing markets to serve the full scope of the public's needs, as well as its reluctance to instigate competition between the public and private sectors or to intrude into markets. Organized in six chapters, Housing After Banking focuses on housing and development through a lens of major 20th century legislation, policy, and economics, as well as on energy and renewable-energy research and legislation that promised to produce not only sustainability but new markets.

The essential hypothesis and thread through this work is that housing as we know it today in the United States, understood as a product of speculative real-estate development, has a relatively short history that is not as homogenous as is often assumed. A closer look at housing's history in relation to economies, political ideology, and major historical events reveals that housing in the decades since the end of World War II is far from consistent in its dependence on debt and appreciation, and its reliability as an asset. It has increasingly become volatile, not only in the post-1970s globalized economy but even more so in the 1990s and during the major economic upheavals of the first two decades of the 21st century. Even as home ownership has clearly produced wealth, its shifting valuations drive major fluctuations in household net worth, especially since the 1990s. Land comprises the largest component of home ownership for single-family homes in much of the nation and is more volatile than the structure, the house itself.

All of this points to a level of risk born by speculation that makes the role of architecture and building far less important to affordability. The profile of this risk is far from consistent. We ask, what can design offer this equation? We suggest that a far more comprehensive scope of design offers an opportunity to rescale housing. Indeed, how is housing scaled today? Is there a new way to imagine a future that accelerates access to research and development—capital-to-seed innovation—as it simultaneously enables a flow of wealth through renewable energy? One side of the equation is market- and profit-driven, based in new industrial benchmarks. The other side is an endless tide of new wealth—an excess that evades markets, if not assigned and measured on behalf of an owner. In this case, a localized owner, the household that purchases the energy-caching house, becomes the end-user of a peer-to-peer or peer-to-industry market.

Housing After Banking offers evidence that the nexus that sustains housing valuations is far less stable than it appears, and that in its current state, housing markets have left a vast number of households underserved, unhoused, or housing-cost burdened. The deep array of federal interventions to support housing markets and home ownership since the New Deal, after World War II, in the post-1970s, and after the Great Recession have dramatically increased the leveraging of speculative markets. In the future, will housing in the United States, broadly speaking, still be able to sustainably fund and reinvent itself within long-running banking and mortgage systems that have fueled its growth over the last 80 years? Moreover, have federal, state, and city-based interventions in what today is broadly called "affordable housing," or previously, "public housing," really ever been capable of spurring the production of anywhere near what was imagined or needed to shelter those that markets failed to reach? What makes us tolerate such levels of housing inequity, and does the steep rise in renewable energy before us offer a new potential to change the very economy of housing?

The contents of **Housing After Banking** take the form of short essays—we like Robert Wilson's term "knee plays," or a series of connected vignettes—that each trace a zone of research in economics and development. This work has been developed over many years and has helped fuel experimental architectural, industrial, and engineering proposals that are in turn guided by expertise in materials, advanced manufacturing, and energy. The short essays in Housing After Banking are not exhaustive but attempt to span a significant scope of what we imagine is pivotal and surprising detail. We hope it allows us to convene future work with others and to expand the discussion of what is possible. The idea of a parallel path for us has meant avoiding convergence on a would-be given—an assumed framing of a problem—instead allowing an eventual, incremental reframing of the problem with new parameters. This method relies on accessing and graphing a body of determining factors that are often outside the domain of any one discipline or any one participant. In this regard, we note our partners and colleagues, especially in the design and engineering body of work.

While we certainly offer professional detail, we also play with the idea of each chapter as a prompt for a would-be *method acting*, the discovering of a character's identity in real time. In this case, one form of motivation (fossil fuels) gives way to an as-yet-unknown protagonist: interaction with renewable energy replaces housing as the object we are designing. This puts the economics of housing on a different stage and leaves the professional conditioning of architecture unbound by a script, which is not just being revised but may be gone and extinguished altogether.

We have assembled each chapter in a linear sequence, but they were written in a non-linear order, and we think they should be read as explorations among these parallel paths. The book can be read out of sequence.

At hand is an overarching question of scale considered from six vantage points. Each chapter offers detail that impacts the others. The final query: how does what has been called housing become rescaled as an industry, producing high-tech jobs and a complex manufactured product that generates renewable energy as an abundant resource? We imagine this resets the creative mind's horizon in the engineering and design of structures and in the assumptions of the underlying economic system. We believe that today we take for granted that a sustainable-energy economy will create enough new advanced jobs and income to host a 30-year mortgage. If such jobs are scarce but energy is abundant, an entirely new form of housing markets is needed.

The primary medium of **Part Two: Encrypting the Sun** is design, but it encompasses engineering, materials science, advanced manufacturing, supply-chain logistics, and most of all, renewable energy. We have long worked closely with partners in economics and housing, but here we have developed a deep connection with peers in advanced manufacturing and engineering, especially the realm of "design for manufacturing" (DFM). Over the course of this book and the development of the work it presents, we have increasingly collaborated with engineering, materials science, and supply-chain partners in Silicon Valley and in the automotive realm, particularly manufacturers of electric automobiles. This period of work brought us into discussions with design-engineering experts as well as financial and venture capital partners who have focused on the fusion of computation and manufacturing. This fusion has had an explosive effect on human productivity, far exceeding any previous level to date.

Encrypting the Sun presents an evolutionary new body of work that began by reverse engineering a work of architecture we completed in 2007.

A steel-and-glass dwelling, the Binocular House, designed for Richard Press and Philip Gefter, was analyzed with the goal of identifying its embodied energy, bill of materials, weights, and quantities of materials and labor. The house's current owners, Young Sohn and Mark Armenante, allowed our team new access to the house. We then began a process of reimagining it completed with dramatic reductions in materials and labor, and its operational energy profile. This work evolved over five years and is ongoing. Here we offer a snapshot of the major steps.

While the design work is informed by academic research, it also instigated new research paths. The design work helped us imagine alternative forms of economy and housing legislation. It caused us to look closer at housing policy and federal policy around renewable energy. We were thrilled as we explored and followed the evolution of 1970s congressional policy during early efforts to promote experiments in renewable energy. Chapter five of **Housing After Banking** covers this carefully, investigating a moment when renewable energy was seen as both "inexhaustible" and bound for commodities and manufacturing markets.

How can one create a market for something not scarce? A thesis of our work was already lodged in 1970s law. Designing with experts in various fields allowed us to imagine alternative ways to recover latent and missed opportunities in historically critical legislation. What, for example, did the 1970s offer in terms of federal funding for solar energy compared to today? How did the legislation encourage cross-disciplinary teams to experiment in ways that markets left untouched? We came to see this work as another form of design: designing teams, designing the parameters of an experiment, designing legislation that could open new products and thereby new markets.

While we found ourselves increasingly agile with economic data and its sources—such as the Federal Reserve Flow of Funds—***8 Minutes, 20 Seconds*** is a design project in every way. We feel more confident of this as we finalize the book: it is devoted to *redesigning what we design*. It has allowed us to offer a pathway to change the replication of scarcity that we have tolerated in housing for decades. We imagine this potential through the invention of a new asset altogether: a personal energy asset, or renewable energy encrypted as universal basic income.

Much of our work was done in collaboration with advisors, but it was fully centered in our office in New York and over the course of many months in Berkeley, California, where we set up a satellite studio. It was a skunkworks to share ideas with Bay Area and Los Angeles partners. The Berkeley studio brought us back to a former home base, the long shadow of UC Berkeley's Bauer-Wurster Hall, and to Catherine Bauer's immense contributions to housing policy and design aimed at rescaling housing as an industrial and social instrument after the Great Depression.

Housing After Banking / Encrypting the Sun

Housing After Banking was not anti-banking at its inception, nor is it anti-banking today. It is not anti-capitalism or anti-innovation. It asked, then and now, what we can make of a housing market that carries mountains of evidence of wealth creation but has done so in increasingly risk-laden markets reliant on the immense public burden of supplying infrastructure, preferential taxes, securitized mortgages, and investor bailouts. The first chapter opens with this focus: the role of debt and leverage, and thereby risk at the personal and federal level, including the highly risk-producing variable interest rates set by the Federal Reserve Bank. The success of housing as we know it today has been achieved in very uneven and often unfair ways. Since the 1970s, it has provided millions of people housing but by way of deeply mortgaged property. It has exposed us to often dramatic fluctuations in valuations. Over the past five decades, the ebb and flow of urbanization and its pressures on valuations, particularly on land and in territories rich with jobs, has turned housing markets into a casino, and one that excludes entry to vast numbers of people.

As governments, industry, and society begin to grapple with new forms of digital automation and their impacts on labor and jobs, a critical inquiry and correlation becomes more and more urgent. The jobs most susceptible to automation and displacement are in the realm of "opportunity employment," professions available to those without a college degree that allow one to live within the area median income. When governments enact legislation to measure affordability, they frequently frame access around area median income. Projections about automation are by necessity speculative and diverse—they emerge with motives—yet regional Federal Reserve Banks and private industry all anticipate extreme vulnerability in lower skilled and less specialized professions. In Phoenix, Arizona, for example, "opportunity employment" accounts for 31 percent of the region's 2,116,640 jobs, according to the Federal Reserve Bank of Atlanta.[2] Their research correlates opportunity employment with cities, offering a window into how labor automation relates to housing costs and the potential loss of housing.

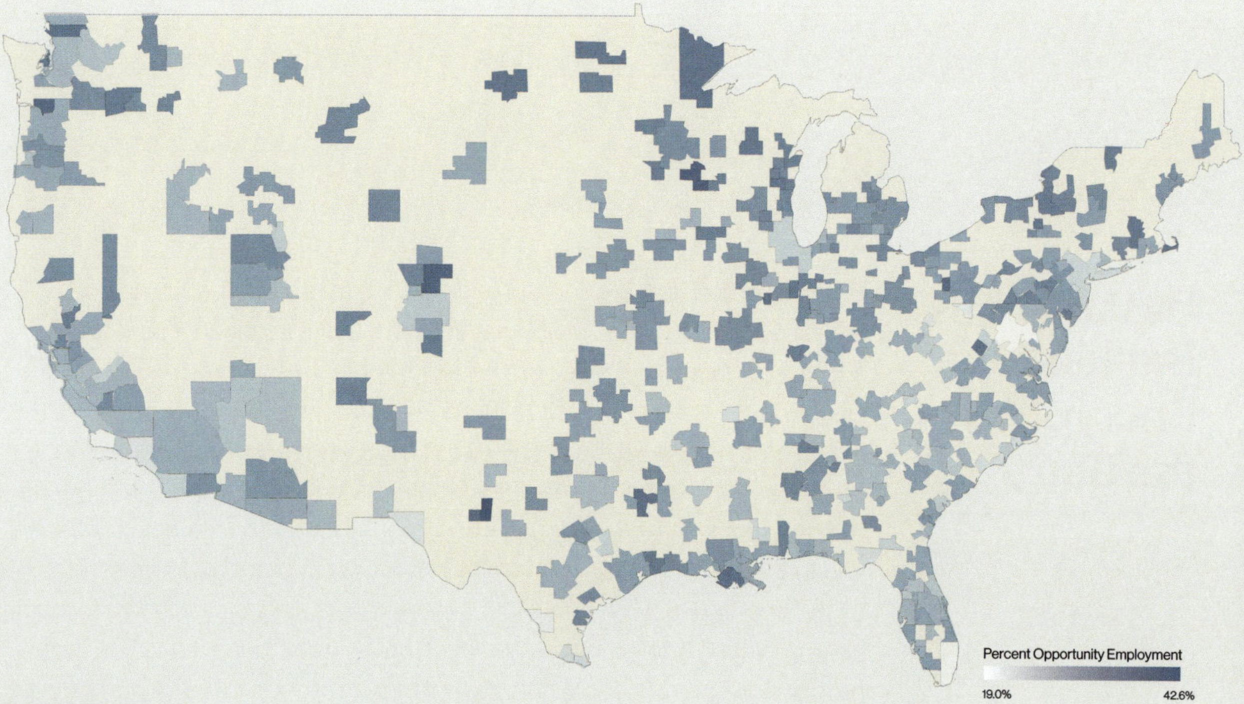
Percent Opportunity Employment
19.0%
42.6%

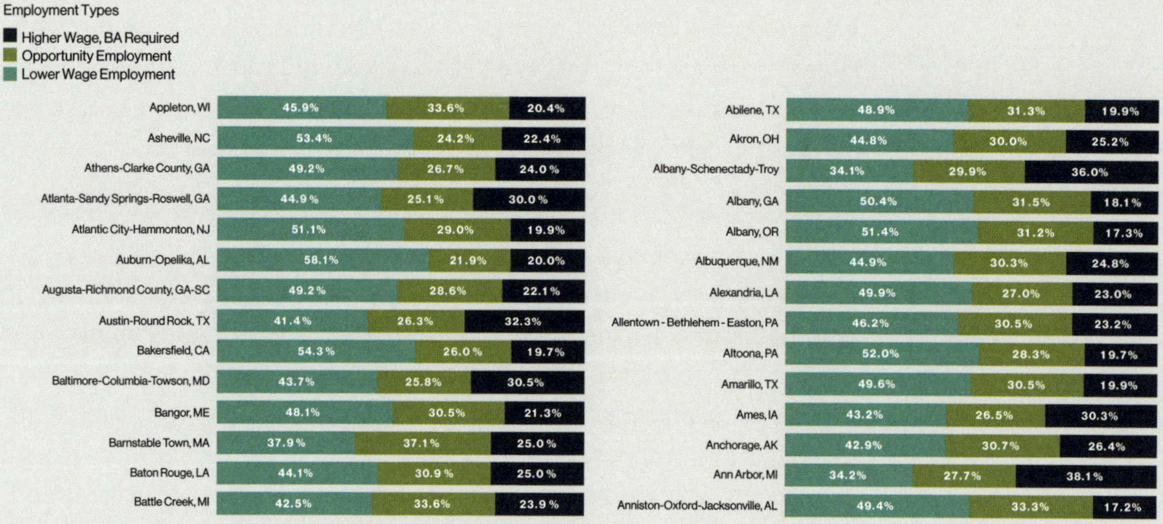
Employment Types
Higher Wage, BA Required
Opportunity Employment
Lower Wage Employment
Appleton, WI 45.9% 33.6% 20.4%
Asheville, NC 53.4% 24.2% 22.4%
Athens-Clarke County, GA 49.2% 26.7% 24.0%
Atlanta-Sandy Springs-Roswell, GA 44.9% 25.1% 30.0%
Atlantic City-Hammonton, NJ 51.1% 29.0% 19.9%
Auburn-Opelika, AL 58.1% 21.9% 20.0%
Augusta-Richmond County, GA-SC 49.2% 28.6% 22.1%
Austin-Round Rock, TX 41.4% 26.3% 32.3%
Bakersfield, CA 54.3% 26.0% 19.7%
Baltimore-Columbia-Towson, MD 43.7% 25.8% 30.5%
Bangor, ME 48.1% 30.5% 21.3%
Barnstable Town, MA 37.9% 37.1% 25.0%
Baton Rouge, LA 44.1% 30.9% 25.0%
Battle Creek, MI 42.5% 33.6% 23.9%
Abilene, TX 48.9% 31.3% 19.9%
Akron, OH 44.8% 30.0% 25.2%
Albany-Schenectady-Troy 34.1% 29.9% 36.0%
Albany, GA 50.4% 31.5% 18.1%
Albany, OR 51.4% 31.2% 17.3%
Albuquerque, NM 44.9% 30.3% 24.8%
Alexandria, LA 49.9% 27.0% 23.0%
Allentown - Bethlehem - Easton, PA 46.2% 30.5% 23.2%
Altoona, PA 52.0% 28.3% 19.7%
Amarillo, TX 49.6% 30.5% 19.9%
Ames, IA 43.2% 26.5% 30.3%
Anchorage, AK 42.9% 30.7% 26.4%
Ann Arbor, MI 34.2% 27.7% 38.1%
Anniston-Oxford-Jacksonville, AL 49.4% 33.3% 17.2%

Housing in expensive, job-rich markets in the United States has been under severe pressure for 50 years. A loss of opportunity jobs along with lack of job migration will couple with climate migration to accelerate the housing crisis. This is an opportunity for a new form of housing as renewable-energy asset to stabilize shelter and secure income for households, while also addressing climate change and settlement patterns. Legislation addressing affordability over the past 50 years has largely incentivized small nonprofit builders, leaving little capital for research and development. Chapter four discusses this in detail. We imagine that decarbonizing development could also mean enhancing housing security and even universal income.

When asked in bare terms, the question is startling. We increasingly felt it was not extreme: What if housing was no longer realized as a form of or add-on of real estate? While we acknowledge that, historically, titles and deeds have been closely tied to household security, we want to ask a new and parallel question: what if shelter is secured by energy and time of a profoundly different duration and character. Assembling parts and materials that harvest renewable energy becomes not a radical rejection of wealth or titles but a highly capitalized new industry and source of jobs itself. But more importantly, it forms a downstream basis for universal income in the form of shelter and energy, when encrypted, digital-token-like, as a distributed renewable-energy network. Renewable energy as housing would constitute a new asset class, a new product. More people would be served and sheltered than in former markets, as well as by public-and- affordable-housing regimes.

In this equation, people are not afforded shelter because of their capacity as real-estate consumers. Housing instead manifests a relationship to the spatial coordinates of the Sun, replacing real-estate models that have often driven municipal land policies and federal and state tax structures.

It would be an immense revaluation of settlements and dramatically alter the grounds of sustainability models.

Housing is not a right in the United States, and government intervention in markets for housing has in countless ways been offered and then been undone or dissimulated in the US. Despite that, the federal government has spent trillions shoring up housing markets, even as it claims it is not a competitor or is unwilling to intervene in housing. We have to ask, when was the last time a new hard asset was made, invented, or discovered? Has capital been endlessly swirling in the nonproductive pools of concrete, timber, and aluminum that we call housing? If this has been productive for wealth creation and some investors, it has also served as punishment for the non-housed, barely housed, and rent-burdened.

As we write these installments, we hope this book unpacks what we learned and unlearned during nearly 30 years of work in housing as researchers, designers, architects, engineers, academics, editors, curators, and at times activists.

In the spring of 2023, the failure of three United States banks—Silicon Valley Bank, Signature Bank, and First Republic Bank—occurred over seven weeks. The rapid succession of three regional bank failures, according to financial reporting, resulted from their vulnerability to Federal Reserve inflation-induced interest-rate hikes that devalued long-term bonds held by the banks. The risk associated with these three banks was quickly described as containable but not without immense government intervention to secure large bank-held accounts that exceeded the levels normally insured by the Federal Deposit Insurance Corporation (FDIC).

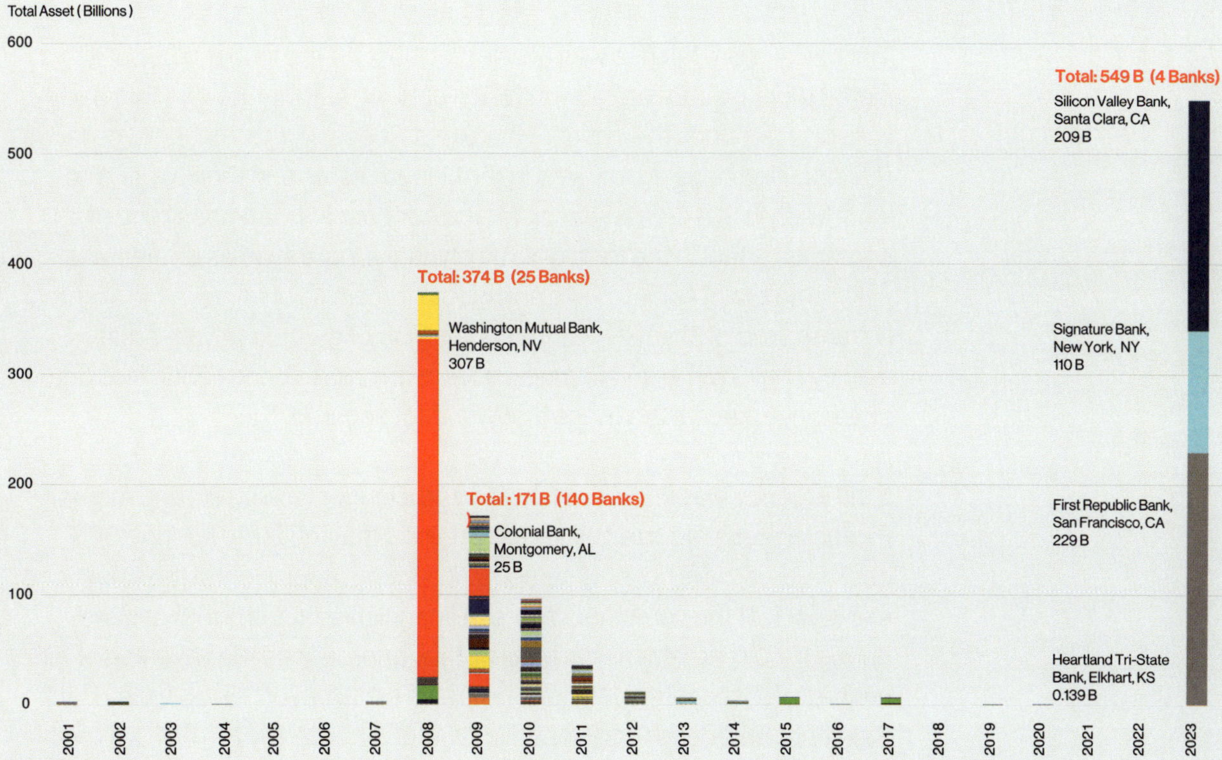

Year	2001	2002	2003	2004	2005	2006	2007	2008	2009	2010	2011	2012	2013	2014	2015	2016	2017	2018	2019	2020	2021	2022	2023
Number of banks	4	11	3	4	0	0	3	25	140	157	92	51	24	18	8	5	8	0	4	4	0	0	4
Approx. Asset (Millions)	$2,358	$2,705	$1,045	$163	$0	$0	$2,602	$373,588	$170,909	$96,514	$36,012	$12,055	$6,101	$3,088	$6,727	$278	$6,530	$0	$214	$458	$0	$0	$548,639

Bank Failures: 2001–2023: 566 banks failed between 2001 and 2023, according to the Federal Deposit Insurance Corporation (FDIC).[3] Graphic by authors

The risk of more failures was averted, at least for the time being, but it raised a lurking concern about overall banking stability in ways that had not surfaced since the onset of the Great Recession, the financial collapse that engulfed housing markets in the United States and then expanded worldwide in 2007. One reason for the concern was the possibility of a contagion effect in the form of a run on banks, portrayed as comparably risky. In an era of social media and global transmission of even the slightest ill-framed rumor, the risk was immense. Major figures in private equity quickly filled Twitter and financial news with calls to bend FDIC rules and cover any losses, even those that were not secured.

If the urgency was immediate, it also had a longer time frame and memory: Financial press reports quickly ascertained that the three spring 2023 bank failures were not only immense in size but approached the valuations and losses of the combined failure of financial institutions that ensued during the Great Recession. Indeed, they approached the valuation of the entirety of 21st century US bank failures. The failure of Silicon Valley Bank, Signature Bank, and First Republic Bank is recorded by the FDIC at a value of $549 billion. Just three regional bank's losses reached the equivalent of 76 percent of the 564 financial institution failures since 2000 and 77.5 percent of the 518 failures between 2007 and 2015, as the housing and the economy at large imploded and then found stability after the Great Recession. In the aftermath of Covid19, a public aware of expenditures to secure jobs was left with an unresolved anxiety. To those with a careful memory of financial markets as recently as 2007, it was one more reason to ask how stable are debt markets and the assets that secure those debts.

Questions about government debt levels are a routine part of politics; many will remember the *Metronome* debt clock by artists Kristin Jones and Andrew Ginzel installed in New York City's Union Square in 1999, or the National Debt Clock installed by real-estate mogul Seymour Durst near Times Square dating back to 1989. That discussion rarely recedes from debate for long and is deeply shaded by political motives (to cut social safety nets, for example), but there are also more recent and subtle framings of issues around debt. Central banks have already raced to secure market stability on three major occasions in the 21st century: in the immediate aftermath of 9/11, as housing markets began to collapse after the mortgage-backed securities crisis of 2007, and as a global pandemic shut down commerce worldwide in 2020. The world's top ten central banks have since 2006—before the housing crash—added approximately $26 trillion to their holdings. In the fifteen years between 2006 and 2022, onboarding of illiquid assets, commercial bank failures, and efforts to prop up bankruptcies and job growth took central bank holdings from $6 trillion to more than $32 trillion. At the private level, households have taken on similar increases in debt, using leverage at levels that reached 100 percent of GDP by 2006, up from 43 percent in the early 1970s and 18 percent in the immediate aftermath of World War II.

The collapse of three regional banks in 2023 may quickly fade from news, but they serve as an ember that economists routinely struggle to put out or to contain. Is the leverage that drives the world economy we know today sustainable? We have been asking this question for some time in our work, and while we originally filtered it through an architectural lens at the scale of financing a building or house, we have fully embraced a deep dive into the economics of housing. The move to an aggregate scale allows us to consider housing as an asset class and a form of national and personal wealth. Here leverage and debt become public and private, and the entire intersection of professional and economic disciplines around housing quickly becomes visible: energy, mobility, materials, and the practices of architecture, engineering, construction, development, real estate, and banking. That nexus has deeply changed structurally since the advent of mass-produced houses in the aftermath of World War II. Its future is far from certain.

We hope this book instigates others to give laws and policy around housing a closer read and address needs that we routinely leave in abeyance and tolerate remaining unfulfilled. Levels of scarcity that can be hard to imagine need to be addressed directly as no longer tolerable. On July 30, 1974, John N. Nassikas, chairman of the Federal Power Commission, described renewable energy as "inexhaustible" in testimony to the Congressional Subcommittee on Energy Committee on Science and Astronautics in the United States House of Representatives. The introduction of something not scarce has been lurking in the discourse around renewable energy for decades. As automation of labor converges with climate change, we believe that sustainability models must adapt and that we can imagine new means to provide security.

Michael Bell and Eunjeong Seong, New York, August 2023

Endnotes

1. Gloria Guzman and Melissa Kollar, Income in the United States: 2022, US Census Bureau, Current Population Reports, US Government Publishing Office, Washington, D.C., September 2023, https://www.census.gov/content/dam/Census/library/publications/2023/demo/p60-279.pdf.

2. "Opportunity Occupations Monitor," Federal Reserve Bank of Atlanta, May 18, 2023, https://www.atlantafed.org/cweo/data-tools/opportunity-occupations-monitor.

3. "Bank Failures in Brief–Summary 2001 through 2023," Federal Deposit Insurance Corporation (FDIC), https://www.fdic.gov/bank/historical/bank/.

Part One
Housing After Banking

One

Debt: 75 Years of Leverage

The two decades before and after the conclusion of World War II saw the percentage of United States households that owned their home change dramatically. Homeownership leading up to the Great Depression in 1929 peaked at 47.8 percent in 1930 before falling to 43.6 percent by 1940. By 1965, 20 years after the conclusion of the war, 63 percent of households owned their home. The era of homeownership, in particular single-family houses, was firmly established. The Depression and World War II formed the backdrop for federal intervention in mortgages and for a decentralized and dispersed population of private single-family house owners. Banks, aided by federal-government-backed mortgages, provided the nation's homeowners access to the leverage required to buy private, almost exclusively single-family homes. The accrual of long-term household debt in the form of mortgages rose in the post-war decades. Mortgage debt collateralized by incrementally appreciating housing assets increased. An increase in automobile debt, leverage ultimately attributed to depreciating assets, rose. Eventually, unsecured debt in the form of revolving credit became a common part of personal finances. Later in the century, newly introduced and then expanded, home-equity loans provided the means to move unsecured debt to mortgages, transferring expanded equity into consumption. Until the 1970s, savings had steadily increased, but by the 1980s it declined to an eventual low of less than $400 per capita. By 2006, households held debt that neared 100 percent of GDP, with little savings. Economic security was almost entirely based in housing wealth.

The post-1970s era in the US saw homeowners enter into a speculative housing market with little backstop in personal savings but a deep use of future income as leverage. This fueled housing prices and, for a time, equity, but it came to a dramatic collapse by 2008.

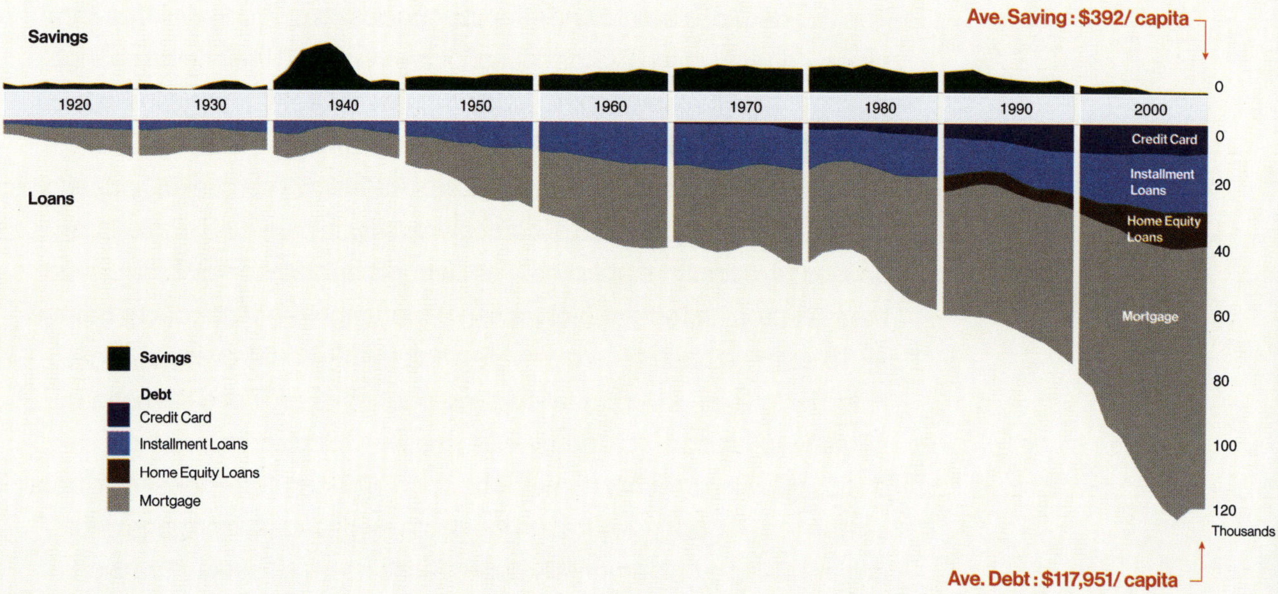

An analysis of household debt by Amy Schoenfeld and Matthew Bloch as published by the *New York Times* on July 2, 2008

The interactive animated graphic is no longer accessible online, but we have recreated a single image here showing the cumulative debt from 1920 to 2008. Schoenfeld and Bloch contributed this analysis to a larger *Times* project titled "The Debt Trap: A series about the surge in consumer debt and the lenders that made it possible."[1] Graphic by authors

Housing After Banking

In the absence of savings, household net worth in the United States is highly tied to real estate and its valuations. In 2023, households that own real estate have a median net worth thirty times greater than those that do not own their home. Classifying the role of housing and its presumed speculative value as a component of household net worth requires a close look at the role debt and leverage play. Since the conclusion of World War II, housing has generally appreciated, but the uses of debt and the exposure to financial risk have also dramatically accelerated. The wealth generated does not exist without this risk. We would ask, is housing as an asset, both the building and the land it occupies, separable from the leverage and risk that afford its purchase? Are design and engineering a factor in housing markets, or are they separate from the financial instruments? Are we investing in the same type of asset if the uses of capital and inherent risk to acquire the asset are dramatically different from decade to decade? In other words, through an economic lens, has risk in the form of a mortgage been the actual asset being acquired, and is housing itself—buildings—still a worthy vehicle for collateralizing financial risk of the magnitude we see today? We think a new asset is possible and needed, but it would require a new research and development structure that current design, real estate, and financial practices don't provide.

While the decade immediately following World War II saw a steep rise in home ownership, housing prices have not increased at the consistent rates we routinely imagine today. The growth in the past 75 years is not a steadily increasing line, and there have been periods where growth stagnated, dropped, or collapsed. Do we need a more nuanced yet also colloquial understanding of how debt and leverage impact the actual asset class and its design? In the context of renewable energy used in housing, we imagine a potential for an entirely new form of asset apart from housing as real estate, a renewable-energy asset that could decrease the uses of leverage and debt and would also be a shelter. But how to design and engineer such a product, and where is its source of research-and-development funding? We could alter how to connect housing to debt by altering what a house is. In examining the uses of debt and leverage in housing over the past 75 years, we imagine the realization of a new type of asset that capitalizes housing as an energy asset rather than as a real-estate asset.

In 1947, two years after the conclusion of World War II and three years after the formation and signing of the Bretton Woods Agreement, aggregate household debt in the United States amounted to 18 percent of the nation's gross domestic product (GDP). Sixty years later, in 2006, as the threat of the Great Recession became evident, household debt had reached nearly 100 percent of the GDP. The steep escalation of private debt in the United States in the early 2000s was unique, but the growth in the uses of leverage since the conclusion of World War II was also not linear. There were unique phases before 2006. In the decades after World War II leading to 1999, uses of leverage and their rate of growth in relation to GDP vary significantly. Household debt as a percentage of United States GDP fell during three eras since the end of World War II. It expanded rapidly after 1947: year-over-year increases form a consistent and linear ascent after the war that plateaus in 1967, twenty years later. Homeownership grew dramatically in the post-war years, and household debt shows this: debt-to-GDP ratios rose from 18 percent in 1947 before peaking in 1967 at 47 percent. The ratio then settled at 43 percent in 1970 before beginning a new steeper ascent later in the decade. It is this new period of post-1970s year-over-year increase that we often assume is normal and that has motivated housing investment instead of savings since. The 1970s and decades that followed also saw household debt increasingly attributed to the purchase of automobiles and the use of unsecured debt, especially credit cards.

By the end of the 1970s, leverage accelerated sharply, and property valuations followed. In the newly globalized, post-Bretton Woods economy, the financialization and worldwide distribution of US financial instruments and derivatives—debt as securities—exploded. The dismantling of the Bretton Woods Agreement in 1971 expanded the United States' ability to shape and participate in a global economy. The end of the gold standard and the rise of global financial, labor, and manufacturing markets embedded the US economy and its debt in a global banking system. Entirely new theories of cities, suburbs, and the cartography of capital and settlement emerged, and everyday experiences of places evolved and shifted. A simple analysis shows that by the mid-1970s, the accrual of household debt again increased and began a second, longer ascent, though it was uneven and episodic. It arrives at an eventual new summit by the middle of the 1990s. Americans began to assume housing was an inherent wealth producer, ignoring the history of uneven growth and the effect globalization of debt securities had in encouraging speculation on an otherwise barely changed physical asset. In 1995, housing begins yet another decade-long incline, this time dramatically steepening its ascent. This third stage collapses in 2008.

Mortgages traded as derivatives and securities enabled and sustained a deeper leveraging of housing markets during the years after the 1970s. Mortgages traded worldwide are originated for and tied to, eventually, 80 million single-family houses and the incomes of their owners in the US.

The market collapse that ensued in 2008 because of the failure of transparency regarding the value of mortgage-backed securities and a range of exotic instruments used by banks in peer-to-peer self-regulatory trading is often understood as resolved, but this requires acknowledging and dismissing the vast sums worldwide central banks invested in buying up failed securities. We think this was also a prelude to the mandate for a new genre of housing asset, which we suggest can form a rationale for a renewable-energy asset that could serve as a productive asset for generating long-term income while offering shelter as a subsidiary. It would in effect reverse rather than accelerate debt. As artificial intelligence and machine learning continue to advance, and new forms of automation threaten household income, it presents yet another horizon that is likely to have catastrophic effects on the already unstable asset of housing. A loss or transference of the labor, jobs, and income that have supported household debt over the past seventy-five years, combined with the destabilizing effects of climate, could lead to another even more tragic collapse.

The exorbitant price increases in housing after 1995 crashed badly. Illiquid housing markets and housing-based securities froze global credit markets, creating a precipice to a second Great Depression just fifteen years ago. Markets have found a level of solvency since, but the emergence of Covid19 in 2020 has created a fourth, unfinished cycle in housing debt, pricing, and access. This is a non-banking crisis that nonetheless required a massive intervention by central banks to moderate housing security. We are currently left with a market that is wholly un-affordable for most, producing a new and more complex form of housing scarcity.

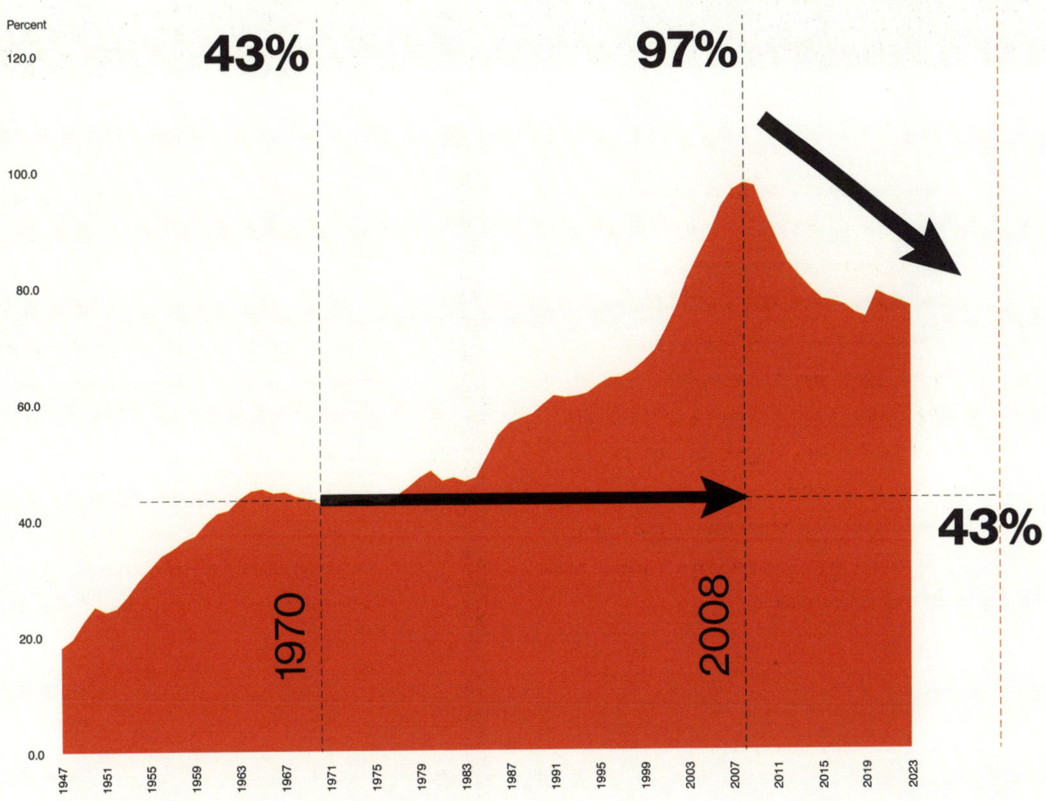

United States Household Debt to GDP, 1947–2019
Can one imagine a retreat in aggregate housing debt? A new type of housing asset could have the effect of lowering debt exposure. *8 Minutes, 20 Seconds* proposes a distributed renewable-energy asset whose potential revenues transact and encrypt the capital investment over time in the manner of a digital currency. A new type of commodity, a renewable-energy asset, would provide housing as a downstream by-product of the production of clean energy. The owner of the energy is housed outside of debt regimes. Even if traditional banking is used, the caching of renewable energy requires a form of encryption to negotiate peer-to-peer and peer-to-industry trade outside of a centralized utility and its price-setting mechanisms.[2]
Graphic by authors

14

What that meant to Detroit in jobs and profits is a matter of painful memory. The United States automobile industry at the peak of the boom employed 470,000 workers. There were only ~~257,000~~ 260,000 many of them at part time, on the depleted payrolls of 1932, but 500,000 were working in 1937.

The 15 major producers showed a profit of more than a billion dollars in 1929. In 1932, they had a net deficit of $130 million, but five years later they were in the black to the tune of ~~$768~~ $770. million.

Can you now doubt that you needed a Bretton Woods in the twenties and thirties?

16

A post-war economy of full production and full employment will require American exports of at least $10 billion.

If the Congress of the United States passes the Bretton Woods legislation, world trade will be freed from restrictive exchange controls and depreciating exchange rates. In that event, the automobile industry can look forward to a steady export market of at least a million cars a year.

We can reach such a trade level only if both the producing and consuming powers of all countries are expanded, not merely restored to their old levels.

Diaries of Henry Morgenthau, Jr., April 27, 1933–July 27, 1945
A post-World War II United States economy required an increased level of exports to sustain full employment. In 1945, Henry Morgenthau, Jr., Secretary of Treasury from January 1934 through July 1945, gave an estimate with remarkable detail in a speech at the Detroit Economic Club to foster support for the signing of the Bretton Woods Agreement: "A post-war economy of full production and full employment will require American exports of at least $10 billion." Speaking to an audience of automobile industry leaders, Morgenthau enunciated that Bretton Woods would ease the impact of fluctuating currency exchange rates on the sale of a Detroit produced car in Europe.[3]

Last summer the best technical experts of 44 United Nations and associates met at Bretton Woods, New Hampshire, to grapple with the problem of postwar money. They worked on the basis of a plan that had been evolved from preliminary discussions extending over two years.

The result was agreement on a program which provides for a Fund to stabilize currencies and an International Bank to help finance reconstruction and development.

To the people of Detroit, it means a foreign market for as much as a million cars a year, and a goodly proportion of your machinery, metal products, and chemicals.

It means that if the foreign branch of a Detroit plant makes money, the company can get its profits out in dollars instead of harmonicas. Under such exchange policies, an American salesman can go to Belgium and sell a thousand-dollar car for 40,000 francs without worrying about cancellations because sudden depreciation has put the exchange value of that thousand dollars up to 60 or 80,000 francs and out of reach of most buyers

. . .

Morgenthau's 1945 address to the Detroit Economic Club outlined goals for a post-World War II economy reliant on exporting manufactured goods. Twenty-five years later as Bretton Woods was dismantled, real estate-based debt securities became easily tradable. Exported in a newly global market, they enabled new heights of speculation in United States housing.

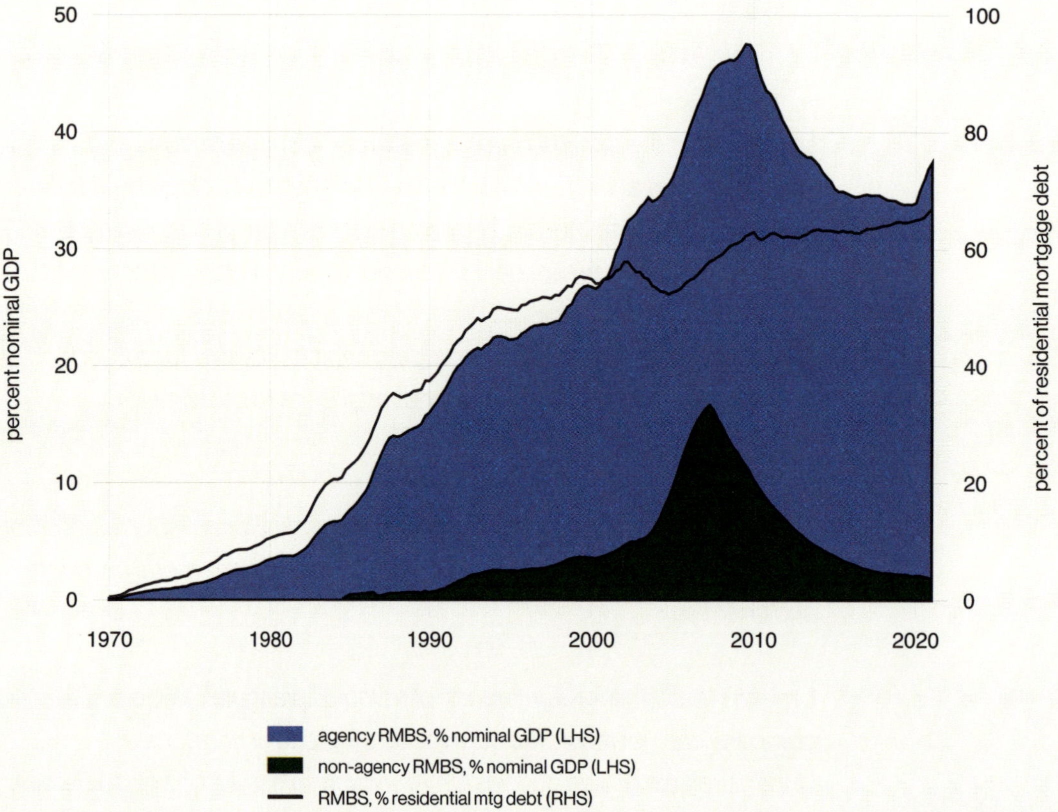

Mortgage-Backed Securities Outstanding

Since 1970, the role of government-guaranteed residential mortgage-backed securities (RMBS) has reached more than 45 percent of GDP. Non-government-guaranteed mortgage-backed securities (non-agency RMBS) are greater than 15 percent. The Federal Reserve Bank of New York described the mortgage-backed security market: "The mortgage-backed securities (MBS) market emerged as a way to decouple mortgage lending from mortgage investing. Until the 1980s, nearly all US mortgages were held on balance sheet by financial intermediaries, predominately savings and loans. Securitization today allows these mortgages to be held and traded by investors all over the world, and the US MBS market is one of the largest and most liquid global fixed-income markets, with more than $11 trillion of securities outstanding and nearly $300 billion in average daily trading volume."[4] The decoupling of mortgage origination and holding not only changes the territory of investment but also is often seen as an increase of moral hazard and weaker incentives to avoid risk.

Central Banks

Since 2006, in the lead up to the housing-market-fueled Great Recession, central banks worldwide have dramatically increased and held immense sums of debt off the public markets. Effectively shoring up assets weakened by financial shock, the world's top ten central banks protected markets whose liquidity had been severely tested. Housing markets have played an immense role in this backstopping.

Many economists believe a would-be second Great Depression was staved off in 2007 by massive infusions of federally backed liquidity to both commercial and investment banks. The United States Federal Reserve removed more than $1.9 trillion in mortgage-backed securities from the markets in 2009, a once-in-a-century action, in an effort to stabilize the unfolding economic crisis. This action was unprecedented in type and scale.

By 2016, as the financial markets began to appear stable, attention was being called to the scale and makeup of central bank holdings in the United States and worldwide. Private debt was transformed into publicly held financial assets in the form of debt securities purchased by central banks. By 2016, the world's top ten central banks had dramatically expanded their holdings by removing illiquid private debt from the markets. While some of these assets were later resold back into the open market, many remained on central bank books for a decade. Before the crash, they collectively held six trillion dollars; by 2016, they held as much as $21.4 trillion of private debt as they progressively stabilized the world markets.[5] It has expanded since: one measure shows major central banks worldwide in 2021 are holding $32 trillion on their books. The 21st century has already seen two major impacts to markets and central bank roles in securing markets: the housing and liquidity collapse and the Covid19 pandemic. Prior to Covid19 and subsequent inflation, the United States had a 12-year period where interest rates were lower than at any time in the last half century. At the time, it was a frequent concern what tools central banks had left to stave off another collapse if reduced interest rates failed.

In the intricate world of central banks, this may be a scenario remediated by *printing* money, but it hard to not ask if capitalism's housing markets have in this century induced increasingly intolerable strains on government. What begs architectural attention is to ask how stable the overall picture is. Is the financial system's stability masked by massive yet arcane market interventions? Is it reliable to imagine the future of housing and, in the wider realm, urban form, as based on leverage to the extent we have witnessed in the post-Bretton Woods era, particularly in the 1990s and early 2000s? If not, what forms of capital will enable development in the future? Automobiles have priced themselves out of sales and into leases, which amounts to leveraged depreciation. The increasing role of services as opposed to purchase in the form of companies like Airbnb, WeWork, and the experience economy invokes an emerging asset-less and possibly wealth-less new generation. The incremental changes that underlie the use of finance in development are conceivably at a peak, masked by the role central banks have played since World War II in establishing and sustaining the possibilities of development.

As of 2021, the world's central banks hold as much as $44 trillion in assets. The impact of Covid19 on global markets and the role central banks played in securing markets has multiplied the ever-increasing capitalization of a scarce asset—the home—making it available to fewer and fewer, and often only those who forgo debt and pay cash.

One can ask, what constitutes a safe asset today?

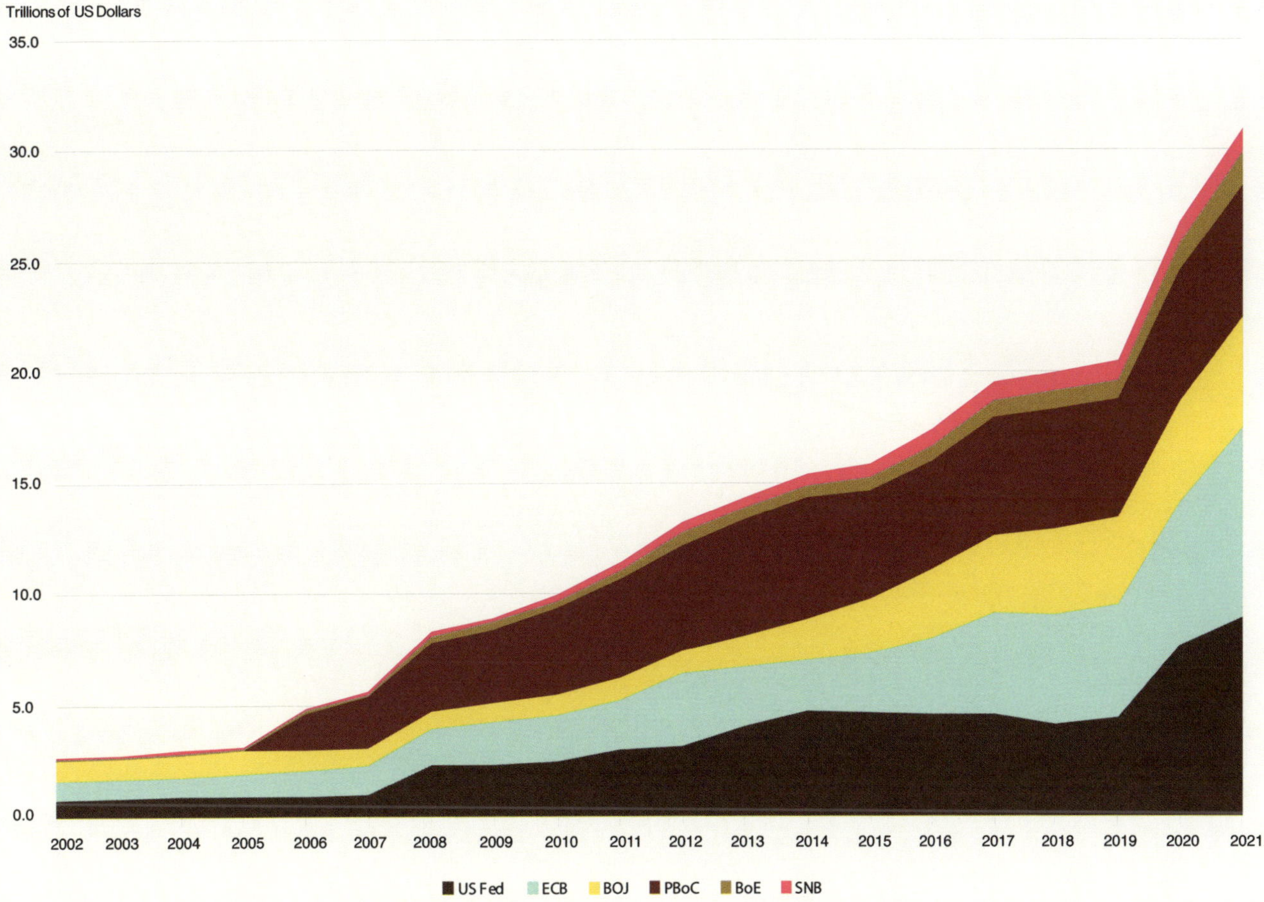

Total Assets of Major Central Banks: United States Federal Reserve, European Central Bank, Bank of Japan, People's Bank of China, Swiss National Bank, 2002 to 2021[6]
Graphic by authors

ECB: European Central Bank
BOJ: Bank of Japan
PBoC: Bank of China
BoE: Bank of England
SNB: Switzerland National Bank

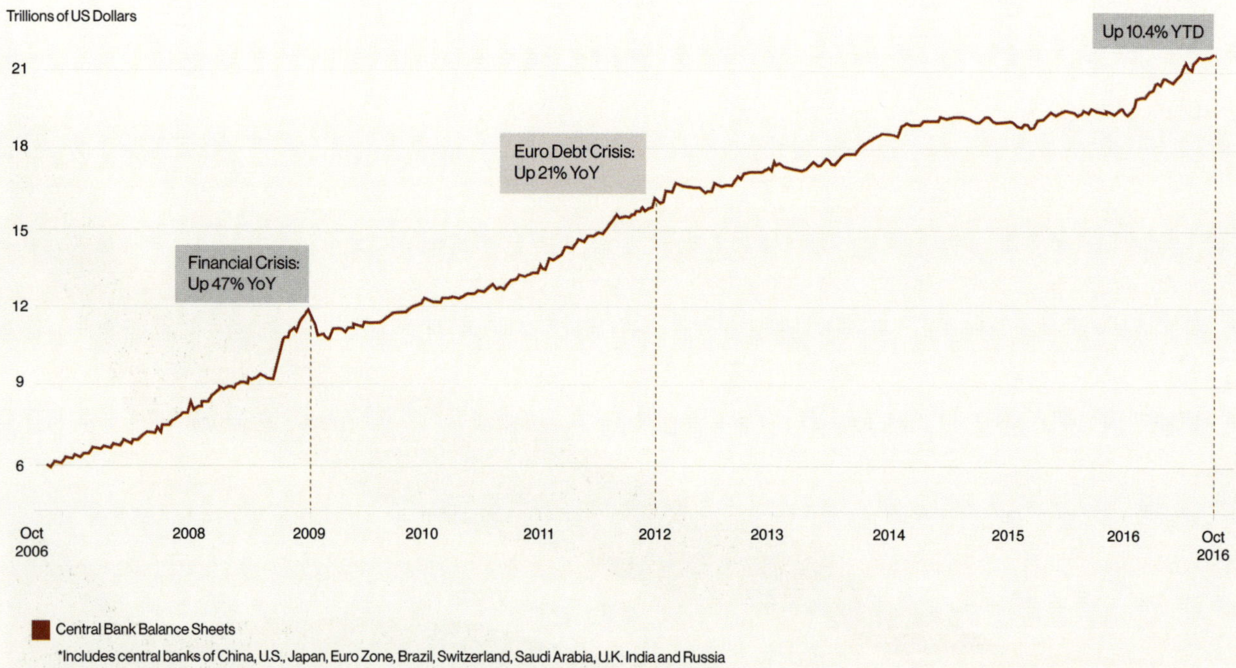

The Combined Assets of the 10 Largest Central Banks
Mainstream Financial News: A Bloomberg news article in 2016 reported that the world's top 10 central banks had increased their holdings by a factor of 350 percent to $21.3 trillion in the decade between 2006 and 2016, dramatically expanding their balance sheets in the aftermath of the Great Recession. According to Bloomberg, the holdings were worth a third of the world economy. Top central banks are effectively shoring up unstable assets and their markets. Alarm about these levels has been reported consistently in the financial press in the aftermath of the Great Recession and continues today after Covid19[7]

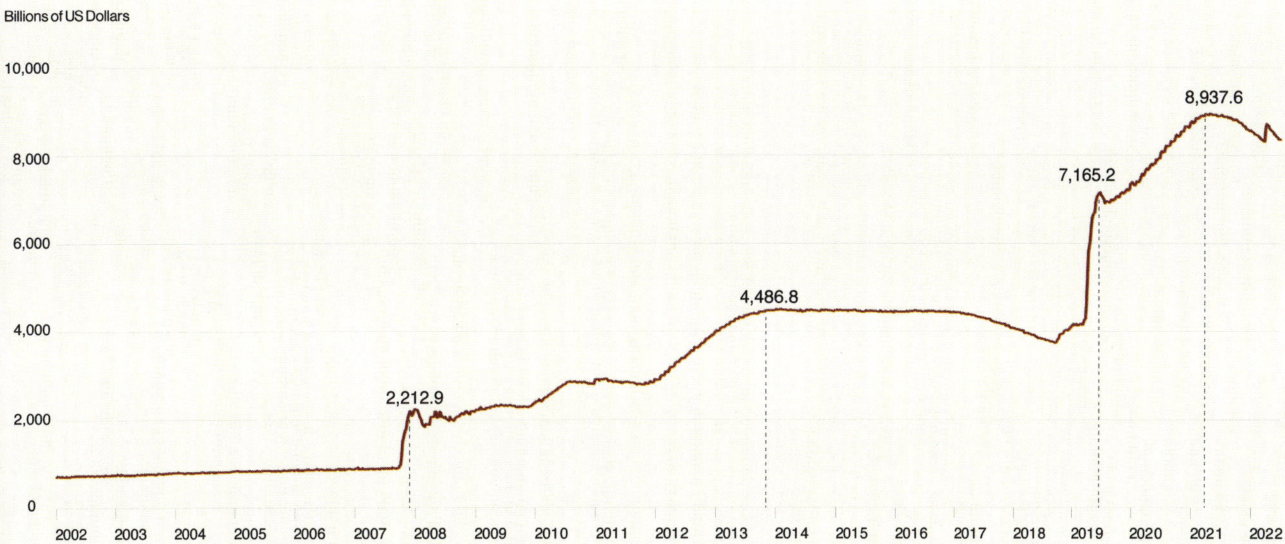

Total Assets of Federal Reserve
In 2008, the Federal Reserve held approximately one trillion dollars in assets. In 2023, it holds nearly $8.4 trillion, declining from a peak of nearly $9 trillion in 2022.[8]
Graphic by authors

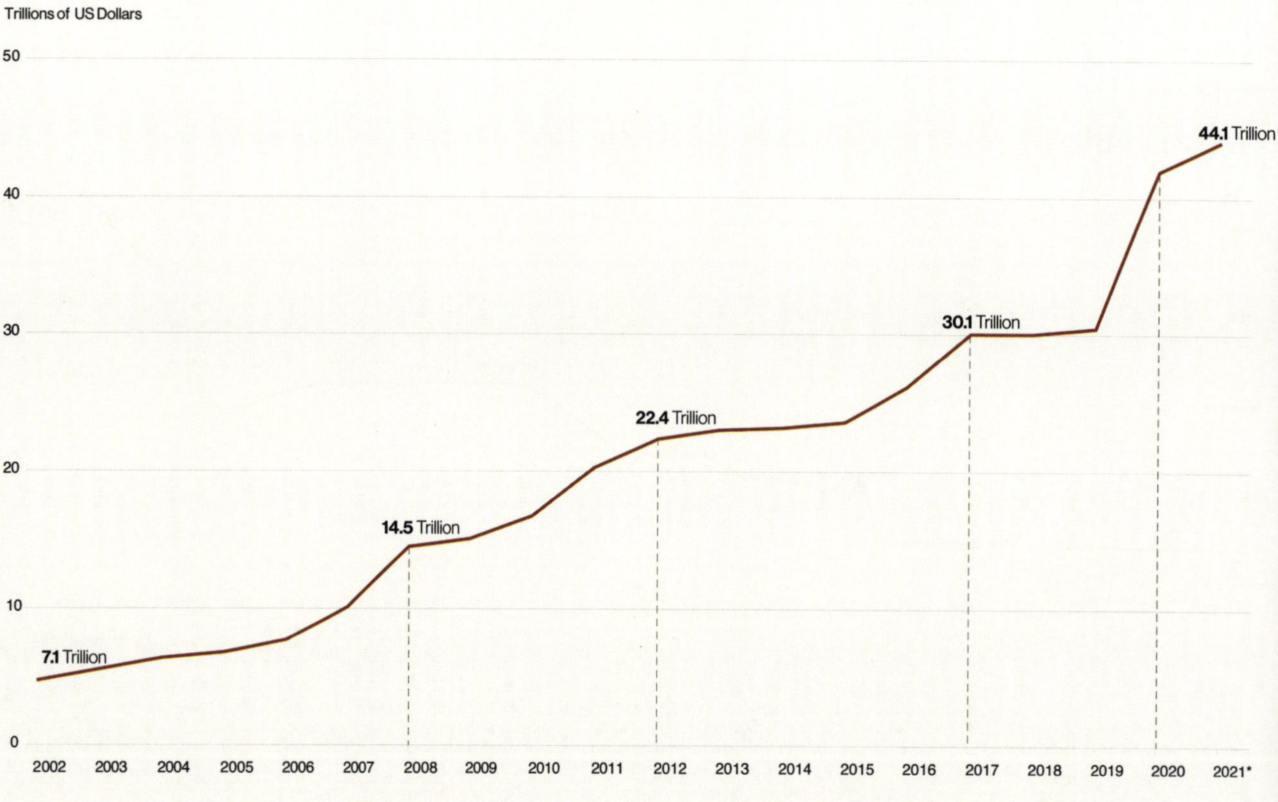

Total Assets of Central Banks Worldwide in Trillion US Dollars from 2002 to 2021
In the twenty years since 2002, central banks worldwide have increased asset holdings from $7.1 trillion to $44.4 trillion, a rise of 621 percent. Banks represented: Argentina, Australia, Brazil, Canada, Cayman Islands, Chile, China, Euro Area, Hong Kong, India, Indonesia, Japan, Korea, Mexico, Russia, Saudi Arabia, Singapore, South Africa, Switzerland, Turkey, the UK, the US. *Does not include data for Russia.[9] Graphic by authors

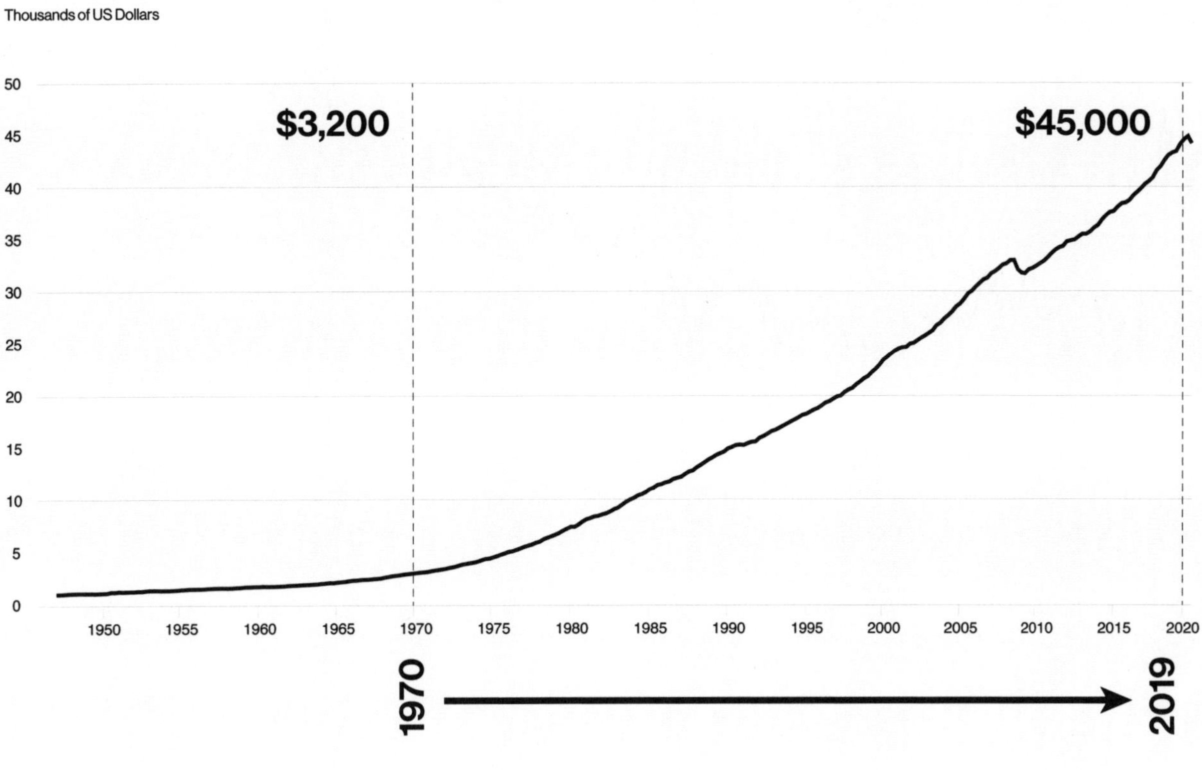

Personal Consumption Expenditures per Capita[10]
Graphic by authors

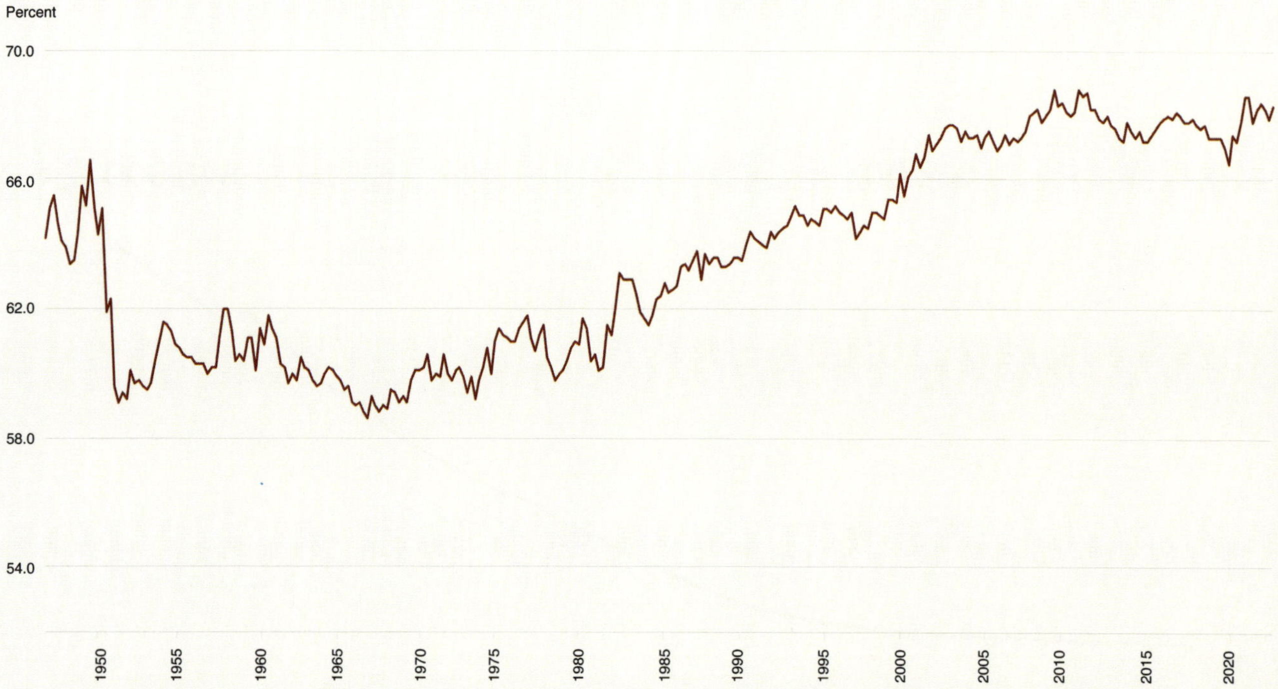

Shares of Gross Domestic Product: Personal Consumption Expenditures: 1947–2023
Consumption in the United States rose sharply after World War II as consumer products were made available again after the war effort. It declined to a low of approximately 58 percent of GDP in the mid-1960s and rose to approximately 68 percent in 2009. It is the largest contributor to the US economy. Housing and home ownership fuel this with expenses related to durable and non-durable goods. Advances in housing sales often run parallel to durable good sales, but consumption more broadly speaking correlates to housing. The relationships have been a major question for economists who find some expenses are not flexible while other are wholly tied to new home purchases.[11]
Graphic by authors

Zeros and Ones - The Flow of Funds

8 Minutes, 20 Seconds begins as a local and essential enquiry. How can we make housing more affordable for people in cities where expensive land and high construction costs put housing out of reach? The questions become far less local very quickly, however, because today more than 39 million United States households struggle to pay for their housing. Three-quarters of a century of expanded leverage and immense government intervention has left nearly one-third of households struggling.

The questions become inevitably global even as they remain discrete and precise when measured against the last 75 years of housing policy in the United States and the political ethos that has long made markets the denominator of the possible. Housing in the United States and increasingly in the world is a capital asset, and while the role of governments in moderating affordability is often significant, it is also indirect and reluctant. The influence of the government is massive in creating markets and regulatory action in markets, but indirect and modest in how it abets actual innovation in construction. Housing is constructed as shelter, but only in light of its value in wealth production. It is realized as a real-estate asset class, and in relatively short order, it is expected to produce a return on investment. The aspiration for housing to be a home and dwelling may underpin the salability and desirability of housing, but that quality, and indeed essential factor, has long been measured against its performance as an investment and would-be commodity. The risk involved in producing housing comes from the market. The development process is quick, the transfer of the property is equally rapid, and then the longer-term occupation lasts perhaps decades. The risk over its lifespan is born by the buyer and owner but also by the federal government in securitizing the long-term debt. Each has a temporal dimension tied to future payback and use, including the land, infrastructure, building, energy, and mobility that serve it.

As designers, in partnership with an engineering and materials team and financial experts, we are proposing a new look at how housing is scaled. This would allow an aggregate view of the market's valuations and, ideally, a convening of potential funds for research and development on par with the automobile, aeronautics, medical, and consumer-electronics industries. Such research-and-development resources could provide entry into advanced manufacturing and the ability to precisely model physical and mechanical systems, a reduction in labor and, ideally, not just lower costs for a higher-quality product, but also access to renewable energy and its integration into housing design: the potential to design for manufacturing, coupled with deep integration with renewable energy.

In 1969, economist Milton Friedman offered an ironic but serious critique of the Federal Reserve: it was a stinging comment that entered into mainstream media and that is still often referenced to today. "We don't need a Fed," Friedman said. "I have, for many years, been in favor of replacing the Fed with a computer." Such a computer "would print out a specified number of paper dollars" to augment the money supply. "Same number, month after month, week after week, year after year." "The Fed has had very few periods of relatively good performance," he continues. "For most of its history, it's been a loose cannon on the deck, and not a source of stability."[12] In the interim 50 years since Friedman's comments, the world has seen entirely new products and assets invented. Computers, their components, and the electronic, satellite-enabled, radio-digital networks that link them have disrupted entire industries. They have also produced newly attenuated financial markets that are themselves more instantaneously tracked and traded. We have remonetized housing debt in a long chain of new instruments. It is time to entirely reinvent what was housing. It may indeed not be housing that we imagine as our future homes, but instead an energy asset that has the downstream effect of offering a place to reside.

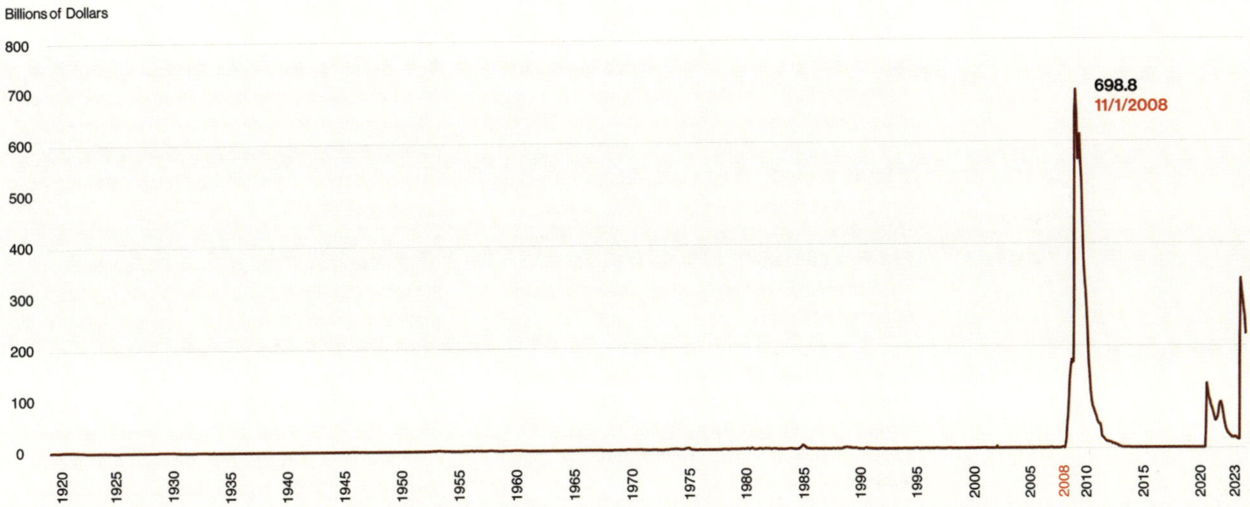

Total Borrowing from the Federal Reserve . Billions of Dollars, Not Seasonally Adjusted
Commercial bank borrowing from the Federal Reserve since 1920 massively increased during the Great Recession and more recently during the Covid19 pandemic. Climate change, labor automation, and future forms of housing stress present challenges for the near future and our wider ability to fund change. Do we have the means to create and fund new teams that can invent assets that might alter our financial reliance on debt and on central banks as the final guarantor?[13]
Graphic by authors

Endnotes

1. Amy Schoenfeld and Matthew Bloch, "The Debt Trap: The American Way of Debt," *New York Times*, July 2, 2008, https://archive.nytimes.com/www.nytimes.com/interactive/2008/07/20/business/20debt-trap.html.

2. "Households and Nonprofit Organizations; Debt Securities and Loans; Liability, Level," Board of Governors of the Federal Reserve System (US), Federal Reserve Economic Data (FRED), Federal Reserve Bank of St. Louis, https://fred.stlouisfed.org/series/CMDEBT, June 25, 2020; and "Gross Domestic Product," US Bureau of Economic Analysis, Federal Reserve Economic Data (FRED), Federal Reserve Bank of St. Louis, https://fred.stlouisfed.org/series/GDP, June 25, 2020.

3. "Diary, Book 823, February 26–28, 1945," Diaries of Henry Morgenthau, Jr., April 27, 1933–July 27, 1945, Henry Morgenthau, Jr. Papers, 1866–1953, Franklin D. Roosevelt Presidential Library & Museum, http://www.fdrlibrary.marist.edu/_resources/images/morg/md1124.pdf.

4. Andreas Fuster, David Lucca, James Vickery, "Mortgage-Backed Securities," Staff Reports, No. 1001, Federal Reserve Bank of New York, Feb. 2022, https://www.newyorkfed.org/research/staff_reports/sr1001.html.

5. Phil Kuntz, "Big Central Bank Assets Jump Fastest in 5 Years to $21 Trillion," Bloomberg, Oct. 16, 2016, https://www.bloomberg.com/news/articles/2016-10-16/big-central-bank-assets-jump-fastest-in-5-years-to-21-trillion.

6. "Assets: Total Assets: Total Assets (Less Eliminations from Consolidation): Wednesday Level," US Federal Reserve-Assets of Central Bank in the US, 2002–2021, Board of Governors of the Federal Reserve System, Federal Reserve Economic Data (FRED), Federal Reserve Bank of St. Louis, June 27, 2023, https://fred.stlouisfed.org/series/WALCL; "Central Bank Assets for Euro Area (11-19 Countries)," European Central Bank, Federal Reserve Economic Data (FRED), Federal Reserve Bank of St. Louis, June 27, 2023, https://fred.stlouisfed.org/series/ECBASSETSW; "Bank of Japan: Total Assets for Japan," Bank of Japan, , Federal Reserve Economic Data (FRED), Federal Reserve Bank of St. Louis, June 27, 2023, https://fred.stlouisfed.org/series/JPNASSETS; "Total Assets of the Central Bank in the United Kingdom (UK) from 2002 to 2021," Financial Stability Board, Statista, Statista Inc., Dec. 20, 2022, https://www.statista.com/statistics/1021009/total-assets-of-the-central-bank-in-united-kingdom/; "Total assets of the central bank in Switzerland from 2002 to 2018," Financial Stability Board, Statista, Statista Inc., Jan. 19, 2020, https://www.statista.com/statistics/1021006/total-assets-of-the-central-bank-in-switzerland/.

7. Kuntz, "Big Central Bank Assets Jump." See also: Christopher Thompson and Claire Jones, "Asset-backed securities: Back from disgrace," *Financial Times*, Sep.. 30, 2014, https://www.ft.com/content/7d9d25f0-4729-11e4-ba74-00144feab7de?siteedition=intl#axzz3F6gavKhp.

8. "Assets: Total Assets: Total Assets (Less Eliminations from Consolidation): Wednesday Level," Board of Governors of the Federal Reserve System, Federal Reserve Economic Data (FRED), Federal Reserve Bank of St. Louis, June 27, 2023, https://fred.stlouisfed.org/series/WALCL.

9. "Total Assets of Central Banks Worldwide from 2002 to 2021," Financial Stability Board, Statista, Statista Inc., Dec. 20, 2022, https://www.statista.com/statistics/421201/assets-of-central-banks/.

10. "Personal consumption expenditures per capita," US Bureau of Economic Analysis, Federal Reserve Economic Data (FRED), Federal Reserve Bank of St. Louis, June 27, 2023, https://fred.stlouisfed.org/series/A794RC0Q052SBEA.

11. Efraim Benmelech, Adam Guren, Brian T. Melzer, "Making the House a Home: The Stimulative Effect of Home Purchases on Consumption and Investment," Working Paper 23570, National Bureau of Economic Research, July 2017, https://www.nber.org/papers/w23570; and "Shares of gross domestic product: Personal consumption expenditures," Federal Reserve Economic Data (FRED), Federal Reserve Bank of St. Louis, June 27, 2023, https://fred.stlouisfed.org/series/DPCERE1Q156NBEA.

12. Deroy Murdock, "Milton and Rose Friedman Offer Radical Ideas for the 21st Century," Cato Institute, Dec. 8, 1999, https://www.cato.org/publications/commentary/milton-rose-friedman-offer-radical-ideas-21st-century.

13. "Total Borrowings from the Federal Reserve," Board of Governors of the Federal Reserve System, Federal Reserve Economic Data (FRED), Federal Reserve Bank of St. Louis, https://fred.stlouisfed.org/series/borrow.

Two

Marketing Scarcity: Density Sustains Leverage

Temple Terrace, Florida, 2011.

Photograph: Michael Bell, Eunjeong Seong.

For *Foreclosed: Rehousing the American Dream*, The Museum of Modern Art

The 2022 United States Census described a national total of 1.39 million privately owned housing units completed that year. Of that total, 747,000 or 54 percent of the units were realized in the census's South region. The census divides housing starts, completions and occupancy into four regions: the Northeast, Midwest, South, and West (including Alaska).

While sustainability arguments predominately point to a need for increased density in land use, especially for housing, the census region of the United States that has grown most rapidly over the past five decades lies in the states and cities where lower density is the norm. Census data shows that the thirty-year period between 1985 and 2015 saw the nation's aggregate housing stock increase from a total number of 97.3 million units to 134.7 million. In just three decades, new housing units added to the aggregate grew the total housing stock by 39 percent. In retrospect, approximately 28 percent of the nation's extant housing units in 2015 were added during only three decades. On aggregate, the South region alone accounts for 51 percent of what was added nationally in that time span.

As the US economy began to recover from the Covid19 pandemic, financial and real estate news reported that the southern areas of the nation were rapidly advancing in renewed housing starts. They also reported and sought to demonstrate migration of the US population to southern states and cities. The motivations, described as larger homes, lower-cost housing, and lower taxes than in other regions like the Northeast, portrayed a new version of a tendency that has been in place for decades. The census-demarcated South has been outpacing the North, Midwest, and West for decades, and the delta of completed housing units has increased virtually every year since 1968, as far back as the authors studied. In fact, it has outpaced every other region since 1968: Compared to the Northeast, the South has built between 238 and 712 percent more housing than the rest of the country as a whole each year since that time. The peak at 712 percent was reached in 2021. A year later, the delta declined to 647 percent.

While any measure of the recent past reveals immense growth in the South and might steel attitudes towards sustainability and its relation to land use and density, looking to the future is even more startling. If we constructed half of the nation's recent housing stock in regions we routinely call low-density sprawl, what do we imagine for the next three decades? If decarbonization is the goal, how do we address even our nation's recent history? Are the jobs and opportunity of higher-cost and denser cities outside the South durable, and will they be a draw in the immediate decades ahead?

We believe there are distinct opportunities delivered in this cartography: a regional access to renewable energy, especially solar and wind, and a higher value of houses as buildings relative to their land cost, particularly in the non-northeast regions, which affords an opportunity to retrofit a form of housing usually built of easily malleable wood-frame and low-cost materials. These houses have, by proportion, less land costs associated with their purchase, a historical attraction that provided more space to households we believe will be renewed if the economy sheds jobs to automation in denser regions of the nation.

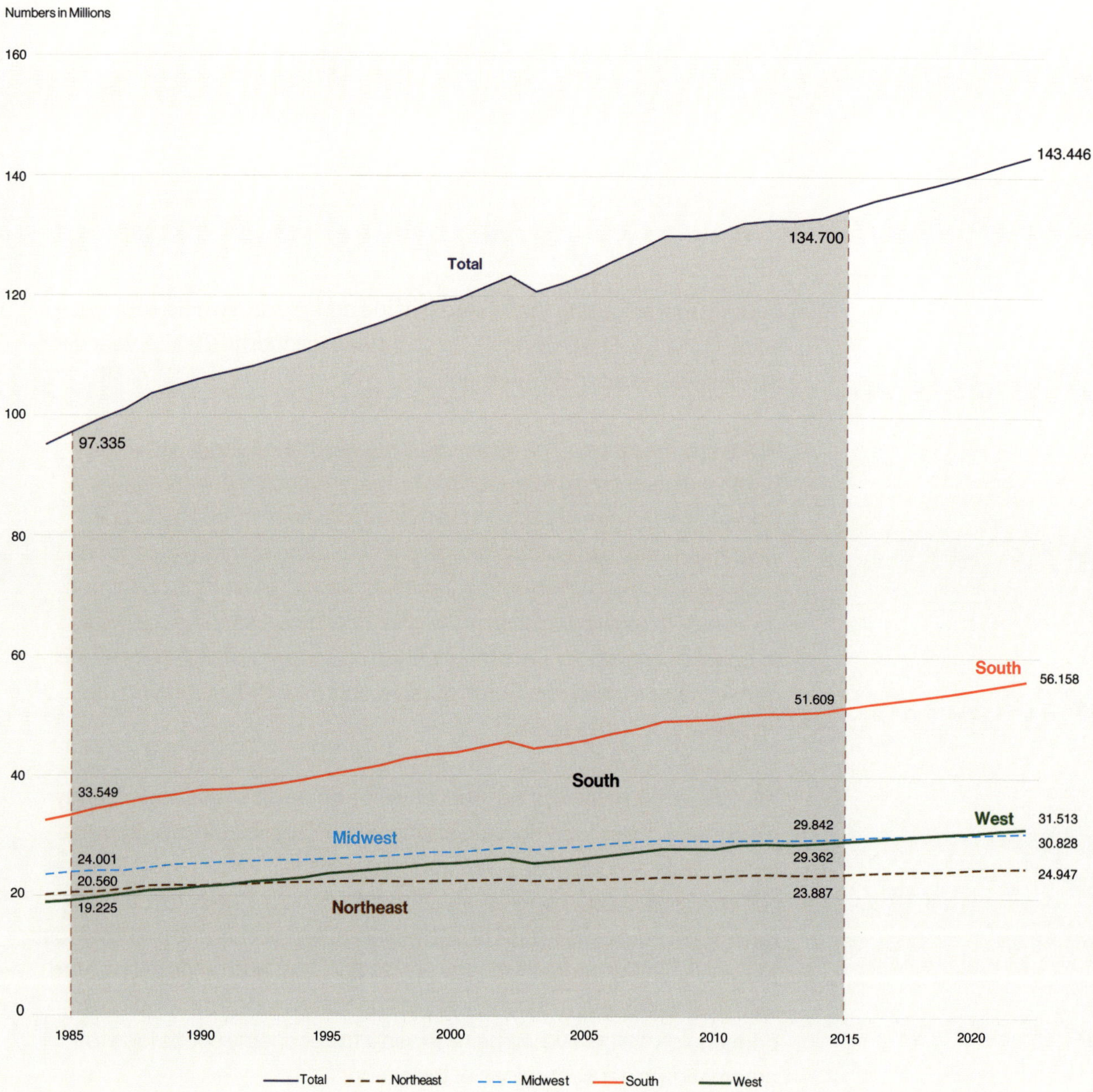

United States Housing Units 1985–2015, Northeast, Midwest, South, and West Regions, and Total

The Census South Region had dramatically outpaced the Northeast, Midwest, and West regions.[1]

Graphic by authors

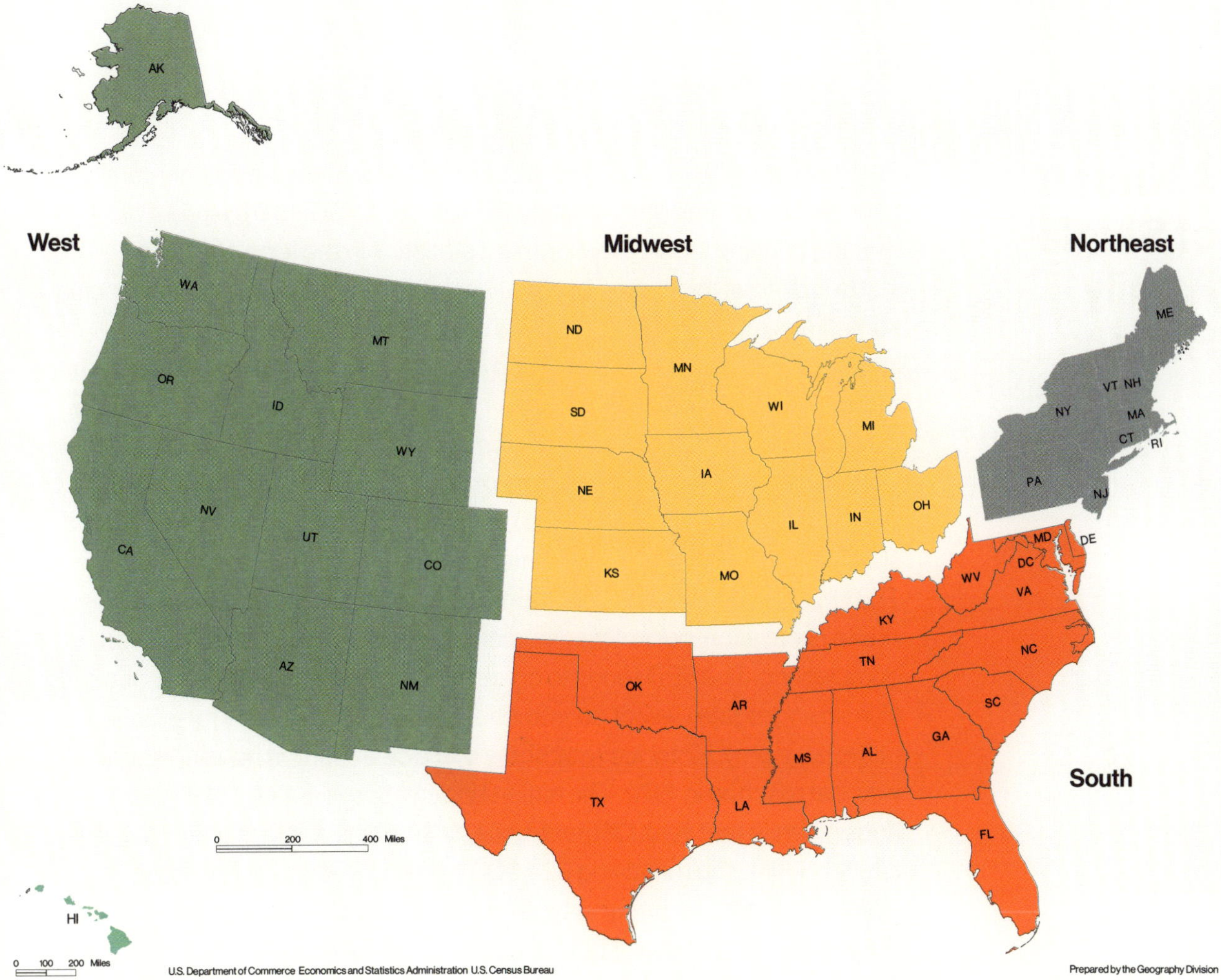

A census map outlines the four regions that the Census South Region is composed of: Alabama, Arkansas, Delaware, District of Columbia, Florida, Georgia, Kentucky, Louisiana, Maryland, Mississippi, North Carolina, Oklahoma, South Carolina, Tennessee, Texas, Virginia, and West Virginia. Alaska and Hawaii are included in the West Region.[2] Graphic by authors

A Nation of Single-Family Houses

The vast majority of existing homes in the US are detached single-family houses. They form approximately 82 million in total and 61 percent of all existing housing stock. Development statistics in the form of housing starts is difficult to generalize; data kept by federal, state, and city agencies sometimes measures housing units rather than households. Private industry and interests track housing counts with a wide range of means and goals. The Federal Reserve, for example, collects information from Zillow, recognizing the reach the private company has in today's markets. Housing starts recorded by the Department of Housing and Urban Development (HUD), the Federal Reserve (FED), and the Census Bureau are at times shared as sources but at other times are generated independently. The US Census, for example, might count a housing start at the time of site excavation, but in other studies the census also counts housing completions. The FED tends to count starts or permitting; permit counts give an aggregate view of construction and also allow some forecasting of the economy. Historically, all show that a clear peak in housing starts was last reached in 1972. The nation began approximately 2.49 million housing units that year. Of those units, 1.41 million took the form of single-family houses; the remaining 924,000 were in buildings of five or more units. A finer grain of housing type can be charted, but today the US is still predominantly a nation of private houses. The cartography that results is a nation of low-density development.

Land and Structure: A Real-Estate Transaction

Any real-estate transaction is composed as an aggregate of land plus a structure, but in the case of a single-family house, this aggregate comprises one transaction and one owner. It becomes a singular form of private property but is in fact two different assets and is identified by the government and taxed as such. That separation of land and structure allows economists to chart the values of each. As a form of real-estate development, municipal tax structures generally term the structure as an *improvement* to the *land*. Each carries its own tax obligations and is demarcated as such in tax levies. Land use, zoning, and taxes as ad valorem provide municipal revenue, a city or town budget derived from taxes on the market values assigned to the combination of land and house, or more generically, land and structure.

But does a structure count as an improvement on land, or is it the other way around?

Over the past five decades, there is clear evidence to show that the structures we call housing or houses are increasingly a smaller and less consequential component of real-estate valuations compared to land. This is especially true in areas of the country that offer access to not just high-paying jobs but diversity in jobs and economic resiliency. In these areas, it is land that adds the majority of value to a housing transaction. The structures we build on top of land in these areas have far less ability to alter the price of being sheltered. It raises a question: how much can efficiency in materials or of labor in building design and engineering lower the cost of housing in high land-value areas?

Often characterized as sprawl, the regions of the country distinguished by a tissue of parking lots and ligature of arterial roads and highways have been awarded immense criticism. From cul-de-sacs to strip malls, there is a routine critique of these zones of development as unsustainable. Indicted as socially alienating, reliant on carbon-intensive automobiles and complex and aging energy networks, there are ready proposals to increase their density and try to limit their reliance on private mobility. These regions of the country have largely relied on lower-cost land, simple, if labor intensive, construction practices, and low-cost gasoline by world standards. Several decades of quantitative easing made for low-cost mortgages. But any attempt to postulate a future for the 82-million-and-growing number of single-family houses needs to acknowledge the matrix of land-and-structure costs. In job-rich states such as California, land costs are such that the structure as improvement upon land often counts for a small fraction of the cost of housing. Can architectural and engineering innovations in means of construction and labor meaningfully lower housing costs in such an equation? Density, when it is employed, becomes a proxy for diminished land costs, but in regions of the country where density has not been a historical factor, we can and should look forward to new techniques, especially if we imagine employment opportunity waning in job-rich locales. Architects routinely embrace cost-savings as a challenge to innovation, but to date we still see vast housing scarcity. Housing is financially out of reach for millions of households. If one projects an economy transformed by automation and artificial intelligence, it will be more so.

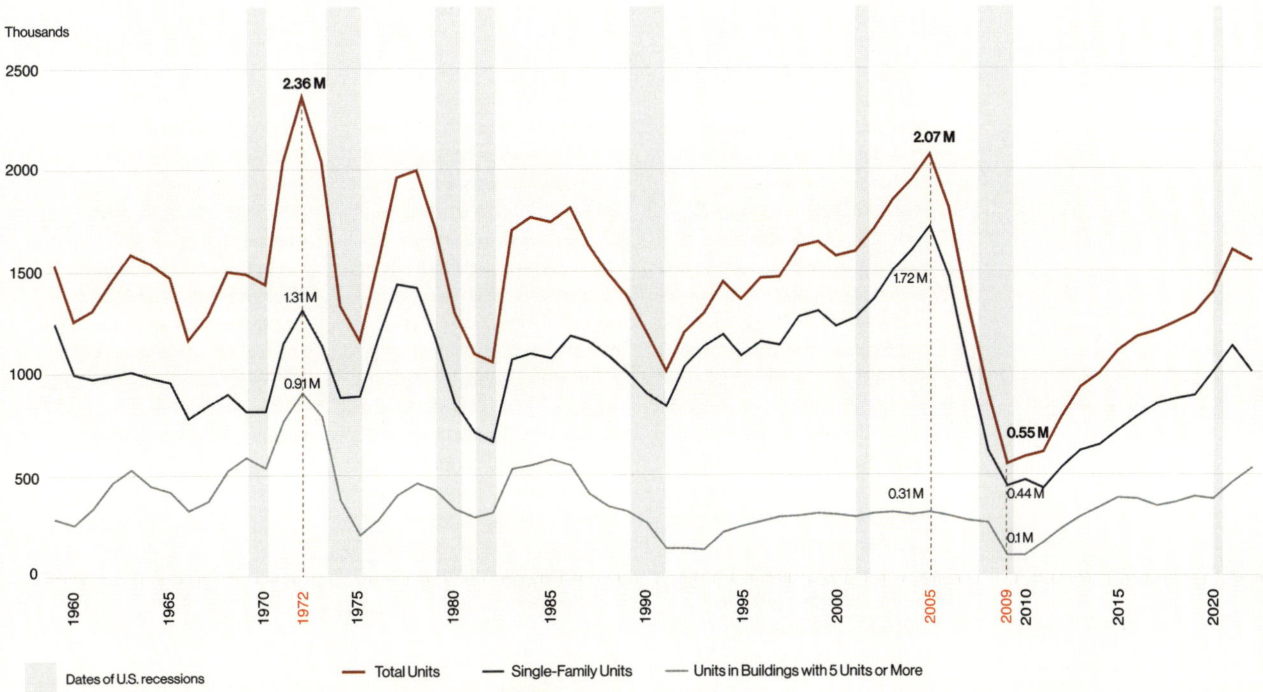

New Privately-Owned Housing Units Started
In the aftermath of the Great Recession, housing starts fell to 555,000 units. The aggregate numbers vary from month to month, seasonally, and over the course of the 2010s, but 2009 marked a plunge and the lowest level in 50 years. As Covid19 took hold in 2020, housing production plummeted again, in part due to lockdowns, supply chain disruptions, and fear. It quickly picked up again, particularly in the South, and more widely as developers recognized the migration made possible by internet-enabled remote work. If one focuses on the volatility, which is quite real, you can also miss the larger picture. Housing in the United States is a perpetual courtship between markets and the various levels of government that adjudicate zoning and land use, permits and density (floor area ratio, or FAR), setbacks, and at times income and other social heuristics and measures. The government ultimately provides a quotient, or set of variables, either by design, simple momentum, its tenor, or in response to need. The parameters of development have limited experiments that set new or other potentials. A deeper implementation of renewable energy as the driver of settlement is a window that will offer a new heuristics and new denominators. More than sustainability, it anticipates migration and adoption of energy sources that are not scarce.[3] Graphics by authors

Simultaneous City, as shown here, was commissioned for the Museum of Modern Art's *Foreclosed: Rehousing the American Dream* and followed curators Barry Bergdoll and Reinhold Martin's mandate to seek a new form of public housing in the post-foreclosure landscape of the United States. In replying to the MoMA inquiry on the potential of a public role in housing development at this late stage, we avoided as untenable direct government expenditure on housing and instead sought to steer the small city of Temple Terrace, Florida, our case study, toward using its local and immediate economic capacity to hold land it had begun to assemble with tax revenue.

The land purchase by the city had been intended to be released into a public-private partnership. Instead of subsidizing the private market through a developer, we proposed the city rezone property setbacks as well as purchase underutilized private property, then reorganize these areas into a new zoning and land use, mandating the development of new housing types for previously underserved constituencies. Architecture in this zone would be realized at a scale that sustains high levels of capital investment but is imagined within the economic capacity of citizens. A 225-acre redevelopment zone that would have been subsidized for a private developer is instead held by the city and a new level of urban density is imagined that takes as its economic basis the collective capacity of the aggregate income of the households. Architecture is reverse-engineered within that capacity. We proposed adding as many as 10,000 new residents to a city of 24,000 and seeking a development model that would optimize the aggregate financial resources of the new constituents, comprising approximately 4,000 new households.

Building within the aggregate and collective income of the households meant that we could engage the innovative resources of material, structural, and environmental engineering and access a far higher level of building technology and quality control. Assuring the privacy and other aspects of suburban living was a design mandate that would be sustained by a much deeper well of experimentation, modeling, and coordination than suburban housing had provided historically. The work was in effect a new form of public housing on publicly-held lands that used private wealth to support the buying capacity and sustain a highly capitalized R & D-laden new work of architecture. *Simultaneous City* was developed with team members including Rosanne Haggerty, Community Solutions; Nadine Maleh, Community Solutions; Matthias Schuler and Erik Olsen, Transsolar; Mark Malekshahi; Zak Kostura, Arup; Brian McLoughlin and Peter Hance, public housing and development; and Jesse Keenan, real-estate economics.

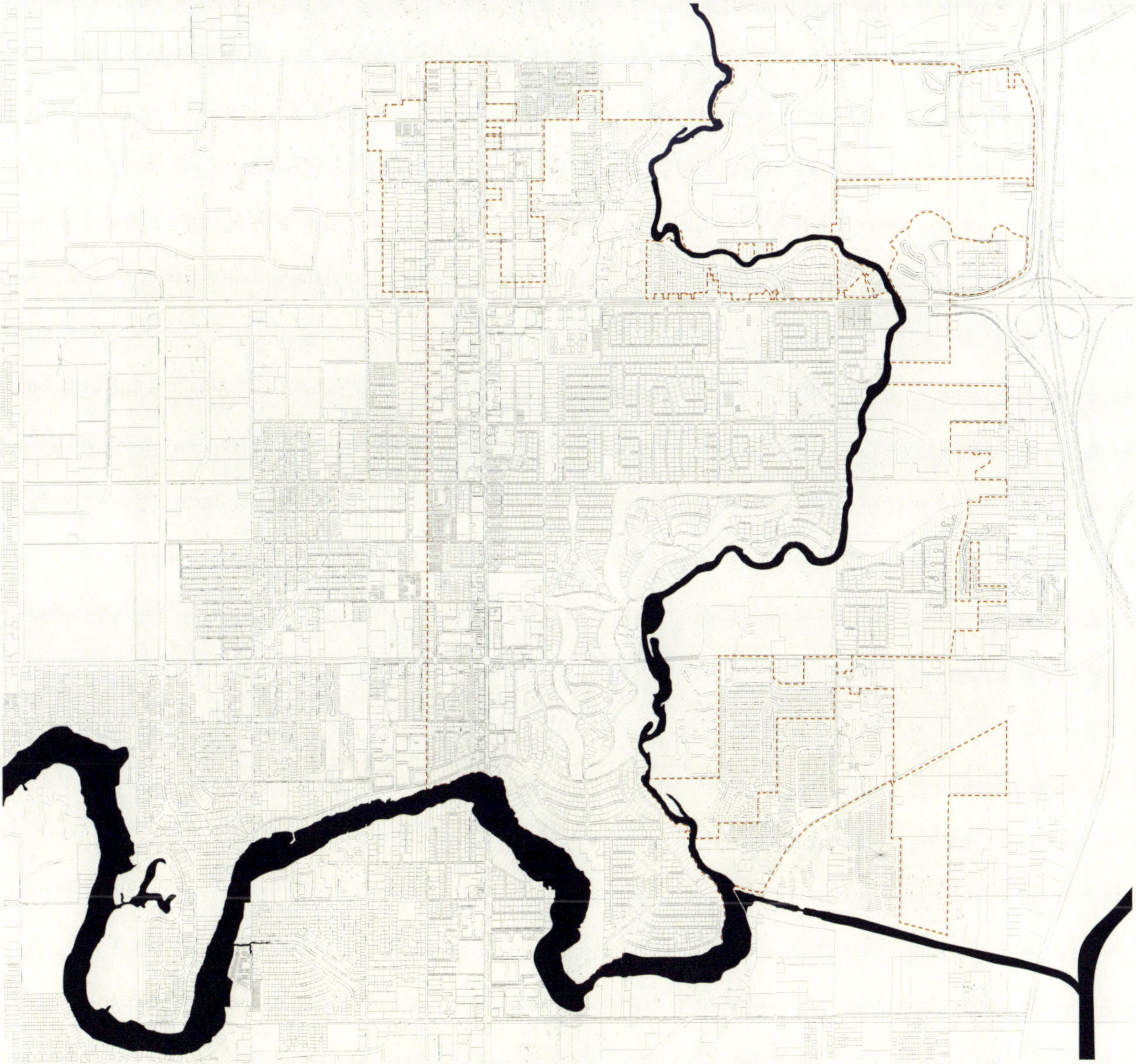

Bell-Seong, Visible Weather, Simultaneous City, Museum of Modern Art, 2012

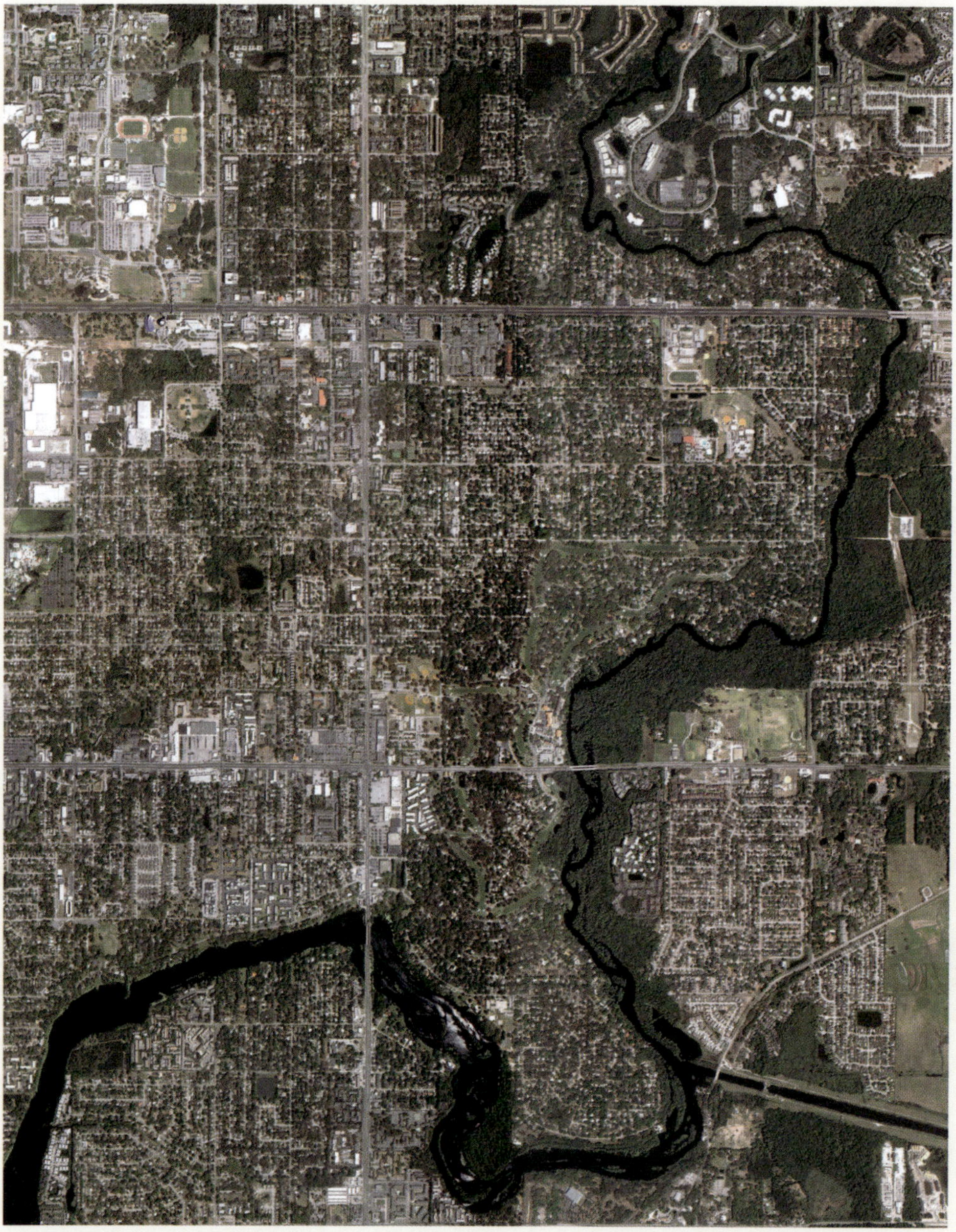

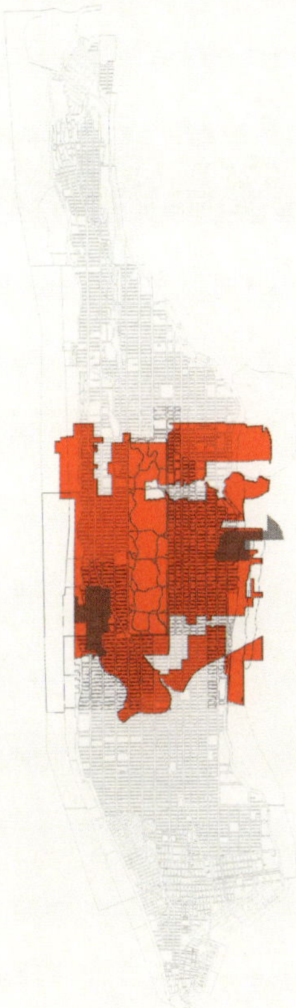

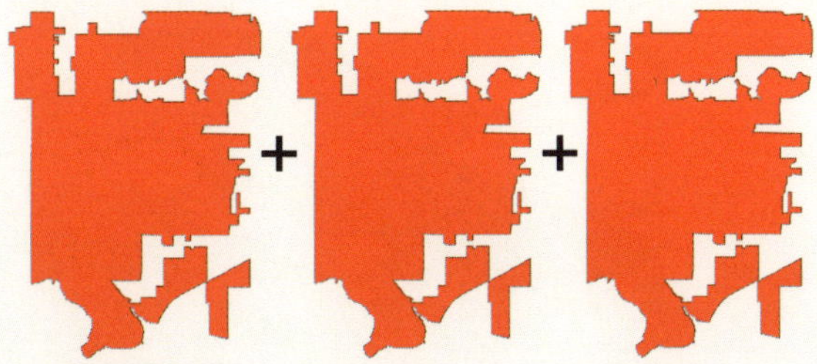

Manhattan
Area
14,720 Acres
23 Sq. Miles

House units
857,000

Population
1,585,873

Density
108 Person/ Acre

Temple Terrace
Area
4,600 Acres
7.15 Sq. Miles

House units
10,551

Population
24,620

Density
5 Person/ Acre

7.15 Sq. Miles
4,600 Acres

1.3 Sq. Miles
833 Acres

0.65 Sq. Miles
417 Acres

Temple Terrace, Florida borders the northeast of Tampa. At 7.7 square miles, or 5,000 acres, it hosts a population of 26,000 residents that form 10,500 households, or five people per acre of land. In comparison, New York City's early-2000s Hunter's Point South development on the East River in Queens opposite the United Nations called for more than 200 people per acre.

Bell-Seong / Visible Weather, 2012. Density is both formal and economic and can be targeted to achieve the specific enhancement of wider regions. Bell-Seong proposed a redeveloped border between Tampa, Florida and Temple Terrace. North 56th Street is sited about 600 feet east of the Tampa border and within Temple Terrace. At approximately 2.9 miles in length, it is similar to the north/south dimensions of Central Park. Our proposal and project, developed for the Museum for Modern Art, sought to re-zone and alter legal property setbacks and land use, adding new development and a new population to this border and creating a new high-density urban area by utilizing underdeveloped property along this axis. Since its founding in 1929, Temple Terrace has struggled to sustain solvency in part due to its provision of full municipal services with such low land occupancy and density. Our proposal would nearly double the population of the city and increase its tax base while also increasing sustainability in new passively cooled housing types. Temple Terrace was modelled as part of Bell-Seong/ Visible Weather's contribution to *Foreclosed Re-housing the American Dream*, commissioned by the Museum of Modern Art.

Land and Structure / A Real Estate Transaction

The single-family house, refined and created in immense numbers in 20th century post-war US suburbs, fuses land and structure as an increasingly normalized, near-commodity asset. The standardized house, sold in immense numbers and built since Levittown within a stream of choreographed sub-contractors, trades, and materials, is first made possible by the acquisition of land as property, a cartographically segregated precinct of the Earth made tradable as a titled territory with precise boundaries described in its legally assigned paperwork. Together, the house and land form the parameters that allow the government to define land use and urban density, the predominant forms of zoning that shape US housing markets and settlement patterns. The local zoning statutes typically involve separating home from work, home from school, home from production, and for nearly a century, rely on private automobiles to connect the discrete uses, and forms of occupancy and ownership. Discussed in cultural terms, the title of the single-family house is easy to relate to a series of agents and actors who perform its development practices, operate within its real-estates indices, and participate as users. For decades, critiques have been put forward of the sustainability of the single-family house, yet in the aftermath of Covid19, we have seen it gain immense stature as an investment, as a social instrument, and a cultural aspiration. All of this belies the actual complexity of its role in real estate and can give us a too-short vantage point on its reliability as an investment.

The single-family house is a product of land and structure: each makes the economic value of the other possible. They also condition a form of land use and density fusing each house to an individual site. Economists Morris A. Davis and Jonathan Heathcote describe this in their 2006 essay "The Price and Quantity of Residential Land in the United States":

"One can conceptualize a house as a bundle comprising a *reproducible tangible structure* and a *non-reproducible plot of land* [emphasis added]. When the value of a home is decomposed this way, land capitalizes the market value of a home's location." They continue: "On the demand side, the physical structure is valued as a capital input in home production and leisure activities, while land capitalizes the market value of local schools and the commuting distance from employment centers. On the supply side, the land-structures distinction is even more stark: structures are easily reproduced, while desirable residential land is not." Their finding: "housing combines both structure and land components whose prices evolve quite differently."[4]

According to their research, in the post-1970s economy, land in what were increasingly becoming metropolitan areas became a greater percentage of housing costs. Land in the post-1971 economy increases at a much steeper rate than structures. Land is also, they believe, more affected in price by contributing factors such as interest rates. Structures (houses) are less affected, if at all. This equation might account for architects, planners, and some activists tending to use increased density to offset land value, turning architecture into a form of spatial arbitrage and financial leverage.
It monetizes land, and its increased valuation drives up municipal tax receipts: land monetizes the city. Meanwhile, the housing *on the land* provides shelter: a home to support a job that monetizes the entire apparatus. Far from being a simple improvement to land, a structure is part of creating the means to carry its costs. A job provides for a mortgage, while the structure as a house instigates consumption, and land fuels value-added revenue to fund the city's institutions.

Davis and Heathcote offer a vantage point on nearly 50 years of escalating land costs and higher density in job-rich areas of the nation.

People who have flocked to urban areas for jobs accept high land costs as normal and inevitable. Land costs are shown to be more volatile: in this equation the risk associated with a mortgage is not attributed to the structure as much as the land. High land costs diminish the role architecture plays in the provision of affordable housing; they also turn buyers into land speculators as we seek shelter. Evidence shows that during a crash, land falls farther and faster. Everyone becomes a speculator in the middle of a deeper, more volatile form of risk. Affordability in expensive housing markets is achieved through increased density, but where single-family houses are concerned, each owner carries the risk associated with their property, especially the house's land. Stacked against globally traded housing debt in the form of financial instruments and derivatives, the arithmetic density of architecture is no match for the calculus of a market where jobs built up over decades may be replaced by automation and where the high cost of urban land is a bet most cannot afford or risk. We have seen a crash tied to a lack of transparency in housing debt and its derivatives. Will we see a crash attributed to historically new drivers of job loss and an associated hit to land values and to the debt tied to land, all in the hands of private households?

Before we were aware of the Davis and Heathcote research, we encountered and began working with what turned out to be their data sets. We had accessed data on structure and land valuations made available by the Lincoln Institute of Land Policy, where Davis and Heathcote had created and publicly shared their database. We began to map the Excel-formatted information, exploring the valuations assigned to the structure and land in different regions of the country. Davis and Heathcote today provide their research and datasets at American Enterprise Institute on a public website, and we have since updated and expanded our use of this data.

The results provide a visually stunning window when simply mapped into graphics and show that today land for housing in major suburban and edge cities can account for as much as 80 percent of housing costs.

In California in 2005–06, at the peak of the pre-Great Recession market, land accounted for 77 percent of housing costs statewide. In the pre-crash market, this left only 23 percent of housing costs going toward actual building. Thirty years earlier, land in California was closer to 27 percent of housing costs. The ratio of structure to land had inverted in 30 years, making the cost of the land three times the cost of the building.

Density can diminish the risk and cost, but density is also seemingly less attractive when the role of jobs to support debt diminishes the hyper-financialization of housing in cities. Debt becomes intolerable when jobs disappear and the value of urban locations shifts. Covid19 is a strong indicator that the public will consider alternatives to expensive land when remote work and joblessness increase. Long linked to the social capital gained through the cultural and economic benefits of living in urban centers, density may today be irretrievably financialized. In other words, has the culture of cities, however socially important, also become a cloak that uses an urban/architectural vocabulary to enable the hyper-financialization of homes? An era of mortgage-backed securities (MBS) and credit default swaps (CDS) demands more return and leverage. What happens when automation makes jobs less available? What buyer or bank will still accept this risk equation? What new product can remake the use of lower-cost land and create climate-positive and income-producing housing?

Davis and Heathcote's 2006 essay and its conclusions were derived and made possible by their wider, carefully curated exploration of historical data on structures and land values in the US. They made use of records that allowed them to discern between the costs of land and structures for housing transactions since 1929. They had particularly precise records and data from 1975 onward, using municipal tax structures that assign separate values to land as distinct from structures. They disaggregate the real-estate asset into its components, allowing them to discern which entity is driving costs and values, and which entity is creating the most financial risk.

Single-family housing emerged as a product of a mechanized, industrial society. If not literally made or manufactured inside a factory, housing was composed of industrialized products that become local when assembled into buildings and architecture. Delivered to a building site—the land component of the property—construction fits otherwise industrial components into a local commodity and congregates it as another form of property, fusing land with the structure: housing. Davis and Heathcote study this history in an aggregate at scale, which we return to in our next chapter.

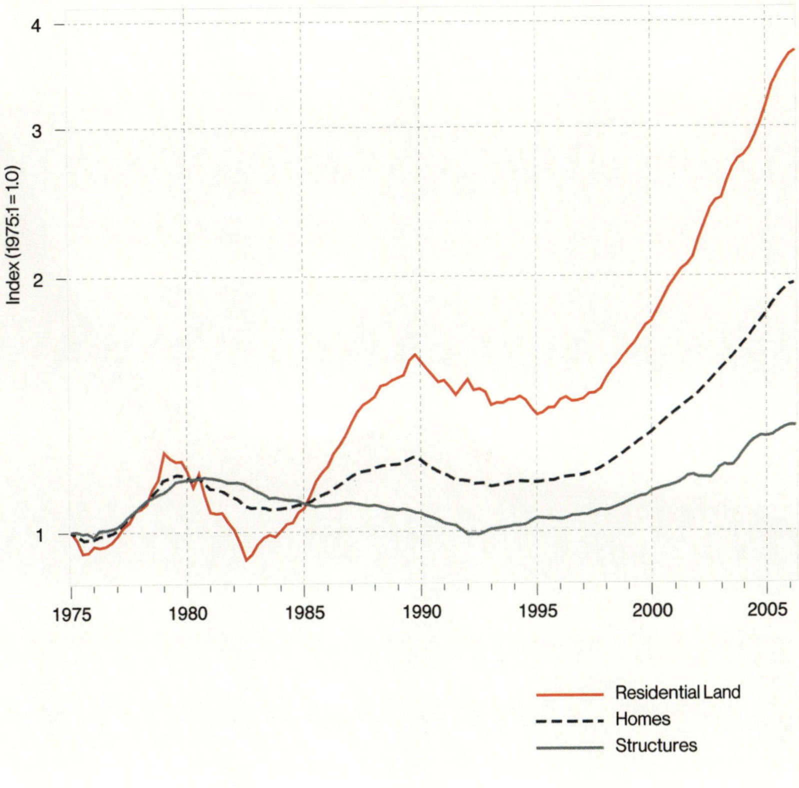

Real Land, Home, and Structures Prices (Log Scale)

In a post-1970s economy, residential land prices and valuations increase at a steeper rate than either the cost of the structure (the house) or the overall "bundle" of the structure and land that forms a real-estate transaction.

Graphic: Morris A. Davis and Jonathan Heathcote, Real Land, Home, and Structures Prices

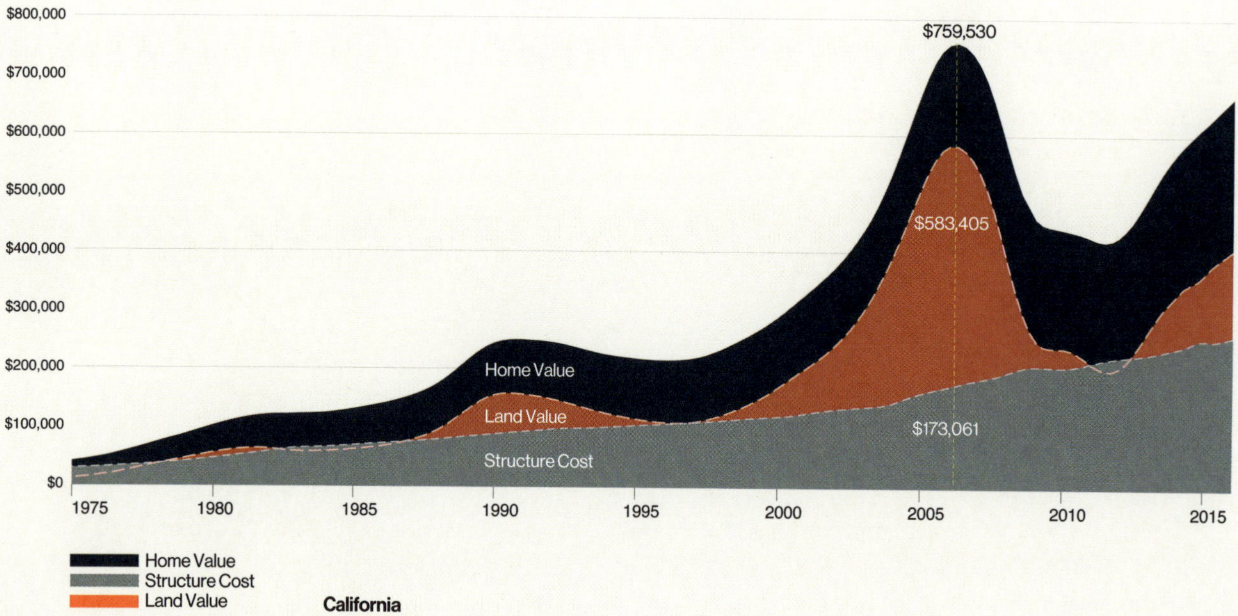

California

Home Value–Structure Cost–Land Value: California
In 2005–06, at the peak of the pre-Great Recession market, land in California accounted for 77 percent of housing costs statewide. In the pre-crash market, this meant only 23 percent of housing costs went toward actual building. Thirty years earlier, land was closer to 27 percent of housing costs in the state. While land values fall in the Great Recession, they sustain high valuations compared to sister states. The value of the structure and land run in parallel, even under economic distress.

Graphic by authors. Data source: Davis and Heathcote; and Davis and Palumbo

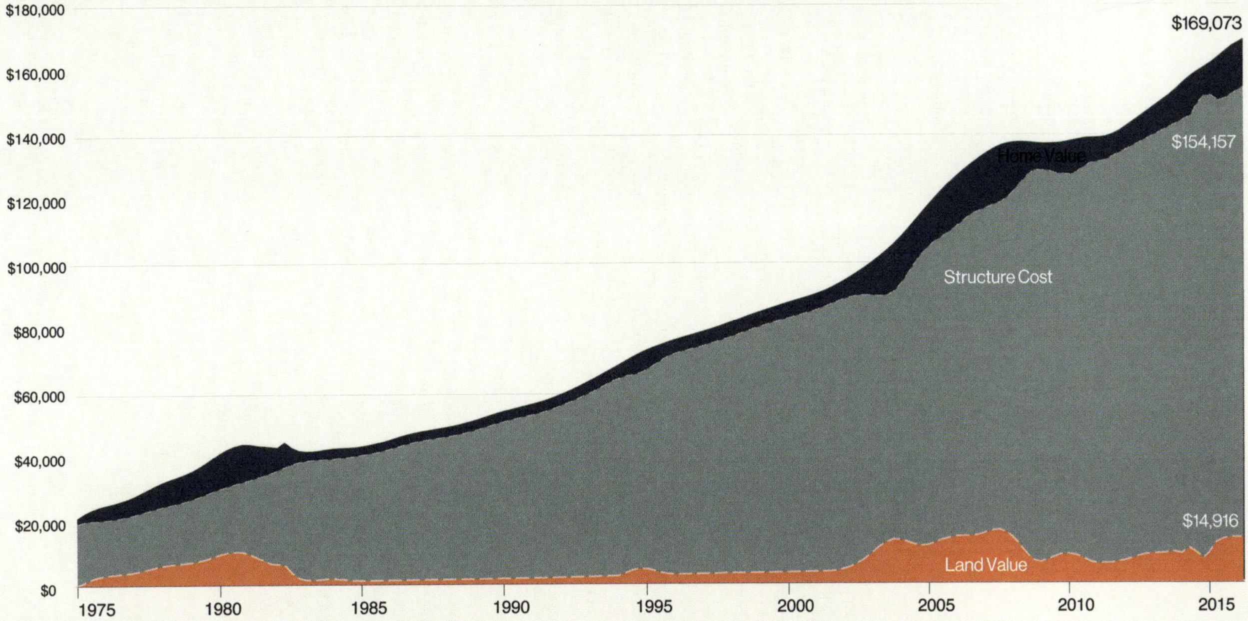

West Virginia

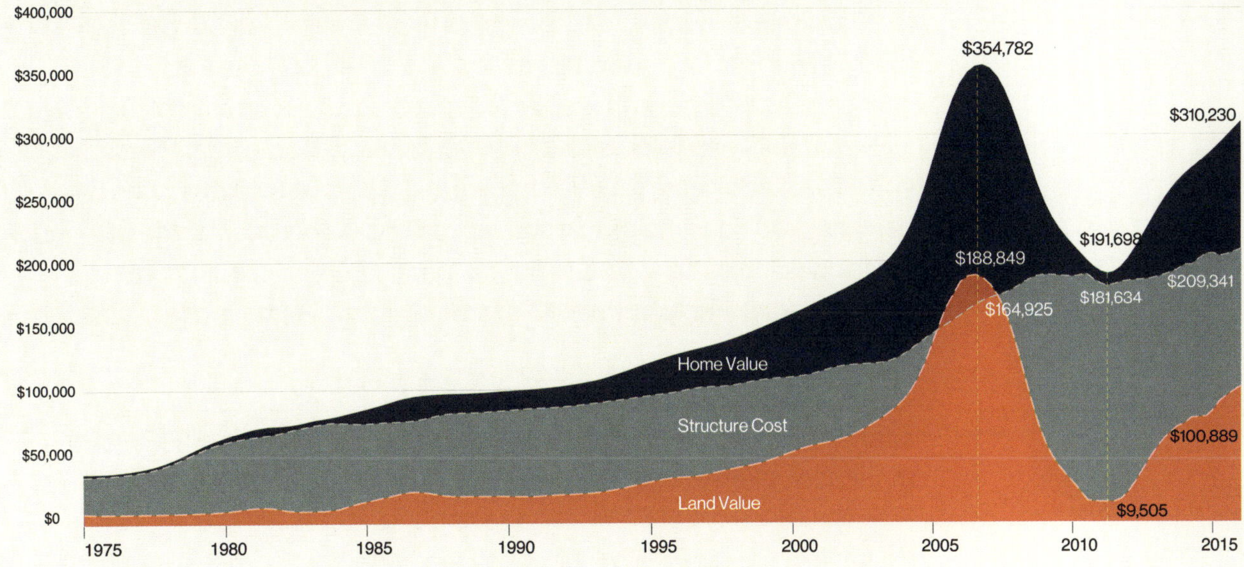

Arizona

Home Value–Structure Cost–Land Value: West Virginia
In West Virginia, the ratios are the inverse of those of California. Land values in the state accounted for 11 percent of a residential real-estate transaction in 2005. They have ranged from five to 25 percent since 1975 and only crested 10 percent between 1975 and 1982, and again between 2003 and 2008.

Home Value–Structure Cost–Land Value: Arizona
In the aftermath of the 2008 financial crisis, residential land values in Arizona plummeted in value. Pre-crash land values were higher than 53 percent of a home purchase. But since 1975, they have been as low as five percent. A 2011 residential real-estate transaction was almost exclusively based on the value of the structure. The volatility of land, as noted by David and Heathcote, was far higher than that of the structure. Between 1975 and 2016, the land fluctuated in value from five percent in recent years to a high of 53 percent.

New Forms of Density

Building in an urban context is today only possible through legal forms and networks of property and wealth, often requiring a rapid return on investment to the developer. The buyer's access to a home usually entails a long-term amortization of debt, spreading out payments over a decades-long mortgage. These two time cycles determine most of the decisions in housing: the need to build outside, regardless of weather conditions, with some control over the process, a degree of rigor, and within tight schedules. A prospective buyer has to be willing to not only buy the property but sustain a mortgage for decades to come. The building needs to be rapidly assembled on site and have the ability to last decades. But housing in this realm today serves a narrow realm of the market. A National Association of Realtors survey showed that the market in 2023 lacked at least 320,000 homes that would be available to the 51 percent of US households that earn up to $75,000 per year.[5] In the US, those households can afford to buy less than a quarter of listings in the current market. Five years ago, this income group could afford to buy half of all available homes.

Households other than white or Asian also are disproportionally affected by a lack of access to market-rate housing at affordable prices. This real-estate industry statistic also undercounts vast sections of the US market that are essentially "under-banked," whether because they do not have or cannot obtain a bank account due to informal sources of income, legal issues, or their citizenship status, or because they are unable to get traditional loans or credit, and therefore are not served by banking and mortgage mechanisms at all. Freddie Mac identifies five major constituencies and regions of the nation where manufactured housing or mobile homes account for as much as 20 percent of households' access to shelter. In 2023, they estimate as many as 8.5 million households lived in manufactured homes. Frequently set on leased pad sites, these households often find financing as non-collateralized debt, similar to an automobile loan, and they incur far higher interest rates charged for a landless housing type valued as a depreciating rather than appreciating asset. The median income of these households was about $30,000 per year in 2023.[6]

Detached single-family houses, built with lumber and a myriad of off-site, pre-engineered, and manufactured products such as drywall and windows, are rarely more than two stories tall. This type of construction requires little in terms of research and development. The single-family house is not capitalized in ways that afford research and development outside of a limited set of components. The machines that aide their construction are straightforward: excavators, power table and chop saws, battery-powered hand-held drills, air compressor-driven nail guns, and paint sprayers. Housing is often built with wide construction tolerances to allow for error and field-based improvisation. Steel is rarely used except for small plates or straps that tie discrete wood members together: a two-by-four or two-by-six is strapped to its foundation sill plate or header to assist in a windstorm or hurricane. Estimates show labor in a typical house as high as 2,000 on-site hours, 1,900 indirect or off-site hours (in components and materials), and 250 managerial hours. The simultaneous pressure of efficiency and speed in housing couples with a practice of looseness and fit. While organized, the processes that form housing benchmarks are dramatically lower than most other scaled products. Toyota, for example, needs approximately 29 hours to produce its vehicles on average. Housing as we know it has never approached either the precision of advanced manufacturing or its scale and speed.

It also does not have any kind of comparable R & D. The wealth production from housing has come from its real-estate values and the trading of its leverage, tied to and derived from property. Architectural concerns with life safety and thermal integrity might follow instrumental means: verification of structural mechanics and life safety are a common goal. But what of the accelerated forms of wealth that scale affords: how do we imagine a new generation of wealth made possible by building housing in new forms that can achieve a greater scale and larger numbers? And where and to whom will that wealth flow? Are these even architectural concerns?

Bell-Seong / Visible Weather, 2012. Simultaneous City, Temple Terrace, Florida. A digital study for a planned exhibition physical model shows new high-density housing and civic and office space adjacent to low-density single-family houses.

1929: An Aesthetics of Scarcity/ Machines Outsource Wealth

In a little-discussed passage written in 1929, Walter Gropius, founding director of the Dessau, Germany-based Bauhaus, captured a confounding scenario in the uses of technology as applied to the design of housing. Gropius became a profound influence in 20th century design and design education in large part by situating the aesthetics and beauty of design closer to industrial manufacturing, processes that are only producible at a large scale with capital and investment in machinery, research and development, a substantial labor force, and a goal of factory production in order to replicate the item in large numbers.

But as Gropius imagined the importance of machines for housing design and production, he framed a problem that persists a century later. In a cascading series of four points, sorted in an arithmetical and architectural order, Gropius delivered the reader to a hard conclusion. Technology, he wrote, "operates within the framework of industry and finance, and since any cost reduction achieved must first of all be exploited for the benefit of private industry (the owner of the technology), it will only be able to provide cheaper and more varied dwelling if the government increases private industry's interest in dwelling construction by increased welfare measures."[7] In the descending series of points, he leads himself to a conclusion: if technology increases the efficiency of making/constructing or manufacturing housing, the increase in productivity and its wealth production will fall to the owners of the technology, not to the owners or users of the end product: housing. A dent in housing costs—access to what he called a "cheaper and more varied dwelling"—will only come, he wrote, with a government ordained provision of land, building sites withheld from markets and speculation by the state.

> *"Since Technology operates within the framework of industry and finance and since any cost reduction achieved must first of all be*

> *exploited for the benefit of private industry, it will only be able to provide cheaper and more varied dwelling if the government increases private industry's interest in dwelling construction by increased welfare measures. If the minimum dwelling is to be realized at rent levels which the population can afford, the government must be requested to: (1) prevent waste of public funds for apartments of excessive size . . . for which an upper limit of apartment size must be established; (2) reduce the initial costs of roads and utilities; (3) provide the building sites and remove them from the hands of speculators; (4) liberalize as far as possible the zoning regulations and building codes."*[8]

Gropius, in his sequence of four points, reaches a conclusion: agents of government should intervene in property and remove at least some land from speculation. In doing so, he effectively locates the potential of architectural experience apart from the land it occupies and apart from the wealth creation that industrial processes export to real estate and its developers, who own the production and its machines. Gropius imagined, perhaps only briefly, alleviating the pressure land costs create as the first gate of architectural experience. Ninety years later, cities worldwide are struggling with the same question in exponential terms. For much of the past 100 years, architecture has been formulated around themes of scarcity, often born of land costs but carried by architecture. Cast as a today diluted-but-*minimum* existence, it can lead to a darker quasi-monumentalizing of loss. We design an aesthetics of what is not possible and create an amnesia of what we imagined and could not sustain. Davis and Heathcote help lift that amnesia: the cost is increasingly not architectural, raising the question, what resolves scarcity if density begins to fail or if density itself becomes less attractive as jobs are lost in urban regions of the nation?

8 Minutes, 20 Seconds did not begin with a query of the Bauhaus, but in assembling the work we share here, Gropius's short passage is one of many parallel paths and points of entry that we balanced that hovers in a matrix of entry points in framing a question: Why is housing so scarce for so many people and how can we remobilize technology toward a future form of housing that would keep the wealth afforded by technology local to the user and resident of housing. We want, in effect, to encrypt that value as a protected asset for the benefit of the user. Would we even call it housing or instead a new type of asset closer in its characteristics to an energy or a productive asset that generates an income and appreciates in value?

Housing as we know it today is a broadly accepted and central term in architecture, planning, and economics, but it has a relatively short history. It forges many specific as well as looser colloquial meanings. It is also routinely understood as something monetized through real estate and figured in matrices of development, as well as in the domestic sphere of private life. Today, automation of labor threatens a vast number of jobs that sustain housing valuations. While the framing can seem to be hyperbolic at times, major economists have asked us to consider this in cold terms: Is it possible that the value of labor might dramatically decrease in a new and deeply accelerated era of automation? If job offerings meaningfully recede in cities, what sustains high land costs? What will fund efforts to address climate change, health, or education if the tax base for housing declines? Is an entirely other economy possible, and where does architecture lead this equation rather than follow it. We think that architecture can provide the next apparatus, but the way we fund and advance design itself needs to change and be capitalized at a large scale in ways it never was during the last century in which housing became hyper-capitalized as real estate.

In the nearly 100 years since Gropius noted a concern about outbound wealth in housing production being captured by the owners of technology, the urbanizing world has only accelerated, and its incantations are often *delirious*. Many say the cultural life of cities makes the cost worth it. They are also pragmatic, viewing density as a sustainability quotient. The urban instigates so much of what we have imagined as a reason for architecture. Our compiled parallel paths warn us today, however, to separate the questions of sustainability from scarcity structures, including former energy paradigms, and governmental or industrial heuristics that have enforced the scarcity mindset of limited assets and land, and a narrow political imaginary. A deep study of renewable energy moves us toward a mathematics and a reality of something of a larger scale and of a quantity that is hard to grasp and is non-human in scope. Scarcity is not a reality. When gauged with a view to the potential of renewable energy, a form of abundance emerges.

The pressures that bear on cities have in the past centuries conspired with real estate and property to make architecture, which should have served as a manifestation of local experience, into an agent of urban wealth. Architecture allowed its profession to be a small-scale provider of occasional relief—to very few people. That makes it urgent it to become a true plastic local agent that offers an alternative.

What forms of land use and density is architecture capable of achieving if the experience of housing were less coupled to real-estate valuations and instead were tied to a far deeper, more intuitive reading of the motion of Earth and Sun? Can architecture go beyond sustainability to grasp its role as one of the very arbiters of life itself that a future less-employed society might need to rely on?

Scarcity

1. After Peak Debt

A Solar Bank

2. After Peak Automobile

Re-Invent the Supply Chain

3. After Peak Labor

Energy Income

4. After Peak Consumption

Personal Trade

Abundance

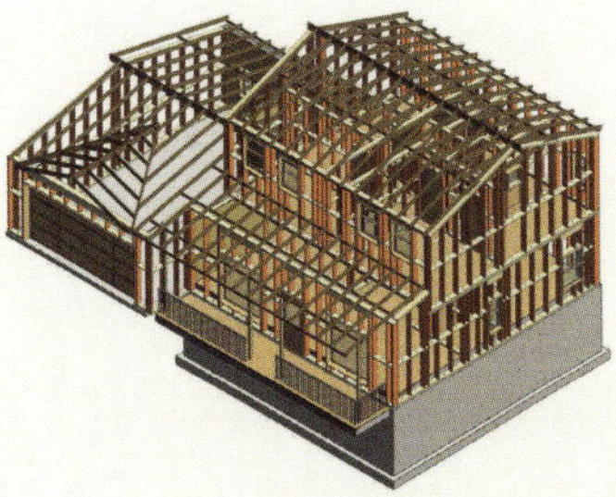

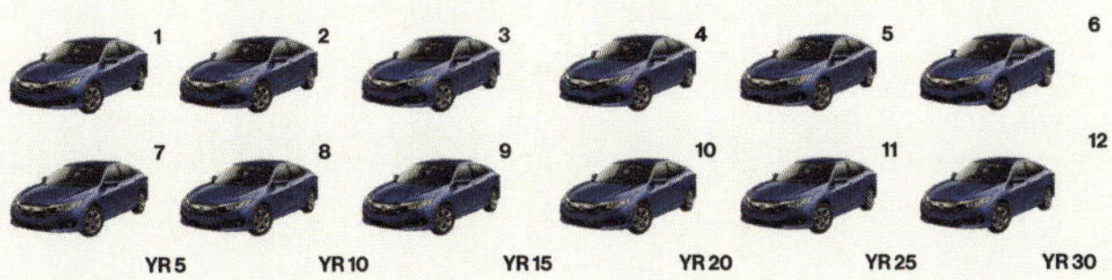

The House (2022-52)

$584,000 →

Single Family House
Houston, Texas
Purchase Price – $314,000
Mortgage (80%) – $251,200
Interest (6.7%) over 30 Years – $332,338

Total Cost – $584,000

Mobility (2022-52)

$396,000 →

Honda Civic – Kelly Blue Book "5 Years Cost to Own" – $33,000
Household – Driver 1 - 6 cars over 30 Years – $198,000
Household – Driver 2 - 6 cars over 30 Years – $198,000

Total Costs Mobility over 30 Years – $396,000

Household Median Income (2022-52)

$1,782,000

Median Income per Year – $59,400

30 Years - Median Income – $1,782,000

Does not included energy, real estate taxes, insurance and maintenance.

The housing and mobility world we live in today emerged in the post-World War II era. It was shaped by a nexus of houses and automobiles. Housing is a province of debt, private mobility (automobiles), labor (jobs), and consumption. Today, each of these foundations of settlement are either thought to have reached peak values or are in the middle of major revisions. Is there a peak private and public debt level? Peak automobile sales are widely predicted to have arrived with the advent of transportation as a widely adopted information technology-based service and longer lasting electric cars. What are the prospects for peak labor? For peak consumption? Or is each being remunerated, re-monetized, and reinvented without economic contraction? Resolving a response to climate change must address these developments, but some are already failing, and few accept the uneven distribution of wealth and housing each provides.

The graphic compares the relative cost to own a single-family house and a private automobile to service mobility over thirty years. In a case study based in Houston, Texas, the cost of a mortgage and interest over thirty years and twelve automobiles effectively parallels thirty years of area mean income. Mobility can easily exceed shelter costs in many parts of the country.
Graphic by authors

Looking Forward

Planning for and mapping potential future renewable-energy generation requires mapping future transmission lines, projecting where energy is generated and where it will be consumed. An investment of trillions of dollars in future infrastructure derived from a geospatial relation to solar and wind energy may be legislated in the federal, state, and municipal tax structures that permit and fund infrastructure, but it also needs to acknowledge a new form of territorial wealth and energy. This may supersede city governance as we know it today.

Princeton University Andlinger Center's 2021 report Net-Zero America: Potential Pathways, Infrastructure, and Impacts maps out scenarios that demonstrate new possible sources and pathways of energy production and delivery.[9] Derived in part from current settlement patterns that possess anticipated capabilities for renewable-energy generation, it traces a decarbonized network of energy production, interpolating past grid-plus-settlement patterns within new grid-plus-settlement patterns. A question we would ask is if the United States added 39 percent on aggregate to its housing stock in the 30 years between 1985 and 2015, what do we imagine can happen in a similar time frame going forward from today? The Princeton Study projects an energy grid for 2050, carefully mapping the progressive changes in five-year increments. The US Energy Information Administration (EIA) estimates that our current grid loses approximately five percent of primary power in distribution and transmission of electricity. As we move to renewable energy will the energy be transported to existing housing stock? Or will new housing stock move toward the energy-creating new settlement patterns? We propose that new housing can in fact serve as the distribution system.

The parallel inquiries that form *8 Minutes, 20 Seconds* lead us to a concern that the job and income sources that have fueled current settlement patterns and real-estate valuations could be far less vital in near-future decades. If so, moving renewable energy over great distances to housing settlement patterns from another era will make less sense. The economics of development in our past century have been based on land as property, and increasingly, on non-home-based labor. We moved from an agrarian and rural nation to an industrial and managerial retail-and-office-based economy. In doing so, the home became a site of repose from work. In future chapters, we try to gauge what the next thirty years might bring to that equation. How many of us will leave home for a job? Does the future of real estate figure land less as property, or as we propose, does housing become more a derivative or downstream by-product of renewable-energy production composed of a new micro-renewable grid of private contributors to the energy sector? Gropius's homeowner becomes a technology owner and is able to harvest its wealth.

It is urgent to reimagine housing for an era that disaggregates dwelling from the cartography of jobs developed in the post-war and post-Bretton Woods eras. As the transmission of energy from fossil-fuel sources and refineries in this era is transformed, we must prepare for large-scale migration. Lower-density development need not be carbon intensive. In fact, it could provide a uniquely regenerative landscape of post-scarcity renewable-energy housing.

Evolution of wind and utility-scale solar projects, E+ Base

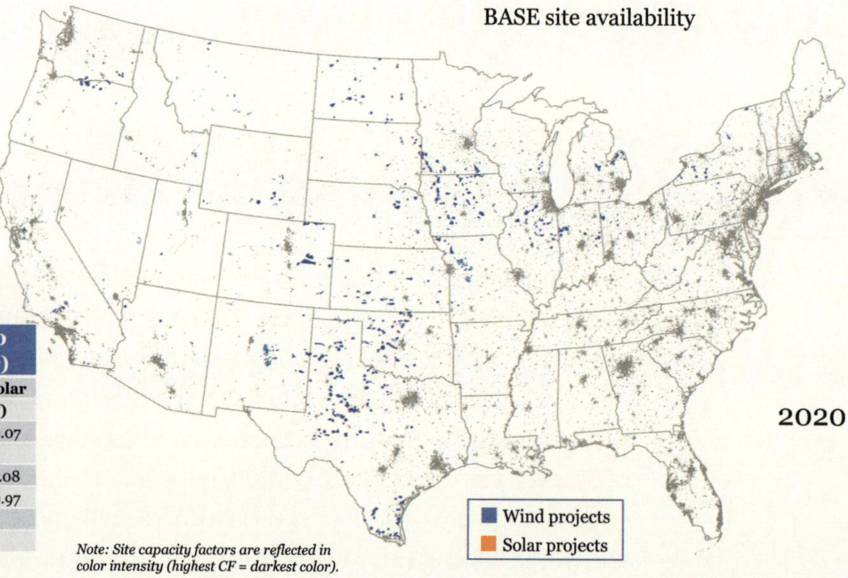

As of end 2020 (modeled year)		
	Wind	Solar
Capacity installed (TW)		
	0.15	0.07
Land used (1000 km²)		
Total	58	1.08
Direct	0.6	0.97

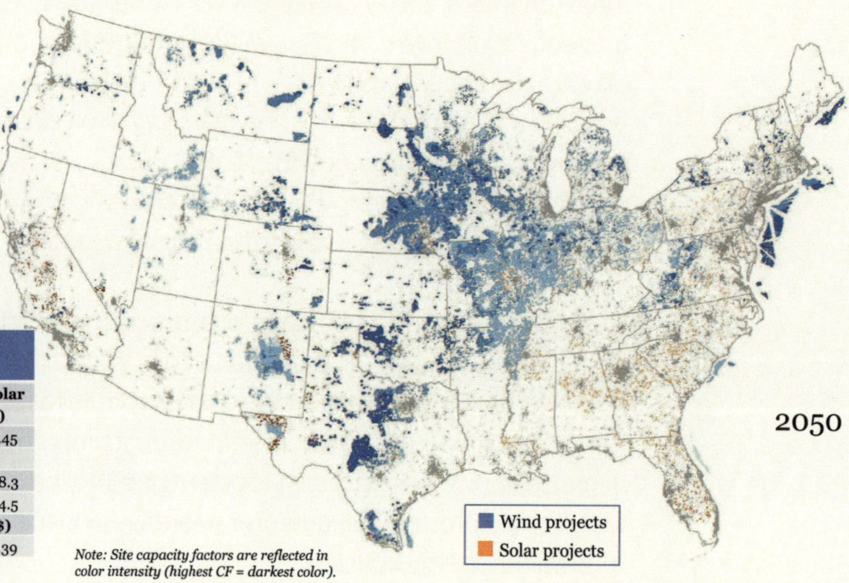

2020 - 2050 (cumulative)		
	Wind	Solar
Capacity installed (TW)		
	1.48	1.45
Land used (1000 km²)		
Total	550	38.3
Direct	5.5	34.5
Capital invested (2018$)		
Trillion $	1.84	1.39

Mapping solar and wind generators and transmission for the E+ pathway with Base land availability

Source: Net-Zero America

Installed solar and wind capacity, top-ranked states, E+ RE+ Base

2050

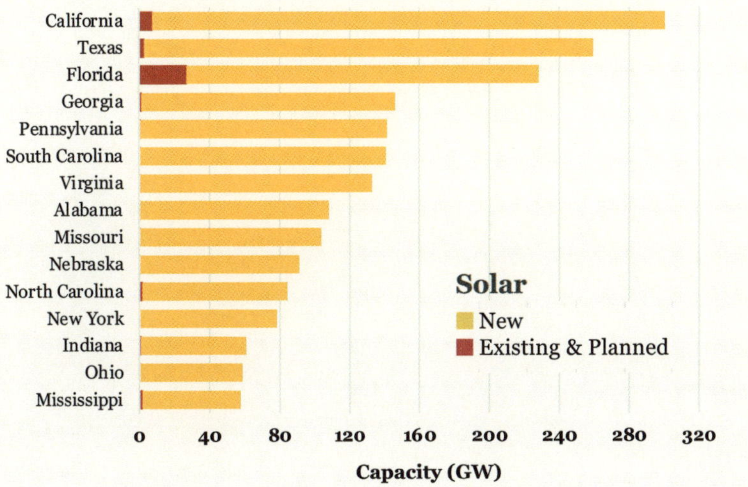

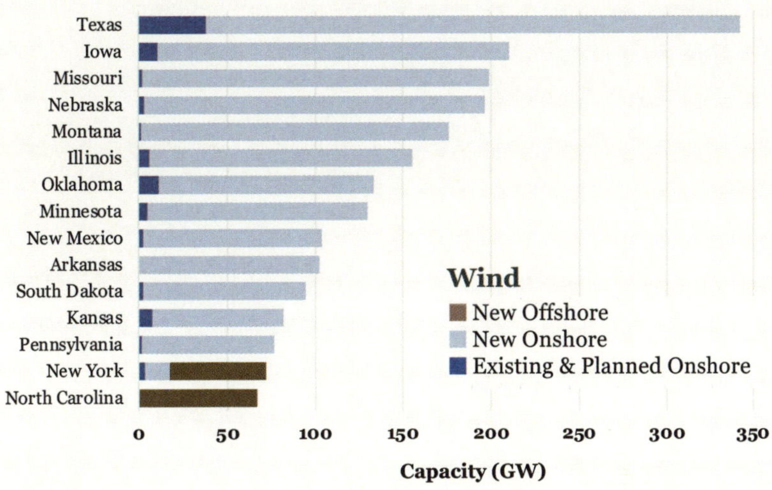

Installed solar and wind capacity, top-ranked states, E+ Base

Source: Net-Zero America

Transmission system in 2020 (≥ 345 kV lines shown)

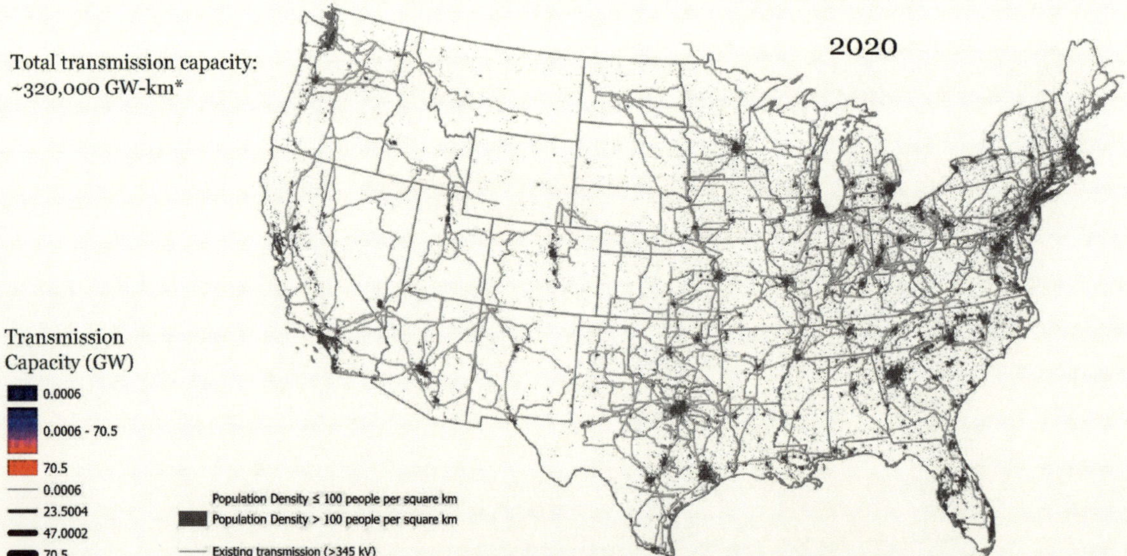

* Homeland Infrastructure Foundation-Level Data (HIFLD), 2008, as cited in National Renewable Energy Laboratory, Renewable Electricity Futures Study, 2012.

Transmission expansions to support wind and solar generation in E+ scenario with Base siting availability, 2050

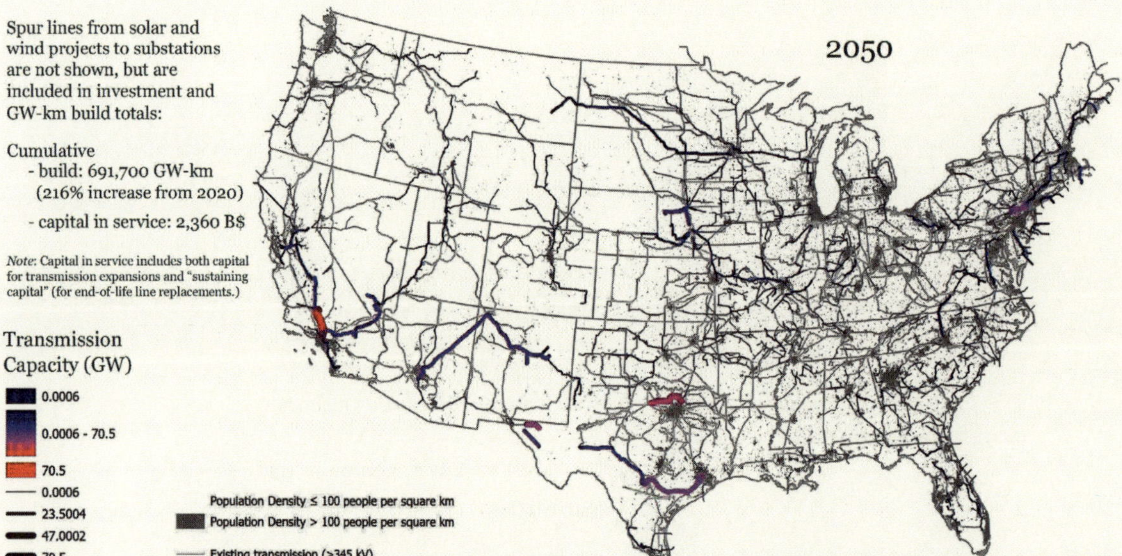

Note: Transmission expansion is visualized along existing rights of way (>160 kV); paths are indicative not definitive.

Transmission expansions to support wind and solar generation in E+ scenario with Base siting availability, 2020–2050

Source: Net-Zero America

Endnotes

1. "Housing Vacancies and Homeownership (CPS/HVS), [Current Population Survey/Housing Vacancy Survey]," Bureau of the Census, Washington, DC 2023, https://www.census.gov/housing/hvs/data/histtabs.html.

2. "Nation," and "Region," Maps, United States Census Bureau, https://data.census.gov/map?q=United+States&g=010XX00US&layer=VT_2022_020_00_PY_D1&basemap=basic&palette=Greens&mode=thematic&loc=37.7214,-99.7282,z4.4430.

3. "New Privately-Owned Housing Units Started: Single-Family Units," U.S. Census Bureau and U.S. Department of Housing and Urban Development, FRED, Federal Reserve Bank of St. Louis, https://fred.stlouisfed.org/series/HOUST1F; "New Privately-Owned Housing Units Started: Units in Buildings with 5 Units or More," U.S. Census Bureau and U.S. Department of Housing and Urban Development, FRED, Federal Reserve Bank of St. Louis, https://fred.stlouisfed.org/series/HOUST5F; "New Privately-Owned Housing Units Started: Total Units," U.S. Census Bureau and U.S. Department of Housing and Urban Development, FRED, Federal Reserve Bank of St. Louis, https://fred.stlouisfed.org/series/HOUST

4. Morris A. Davis and Jonathan Heathcote, "The Price and Quantity of Residential Land in the United States," *Journal of Monetary Economics,* vol. 54, no. 8, 2007, 2595-2620, 41. See also: Morris A. Davis and Michael G. Palumbo, "The Price of Residential Land in Large US Cities," Finance and Economics Discussion Series, Divisions of Research & Statistics and Monetary Affairs, Federal Reserve Board, Washington, D.C., May 2006, https://www.federalreserve.gov/pubs/feds/2006/200625/200625pap.pdf.

5. Clare Trapasso, "Affordability Crunch: Where Middle-Class Buyers Can Afford Homes the Most—and the Least," realtor.com, Jun. 8, 2023, https://www.realtor.com/news/trends/affordability-crunch-where-middle-class-buyers-can-afford-homes-the-most-and-the-least/.

6. Duty to Serve; Underserved Markets Plan, 2022–2024, Fannie Mae, Jan. 12, 2023, https://www.fhfa.gov/sites/default/files/2023-12/Freddie-Mac-2022-2024-UMP-Redline-Jan2023.pdf.

7. Walter Gropius, "Die Soziologischen Grundlagen der Minimalwohnung" [The Sociological Basis of Minimum Housing], *Die Wohnung für das Existenzminimum* (Frankfurt, Englert & Schlosser, 1930). The passage appears and was here sourced from Kenneth Frampton, *A Critical History of Modern Architecture* (New York: Oxford University Press, 1980), 141.

8. Gropius, "Minimalwohnung."

9. E. Larson et al., Net-Zero America: Potential Pathways, Infrastructure, and Impacts, Final Report, Princeton University, Princeton, NJ, Oct. 2021, https://netzeroamerica.princeton.edu/the-report.

Three

Aggregate Scale: Vast Fluctuations in Valuations

Michael Lewis's 2010 book *The Big Short: Inside the Doomsday Machine* helped lodge the banking industry's language of mortgage securities in mainstream culture and eventually a popular film. With an edge of dark comedy, the film in particular left an unresolved warning. The audience is invited to observe as Michael Burry, the real-life founder of the hedge fund Scion Capital, begins to suspect the accuracy of the ratings of hundreds of thousands of mortgages bundled and sold as mortgaged-backed securities (MBS). The year is 2005, and Burry has begun to unpack a series of securities with a laser focus, tracing each of the mortgages back to their origins, checking their delinquency rates and originating credit scores, if they existed, and the ratings assigned by Wall Street's top ratings agencies. He disaggregates the securities, examining the ratings of each individual mortgage. He finds a "doomsday machine," a AAA-rated financial security whose ratings are often unverifiable or false, holding tranches of mortgage debt whose risk levels he can't quantify.

The drama emerges as Burry bets against the housing market at large and its mortgage securitization procedures. He forecasts a collapse of the securities and their overall ratings. The film emerges just five years after the book and approximately 10 years after Burry's audit and forecast proved correct. *The Big Short* brings years of financial and banking complexity to a mainstream audience, relaying a trenchant understanding of how housing markets became illiquid, the propensity to leverage, and the opacity rife in the industry. Mortgages were sold so quickly in those years that records were barely able to keep track of who owned the proceeds of the debt. In the dramatic sphere, the audience observes a quasi-maniacal Burry, portrayed by the method-acting Christian Bale, as he looks closer. Dramatic turns bring us to the realization of what he is seeing and the humiliation of going against conventional and ill-informed wisdom. The film ingeniously shows the big picture and the detail, commanding attentiveness from the audience.

In the decade prior to the release of the 2010 book and 2015 film, the global news media and an increasingly curious public were already attempting to decode an array of banking and securities acronyms and terms: MBS (mortgage-backed security), CDO (collateralized-debt obligation), tranches of debt timed for repayment to investors, and leverage. The 1999 repeal of the New Deal-era Glass-Steagall Act, made null and rescinded in wake of the merger of Citicorp and Travelers insurance in the early 1990s, took on a new resonance.[1] As the subprime-mortgage crisis unfolded, the wider public was increasingly asked to react to deep losses attributed to terms that were often barely understood but widely reported in mainstream news. The Lewis book and film were heralded for making a complex story broadly accessible, revealing the levels of risk present in the vast scale of housing markets. Those who wrote off the crisis as a rare "black swan event" or as unforeseeable had to reconsider.

As the mortgage crisis undermined markets at large, the broad public was also incrementally coming to terms with the prospect of immense corporate bankruptcies beyond housing markets, which they had long been warned might be possible and now were actual. The long-term structural problems of companies like General Motors and Chrysler had been publicly discussed as increasingly untenable. These shocks were not without historical explanation or precedent. But they also learned of more wicked terms and instantaneous, pivotal types of failures: derivatives and credit default swaps where the onset of failure could be immediate and form a rapidly reversing tide, an exponential deluge in the wrong direction. Credit default swaps, financial instruments created as peer-to-peer insurance between banks, were valued at multiples of the gross national product. As housing and housing-credit markets began collapsing in 2008, Erik Sirri, director of the division of trading and markets at the US Securities and Exchange Commission, testified to Congress that the "total notional value of CDSs is estimated to be approximately $55 trillion, according to the International Swaps and Derivatives Association (ISDA), doubling its size in only two years."[2]

It was a figure twice that of the US stock market that year and more than 3.5 times the nation's GDP, growing from $6 trillion in 2004. Sirri added detail to the nature of CDSs and the risk to wider markets: "CDSs are executed bilaterally with derivatives dealers in the OTC market, which means that they are privately negotiated between two sophisticated, institutional parties. They are not traded on an exchange and there is no required recordkeeping of who traded, how much, and when. The dealers include more than a dozen large, globally active banks. London and New York are the centers of CDS trading. In addition to the dealers, active participants in the CDS market include hedge funds and registered investment companies, as well as insurance companies, among others."[3]

While a credit default swap can create liquidity in markets by transferring risk from one party to another, by 2008, they had reached such a scale that no bank was understood to be capable of upholding its agreements. Untenable payouts would emerge if, for example, mortgage-backed securities failed at scales that bankrupted banks. If all of this were the subject of an economics or mathematics PhD, one might have to absorb and learn the detail and real risk, but as 2008 unfolded, it became common to encounter the haunted specter of a financial crisis that would eclipse the Great Depression. The Federal Reserve stepped in, its then-Secretary Hank Paulson declaring he didn't know how much money it would take to stabilize markets as he requested $700 billion to purchase and remove mortgage-backed securities from banking books and US markets. Surely, in Paulson's mind, the $700 billion was small compared to a collapse of $55 trillion CDS agreements.

The public lessons in the terms of financial instruments revealed a deeper concern: the inventors of these often-exotic forms of finance claimed they often didn't understand them either nor foresee the calamity of their failure. "Too big to fail" became a common phrase in daily mainstream news cycles. A form of ironic comeuppance and retribution nonetheless wounded the entire nation and global economy, with billions of people's aspirations undone by the failure of millions of mortgages tied to houses.

Deep and chaotic aspects of volatility added a level of anxiety to the equally devastating loss of household wealth and shelter. Security in the form of leveraged housing, an underwater mortgage led to everyone coming up short.

Scale did not guarantee stability. Homeowners were blamed for unpaid debts as banks raced to shed responsibility for what they knew they never should have lent. And it was all quite clearly imaginable: The rise in debt since the end of World War II would seem to have hit a limit. Mortgage-backed securities shielded and attenuated the rise, but it all eventually returns to someone with income from a job paying a mortgage.

Scale: An Existential Architect Begins an Exit from Scale

In 2005, the Netherlands Institute of Architecture (NAI) published archival materials from Team 10, the architectural group formed by a second generation of then-younger modernist architects and planners. Working in the post-war period, Team 10's members are broadly understood to have adopted and sustained a modernist project of increase in scale while seeking a more subtle and nuanced understanding of everyday life. They adopted an anthropological approach to scale and action in the context of often immense works of urban planning and architecture. The NAI publication *Team 10, 1953–1981: In Search of a Utopia of the Present* was edited by Max Risselada and Dirk van den Heuvel and shares interviews, letters, meeting photographs, and texts from an array of Team 10 members. These fragments of information illuminate Team 10 confronting what was already in the 1960s a shrinking welfare state in France and Europe. The political culture that enabled works of immense scale for large populations of people was being reevaluated, a seeming retreat from the levels of scale we often imagine as a quality of Modern design and development. They form a parallel to events in the United States bearing on architecture and scale, especially the deconstruction of New Deal public housing policies that since the 1960s laid the grounds for more privatized forms of affordable housing.

The archive covers Team 10 activities and correspondence up to 1981, but its most resonant and unresolved portions today involve the group's doubts expressed in the late 1960s and early 1970s. Archival notes show Team 10 member Georges Candilis addressing an emerging but overt sense of vulnerability. In the late 1960s, the firm's immense housing project at Toulouse le Mirail, France—still under construction—forms a backdrop to Candilis reimagining his role in the design of works of such massive scale. Largely but not fully realized, Toulouse le Mirail could now house 20,000 people, a significant portion of the 70,000 it was planned for. Candilis resigned from the project, acknowledging a need to reappraise

George Candilis, Candilis-Josic-Woods architects. A billboard shows the site plan in front of the Pergaud buildings of the Toulouse Le Mirail development in the Bellefontaine district of Toulouse.

Photograph: André Cros, November 13, 1970

the times and the "brutality and complexity" of the problems. A newly empowered conservative government, according to the archives, had forced a reanalysis of the project's future. These notes occur in a chapter discussing a burgeoning awareness that the work had taken a decade to build and was possibly "obsolete even while under construction." The ideas and apparatus that propelled works of such scale, a post war reconstruction and welfare state, were waning.

Team 10, 1953–1981 uses archival notes to bring the reader close to Candilis's thoughts and experience. Protesters called for less central control over urban development; Team 10 members who served as professors faced castigation as students asked them to disengage from work so centrally authored and controlled. Aldo van Eyck and Jacob Bakema were censured by TU Delft for acting as a "lackey of capitalism." Candilis speaks in an interview of people having more to contribute to the design of where they live and of them having some hand in building it. Candilis was asking Team 10 to face the grand scale and social ambition of their work, as well as their own viability in the politically contracting welfare state that had been their patron and a proxy form of conscience. That welfare state was under duress: it was shrinking, while at the same time Candilis was privately doubting the outsize role he and his colleagues played in thousands of people's lives. Mass housing was in effect architecture and planning enacted upon rather than for and with populations.

Anyone who has experienced architectural or urban planning education since has encountered an aftereffect of the sensibility and doubt of this era. Works of immense scale have not ceased to exist, but broadly speaking, designers and development agents (the state, legislators, developers, investors, buyers, and designers) that *might* routinely work at a large scale try to imagine they are offering something other: design that is more responsive to need, more local in aspiration and technique, or at least visually if not operationally disaggregated into smaller physical forms. As the 1960s unfolded, urban design scholars and writers were far less hesitant as they equipped a wider and more mainstream audience with terms and language to dismantle scale. Jane Jacobs most prominently but also sociologist Francis Fox Piven confronted and condemned the larger-scale mechanisms of the welfare state, vividly showing works and policies that operate at the scale of populations often manifest a convertible quality, reenacting and mirroring forms of segregation, and locking people into stratifications they had promised to undo. Concern about scale is a deeply complex part of the design ethos today, but if housing appears to be individuated into smaller units and single-family houses, the banking and procedural means of extracting wealth and procedural compliance remain immense. Financially, housing markets and their derivatives eclipse anything imagined in the era of Team 10.

If the state has since retreated from housing, it is possible to say that so too did architects. An evolved endgame emerged, a treatment of scale that is troubled and in effect existential. As a result, housing as we know it today is still, almost inevitably a concern realized at a wide scale but without the faith that it should be. In most industries, scale affords the financial capacity for research and development. Scale can provide access to new technologies, new means and methods, or simply more didactic forms of testing and prototyping. How architecture benefits from scale today is a matter of dissonance: the financial and capital aspects of housing finance are deeply and technologically enabled and bolstered by it, but the outward forms of housing design and engineering practices are thwarted if not wholly marginalized. If the benefits of scale are present in housing subcomponents, it leaves designers to weave together disparate parts in an uncoordinated supply chain often engineered to the least common denominator.

The benefits that accrue to research-and-development-laden and manufactured products makes it into architecture episodically, as adjacencies. Automobiles, appliances, computers, electronics and software, medical research, and health care all intersect with housing with the benefits of large-scale production. Meanwhile, housing is still realized with a rudimentary form of construction by companies that at their largest are still small by comparison. Only five of the top home builders in the United States have larger than eight billion dollars in market capitalization. The mid-century writings of John Kenneth Galbraith describe the emergence of scale in large corporations as a necessity to assure stability of capital investment. He described General Motors and Detroit's auto industry more generally as operating in the post-World War II-era at such a scale as to provide health care, retirement, and high wages to hundreds of thousands. But he also described a more ruthless invention of seemingly heterogenous customer profiles, each ascribed to a product line that inoculate the corporation from instability born of consumer choice. Scale in Galbraith's description operated to assemble capital, and capital allowed research and development. He saw this in education and health care, structures beyond the corporation. Housing today seems to reside in a similar emulation and dissimulation of scale, but today the volatility of the past few decades reveal housing markets as far from stable, and the largest housing developers themselves are not very large. How a next generation assembles capital for research and development and designs a product that can bear the debt structures dependent on it is an urgent question.

Builder/ Revenue	2021 Leading home builders in the United States in 2021 by gross revenue (in billion U.S. dollars)			2020 Leading home builders in the United States in 2020 by gross revenue (in billion U.S. dollars)			2019 Leading home builders in the United States in 2019 by gross revenue (in billion U.S. dollars)		
	Revenue	No. of Units	$/ Unit	Revenue	No. of Units	$/ Unit	Revenue	No. of Units	$/ Unit
D.R. Horton	$27.93	81,981	$340,689	$21.58	71,292	$302,671	$17.38	58,434	$297,395
Lennar Corp	$25.35	59,825	$423,736	$20.84	53,376	$390,438	$20.56	51,491	$399,293
PulteGroup	$13.38	28,894	$463,072	$9.92	24,624	$402,656	$9.92	23,232	$426,825
NVR	$8.70	21,540	$403,900	$7.33	19,766	$370,738	$7.22	19,668	$367,145
Toll Brothers	$8.43	9,986	$844,182	$6.94	8,496	$816,502	$7.22	8,107	$891,082
Top 5 Builders	**$83.79**	**202,226**		**$66.61**	**177,554**		**$62.30**	**160,932**	
Taylor Morrison	$7.27	13,699	$530,696	$6.13	12,524	$489,380	$4.62	9,964	$463,970
KB Home	$5.71	13,472	$423,842	$4.17	10,672	$390,461	$4.54	11,871	$382,276
M.D.C. Holdings	$5.10	9,982	$510,920	$3.77	8,158	$461,510	$3.21	6,974	$459,564
Meritage Homes	$5.09	12,801	$397,625	$3.03	11,834	$255,788	$3.61	9,267	$389,015
Century Communities	$4.22	10,805	$390,560	$3.03	9,453	$320,216	$2.48	8,000	$310,125
Top 10 Builders	**$111.18**	**262,985**		**$86.74**	**230,195**		**$80.76**	**207,008**	

Private Construction
$ 1.046 Trillion

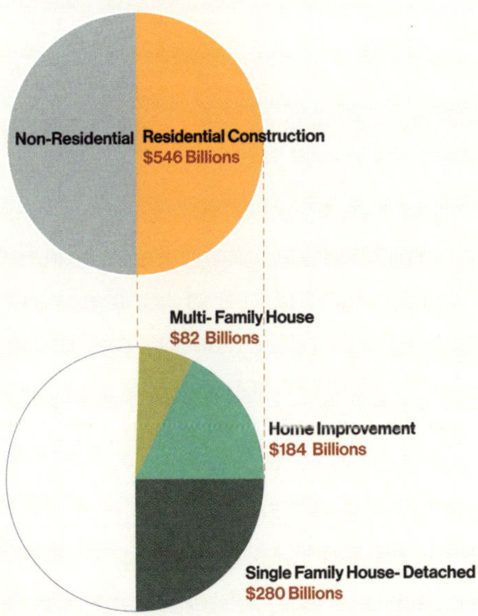

The top ten home builders in the United States by revenue, number of units, and cost per unit in 2019, 2020, and 2021.[4]

United States Census: Value of Construction Put in Place in 2019. Residential housing accounted for $546 billion dollars in construction. Single-family houses accounted for 51 percent of all residential construction. Home improvement spending accounts for 34 percent of all residential construction spending.[5]

Scale: NYCHA and Levittown

"This title amends the United States Housing Act of 1937 by authorizing Federal contributions and loans for local programs involving not to exceed 810,000 additional units of low-rent public housing over a six-year period. The Public Housing Administration may authorize local authorities to commence construction of 135,000 units each year. The President, however, is authorized to accelerate the program to not more than 200,000 units per year or to retard the program to not less than 50,000 units per year, subject to the total authorization of 810,000 units, if he determines, after advice from the Council of Economic Advisers, that such action is in the public interest."[6]

—Housing Act of 1949, Public Law 171 (63 Stat. 413)

If read without specifics of context or human need, the Housing Act of 1949, enacted by the United States Congress seems immense in scale. It created a political apparatus to fund, plan, and create as many as 810,000 new Public Housing Authority (PHA) units in cities across the nation. Set atop approximately 125,000 units of public housing already realized under the New Deal Housing Acts of 1934 and 1937, the 1949 legislation created the potential of nearly one million new PHA units. A year later, the 1950 Census estimated a total of 46 million housing units in the country. At the outer limits of their funding and authorizations, the Housing Acts of '34, '37, and '49 created a path for the US government, in partnership with states and cities, to enact housing on a scale equivalent to approximately two percent of the nation's existing housing.

If measured as a private business, public housing in 1949 had no comparable enterprise among private companies engaged in home building. Levittown, New York, begun in 1947, reached a total of approximately 17,000 units over four years at its completion in 1951. As a forerunner to the industrialization

HOUSING ACT OF 1949 3

increase in its title II insurance authorization. The extensions under title I relate to small loans for alteration and improvement and new construction and under section 608 to rental housing. The increase in insurance authorization applies to all types of housing under title II, owner-occupied, small and large scale rental and sale housing, including cooperative housing.

TITLE III. LOW-RENT PUBLIC HOUSING

This title amends the United States Housing Act of 1937 by authorizing Federal contributions and loans for local programs involving not to exceed 810,000 additional units of low-rent public housing over a 6-year period. The Public Housing Administration may authorize local authorities to commence construction of 135,000 units each year. The President, however, is authorized to accelerate the program to not more than 200,000 units per year or to retard the program to not less than 50,000 units per year, subject to the total authorization of 810,000 units, if he determines, after advice from the Council of Economic Advisers, that such action is in the public interest.

Federal annual contributions may not exceed the amounts which, with the required local tax exemption, are necessary to make up the difference between the rents which the low-income families can afford to pay and the annual costs incurred in the operation of the projects, including interest and amortization of all capital borrowings. In no event may they exceed the aggregate annual contributions authorization, reaching a maximum rate of $308,000,000 per year after the total program is in operation.

The act reduces the maximum period for loans and annual contributions from 60 to 40 years and adjusts the basis for Federal contributions in accordance with the increased annual amortization requirements.

Provisions in this title strengthen the statutory safeguards to assure that occupancy of projects is limited to low-income families in need of adequate housing. As in the past, annual incomes of families on admission may not exceed five times the rent, including utilities, but the act recognizes the needs of larger families by exempting from income $100 per year for each minor dependent. The title further requires local authorities (1) to establish upper rental limits for admission to projects at least 20 percent below the lowest rents at which private enterprise unaided by public subsidy is providing an adequate supply of decent housing in the respective localities, (2) to provide maximum income limits for admission and continued occupancy, (3) to require the removal of families found to be ineligible as the result of periodic reexaminations of tenant incomes, (4) not to discriminate against welfare cases, and (5), subject to specific preferences stated below, to give preference to families having the most urgent needs. In determining the eligibility of families for continued occupancy, the local housing authorities may exempt $100 for each minor or any part of the income received by minor members of the families (since such income normally will be available to the tenant families only for a short period).

Families who are otherwise eligible and who are displaced or are about to be displaced by public slum clearance, redevelopment, or low-rent housing projects will be given a first preference for admission

3640

The Housing Act of 1949 was immense in scope, enacted concurrent with a steep rise in the development of suburban communities. Its planned scale in terms of creating new public housing units was overshadowed by its urban planning. Under the auspices of urban renewal, the 1949 Housing Act caused immense displacement of non-white households. Structurally erasing historical neighborhoods and communities, it relied on complex and nuanced terms to define the legal and economic grounds for wholesale destruction of neighborhoods, while simultaneously seeking new means to review and limit eligibility for public housing.

of housing, William J. Levitt built housing in the hundreds of units per year in the pre-war period. Levittown, realized on 1,200 acres in Nassau County, New York, brought this figure into the thousands. The New York City Housing Authority (NYCHA) in 1950 was already far larger. NYCHA's 1950s Development Data Book showed a total of 75,952 apartments under NYCHA management. 30,730 were already completed, and 34,967 new units were under construction or pending construction, intended as additional permanent housing. Another 10,255 were for Temporary Veterans Emergency Projects. In 1950, NYCHA accounted for approximately 3.12 percent of New York City's estimated 2,433,465 housing units.

Scale in the post-New Deal and post-World War II eras takes on completely new denominators as housing becomes industrialized and imagined for entire populations. Construction became a form of would-be manufacturing, combining the state and private enterprise. Housing's new impact on the social life and circumstances of millions creates the nexus of a then-uniquely American way of life: housing as mass produced real estate, housing as a by-product of governmental policy, and housing as a downstream product of a quasi-assembly-line labor stream. By 1949, the United States Housing Acts had each increasingly addressed concerns of a federal authority operating at a large scale, upending smaller and local private markets, while stating internal limits on scale and building activity. The 1949 and subsequent '54 acts in particular caused immense and racially targeted displacement, at the same time that their language declared government-backed development would not build more than was removed. The cruelty and racism of the displacement included language of supposed deference to markets. If Levittown became a model for vast regions of the country, public housing increasingly disguised its scale even as it continued to grow. It became a target for conservatives who saw it as government market-making and understood the production of entire precincts and the conditioning of entire environments and populations as structurally intolerable, a prelude to a critique of what became known as structural racism. Housing at the scale of PHA is increasingly suspected of being tantamount to the construction of a population by an outside agent. Levittown persists as a model perhaps most poignantly by way of the isolation afforded by a single-family house and the discrete assignation of a mortgage to the family unit, and thereby responsibility for its related financial transactions, asset value, and proceeds of debt. If NYCHA and Levittown introduced a new scale to housing, each quickly found complex reasons to be wary of that scale, even if few alternatives arose.

Scale has many implications in business and is of particular focus today in computationally enabled practices and economies. A central aspect of this is unchanged since the 1940s: successfully applied, an increase in scale, in for example, production capability, increases revenue at a rate greater than the inherent cost of increasing output. Scale changes the return on investment. It enhances it. The acceleration in scale is literal—more units of something are produced—but the capital return is greater than the stepped multipliers. When this is applied to business, it is understood as innovation. If applied by the government in the realm of housing, it has often been witnessed as unwelcome federal intervention in private markets. In the US case, the market is understood to have constitutional protections broadly afforded by the Fifth Amendment's protection of the right to property, shielding both the wealth it affords and largely prohibiting eminent domain, or the public taking of private property. A landowner is understood to have the right to seek the highest and best purpose for property. The Public Housing Authority owning 3.12 percent of New York City's housing units and a developer whose 1,200-acre real-estate transaction approaches the scale of a small city tests these principles. Property and development approach industrial scales in the post-war era, but the parameters that shape scale in housing and where the terms are drawn in the near future remain a very open concern.

Scale: Vast Creation of Wealth (For Some)

The economics of housing as shelter and instrument of personal wealth and household net worth are a defining aspect the US economy. It has been a prevailing characteristic since the rise of the single-family house and suburban development, when land and house ownership in the form of private real estate took their contemporary form. Wealth accrued in housing ownership has been especially important in the post-1970s as speculative practices and expansive financial instruments around housing grew in the United States and worldwide. This environment of everyday speculators and trade around home values has also created and exposed everyone, homeowners or not, to real-estate risk. The prospect of housing realized at large scales, offering security or less exposure to the downside of arbitrage, seemed more convincing in the years leading up the mid-1980s. The post-war and mid-century housing markets offered more consistent valuations but also less appreciation.

A now-foundational measurement of housing markets, the Case-Shiller Home Price Index, helps visualize this. It sets housing valuations at a historical origin, establishing a benchmark in the year 1890. From this anchor, economists Karl Case and Robert Shiller measure fluctuations in valuations in repeat sales, creating what has become a barometer for US housing, depicting 134 years of housing valuations. From an origin of 100 in 1890, the Index chart's values reached 224.40 in May 2022, during the still-recent run-up in housing prices in the Covid19 era. The prior peak had been 195.82 in December 2005.

But for the years between 1945 and 1985, homeowners saw far less speculation and steep price changes of any duration that were not offset by declines. A peak set in the immediate post-war period matches a peak set in the mid-1980s, 40 years later. From the 1910s to the mid-1940s, there was little if any rise in housing valuations. The volatility that characterizes our recent decades is unique. Knowing this diminishes acceptance of the widely held assumption that prices will inevitably rise. It also instigates a concern: does housing at an increased scale offer the type of security we could expect from such a mass project and investment? As we develop this research, we increasingly think housing has only scaled up in isolated and fragmented ways: in its sub-components, for example, but not the ways it uses on-site labor, curates land purchases, and sells final houses.

Today there are well-documented shortages of housing that show the market abandoning activity in some price arenas. Real-estate location can drive prices, but if scarcity was improved through current practices, would appreciation continue as it has? Has scarcity been maintained in part to assure valuations? The Case-Shiller Index, here, demands closer interpretation as to what drives the index to the heights it reached in the 1980s and beyond. If the supply of housing was dramatically increased, what would occur with valuations and the accumulated debt instruments and obligations tied to each house and its mortgage? Those holding a housing asset over time have by and large accumulated immense equity: any devaluation of asset value would diminish that equity. If a new denominator is added to the wealth equation—renewable energy, in this case—would housing markets find a new level? Would the "stock" that constitutes the housing industry at large increase with a new kind of equity and asset? The house as energy-generating asset disaggregates a part of the value of real estate as we know it while expanding the provision of shelter.

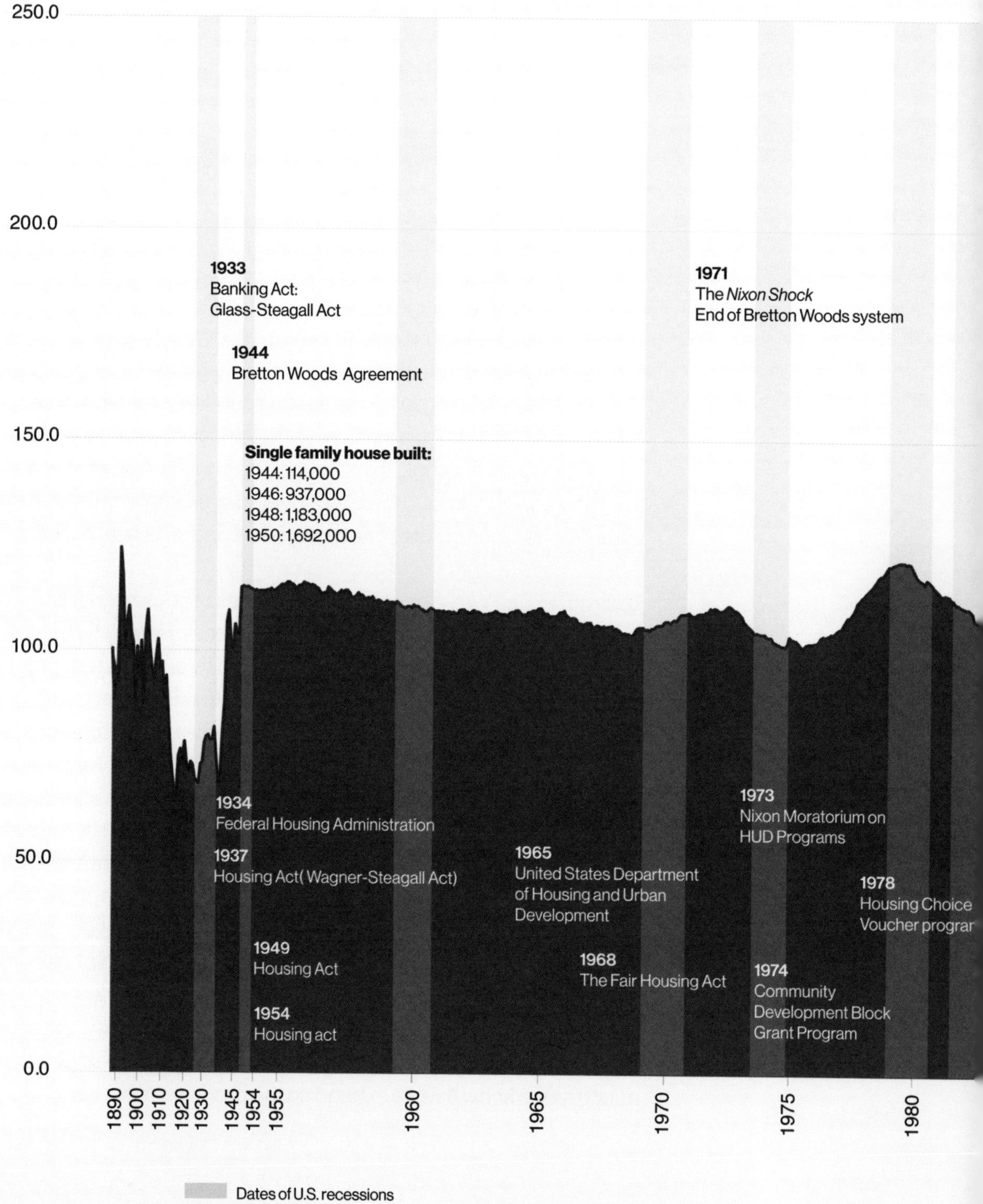

Case-Shiller Index, Real Home Prices showing home prices from 1890 to 2023[7]
Graphic by authors

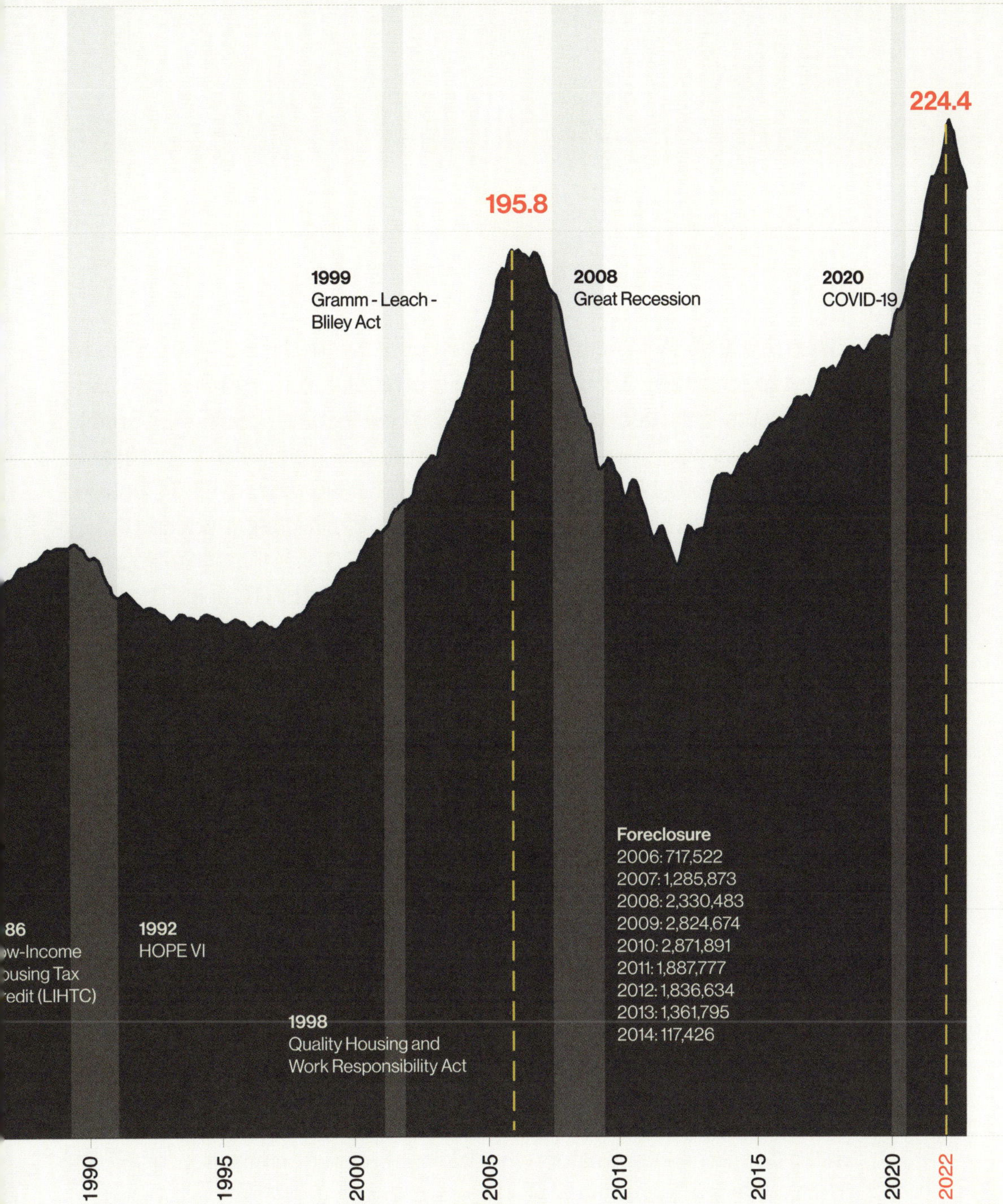
224.4
195.8
1999
Gramm - Leach - Bliley Act
2008
Great Recession
2020
COVID-19
Foreclosure
2006: 717,522
2007: 1,285,873
2008: 2,330,483
2009: 2,824,674
2010: 2,871,891
2011: 1,887,777
2012: 1,836,634
2013: 1,361,795
2014: 117,426
1992
HOPE VI
1998
Quality Housing and Work Responsibility Act
1990
1995
2000
2005
2010
2015
2020
2022

Volatility: Erasing 75 Years of Progress in Five

Since Public Housing Authorities (PHAs) were founded in 1937, the US has realized approximately 1.3 million hard units of federal, state, and city PHA-owned apartments. In the decades since the 1986 Low-Income Housing Tax Credit (LIHTC) laws were inaugurated, creating the modern equivalent of publicly subsidized affordable housing, as many as 3.55 million units of LIHTC housing have been built. During that period, the Clinton Administration reduced the PHA count of hard units by approximately 300,000 units through a program of demolition, replacing them with an increased count of LIHTC units. The 2008 financial crisis threw as many as 16 million homes into foreclosure proceedings, and more than six million were foreclosed. As the crisis ebbed, hundreds of thousands of single-family homes were purchased by hedge funds and often remanded back to the former owners as rental properties. A vast wealth transfer took place: What were privately owned single-family houses were transformed into institutional assets owned by hedge funds. This occurred at then-dramatically reduced post-crash valuations.

Estimates for this are fluid, and it is difficult to count, but a study by the Urban Institute published in 2017 estimated that private equity firms and institutional investors had purchased approximately 200,000 single-family houses. In 2017, the authors estimated the investment reached $33 billion. Today's estimates place the number of investor-owned single-family houses far higher: an Urban Institute estimate puts the number at approximately 574,000 units, as much as 3.8 percent of their estimated 15.1 million single-family house rentals.[8] Their estimate only counts investors who own one hundred or more houses. HUD's Office of Policy Development and Research publication, *Evidence Matters*, offers both current estimates and projections from a variety of real-estate investment firms.[9] MetLife Investment Management, for example, estimates institutional investors own as many as 700,000 single-family houses and forecasts ownership of as many as 7.6 million homes by 2030. The MetLife estimate is 4.6 percent and projects more than 50 percent. The Joint Center for Housing

Studies of Harvard University offers more granular detail. They estimate that in 2021 sales of single-family houses to institutional investors reached "67 percent in Lincoln County, Mississippi; 63 percent in Van Buren County, Iowa; and 52 percent in Tarrant County, Texas." Regardless of source or location the rise of institutional investment in what has been the bedrock investment of a household to secure wealth accumulation is in serious jeopardy. It is not at all clear how the current housing markets can innovate to address this.[10]

Working at a scale that is still far smaller than the number produced through Low-Income Housing Tax Credits or the nation's extant public housing, KB Homes, one of the nation's top home builders, constructed 670,000 housing units over its 65-year history. The few years after the financial collapse appears to have transferred nearly as many single-family houses to hedge funds in a few short years. There are some that herald the hedge funds' accumulation of houses as a market risk-taking and a stabilizing force in the aftermath of crisis. If so, it still raises concerns about the rapidity of the transactions, and the volatility and risk-taking that home buyers enter into unwittingly merely to seek shelter.

As home prices rose in the aftermath of the Great Recession, large numbers of investor-purchased houses were traded to new investors, creating a complex ownership trail and reorganization of unit counts. In some cases, homes were sold and then recombined en masse, with the sellers in effect joining new corporate entities. The net result made single-family houses held in large numbers a new asset class in real-estate. This was accomplished with little if any change to the hard asset itself but only how its value was held, securitizing rental streams into a new financial instrument. A former homeowner could be standing in the same kitchen with less wealth, security, or prospects for the future. The Urban Institute team titled the new asset, "US Single Family Rental—An Emerging Institutional Asset Class," assigning it the acronym SFR.[11]

The asset became the rental income more than the house.

The story is very much unfolding. The rush to the suburbs and single-family houses created in the Covid 19 era accelerated institutional buying. News accounts showed how regional and place-specific activity increased in recent years. CoreLogic research shows that between 2019 and 2022, investor purchases of single-family houses were between 18 and 28 percent of sales, which were made in cash, ironically if not cruelly freezing out those reliant on mortgages, the very people who were exploited fifteen years prior.[12] More homes were foreclosed over just a few years during the Great Recession than were ever realized during the entire 75 years of federally assisted public and affordable housing programs. Units and homes lost to foreclosure in those few years totaled more than were ever built in the nation's seven decades of public housing construction and Low-Income Housing Tax Credits combined. It suggests that the system is broken and needs to be replaced.

We would argue it also shows that, from Levittown to NYCHA to private-equity single-family rentals, housing has neglected the actual benefits of scale, which has enabled innovative products in manufacturing, industrial processes, materials science, energy, and virtually any industry even remotely as capitalized as housing. We think the SFR as an investment asset class and the myriad denominators that have unfolded to create the current milieu are devastating for many, but we optimistically believe that housing is again poised to reengage questions of scale, if only because we need new wealth mechanisms. Too few people are well-housed, which is an ethical question. One has to ask, can housing as we know it produce wealth for investors with less volatility if does not change? We believe it can and must change into an energy asset, gaining status in an entirely other dimensional space—from the Sun and wind—and an economy of an entirely other and larger measure.

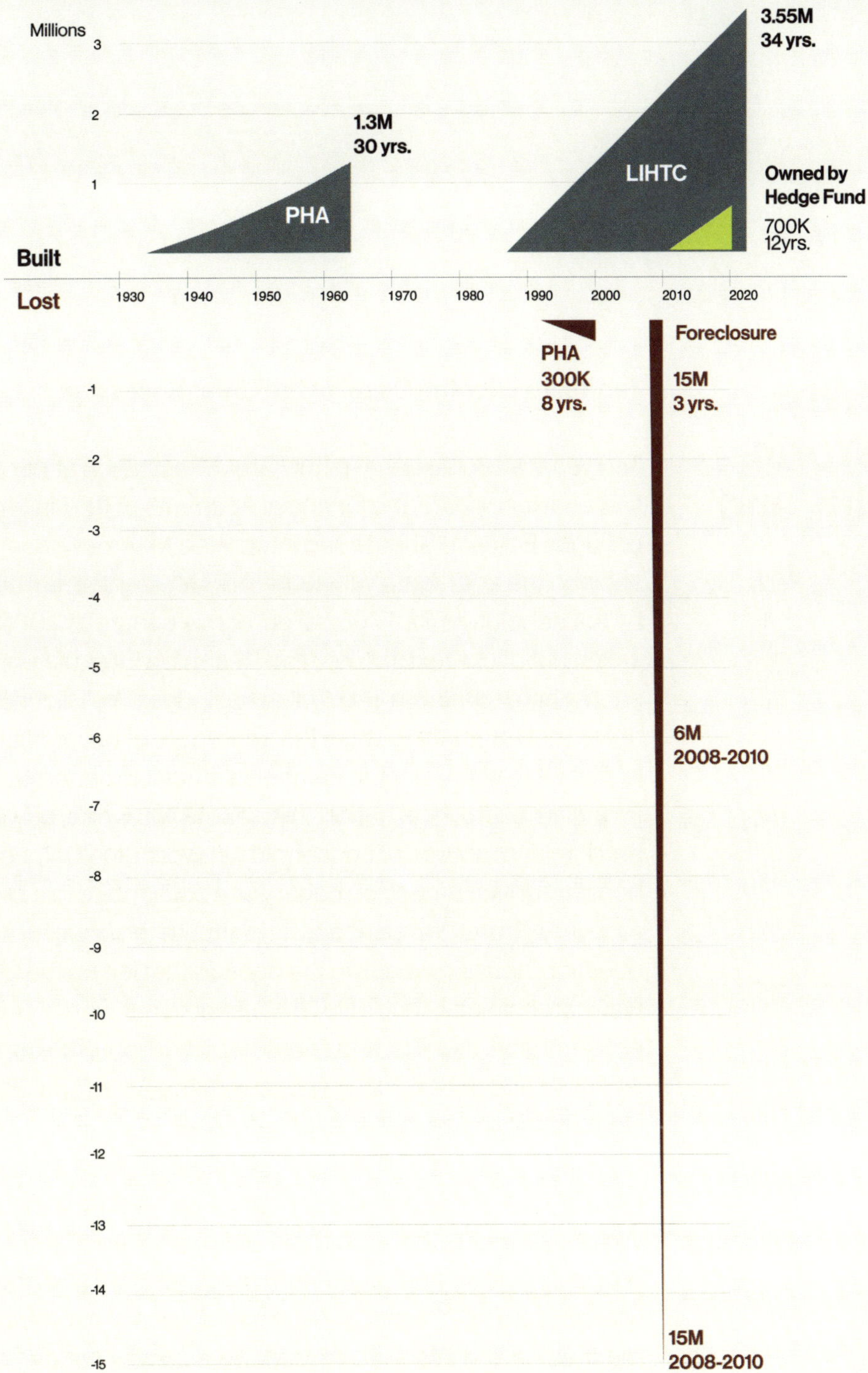

75 Years: Gain and Loss
New housing units added by Public Housing Authority and Low-Income Housing Tax Credit developments (LIHTC) compared to PHA unit reductions and foreclosures.
Graphic by authors

Volatility: Net Worth, Wealth, and Housing

Ten Years after the Onset of the Great Recession

Ten years after the onset of the Great Recession at the close of the first quarter of 2017, the Financial Accounts of the United States Flow of Funds Balance Sheets and Integrated Macroeconomic Accounts showed the aggregate valuation of US residential real estate held by households as $26.765 trillion, or more than $80,000 per capita. Taken out of context, the Federal Reserve's Flow of Funds number seems hard to fathom yet alone even judge. The Federal Reserve itself notes that attempts to value the aggregate of residential real estate is difficult to verify, but the number is crucial to understanding the financial health of the nation. In a post-1970s world, private housing is the predominant source of household net worth. In 2017, a decade after the housing-driven recession began, one could point to a broadly termed recovery. Broad comparisons help situate the housing and net-worth question: housing wealth in the decade that led up the 2008 crash was approximately half of total household net worth. Tied directly to consumption, mobility, amortized debt, and jobs, the contours of wealth as real estate directly correspond with the American urban form of the single-family house set atop private land.

Housing valuations are wholly imbricated if not defined by and as time. We talk about the flow of income and money, geography, property, proximity to jobs, and social life in these terms. If one draws back four years before 2017, when the estimated value of residential real estate reached $26.8 billion, the aggregate value was pegged at $20.3 trillion in 2013. Draw back further to 2011 and the value had declined to a post-crash low of $18.14 trillion. During the post-crash era, in the course of six years from 2011 to 2017, aggregate US residential real-estate valuations rebounded from their collapse by $8.625 trillion, or more than 53 percent. But to imagine the growth between 2010 to 2017 as a recovery and verification of the market's resiliency is to miss the bigger catastrophic picture. To appreciate the severity of the ongoing crisis of risk, debt, and insecurity from over-financialized housing, one must draw back to the apex of the Great Recession between 2006 and 2008, in particular the fourth quarter of 2008, when the rapid descent into financial crisis accelerated, and the media began to unmask the mortgage industry's opacity and the finance industry's trade in mortgage-backed securities and an array of derivatives.

During the inflation of housing valuations leading to the Great Recession, residential real-estate valuations had peaked in 2006 at approximately $24.134 trillion. Ten years earlier, in 1996, the value was approximately one-third of that at $8.89 trillion. The ten-year period leading up to the collapse constituted a 271 percent increase in housing valuations.

As the post-recession "recovery" emerged, aggregate values were well above those of the year 2000 and have since exploded, increasing equity while also increasingly limiting a range of potential buyers from the market. In the aftermath of the Great Recession, the uneven distribution of equity based on when a house was purchased and financed meant that many US households had by and large entered an era of negative equity that took years to eclipse. Equity in homes financed a decade prior the recession was more protected, assuming they had not refinanced. Equity—even if based in the run-up of valuations beginning in the 1990s—might not have entered negative territory, but different regions of the nation faced more severe foreclosure rates and shorter tenure of occupancy. For many, Covid19 has helped solve this, with remote work enabling a new migration to the suburbs and inflation driving up valuations.

In the 21st century's first two decades, housing values in the US have fluctuated violently. The increased valuations between 2000 to 2006 were unprecedented, but nothing in our history has approached the fluctuations up and down that followed the credit seizure. It is reflected in household net worth, particularly if one looks at the years from 1952 to the 2023.

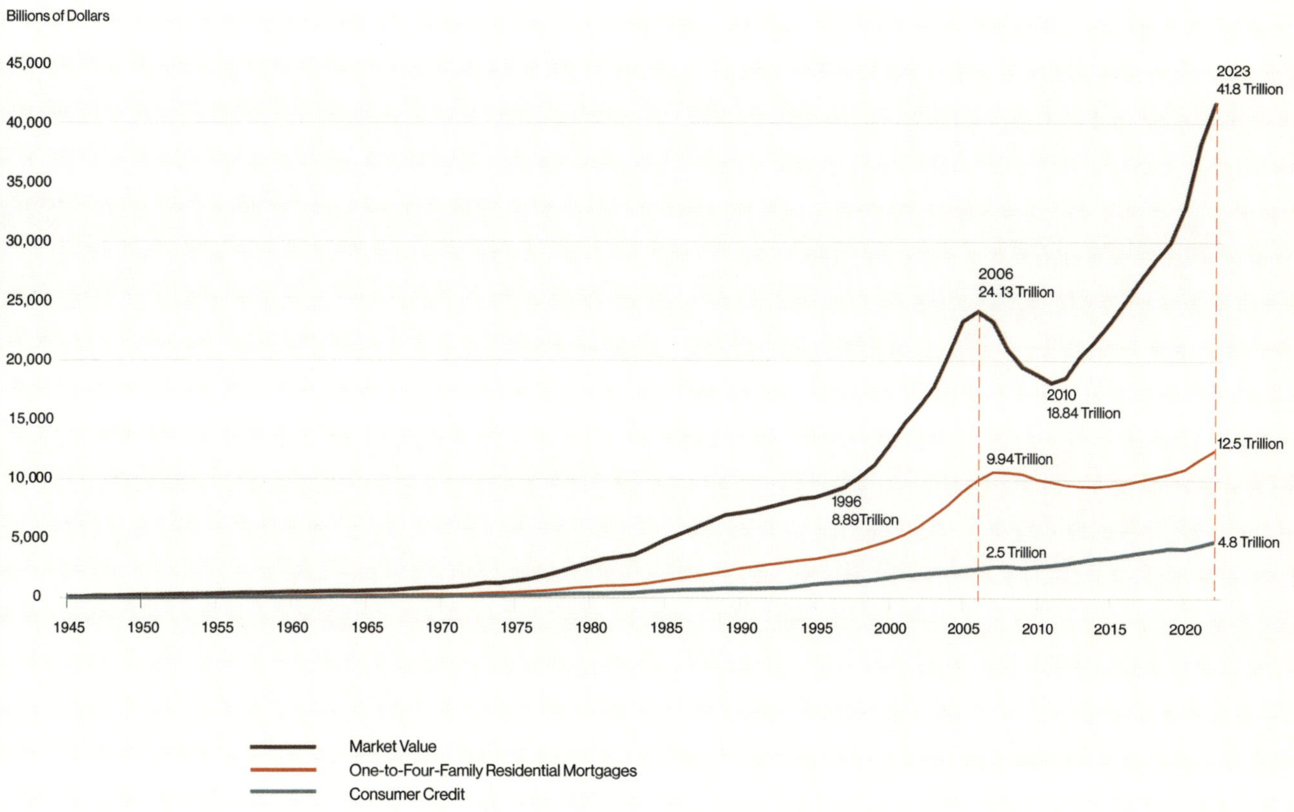

Households and Nonprofit Organizations Real Estate Market Value-Mortgage-Consumer Credit

Three distinct Federal Reserve datasets were combined and illustrated by the authors: one-to-four-family residential mortgages held by households and nonprofit organizations, consumer credit liability of households and nonprofit organizations, and owner-occupied real-estate of households, including vacant land and mobile homes.[13]
Graphic by authors

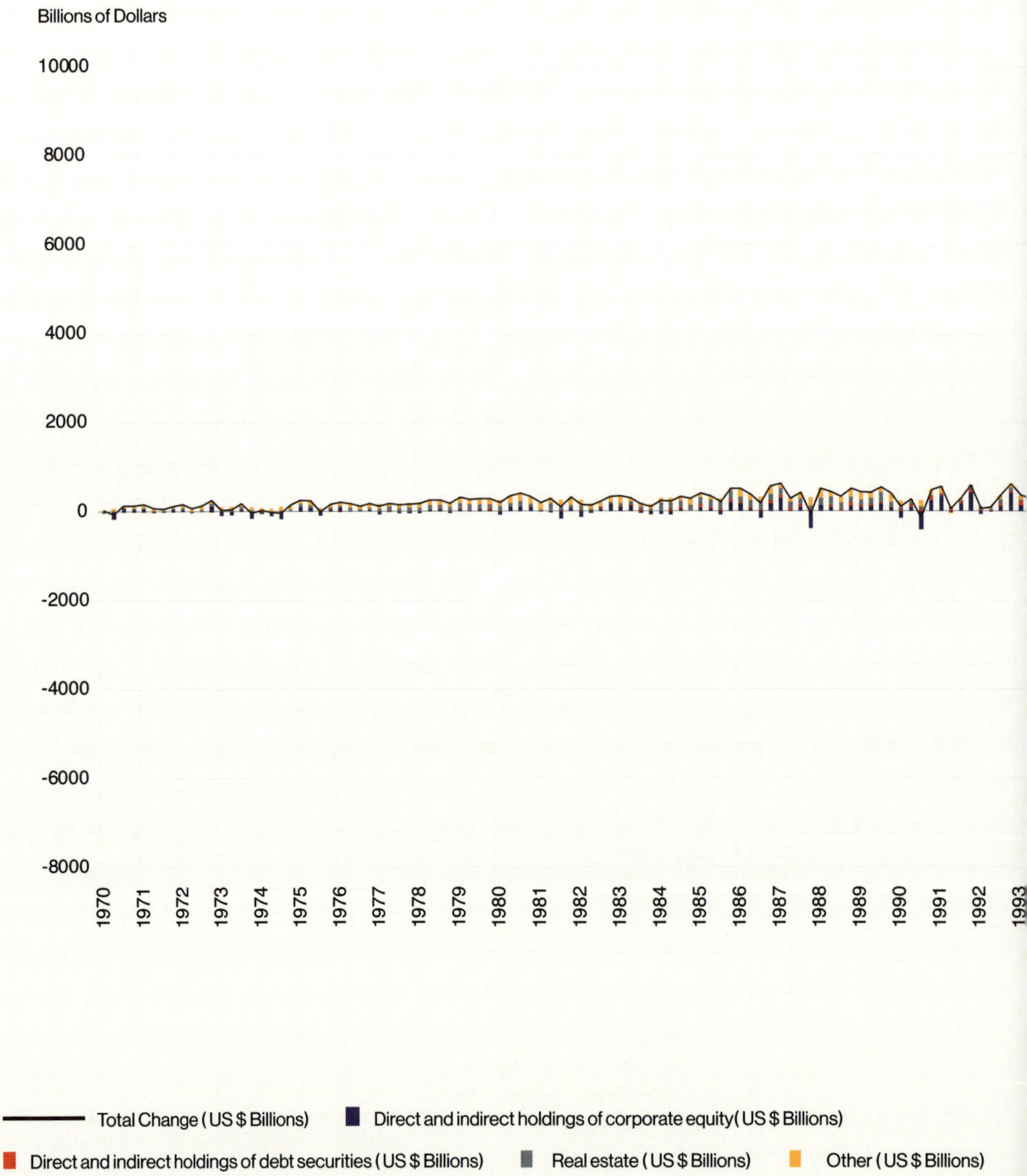
Billions of Dollars
10000
8000
6000
4000
2000
0
-2000
-4000
-6000
-8000
1970
1971
1972
1973
1974
1975
1976
1977
1978
1979
1980
1981
1982
1983
1984
1985
1986
1987
1988
1989
1990
1991
1992
1993
Total Change (US $ Billions)
Direct and indirect holdings of corporate equity(US $ Billions)
Direct and indirect holdings of debt securities (US $ Billions)
Real estate (US $ Billions)
Other (US $ Billions)

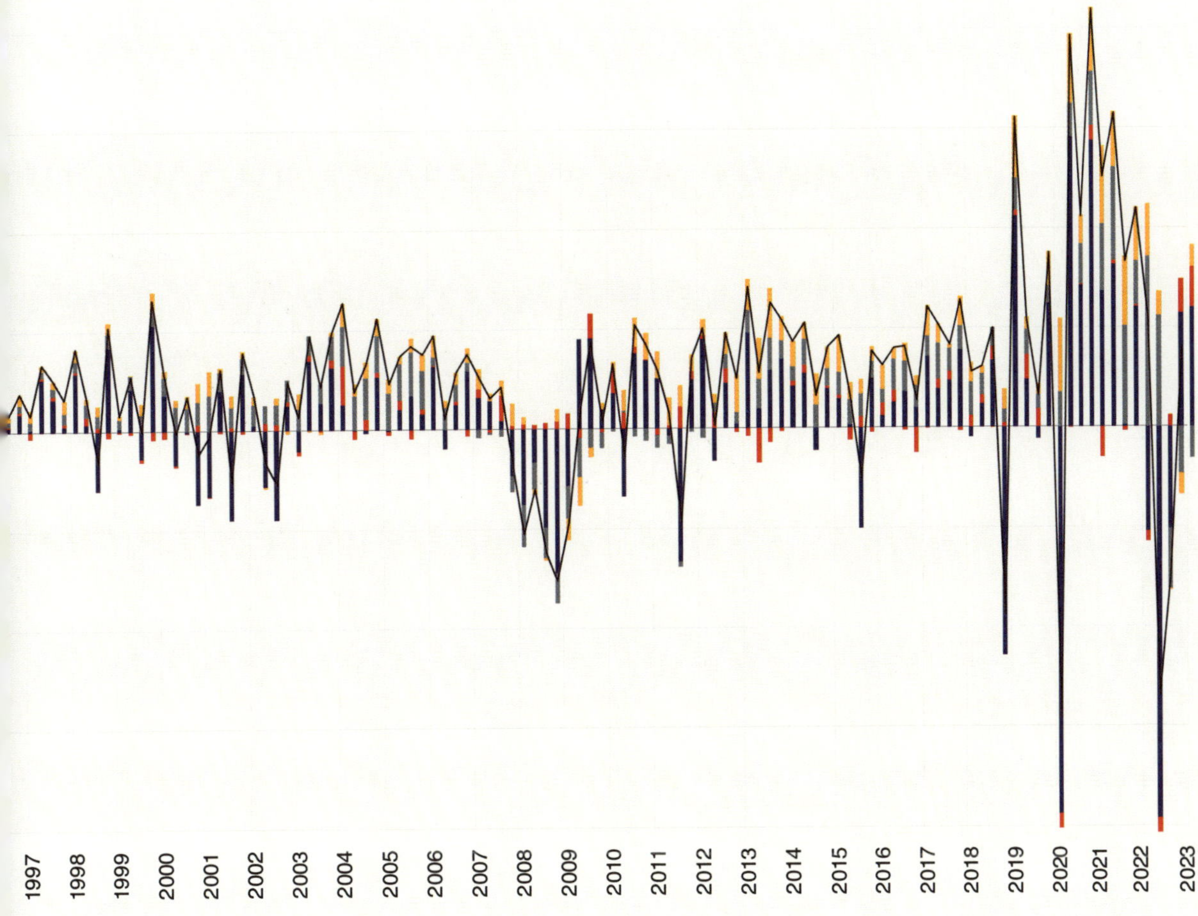

Changes in Net Worth of Households and Nonprofit Organizations, 1952–2023[14]
Graphic by authors

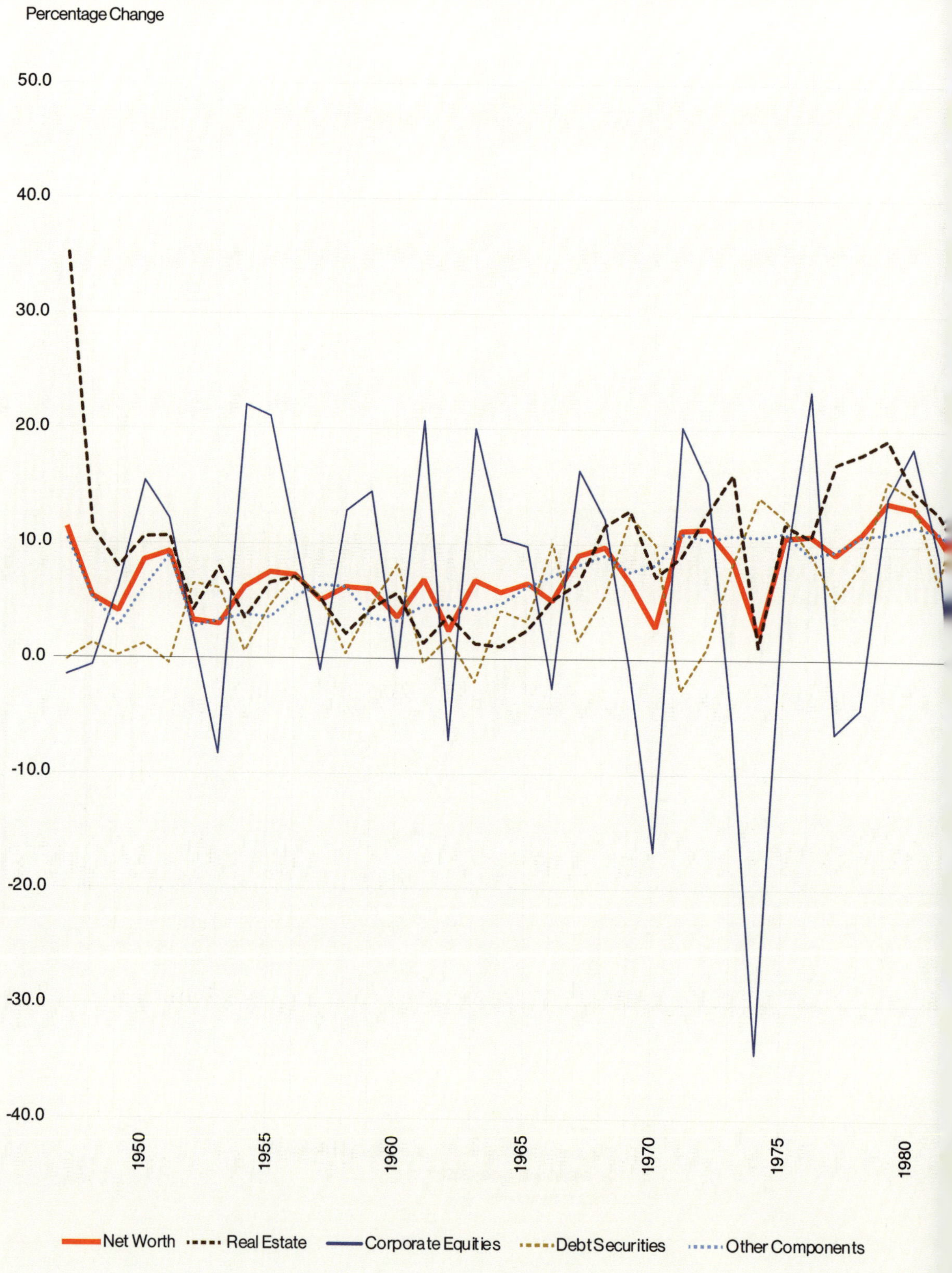
Percentage Change
50.0
40.0
30.0
20.0
10.0
0.0
-10.0
-20.0
-30.0
-40.0
1950
1955
1960
1965
1970
1975
1980
Net Worth
Real Estate
Corporate Equities
Debt Securities
Other Components

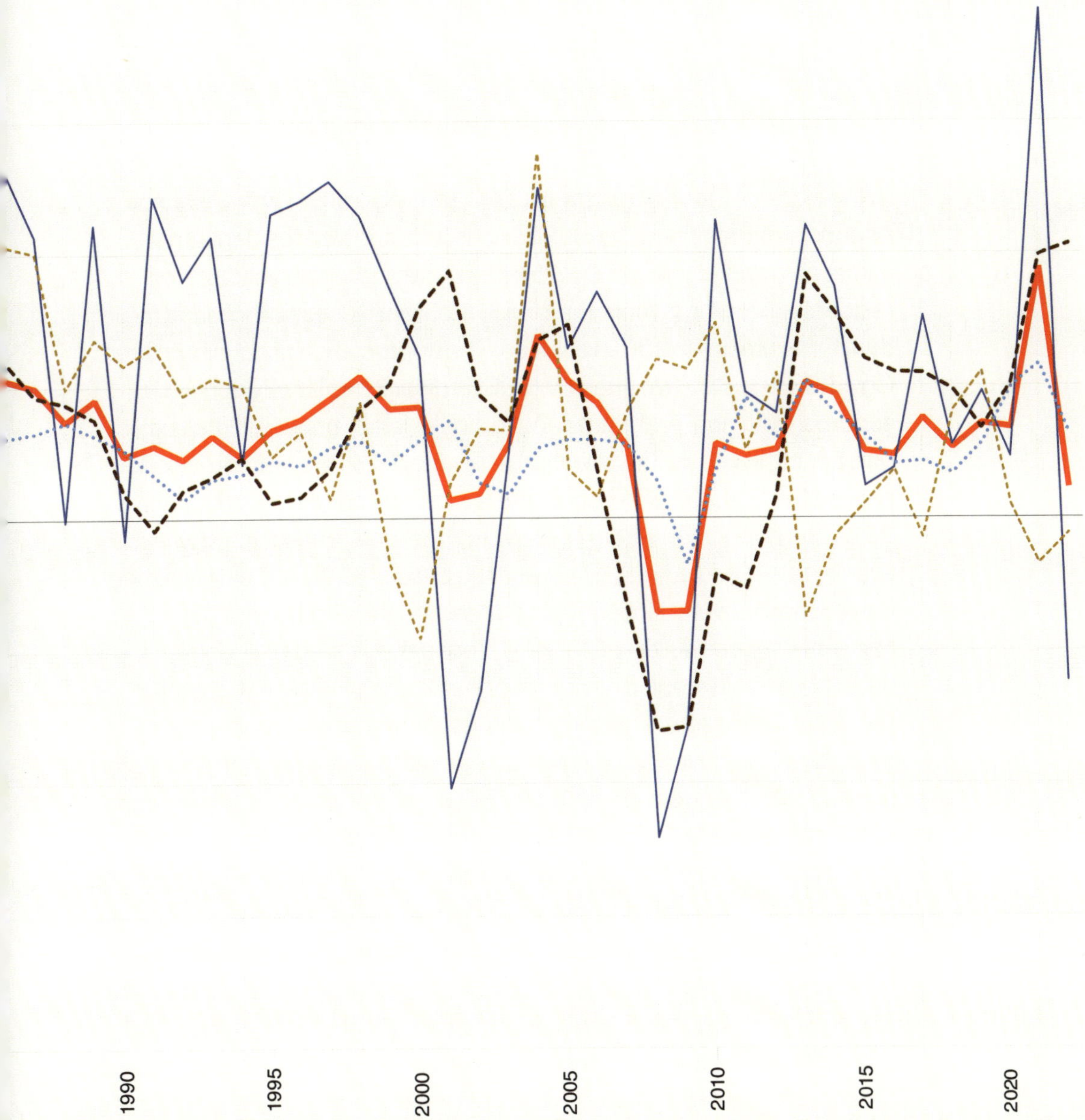

Annual Percent Change in Net Worth of Households and Nonprofit Organizations[15]

Four distinct Federal Reserve datasets were combined and illustrated by the authors.

15 Years After the Great Recession (and a Pandemic)

At the close of the first quarter of 2023, the Federal Reserve Financial Accounts of the United States Flow of Funds showed residential real estate at a market value of $41.75 trillion. The aggregate valuation of residential housing is more than twice its Great Recession low and more than three times the 2000 valuation. The appreciation of housing in the Covid19 era is still a live question, but it is clear it has largely applied to suburban and rural real estate and to single-family houses. If measured on a per capita basis, the valuation assigns a $124,883 market value to each of the 334,233,854 people the US census projected in January 2023. But of course, neither housing nor the wealth associated with it is evenly distributed among owners; in the case of renters, the divergence is even more severe. Households that owned their homes in 2020 had a median net worth of $137,400. Those that rented their home had a household median net worth of just $5,728.[16] Fifteen years after the Great Recession, a housing crisis instigated largely by a myriad of mortgage derivatives, housing and the wealth associated with it has been dramatically upended again. For some it produced immense new wealth, and for others it made the possibility of owning a home far more remote, if impossible. The volatility can be assuaged if one holds the asset on either side of the fluctuation, a forbearance that bypasses the losses. But it also fundamentally reveals that the complexity of financial instruments used to expand the scale of housing production are fraught. So too are the jobs that fund mortgages and are possibly facing risk from automation. And in 2023, the ability to acquire and hold onto housing assets is being impacted by the potential of remote work and new investors in housing markets such as hedge funds, whose financial means and ability to act fast edges out many who can't compete with cash offers.

Housing is a pivot point in financial security for individuals; it's also a source of national wealth. Vast amounts of lending are secured by it as an asset class. Ownership of a home has been a major factor in creating household net worth, but in recent decades it has also exposed owners to inordinate risk. Over the last two decades, it has episodically been an extraordinarily volatile asset, even if its returns have at times been exorbitant for owners. The divide between owners and renters has become more severe in the Covid19 era as ownership has become more out of reach. It becomes difficult to call any of the swings since the 1990s a recovery because in each case there was extraordinary investment by central banks and the government that incentivized new trade through quantitative easing and acquiring or "mopping up" illiquid assets. This was true in the wake of Great Recession and Covid19.

The rapid changes in valuation have been staggering, and while deeply complex, it is quite simply far more volatile in recent decades than it had been in the two primary periods that defined 20th century housing markets: the post-World War II era and the post-1970s era of globalized finance that spread US mortgage securities worldwide. If the volatility of housing is seen as temporary—set in the background of a banking and liquidity crisis, a lack of transparency in mortgage markets and mortgage-backed securities in 2008, or against a global pandemic in 2020—we might imagine a slow return to the normal. But in housing's relatively short history as a discrete industry and denominator of an economy, the normal is not something that has lasted for that long.

Presumptions about housing as "a good investment" or "always rising" are deceptive. In the post-World War II era and up to the 1970s, housing valuations did not rise that steeply. With less access to mortgage liquidity and less ability to trade mortgages nationally and globally, the impetus to buy and sell houses was less. On its surface, the 1970s era saw housing valuations rise at a faster rate, but it also saw a decline in middle-class wealth from labor and an exporting of jobs in a post-Bretton Woods, post-gold standard economy. Labor as a percentage of gross domestic product has declined since the 1970s. It recovered in the 1990s and declined to new lows since 2000.[17] The post-1970s era increased housing wealth and tied that wealth to a more indexed, attenuated form of risk. For owners, banks, and governments that act as a backstop, the image of a house as an asset has often appeared to be a wealth-production mechanism. But the asset itself has not benefitted from the same level of research and development that large-scale production affords other commodities or asset classes. The financial instruments that underlie housing valuations have been exotic and deeply enabled by computation, housing itself less so.

Again, scale and research and development have deeply affected an array of commodities that support housing, including communication systems integrated into households like internet networks, smartphones, computers, and televisions; aspects of mobility integral to the location of communities, such as micro-processor-enabled aspects of cars, anti-lock brakes, fuel and electric motor controls; and household appliances and technologies, such as cameras, thermostats, heat pumps, and refrigerators. But the actual production of houses themselves has not achieved a similar level of technological innovation, reinforcing and accelerating the deeply stressed forms of inequity endemic to housing markets, without offering a counter-argument, a political vision, or an architectural imaginary to counter it.

Scale—Computational Control

Private equity has made sophisticated use of a wide range of publicly available data to guide property acquisitions and determine price points for purchase, potential rental income, and appreciation. This includes uses of the prices of comparable houses and a range of scores from local credit-report profiles, health-data variables, crime statistics, and insurance premiums. Hedge funds create a depth and diversity of actuarial guides that inform a decision to invest in a large number of properties, scaling up to a set of assets using data to measure their value and evaluate the populace and constituency: scores from SATs and other standardized educational testing are extrapolated from school-district rankings. In short, they amortize capital allocation in territorial ways, creating a plateau upon which to trade vast sums of money at scales never seen in single-family housing.

This depth-of-technologically-aided trading takes advantage of a now decades-long trend of governments shedding state assets and being less inclined to move contrary to markets. In Europe and the United States, forms of social and public housing are being sold by cities to private investors. In the US, a public housing authority might sell its developments, dispensing of its hard units and replacing them with congressionally allocated rental vouchers. The former is a permanent house, the latter, a stipend that might not survive a future congressional vote. German cities have sold entire public housing sites to private-equity firms.

But if one focuses on the housing type or immediate threat, you can miss the larger threat. From Dresden, Germany to Washington Heights in Upper Manhattan, the uses of data and distributed, networked, web-based forms of property management have allowed housing transactions at scales that have never been seen. While hedge funds and other non-transparent forms of wealth are not new, the multiplication of computational control is.

The software and near-zero costs of communication is reinventing the ability of finance to scale up its transactions in the housing market, creating a more distributed form of ownership in housing. We believe this creates an opportunity, but also presents a great risk to the very generational wealth that a substantial population expects to be preserved through homeownership. While legislation can intervene, the propensity of the market to use computation will not decrease. What can we make of this new form of capitalization?

The New York Times

Public Housing in Private Hands

Give this article

By Mark Landler
May 5, 2006

DRESDEN, Germany, April 28 — Ingolf Rossberg is the mayor of this majestic eastern German city. But watching him stride around his ballroom-size office, wreathed in smoke from his cigarillo, one could mistake him for a European real estate tycoon.

Yet he is that after a fashion. Mr. Rossberg reached a deal in March to sell Dresden's entire stock of 48,000 city-owned apartments to an American private equity firm, the Fortress Investment Group, for $1.2 billion. In a single stroke, Dresden wiped out its burdensome public debt.

"We had to move fast," he said, "because if you had 10 German cities selling their property, it would be a buyer's market."

Moreover, Fortress must hold on to 34,000 of the apartments for 10 years before it sells them. And when it does, it must offer existing tenants a 15 percent reduction from the market price. Finally, it cannot renovate the apartment complexes into luxury condominiums.

A refurbished residential and office building in Dresden, Germany, evidence that urban design has come some way from post-Stalinism.
Matthias Rietschel for The New York Times

Analysts say the rights granted to the residents are not much different from those that govern Germany's highly regulated rental market. But that raises a question: How will Fortress recoup its billion-dollar investment?

Dresden / Germany: 2006
Ingolf Rossberg is the mayor of this majestic eastern German city. But watching him stride around his ballroom-size office, wreathed in smoke from his cigarillo, one could mistake him for a European real estate tycoon. Yet he is that after a fashion. Mr. Rossberg reached a deal in March to sell Dresden's entire stock of 48,000 city-owned apartments to an American private equity firm, the Fortress Investment Group, for $1.2 billion. In a single stroke, Dresden wiped out its burdensome public debt. "We had to move fast," he said, "because if you had 10 German cities selling their property, it would be a buyer's market."[18]
— Mark Lander, "Public Housing in Private Hands," *New York Times*, May 5, 2006

The New York Times

Questions of Rent Tactics by Private Equity

Give this article

Tenants of an apartment building in the Washington Heights neighborhood of Manhattan gather in their lobby to discuss allegations of harassment by the building's owner. Hiroko Masuike for The New York Times

By Gretchen Morgenson
May 9, 2008

Private investment firms have been amassing what may seem like unusual stakes in New York real estate: they have bought hundreds of apartment buildings with thousands of rent-regulated units across the city that produce decidedly meager returns.

As regulatory filings and promotional materials show, the companies expect to generate higher returns quickly by increasing rents after existing tenants vacate their units. Their success depends upon far higher vacancy rates than are typical in rent-regulated apartments in New York.

Some residents and tenant advocates say that they began seeing what they consider a pattern of harassment of low-income tenants this year and suspect that it is a result of the new owners' business models. Tenants have been sued repeatedly for unpaid rent that has already been received by the landlords; they have been sent false notices of rent bills, lease terminations and nonrenewals; and

New York City: 2008
In the last four years, developers backed by private equity firms have acquired almost 75,000 rent-regulated apartments, Mr. Dulchin said, or about 6 percent of the city's 1.2 million such units. Major private equity-backed participants in this market include Vantage Properties, which has partnered with Apollo Real Estate Advisors; the Pinnacle Group, a unit of Praedium Capital; and Normandy Real Estate Partners. Private investment firms have been amassing what may seem like unusual stakes in New York real estate: they have bought hundreds of apartment buildings with thousands of rent-regulated units across the city that produce decidedly meager returns.[19]

— Gretchen Morgenson, "Questions of Rent Tactics by Private Equity," *New York Times*, May 9, 2008

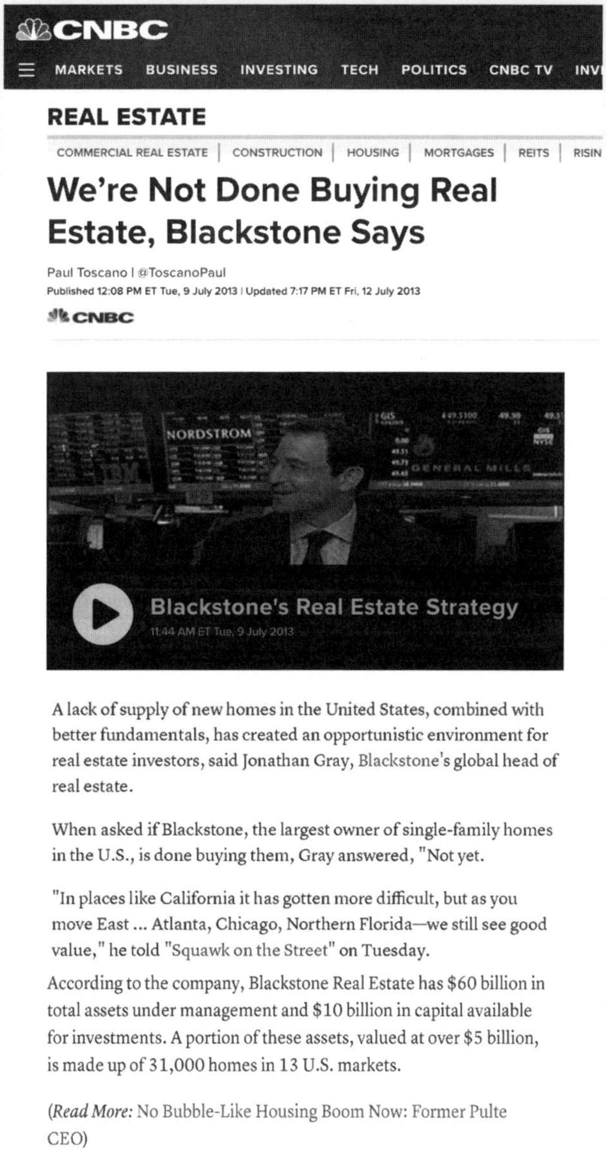

CNBC

MARKETS BUSINESS INVESTING TECH POLITICS CNBC TV INV

REAL ESTATE

COMMERCIAL REAL ESTATE | CONSTRUCTION | HOUSING | MORTGAGES | REITS | RISIN

We're Not Done Buying Real Estate, Blackstone Says

Paul Toscano | @ToscanoPaul

Published 12:08 PM ET Tue, 9 July 2013 | Updated 7:17 PM ET Fri, 12 July 2013

CNBC

Blackstone's Real Estate Strategy

11:44 AM ET Tue, 9 July 2013

A lack of supply of new homes in the United States, combined with better fundamentals, has created an opportunistic environment for real estate investors, said Jonathan Gray, Blackstone's global head of real estate.

When asked if Blackstone, the largest owner of single-family homes in the U.S., is done buying them, Gray answered, "Not yet.

"In places like California it has gotten more difficult, but as you move East ... Atlanta, Chicago, Northern Florida—we still see good value," he told "Squawk on the Street" on Tuesday.

According to the company, Blackstone Real Estate has $60 billion in total assets under management and $10 billion in capital available for investments. A portion of these assets, valued at over $5 billion, is made up of 31,000 homes in 13 U.S. markets.

(*Read More:* No Bubble-Like Housing Boom Now: Former Pulte CEO)

United States: 2013

Since the buying frenzy began, no company has picked up more houses than the Blackstone Group, the largest private-equity firm in the world. Using a subsidiary company, Invitation Homes, Blackstone has grabbed houses at foreclosure auctions, through local brokers, and in bulk purchases directly from banks the same way a regular person might stock up on toilet paper from Costco.

In one move, it bought 1,400 houses in Atlanta in a single day. As of November, Blackstone had spent $7.5 billion to buy 40,000 mostly foreclosed houses across the country. That's a spending rate of $100 million a week since October 2012. It recently announced plans to take the business international, beginning in foreclosure-ravaged Spain.

"A lack of supply of new homes in the United States, combined with better fundamentals, has created an opportunistic environment for real-estate investors," said Jonathan Gray, Blackstone's global head of real estate. When asked if Blackstone, the largest owner of single-family homes in the US, is done buying them, Gray answered, "Not yet. In places like California it has gotten more difficult, but as you move east . . . Atlanta, Chicago, Northern Florida—we still see good value," he told "Squawk on the Street" on Tuesday. According to the company, Blackstone Real Estate has $60 billion in total assets under management and $10 billion in capital available for investments. A portion of these assets, valued at over $5 billion, is made up of 31,000 homes in 13 US markets.[20]

— Paul Toscano, "We're Not Done Buying Real Estate, Blackstone Says," CNBC News, July 9, 2013

The Disruptive Object Developed at Scale: Architecture Overtakes Planning's Relation to Economics

The fields of urban planning and economics have long worked together to support attempts to improve resource allocation, achieve adequate population distribution, and build wealth equity. In relation to these goals, architectural practice becomes more strategically financial and focused on the analysis of specific sites and buildings, taking into account the costs of labor, materials, and the efficient use of tectonics and detail in the context of a project budget and bids. The scale, equity, and security of economies combine in housing as buildings and asset classes and primary sites of consumption that drive the US economy. The house is an economic engine; at its core it is a private financial mechanism where the architect and the users balance the books. Increasingly, we imagine that housing's future as a social benefactor—as something more than shelter—requires access to research and development. The house and architecture as a whole enacted social compact of urban planning and collective economies bears an extraordinary purpose. In its isolated form, it has to disrupt and speak in terms of an equity we imagine belonging to the aspirational governance of cities. The individuated house becomes a lens to collective wealth, not just the wealth of its owners.

We imagine that the house and its evolution as an energy producer and asset will require a far deeper engagement with technology to become not just sustainable but energy positive. Its scale of production can increase not as a shelter has—in terms of density, number of units, and as a financialized asset—but as a distributed renewable-energy production. We see a horizon where the energy-productive would-be house becomes a form of universal income, achieved without a central bank's overly extended mortgage-backed securities. It would be capitalized at scales sufficient to the task of combining energy production and shelter as an affordable renewable-energy housing system, enabled by efficient industrial manufacturing, chemical engineering, and the physics of the photon light waves of photovoltaics.

Such a house-as-energy-asset would be scalar, having the capacity to be mass-produced and networked, and discrete, in the sense of being designed for the individual household and protected as an investment. A beneficiary of advanced engineering and collective cost-sharing by being packaged as a large group of properties, it would also be a private product, air-gapped from utilities and other municipal systems from which we extrapolated the past century of development. The house becomes a localized, encrypted type of wealth in the form of proprietary renewable-energy generation. Solar-rich southern regions from Phoenix and Los Angeles north into New Mexico and Colorado are one example of a region of the nation that can be activated in new ways, not by pilot urban planning, rezoning, and speculative development but through a new technologically enabled form of renewable energy that offers the downstream benefit of shelter as an externality.

Architecture in this equation leapfrogs beyond planning to become an economic agent. A post-carbon urbanism would emerge as an architectural generator of form. The dwelling is coordinated with earth-based territorial aspects of renewable energy; the sky and geospatial aspects of the solar system exert a new authority over what had been a province of land as property and structure as house: municipally organized real-estate. What was housing becomes a kind of enzyme that alters its host. Former realms of authority, development practices, mobility, communications, finance, economics, and, most importantly, energy become phantoms that had limited architectural imagination. Housing options are no longer limited by income and monetized as a form of scarcity inaccessible to a vast number of people.

Such an advanced form of would-be housing cannot emerge without the benefits of scale, but it is a bifurcated form of scale. Once achieved, it moderates further participation in the economy that produced it. If designed as renewable, such a structure could be upcycled and resold to be reallocated and renewed.

Older power structures in real estate are not failing, but they are showing what we believe is an attenuated life span whose viability is about to be further challenged by the real demands of climate change and automation's threat to income and the existing job base.

Endnotes

1. The merger of Travelers and Citicorp actually took the form of Travelers becoming a bank holding company and acquiring Citicorp. The "merger" conflated insurance and commercial banking activities in one company, the separation of which were key conditions of the Glass-Steagall Act of 1933. The Federal Reserve describes the original goals of Glass-Steagall: "These restrictions were a response to the perception that commercial and investment banking had become too intertwined leading up to the 1929 stock market crash—that banks had taken undue risk with depositors' savings in the financial markets or were promoting the securities they underwrote to their customers, leading to conflicts of interest." The approved new bank holding company that combined Travelers and Citicorp forced the rescinding of Glass-Stegall under the Financial Services Modernization Act of 1999. Texas Senator Phil Gramm, a former economics professor at Texas A&M, was a primary sponsor of the act. The global hedging of mortgage-backed securities ultimately threated and caused collapse in every form of banking. The divisions that Glass-Steagall had offered were taken down and overrun. See "Order Approving Formation of a Bank Holding Company and Notice to Engage in Nonbanking Activities," Federal Reserve Press Release, September 23, 1998, https://www.federalreserve.gov/boarddocs/press/bhc/1998/19980923/19980923.pdf; and "Financial Services Modernization Act of 1999 (Gramm-Leach-Bliley)," Federal Reserve History, Nov. 22, 2013, https://www.federalreservehistory.org/essays/gramm-leach-bliley-act.

2. Erik Sirri, "Testimony Concerning Credit Default Swaps," US Securities and Exchange Commission, Oct. 15, 2008, https://www.sec.gov/news/testimony/2008/ts101508ers.htm.

3. Sirri, "Testimony."

4. "2021 Builder 100: The Top 100," Builder, https://www.builderonline.com/builder-100/builder-100-list/2021/.

5. "Construction Spending, also referred to as Value of Construction Put in Place (VIP)," United States Census Bureau, https://www.census.gov/construction/c30/about_the_survey.html. "The key statistics produced for Construction Spending are monthly estimates of

the total dollar value of construction work done in the U.S. The survey covers construction work done each month on new structures or improvements to existing structures for private and public sectors (in 50 states and the District of Columbia). Data are shown by type of construction as seasonally adjusted annual rates and in unadjusted dollars." "Construction spending estimates include the cost of labor and materials, architectural and engineering work, overhead, interest and taxes paid during construction, and contractor's profits."

6. Housing Act of 1949, US Government Publishing Office, https://www.govinfo.gov/app/details/COMPS-10349.

7. S&P/Case-Shiller US National Home Price Index, S&P Dow Jones Indices LLC, Federal Reserve Economic Data (FRED), Federal Reserve Bank of St. Louis, Nov. 21, 2023, https://fred.stlouisfed.org/series/CSUSHPISA; and Robert Shiller, *Irrational Exuberance* (Princeton, NJ: Princeton University Press, 2000).

8. Laurie Goodman, Amalie Zinn, Kathryn Reynolds, Owen Noble, "A Profile of Institutional Investor-Owned Single-Family Rental Properties," Urban Institute, Apr. 2023, https://www.urban.org/sites/default/files/2023-08/A%20Profile%20of%20Institutional%20Investor%E2%80%93Owned%20Single-Family%20Rental%20Properties.pdf.

9. *Evidence Matters*, Office of Policy Development and Research, Department of Housing and Urban Development, Winter 2023, https://www.huduser.gov/portal/periodicals/em/winter23/highlight1.html.

10. *Evidence Matters*, 2023.

11. Sandeep Bordia, "US Single Family Rental—An Emerging Institutional Asset Class," Urban Institute Data Talk Presentation, Washington, D.C.: Urban Institute, Sep. 26, 2017, https://www.urban.org/sites/default/files/2017/09/26/final_presentations_-_single-family_rentals_2.pdf.

12. Thomas Malone, "US Home Investor Share Reached New High in Q4 2023," CoreLogic, Apr. 9, 2024, https://www.corelogic.com/intelligence/single-family-home-investor-share-remained-high-in-q4-2022-with-smaller-investors-driving-demand/.

13. "Households and Nonprofit Organizations; One-to-Four-Family Residential Mortgages; Liability, Level," Board of Governors of the Federal Reserve System, Federal Reserve Economic Data (FRED), Federal Reserve Bank of St. Louis, July 5, 2023, https://fred.stlouisfed.org/series/BOGZ1FL153165105A; "Households and Nonprofit Organizations; Consumer Credit; Liability, Level," Federal Reserve Economic Data (FRED), Federal Reserve Bank of St. Louis, Board of Governors of the Federal Reserve System, July 5, 2023, https://fred.stlouisfed.org/series/HNOCCIA027N; "Households; Owner-Occupied Real Estate Including Vacant Land and Mobile Homes at Market Value, Market Value Levels," Federal Reserve Economic Data (FRED), Federal Reserve Bank of St. Louis, Board of Governors of the Federal Reserve System, July 5, 2023, https://fred.stlouisfed.org/series/BOGZ1LM155035015A.

14. "Changes in Net Worth: Households and Nonprofit Organizations, 1952–2023," Financial Accounts of the United States, Board of Governors of the Federal Reserve System, https://www.federalreserve.gov/releases/z1/dataviz/z1/changes_in_net_worth/table/.

15. "Households and Nonprofit Organizations; Net Worth, Level," Board of Governors of the Federal Reserve System, Federal Reserve Economic Data (FRED), Federal Reserve Bank of St. Louis, July 8, 2023, https://fred.stlouisfed.org/series/TNWBSHNO; "Households; Owners' Equity in Real Estate, Level," Board of Governors of the Federal

Reserve System, Federal Reserve Economic Data (FRED), Federal Reserve Bank of St. Louis, July 7, 2023, https://fred.stlouisfed.org/series/OEHRENWBSHNO; "Households and Nonprofit Organizations; Directly and Indirectly Held Corporate Equities; Asset, Market Value Levels," Board of Governors of the Federal Reserve System, Federal Reserve Economic Data (FRED), Federal Reserve Bank of St. Louis, July 7, 2023, https://fred.stlouisfed.org/series/BOGZ1LM153064475Q; "Households and Nonprofit Organizations, Directly and Indirectly Held Debt Securities; Asset, Market Value Levels, Board of Governors of the Federal Reserve System, Federal Reserve Economic Data (FRED), Federal Reserve Bank of St. Louis, July 7, 2023, https://fred.stlouisfed.org/series/BOGZ1LM154022375Q; "Households and Nonprofit Organizations; Other Components of Net Worth, Excluding Real Estate and Direct and Indirect Holding Holdings of Corporate Equities and Debt Securities, Level, Percent Change Annual," Board of Governors of the Federal Reserve System, Federal Reserve Economic Data (FRED), Federal Reserve Bank of St. Louis, July 7, 2023, https://fred.stlouisfed.org/series/BOGZ1FL152090045Q.

16. Donald Hays and Briana Sullivan, "The Wealth of Households: 2020," Current Population Reports, P70BR-181, US Census Bureau, Washington, DC, Aug. 2022, https://www.census.gov/content/dam/Census/library/publications/2022/demo/p70br-181.pdf.

17. "Share of Labour Compensation in GDP at Current National Prices for United States," University of Groningen and University of California, Davis, Federal Reserve Economic Data (FRED), Federal Reserve Bank of St. Louis, Oct. 29, 2023, https://fred.stlouisfed.org/series/LABSHPUSA156NRUG.

18. Mark Lander, "Public Housing in Private Hands," *New York Times*, May 5, 2006, https://www.nytimes.com/2006/05/05/business/worldbusiness/05property.html.

19. Gretchen Morgenson, "Questions of Rent Tactics by Private Equity," *New York Times*, May 9, 2008, https://www.nytimes.com/2008/05/09/business/09rent.html.

20 Paul Toscano, "We're Not Done Buying Real Estate, Blackstone Says," CNBC News, July 9, 2013, http://www.cnbc.com/id/100873475.

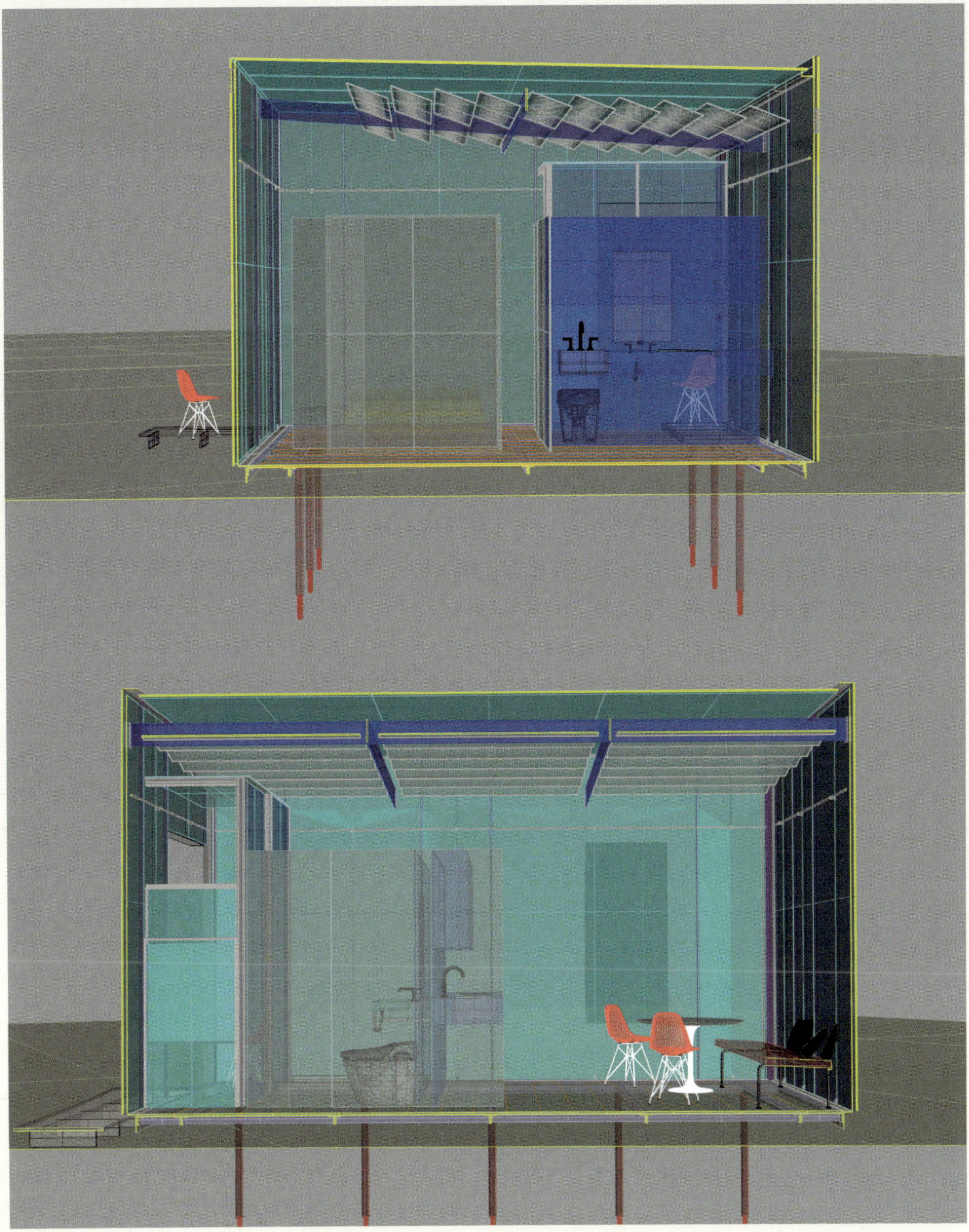

Model C, ADU, 410 square feet. Screen captures show its structure and helical foundations.

Prototype: Liquid heated and cooled insulated glass unit with integral heat pump

Four

Structural Empathy: A Retreating Welfare State Leaves Little Funding for Research

Ronald Reagan signing the Tax Reform Act of 1986

Ronald Reagan signing the Economic Recovery Tax Act of 1981

The IRS as Affordable Housing Agency

A memorable photograph taken in October of 1986. President Ronald Reagan, sitting outdoors at a rectangular wooden table at the edge of a stage set on the South Lawn of the White House. He is signing the Tax Reform of Act of 1986. Five years earlier, in August 1981, Reagan again outdoors at a table. In this photograph, he is signing the Economic Recovery Tax Act of 1981, this time at his ranch in Santa Barbara, California. A tall stack of legislative documents is stacked high, not quite aligned and canting away from him. The stack seems unstable. Set on a circular table top, the seemingly plywood top and chair are supported by a basket-like structure. You feel the weight and imagine the use of gravity as a binding agent.

A provision of stagecraft at major bill signings is not unique, but here the outdoor sites offer an aura of liberation, each bill promising a new level of autonomy and privatization in markets and business. Less government intervention and less government competition. In 1981, at the coastal ranch, the fog engulfs the press conference, requiring the photographers to use small spotlights to record the event. Weather creeping in—nature.

The '81 and '86 Tax Acts have lasting effect, still today, on our entire last century of public intervention in poverty and low-income housing development. The incentive to entrepreneurship each sought to instigate is not without potential, but each had an effect of disaggregating the immense sums the government allocated to housing; it has not helped an already disaggregated and undercapitalized housing industry innovate.

1937: Public Housing: Centralized, Immense, But Increasingly Scarce

It is difficult to imagine a more vivid but constrained bill to cross a president's desk. A thirteen-page document that was destined to affect the political ethos and ethical liability of the country for generations to come but that had to be masked. A bill sprung from ambitions to literally build housing for what would be millions of people in need, yet was simultaneously rife with conflict. How would a government enter into and seemingly compete with the markets it was constitutionally obligated to protect? The Housing Act of 1937, a New Deal reform also known as the Wagner-Steagall Act, emerged in the aftermath and devastation of the Great Depression, and is broadly understood as a new federal reaction to poverty and the need to reform access to housing for the lowest income groups in the United States. State laws on housing and poverty have existed since the middle of the 19th century but were county-based and generally limited to the provision of essential food, water, and lodging. The '37 Act outlined the formation of the nation's first public housing authorities (PHAs), forming a federally instigated mass-housing project that in partnership with states and cities would offer housing to the nation's working poor. PHAs were planned, created, owned, and operated by all three forms of government: federal, state, and city. In the case of New York City, the New York City Housing Authority (NYCHA) became in time the city's largest landlord. At its origin, PHA housing was highly concentrated in New York City, Chicago, and Philadelphia but intended to span the nation. To understand the scope, one can look to more than 3,300 public housing sites and approximately 1.3 million apartments realized before the program's growth was frozen under the Nixon Administration.

If the page count of the '37 Act seems spare, it was not without complex political and ethical dimensions. In unleashing at the outset as much as five million dollars annually, it would instigate a construction project of national scale and ambition. It offered housing for the country's poor, especially its urban poor. Its legal cause of action was not for construction of housing, per se, but in a more circumscribed way, it was created to promote the "general welfare of the nation." The '37 Act took the form of a "declared policy" in which the United States would "promote the general welfare of the Nation by employing its funds and credit" in order "to assist the several States and their political subdivisions to alleviate present and recurring unemployment and to remedy the unsafe and insanitary housing conditions and the acute shortage of decent, safe, and sanitary dwellings for families of low income, in rural or urban communities, that are injurious to the health, safety, and morals of the citizens of the Nation."[1]

Thus the Act described a constituency of those in need, but in terms its capacity to actuate a market, it specifically sought to provide housing to those who lacked the ability to cause the market to produce housing for them. The document describes its terms and denominations, including its projected users, as seeming counterparties in a contractual language:

The term "families of low income" means families who are in the lowest income group and who cannot afford to pay enough to cause private enterprise in their locality or metropolitan area to build an adequate supply of decent, safe, and sanitary dwellings for their use.

In that sense, the '37 Act is framed as an expedient in service to the economy: the economy of building housing. It did not compete with the housing-development market so much as alleviate the need for the market to act on behalf of customers that lacked means to motivate them.

The '37 Act placed on the president's desk fluctuates between declaring a mass project to build housing and simultaneously a need to limit scale. This occurs at the personal-user level in the clearest terms. No apartment built by a PHA was to exceed $4,000 or $1,000 per room to construct.

The document for the president's approval notes that land, development, and community costs were excluded from this limit, and in cities that exceed 500,000 people the provision per apartment was increased to $5,000 and $1,250 per room. In pricing an apartment and its rooms, assigning strict spending and cost limits was anchored not to the provision of housing for the poor but instead to the welfare, safety, cleanliness, and moral timbre of the nation. Housing in this sense is not so much a thing or construction but an action to reduce poverty and increase the health of the nation.

The 1937 Act can be read as explicit but simultaneously reluctant and self-canceling, a policy perhaps enacted at a large scale with contortions that seemed to dissimulate its goals. The 86 years since its signing reveal a slide to a deeper and increasingly market-based logic in dealing with the provision of housing for those that the market fails to serve. If one fast-forwards 49 years later to the Tax Reform Act of 1986, non-market or low-income housing aid moves fully towards a federal provision of market-based incentives that in turn follow the population of congressional districts. Tax credits are provided to non-profit builders who syndicate them for sale to raise seed capital and equity against which to borrow. Over the course of 49 years, the reluctance to compete with markets, even markets that the housing development does not serve, increasingly leads to a disaggregation of aid in the form of a financial instruments administered by federal block grants to local jurisdictions.

By the early 1960s, more than 1.3 million public housing units had been built in the United States. The New York City Housing Authority, the largest of the country's public housing authorities, alone accounted for as many as 189,000 apartments in more than 340 developments. NYCHA is larger than all of the nation's others PHAs combined and in itself once represented more than seven percent of the city's dwellings. An immense urban edifice

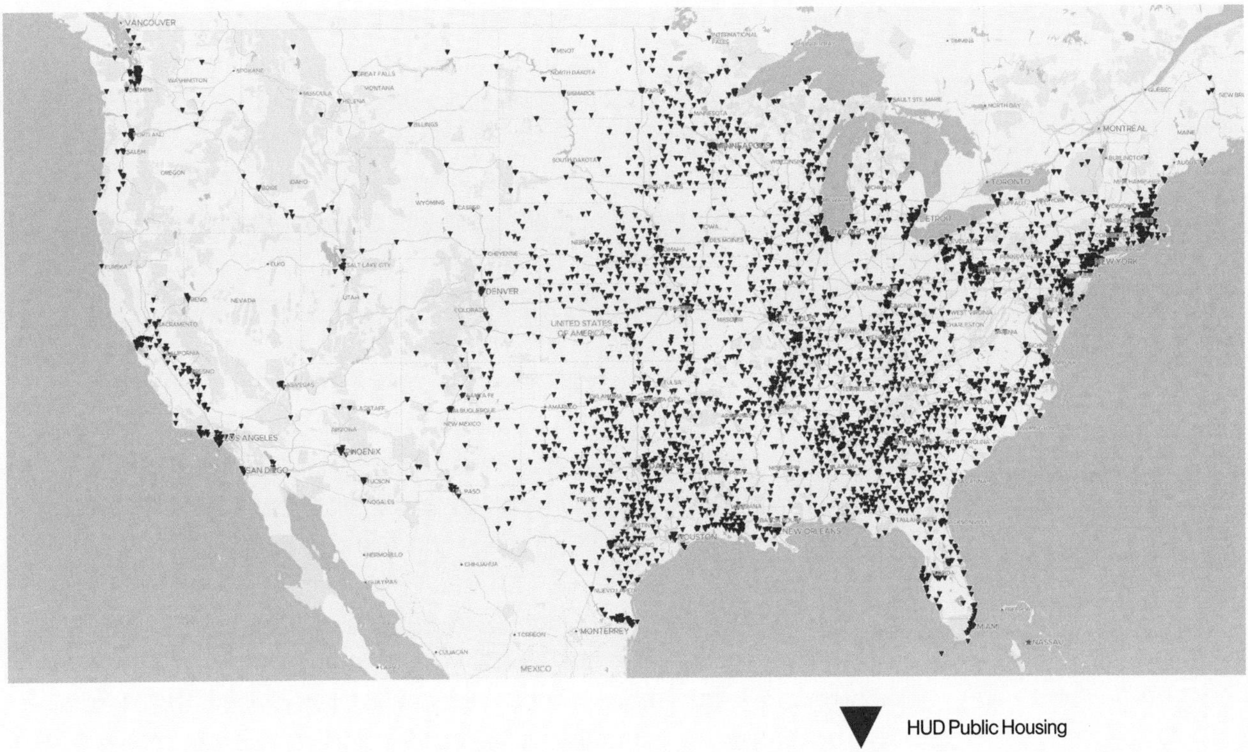

Public Housing Developments
Department of Housing and Urban Development (HUD), United States Housing Authority development sites for public housing. There are more than 3,300 public housing sites in the United States.

Each is owned and operated by a hybrid of federal, state, and city governments.

Source: Department of Housing and Urban Development
Graphic by Authors. This map was prepared using PolicyMap.

and property owner, it is, like most PHAs, often misunderstood. Its presence in the press and the collective imagination of the public is often generalized, yet it was developed in distinct phases corresponding to each of the federal housing acts. Its architecture is often understood as a derivative of the "towers in the park" modernist space planning. A generalized knowledge that it serves poor or working-poor residents is prevalent, but PHAs have over their life span enacted a complex array of rent-pricing means. They are not monolithic even as the developments impart such an image.

PHAs were at their origin a product of three modes of government. They are federal, state, and city-based, and as such they have a local territorial aspect even as they are federal in scope. As with all federal policy, the reach of the federal government in this regard was by design brought into negotiation with states and cities. Bringing empathy and acknowledgement of the need to house those who are not reached by markets, federal housing acts thread their provisions between constitutional terms protecting property rights and the New Deal's recognition of a need to create a public safety net. The provision of housing at a personal and human scale is framed in the 1937 Housing Act as benefitting the "general welfare of the Nation" as much as individuals.

> *It is hereby declared to be the policy of the United States to promote the general welfare of the Nation by employing its funds and credit, as provided in this Act, to assist the several States and their political subdivisions to alleviate present and recurring unemployment and to remedy the unsafe and insanitary housing conditions and the acute shortage of decent, safe, and sanitary dwellings for families of low income, in rural or urban communities, that are injurious to the health, safety, and morals of the citizens of the Nation.*
>
> — September 1, 1937, Housing Act of 1937

At the core of the federal enterprise, in the scope of the 1937 Act, its evolutions in 1949 and 1954, and the ensuing 1.3 million homes, was the raw social and ethical dimension of a city. The succession of acts can be read as progressive and simultaneously self-canceling. By the 1960s, a deepening level of critical philosophy concerning social control and description of populations was as evident as a conservative rejection of government action on housing development. Frances Fox Piven and Richard Cloward, writing in *the Nation* in 1966, published "The Weight of the Poor: A Strategy to End Poverty," outlining what they saw as a path to create a fiscal crisis in the New York City budget by elevating the welfare rolls in the city, shining a light on what they saw as "distorted" New Deal policies.[2] Their 1971 book, *Regulating the Poor* described forms of welfare and housing aid (policies for entry into public housing, for example) that became structurally reinforcing of poverty rather than alleviating it. They accused it of segregating people and populations in soft prisons by way of structural and often racial or racist means, all under the auspices of punitively insufficient yet also structurally necessary social welfare. Housing as architecture created by and apart from markets became federal, state, and city policy, and thereby an explicit form of control and segregation over three short decades.

Piven and Cloward choreographed their research as sociologists in conjunction with door-to-door interviews and community organizing, but questions of social control and its manifestation in design emerge in multitudes of urban planning and architectural criticism and literature during the era. Reflecting on their work in 2010, Piven wrote that they had "at least tried to tackle the difficult strategy problems that an urban-based movement of poor people confronted in a centralized economic and political system."[3] The election of Richard Nixon in 1972 heightened an attack on public housing from a conservative vantage point, and while it adopted immensely different goals, it too attacked the centralization of aid in the form of housing and welfare.

The Nixon Administration declared a moratorium on public housing construction immediately upon taking office, but they did so in a bifurcated public-facing series of complex laws that made it difficult to actually see. While phasing out PHA programs and buildings that were yet to be realized, the administration also advanced several new laws through Congress. One titled the 312 Rehabilitation Loan Program offered loans for rehabilitation of public housing but only within a very limited spectrum defined by Federal Code Enforcement (usually a local government concern) or under federal Model City programs, part of his Democratic predecessor Lyndon B. Johnson's Great Society and War on Poverty agendas. In short, the funds seemed by definition to have a limited reach, modeled as ambition tempered by federal restraint.

As early as 1973, provisions to decentralize public housing further emerged in Congress, acts that serve as precedents for today's Low-Income Housing Tax Credits. A bill introduced by Representative Thomas Ashley and Senator John Sparkman in 1973 proposed the federal provision of block grants in three-year durations, a move that would replace revenue sharing between federal and state governments and instead allocate funds for specific projects. Revenue sharing represented a decentralization of federal funds distributed to states, and in turn allowed states purview regarding their use. Block grants instead move federal funds to states but only for specific goals. Sparkman was quoted in the *New York Times* in March of 1970: "Senator Sparkman said he had never liked the idea of the Government's deciding where people should live. But he said the population projections [of] 10 million more Americans in the next 30 years—were so great that he had come to accept the concept of incentives to guide people to settle in unused areas that could be developed into attractive communities."[4]

The double-sided nature of this time, characterized by a critical rejection of "distorted" and centralized welfare and New Deal laws, and the Nixon Administrations contortions of moratoriums mixed with self-limiting new programs, has left a deep lack of political resolve since.[5] A 1974 *New York Times* article on Michel Foucault's *The Birth of the Clinic* introduced the first English edition of Foucault's 1963 book.[6] The review in a mainstream newspaper appears alongside articles depicting the Nixon Administration's disassembly of housing institutions in real time, offering a window into a philosopher whose work helped shape several generations' ability to dissect and reframe the practices and procedural methods of institutions. Distrust and skepticism of the clinical procedures and observational practices in medical clinics enacted as prelude and rationale for the control of populations was easily transposed to incarceration, housing, land use, and zoning. What becomes of the capacity for the meaningful production of housing at an effective scale to confront the enormity of the problem of the unhoused, rent-burdened, and homeowners subject to the risk of an underwater, illiquid, or rapidly traded mortgage asset in the aftermath of this era is still an evolving question.

The 1937 Housing Act portrays its goals as a form of action more than a form of construction. These attributes are vivid in the Housing Acts of 1949 and 1954, as public housing increasingly becomes a form of urban design couched as renewal and slum clearance, when it was often a form of selective population displacement and structural racism. A lawsuit brought in the early 2000s in Ohio's Supreme Court turned the '37 Act's language against a resident whose children had lost their lives in a tragic fire in a PHA building. The lawsuit framed a PHA's role as a "ongoing governmental function" to reduce poverty rather than a proprietary function as landlord.

Casting an argument in terms that are directly borrowed from the '37 Act, the lawsuit defines unique features of a PHA that would potentially limit its civil liability. The case debated whether a PHA, as a form of government action created with the intention to reduce poverty and increase health, altered its role as a landlord or housing provider. A PHA's administration here, in the language of the '37 Act, "means any or all undertakings necessary for management, operation, maintenance, or financing, in connection with a low-rent housing or slum-clearance project, subsequent to physical completion." In other words, the PHA occurs, at least in part, *after* the completion of the building. Is the PHA separate from the building? In the Ohio lawsuit, the PHA framed itself as having a unique status: "buildings that are used in connection with the performance of a governmental function" were discussed as possibly not subject to the same liability. An intricate case unfolds, and with deference to the family's loss, we mention this hearing only to portray the interwovenness of the major federal housing acts and how deeply conflicted they are in both ethical goals and concern about market intervention. This tendency is as vivid today as it was 1937. It inhibits how the federal government's wealth and economic power might instigate creativity and entrepreneurial behavior given the immense sums that flow to housing aid and to people.

[CHAPTER 896]

AN ACT

September 1, 1937
[S. 1685]
[Public, No. 412]

To provide financial assistance to the States and political subdivisions thereof for the elimination of unsafe and insanitary housing conditions, for the eradication of slums, for the provision of decent, safe, and sanitary dwellings for families of low income, and for the reduction of unemployment and the stimulation of business activity, to create a United States Housing Authority, and for other purposes.

United States Housing Act of 1937.

Be it enacted by the Senate and House of Representatives of the United States of America in Congress assembled,

DECLARATION OF POLICY

Declaration of policy.

SECTION 1. It is hereby declared to be the policy of the United States to promote the general welfare of the Nation by employing its funds and credit, as provided in this Act, to assist the several States and their political subdivisions to alleviate present and recurring unemployment and to remedy the unsafe and insanitary housing conditions and the acute shortage of decent, safe, and sanitary dwellings for families of low income, in rural or urban communities, that are injurious to the health, safety, and morals of the citizens of the Nation.

Definitions.

DEFINITIONS

SEC. 2. When used in this Act—

"Low-rent housing."

(1) The term "low-rent housing" means decent, safe, and sanitary dwellings within the financial reach of families of low income, and developed and administered to promote serviceability, efficiency, economy, and stability, and embraces all necessary appurtenances thereto. The dwellings in low-rent housing as defined in this Act shall be available solely for families whose net income at the time of admission does not exceed five[1] times the rental (including the value or cost to them of heat, light, water, and cooking fuel) of the dwellings to be furnished such families, except that in the case of families with three or more minor dependents, such ratio shall not exceed six to one.

"Families of low income."

(2) The term "families of low income" means families who are in the lowest income group and who cannot afford to pay enough to cause private enterprise in their locality or metropolitan area to build an adequate supply of decent, safe, and sanitary dwellings for their use.

"Slum."

(3) The term "slum" means any area where dwellings predominate which, by reason of dilapidation, overcrowding, faulty arrangement or design, lack of ventilation, light or sanitation facilities, or any combination of these factors, are detrimental to safety, health, or morals.

"Slum clearance."

(4) The term "slum clearance" means the demolition and removal of buildings from any slum area.

"Development."

(5) The term "development" means any or all undertakings necessary for planning, financing (including payment of carrying charges), land acquisition, demolition, construction, or equipment, in connection with a low-rent-housing or slum-clearance project, but not beyond the point of physical completion. Construction activity in connection with a low-rent-housing project may be confined to the reconstruction, remodeling, or repair of existing buildings.

"Administration."

(6) The term "administration" means any or all undertakings necessary for management, operation, maintenance, or financing, in connection with a low-rent-housing or slum-clearance project, subsequent to physical completion.

[1] So in original.

The Housing Act of 1937, also referred to as the Wagner–Steagall Act, established the first federal public housing.

The '37 Act directly linked PHAs to "subdivisions" as well as other municipal structures. In doing so, it further raised the issues of immunity from liability afforded to a municipal structure as opposed to a landlord or housing developer. This was also a pivot point taken up in the Ohio lawsuit. At each turn, issues of scale and intimacy emerge in the effects of the '37 Act. At the same time that it guides a national plan to build what became 1.3 million housing units, it also erects punitive-seeming structures to limit costs per room and set income limits at no more than five times rent. These all recall themes of manufactured scarcity and a concern that a would-be government handout might instigate a failed ethics in the people it serves, a theme equally present in early New York poorhouse laws, when, in the 1850s, counties were ordered to create refuge for the destitute but also to limit comforts of food and shelter so as to not induce false need.

Scale is an inherent aspect of innovation in housing, influencing access to capital, access to the research and development capital affords, and an ability to imagine and respond to needs at a meaningful scale of production, as any automobile or technology company would today. The conflict inherent in the '37 Act might still be better adjudicated today if we could further imagine and reinvent housing as a form of action. There are designers and collectives today that do just this, but not at the scales required to address the public need, as the '37 Act once did. Climate change and the need to address the future of renewable energy presents a moment to do this, but that will take an immense investment by government at scales we see in industries like electric automobiles but not, inexplicably, in housing.

What the '37 Act did provide that is deeply relevant today is its focus on a triadic structure of federal, state, and city government. Can we replace this today with new multi-scalar means and capital to provide the industrial capacity for R & D, combined with an ethical means to imagine fund distribution and access? Can we imagine manufacturing that is both local and based in communities, but that also benefits from tooling, materials science, and computational controls that require far more than any single PHA or small building owner could enact?

The operation of a public housing authority is a governmental function under R.C. [Ohio Revised Code] 2744.01(C)(2) for purposes of political subdivision immunity under R.C. Chapter 2744.

The Act sets forth the defenses and immunities available to political subdivisions in civil actions for injury, death, or loss to person or property allegedly caused by any act or omission of the political subdivision in connection with a governmental or proprietary function.

...

A political subdivision is "a municipal corporation, township, county, school district, *or other body corporate and politic* responsible for governmental activities in a geographic area smaller than that of the state." (Emphasis added [in original text].) ... LMHA [Lorain Metropolitan Housing Authority] is a metropolitan housing authority, defined in R.C. 3735.31: "A metropolitan housing authority created under sections 3735.27 to 3735.50 of the Revised Code, constitutes a body corporate and politic." The parties do not dispute that LMHA is a political subdivision.

...

LMHA, as a metropolitan housing authority, performs a specified "governmental function" under R.C. 2744.01(C)(2)(q). The statute provides that "urban renewal projects and the elimination of slum conditions" are governmental functions. LMHA performs these functions.

...

Before creating a metropolitan housing authority, the director of development must determine that either "unsanitary or unsafe inhabited housing accommodations exist" or there is "a shortage of safe and sanitary housing accommodations in that area available to persons who lack the amount of income that is necessary * * * to enable them, without financial assistance, to live in decent, safe, and sanitary dwellings without congestion."

...

This analysis finds further support in R.C. 2744.01(C)(2)(g), which provides that governmental functions include the "repair, renovation, maintenance, and operation of buildings that are used in connection with the performance of a governmental function." Housing projects are designed to eliminate slum conditions, and the repair and maintenance of public housing are attendant powers of the public housing authority, performed to further the elimination of slum conditions.

Once created, a metropolitan housing authority is required to use its power in order to "clear, plan, and rebuild slum areas within the district in which the authority is created, to provide safe and sanitary housing accommodations to families of low income within that district, or to accomplish any combination of the foregoing purposes."[7]

MOORE, ADMR., APPELLEE, *v.* LORAIN METROPOLITAN HOUSING AUTHORITY, APPELLANT, ET AL.

[Cite as *Moore v. Lorain Metro. Hous. Auth.*, 121 Ohio St.3d 455, 2009-Ohio-1250.]

Political subdivisions — Immunity from suit — R.C. Chapter 2744 — Metropolitan housing authority is a "political subdivision" for purposes of sovereign immunity — R.C. 2744.01(C)(2) — Operation of metropolitan housing authority is governmental function.

(Nos. 2007-2106 and 2008-0030 — Submitted October 8, 2008 — Decided March 25, 2009.)

APPEAL from and CERTIFIED by the Court of Appeals for Lorain County, No. 06CA008995, 2007-Ohio-5111.

SYLLABUS OF THE COURT

The operation of a public housing authority is a governmental function under R.C. 2744.01(C)(2) for purposes of political subdivision immunity under R.C. Chapter 2744.

LANZINGER, J.

{¶ 1} The Ninth District Court of Appeals certified that a conflict exists between its judgment in this case and the judgments of other appellate districts[1] on whether operation of a public housing authority is a proprietary or a

1. The conflicting cases are *Rhoades v. Cuyahoga Metro. Hous. Auth.,* 8th Dist. No. 84439, 2005-Ohio-505; *McCloud v. Nimmer* (1991), 72 Ohio App.3d 533, 595 N.E.2d 492 (8th District); *Jones v. Lucas Metro. Hous. Auth.* (Aug. 29, 1997), 6th Dist. No. L-96-212, 1997 WL 543049; and *Country Club Hills Homeowners Assn. v. Jefferson Metro. Hous. Auth.* (1981), 5 Ohio App.3d 77, 5 OBR 189, 449 N.E.2d 460.

Moore, Admr., Appellee, v. Lorain Metropolitan Housing Authority, Apepellant, et al[8]

Low-Income Housing Tax Credits Disaggregate Federal Funding for Housing Innovation

Of the millions of photographs that preserve the action of a presidential administration, the signing events for the Economic Recovery Tax Act of 1981 and Tax Reform Act of 1986 remain vivid. These two events have had an immense impact on housing. They set the stage for what we still can expect: the limited means available in housing development from the federal government, in particular from the IRS, which in effect became the clearinghouse for affordable-housing tax credits.

The dramatic settings of a California ranch and the White House lawn helped make the images memorable beyond their deep and lasting impacts. By moving what had been federal, state, and city public housing closer to market-rate housing and disaggregating the way federal funds impact housing development, they would incentivize and accelerate what became known as affordable housing and stimulate an immense new market constituency: non-profit housing developers.

Among the provisions of the sprawling Tax Reform Act of 1986 was the initial definition and allocation of Low-Income Housing Tax Credits (LIHTC). Taking the financial form of a pre-payment of taxes to the IRS, the credit was convertible into payment for federal taxes, essentially substituting a tax offset for an outlay of federal dollars. Low-Income Housing Tax Credits are often referred to by the acronym LIHTC (verbally stated as "lie-tek"). In the 37 years since, Low-Income Housing Tax Credits have become the largest and virtually the only financial subsidy to create non-market rate housing for those who the market excludes. They have redefined public housing, and in the colloquial language of politics, blurred the public's imagination or its ability to know how and where federal intervention in housing occurs in vast sums.

The tax credits are allocated in denominations ascribed to a single year, but their ultimate value is found in amortizing them over a decade. A one-dollar credit is worth $10 in tax relief over a ten-year period to its owner. Amortized over a decade, the allocations are far larger than they appear in a single federal-budget year. At the aggregate scale, credits are allocated in each federal budget, and they can eclipse the scale of major federal programs such as the National Science Foundation.

The credits are awarded only to non-profit builders and are syndicated in proportion to an area's population, in effect following population settlement maps and density. They mirror where the population already lives and are awarded on a per-capita basis. Since non-profit builders are themselves exempt from taxes and therefore do not have a tax liability, the tax credit itself is awarded as a salable equity that is fungible and intended for exchange. Once sold, it provides the seed money for a development and provides the initial capital and equity that replaces direct government investment. The funds come from the buyer of the credit. For the federal government, it is deferred revenue rather than a direct expenditure. It becomes equity for an otherwise market-based practice of development that fills in the remaining capital costs with conventional loans, as any market-rate developer would. The tax credit can be especially appealing when acquired for less than face value. While other forms of financial support are possible—such a private grants and other tax credits—debt attributed to a LIHTC project is financed effectively as a market-rate project. Public housing under the federal acts of 1937, 49 and 54 was not legally able to procure debt.

One impetus behind LIHTC: to create and distribute tax credits as financial instruments that provide equity to non-profits, then in turn spur the creation of a two-sided venture. One side of the venture turns toward affordable housing, the other toward successful companies that would purchase the tax credits. Google has, for example, purchased Low-Income Housing

Tax Credits to offset its otherwise potentially gargantuan tax liabilities: the tax credits underwrite affordable housing while benefitting expansion and investment on the part of entrepreneurial non-housing corporations. We have continually asked, is there a way to underwrite entrepreneurial work in housing, funding research and development in housing itself, which Congress imagines flows to the non-housing side of tax credits, rather than expecting it to come from normative real-estate market?

To some extent, the LIHTC programs were created as a hedge and a reaction to the 1986 Tax Reform Act's closing of a series of tax pass-through laws that had incentivized passive-investment housing. A passive investor in lower-income housing markets had been able to move this loss to personal-income taxes. In short, the federal government disincentivized passive investment in lower-income rental housing in the 1986 Tax Reform Act. LIHTC was intended to fill that void with innovative tax laws, tax breaks between two non-governmental parties. A non-profit and a for-profit company become counterparties by way of a parlayed tax instrument.

In 1993, Low-Income Housing Tax Credit programs were made permanent. Novogradac, a predominant accounting firm that administers a great deal of LIHTC syndications, offers a description of why LIHTC is so important today: "Without the incentive, affordable rental housing projects do not generate sufficient profit to warrant the investment."[9]

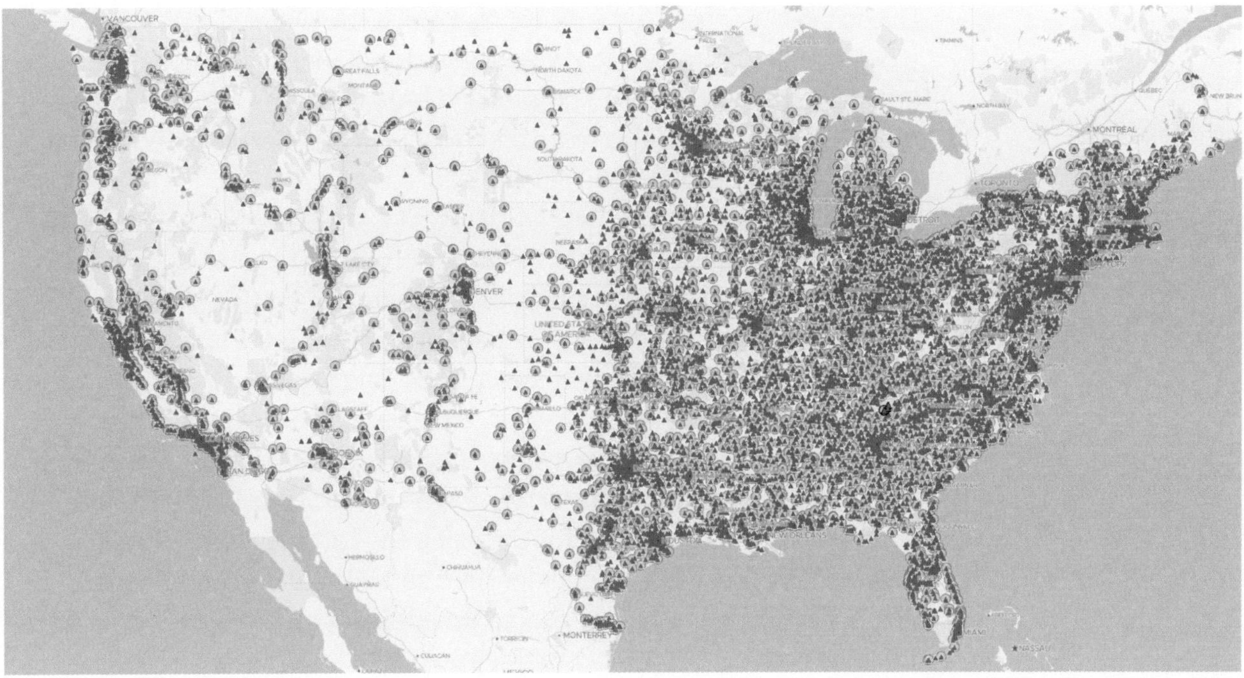

LIHTC (1987-2021)

Low-Income Tax-Credit Housing vs. Solar Map of United States
The cartography of Low-Income Housing Tax Credit developments realized between 1987 and 2021 follows the population distribution. It is a per capita expenditure based on state population. The distribution of renewable energy follows no such state or legal boundaries. We will need to find the legal framework to imagine how these two cartographies are coordinated as the source and geography of energy production shifts at a continental and geospatial scale.[10]

The Cartography of the Sun, the Cartography of Low-Income Tax-Credit Housing

Due to their emergence in an era concurrent with electronic records and digital mapping, it's possible to visualize and track immense amounts of information on LIHTC developments and see the scale of the endeavors over time. HUD's website offers a deep reservoir of housing data and allows one to geo-locate LIHTC allocations:

"HUD's LIHTC database contains information on 52,006 projects and 3.55 million housing units placed in service between 1987 and 2021. Data for properties placed in service in 2022 will be collected in the fall of 2023 and added to this database in the spring of 2024. The database includes project address, number of units and low-income units, number of bedrooms, year the credit was allocated, year the project was placed in service, whether the project was new construction or rehab, type of credit provided, and other sources of project financing. The database has been geocoded, enabling researchers to look at the geographical distribution and neighborhood characteristics of tax-credit projects. It may also help show how incentives to locate projects in low-income areas and other underserved markets are working. With the continued support of the national LIHTC database, HUD hopes to enable researchers to learn more about the effects of the tax-credit program."[11]

Regardless of Party

The 1981 and 1986 Tax Acts were framed around calls for greater privatization and less government intervention in markets of all kinds. Each act was accompanied by a rhetorical call for greater proffering of economic policies that would spur more innovation in private markets. The presidential administrations that have followed have offered broadly different goals in terms of housing, its markets, and addressing housing and human need, but there are few options other than market-based or quasi-market-based LIHTC pro-

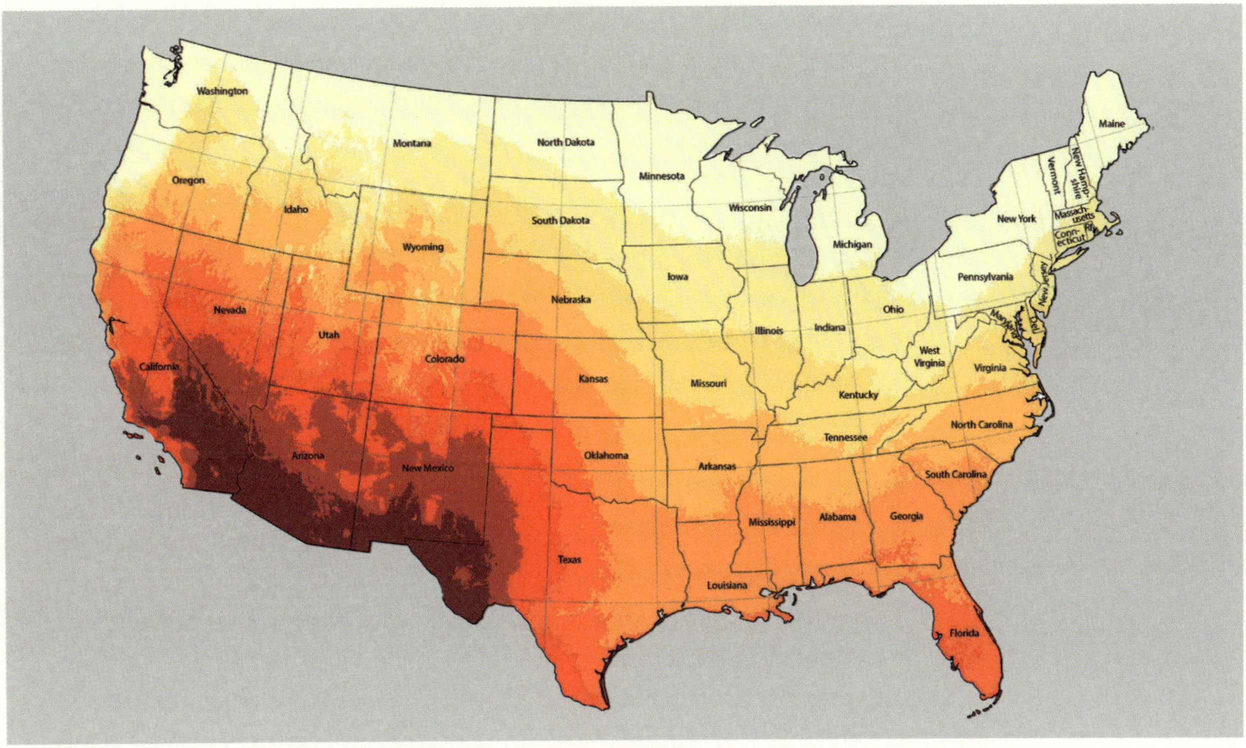

kWh/m^2/Day

- ≥ 5.75
- 5.50 to 5.75
- 5.25 to 5.50
- 5.00 to 5.25
- 4.75 to 5.00
- 4.50 to 4.75
- 4.25 to 4.50
- 4.00to 4.25
- < 4.00

Average Global Horizontal Solar Irradiance [12]
Credit: National Renewable Energy Laboratory

grams available today. Regardless of party and since the 1980s, these are the standing options. An answer going forward, we may well need to take for granted, must come from markets, but it could be deeply assisted by forms of venture capital for climate-based research and by development funds from governments, with a goal of seeking new ways to build and use advanced manufacturing, rather than new ways to underwrite existing real-estate and construction practices. These are the types of R & D needed today.

LIHTC programs are scaled in proportion to the populations and territories they serve. They effectively reaffirm existing population densities and mirror the settlement patterns of the present and recent past. Going forward, we would ask, can such a tax structure devoted to the territorial matrices of the past be recast for a future form of settlement, in particular, for climate change, renewable energy, new labor, and post-labor migration away from expensive coastal land and cities in an era of depleted jobs and incomes? The map of LIHTC's 3.5 million housing units has little overlap with the map of potential renewable-energy generation. Consider this in regard to a map of solar or wind potential: federal policy as we know it follows the apportionment of representation to Congressional districts, which follows population flows. In this sense, housing aid follows a quasi-electoral map. We need to find ways to legislate energy potentials that precede the state formations and electoral processes dividing federal wealth.

Can we do this within the limits of constitutional law and procedure in light of the post hoc relation between populations, congressional representation, and housing support? This seems to be a defining challenge of the immediate decades ahead: adapting federal and state governments to an energy map that is geospatial, based on energy transfers from the sky and space more than Earth and property.

The Scale of the Allocation: Can This Become R & D Rather Than a Development Fund?

In 2023, the federal allocation of Low-Income Housing Tax Credits to states was calculated at $2.75 per capita. Arizona was allocated $20,697,651 in credits in 2023. Over the ten-year amortization, this amounts to $206,976,510 in total aid to Arizona LIHTC investors. Texas was allocated $81,201,838. A total of $812,018,380 over ten years. Novogradac's website depicts the history of LIHTC development, making use of a geo-coded map of the United States. They allow a view over several decades of LIHTC projects. A project funded by LIHTC in 2001 in Wichita, Kansas received $72,091 in credits. Amortized over a decade, the value would be $720,910. The development provided 26 housing units out of 115 total aimed at income levels that were 50 percent of the area gross median income. The mapping provides address, scale, bedroom count, and unit types. We have at hand detailed public and private records of LIHTC.

Syndicators of these credits earn a proportion of these sums, and in managing the life span of the credits, they form a new financial industry, playing a managerial role in supervising compliance with LIHTC regulations. Can this become instead a new form of climate investment, seed capital for new energy instruments, and new means to study and define property's access to renewable energy? It is time to re-imagine what LIHTC was and could be, and to recreate its purpose and means. The funds might seed collaboration between university-based energy consortiums and specialization on geography and geospatial understandings of solar and wind energy.

The smaller scale of LIHTC grants provided a level of local control, assuring a close relationship between government, developer, and owners or tenants. The disaggregation of funds into smaller block grants and developments, however, also pushed LIHTC closer to market-rate practices in design, engineering, and construction. In short, the developments make use of standard practices from architecture to engineering that have long been present in market-rate housing. The centralized funds present at the early days of public housing are here dispersed into lower-rate market-based design and engineering fees. The author's 1990s work in Houston, Texas found that single-floor speculative housing was often built, as expected, with few architectural or engineering services.

LIHTC accounts for more than 3.55 million housing units in the US as of 2021. What can we imagine for the next 3.55 million units? LIHTC accounts for approximately 2.7 percent of all housing in the U.S. It is larger than public housing. PHAs and LIHTC together span approximately 90 years of federal action on housing.

Architects (Finally) Help Dissimulate the State

An economic aspect of LIHTC seems to have barely registered in architectural discourse. LIHTC was used to alter the face of architectural work on housing. Centrally funded, planned, developed, owned, and managed PHA developments, a derivative of modern architecture, would over time be reborn as products of smaller-scale non-profit developers seeded by the sale of tax credits. If LIHTC programs were intended to break down the standardization characteristic of PHA housing, we have witnessed the opposite effect on architecture, leading to a new mass standardization of market-based housing construction techniques. An architectural heterogeneity has been applied to the elevation atop a very uniform set of financial and construction practices.

At the federal level, LIHTC has also been conflated with steps to diminish concentrations of poverty in public housing developments. These were instigated by the center-left Clinton-era federal law on housing. Funds made available by the Clinton-era Department of Housing and Urban Development for public housing administrations during this period were designed to address decades of deferred maintenance in PHA developments. Unable to take on debt, aging public housing sites in the United States long suffered a deficit in funding maintenance from rent rolls. Within HUD's new Clinton-era Housing Opportunities for People Everywhere (HOPE) VI program, funding streams were targeted for renovation and repair, but the policies also required demolition of a portion of each development's "hard units." The funding was only available if the PHA also agreed to remove actual aging PHA apartments and replace them with new housing intended for a higher-income constituency rather than the original tenants.

These goals paralleled a wider move by HUD toward using vouchers and other subsidies to alleviate rent. As "soft units," these new dwellings, now subsidized quasi-market apartments, had an attached but portable subsidy known as a voucher. Outwardly, they were intended to appear as part of the wider and generalized housing market. The Quality Housing and Work Responsibility Act (QHWRA) of 1998 coupled with HOPE VI was designed to offer a means to "deconcentrate" the poverty that had become endemic in much public housing by allowing PHAs to more actively distribute their populations and effectively become a participating public owner within an LIHTC non-profit corporation. Created to realize the new public-private housing required by HOPE VI, and now enabled by QHWRA, together they were a quasi-private form of LIHTC housing that took the place of new public housing.

The changes in development mechanisms meant that PHA housing, centrally funded, planned, and managed since its origins 60 years earlier, was increasingly built within the same labor, material, and financial building logics as speculative housing. The often-referenced broad declaration of a decline in welfare-state funding in recent decades was actually more accurately a shift of that funding from direct expenditures to a myriad of deferred-income instruments. It creates quasi-public housing realized through the same ways and means as speculative housing—long seen as inadequate at serving lower-income constituencies but here propped up to do so—which has shown little capacity for innovation in design, engineering, and energy use or production.

Has the federal government, in seeking to disaggregate concentrations of poverty and incentivize the entrepreneurial aspects of capital markets via LIHTC, also diminished the role of architects and professionals who might bring a capacity for R & D to the deeply social, material, and energy-intensive aspects of housing? A case study from our earlier book, *16 Houses: Owning a House in the City* (Monacelli Press, 2004) showed one housing development paid design/architecture fees at approximately $13

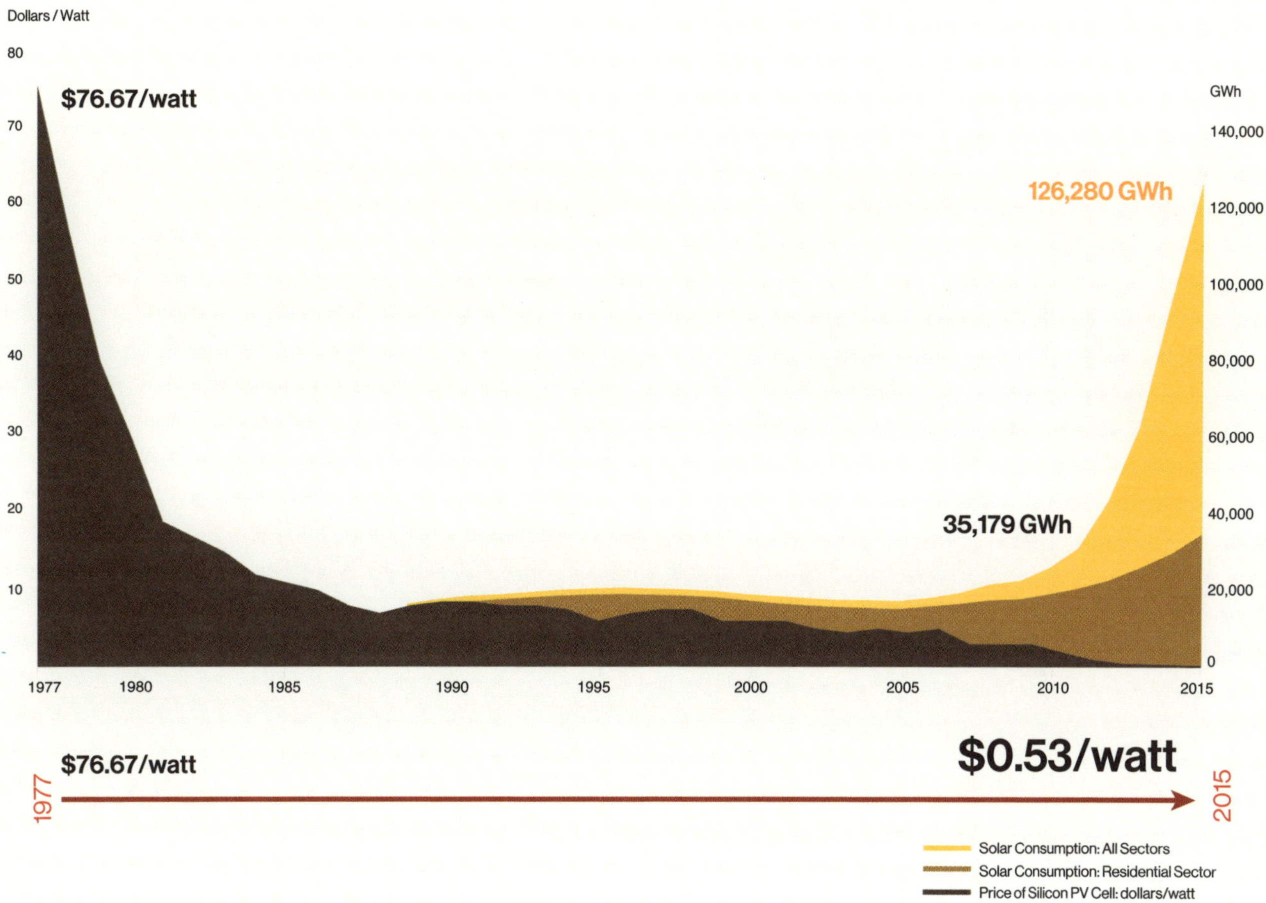

Silicon Photovoltaic Cell Cost per Watt and Solar-Energy Consumption
A declining logarithmic curve depicts silicon PV-cell pricing (dollar/watt). Lower prices are possible, but they will arrive at a slower pace. A rising exponential curve in solar-energy consumption could accelerate, but what relation will that curve have to PV-panel pricing? When does housing cease to be a real-estate asset and instead become a downstream product of an energy asset?[13]
Graphic by authors

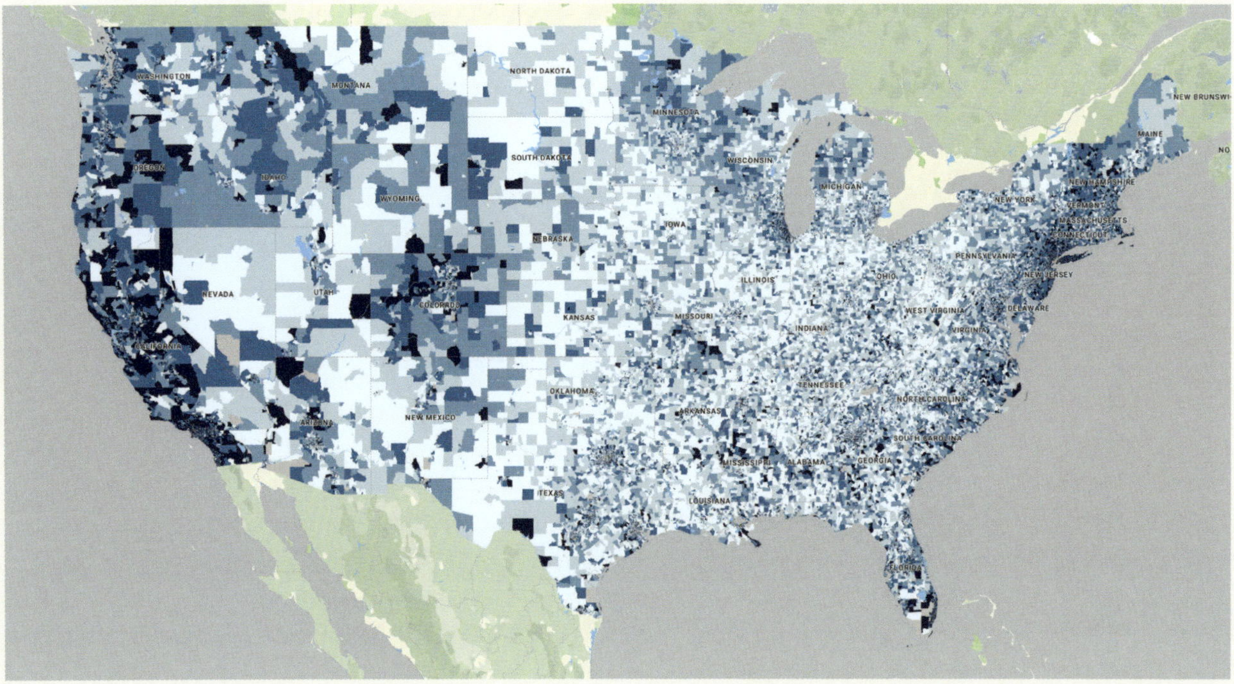

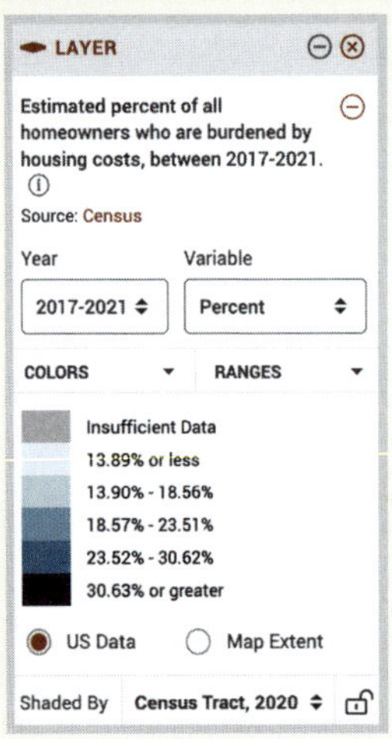

A near-century of federal, state, and city aid to improve housing affordability finds an immense number of households that are still "housing-cost burdened" or "severely housing-cost burdened," the official HUD terms for households that spend more than 30 percent of their gross income on housing costs. Renters (shown in red) are far more at risk of economic insecurity, but homeowners (shown in blue) face financial demands that sustain anxiety and risk in every job-rich region of the nation.[14]

We need to create new programs for the decades ahead.

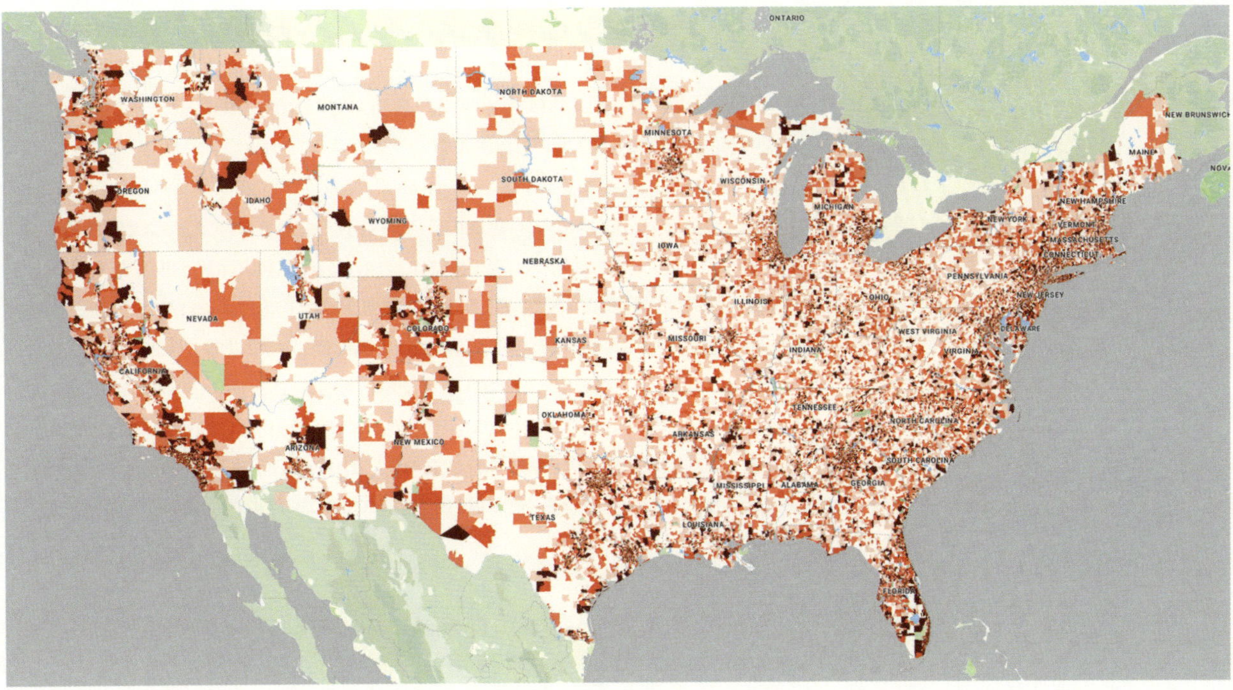
ONTARIO
WASHINGTON
MONTANA
NORTH DAKOTA
MINNESOTA
NEW BRUNSWICK
MAINE
OREGON
IDAHO
SOUTH DAKOTA
WISCONSIN
MICHIGAN
WYOMING
IOWA
NEW YORK
VERMONT
NEW HAMPSHIRE
MASSACHUSETTS
CONNECTICUT
NEBRASKA
PENNSYLVANIA
NEVADA
UTAH
ILLINOIS
OHIO
NEW JERSEY
COLORADO
KANSAS
MISSOURI
INDIANA
WEST VIRGINIA
DELAWARE
VIRGINIA
CALIFORNIA
TENNESSEE
OKLAHOMA
NORTH CAROLINA
ARKANSAS
ARIZONA
NEW MEXICO
SOUTH CAROLINA
MISSISSIPPI
ALABAMA
GEORGIA
TEXAS
LOUISIANA
FLORIDA

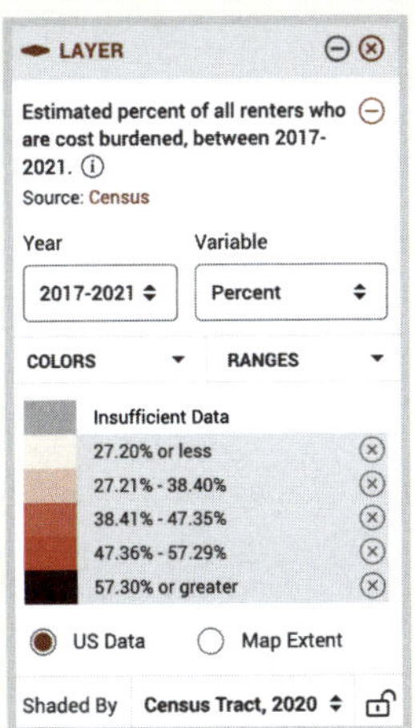
LAYER
Estimated percent of all renters who are cost burdened, between 2017-2021.
Source: Census
Year
2017-2021
Variable
Percent
COLORS
RANGES
Insufficient Data
27.20% or less
27.21% - 38.40%
38.41% - 47.35%
47.36% - 57.29%
57.30% or greater
US Data
Map Extent
Shaded By
Census Tract, 2020

per house. A shocking number but also not unexpected given that several single-story house types were replicated hundreds of times. Market practices in speculative housing that LIHTCs endorse do not offer fees that would sustain design or engineering innovation.

We increasingly believe the term housing has become a hindrance: while shelter is the ultimate concern, our work moves towards imagining shelter as an outcome or downstream product of renewable energy. Renewable energy becomes the driver of settlement. Legacy practices working in isolation can't fulfill the mission ahead of us. But we also need to imagine new ways to ethically and politically advance aggregation and access to R & D funding. Structural changes already present in our economy can be imagined to provide specific and actionable new design and technologically enhanced design practices.

During the past 40 years, the cost to produce a watt of solar energy via a photovoltaic cell has dropped from $77 per watt to 53 cents. Recordings of this decline begin in the 1970s, when the US Department of Energy began officially tracking solar production and consumption. This is the emergence of a new asset class, a new layer of energy applied atop infrastructure developed during the past century. As the cost to capture solar energy decreases, it forms a logarithmic curve: the rate of change in price slows even as the consumption of solar energy advances, making future price drops asymptotically more difficult to achieve. During this same period, the increase in consumption of solar energy was exponential: the rate of increase shown in the curve forms an ostensible mirror relative to the lowering costs. Literal pricing aside, the rates of change are startling. They in effect give a measure to renewable energy as an entirely new asset. Emerging in the context of latter-day urbanization, photons—a silent, persistent, and barely acknowledged optical presence—were becoming usable as energy and, increasingly, as wealth.

Cities are often defined by and debated as corollaries of economic globalization. Today, energy from the Sun has been increasingly registering as a new commodity. In each era of industrialization, cities have been rearranged by a new cartography of industry and globally redistributed labor. In the face of deindustrializing sectors of developed economies, architectural debates have often become urban in character, turning to sociology in an attempt to speak for constituencies destabilized by economic and cartographic shifts that altered labor markets. In this context, a building becomes a participant in larger urban equity issues. It seems we often debate works of architecture as sociological and economic side-effects of money, as the curation of an equity crisis rather than a deep analysis of that crisis.

Renewable energy, as a newly present and immensely valuable asset, brings us to a new place. Will we allow it to be used to sustain the status quo or does it portend a new way to think about collective wealth at geospatial scales? Real-estate industries are not prepared for this. Government has the ability to speak to and for its citizens and needs to find new ways to consolidate and use our collective wealth, imagining equity in the coming decades. Architectural practices have made major advances in using technology to enhance building performance. Can we do more to move them into a deeper real-time collaboration with engineering, energy, materials sciences, and a future-oriented economics, with an eye toward the shared benefits of yet-to-be-realized wealth?

Endnotes

1. US Housing Act of 1937, Public Law 75–896; Sep. 1, 1937, https://www.govinfo.gov/content/pkg/COMPS-10348/pdf/COMPS-10348.pdf and https://ia800708.us.archive.org/17/items/Housingact1937/housingact1937.pdf.

2. Frances Fox Piven and Richard Cloward, "The Weight of the Poor: A Strategy to End Poverty," *The Nation*, May 1966.

3. Frances Fox Piven and Richard Cloward, "The Weight of the Poor: A Strategy to End Poverty," *The Nation*, (republished) Mar. 8, 2010, https://www.thenation.com/article/archive/weight-poor-strategy-end-poverty/.

4. John Herbers, "Democrats Offer City Growth Plan," *New York Times*, Mar. 26, 1970.

5. The specifics of the Nixon era policies are sourced in an essay published by the American Bar Association. See Eugene J. Morris, "The Nixon Housing Program," *Real Property, Probate and Trust Journal* 9, No. 1 (Spring 1974), 2–6, https://www.jstor.org/stable/20781297.

6. Christopher Lasch, "After the Church the Doctors, After the Doctors Utopia," *New York Times*, Feb. 24, 1974.

7. Moore v. Lorain Metro. Hous. Auth., 121 Ohio St. 3d 455, 2009-Ohio-1250, https://www.supremecourt.ohio.gov/rod/docs/pdf/0/2009/2009-ohio-1250.pdf.

8. Moore v. Lorain.

9. Novogradac, Affordable Housing Resource Center, https://www.novoco.com/resource-centers/affordable-housing-tax-credits/lihtc-basics/about-lihtc#:~:text=Without%20the%20incentive%2C%20affordable%20rental,to%20develop%20affordable%20rental%20housing.

10. Low-Income Housing Tax Credit developments, 1987 to 2021. This map was prepared using PolicyMap based on data from HUD, July 14, 2023, https://www.policymap.com/.

11. Low-Income Housing Tax Credit (LIHTC): Property Level Data, U.S. Department of Housing and Urban Development Office of Policy Development and Research, Oct. 28, 2023, https://www.huduser.gov/portal/datasets/lihtc/property.html.

12. Billy J. Roberts, "Average Global Horizontal Solar Irradiance," National Renewable Energy Laboratory (NREL), Feb. 2018, https://nsrdb.nrel.gov/.

13. Composite graphic produced using data from Geoffrey Carr, "Sunny Uplands: Alternative energy will no longer be alternative," *Economist*, The World in 2013, https://www.economist.com/news/2012/11/21/sunny-uplands; and
Energy Consumption by Sector, US Energy Information Administration, Nov. 2012,
https://www.eia.gov/totalenergy/data/monthly/dataunits.php.

14. Estimated percent of all homeowners who are burdened by housing costs, between 2017–2021, Census: US Bureau of the Census, American Community Survey, PolicyMap, July 14, 2023, http://www.policymap.com/; Estimated percent of all renters who are "housing-cost burdened" or "severely-housing cost burdened," between 2017–2021, Census: US Bureau of the Census, American Community Survey, PolicyMap, July 14, 2023. http://www.policymap.com.

Five

Inexhaustible Supply: Renewable Energy Before Sustainability

As the 1970s emerged, the United States was more than a decade into what would become a 60-year era during which energy consumption eclipsed production, a window in the nation's history. In the early 1970s, the imbalance was already accelerating, the delta between production and consumption becoming increasingly clear to Congress and the public at large. Then, in 1973, the US faced an oil embargo imposed by the Organization of Petroleum Exporting Countries (OPEC), which quickly caused the price of imported oil to quadruple.

The oil embargo propelled an immediate crisis of fuel availability, but it also brought on a practically existential threat of austerity, which unsettled a country used to excess. The first political reaction was to ask the public to conserve fuel, if not to outright diminish its expectations of human comfort and ease of mobility. The specter of geopolitical conflict playing out through fuel supplies cast the crisis in phantom terms: the US State Department's Office of the Historian described this moment in bare language, with the government effectively asking the public to accept new conservation standards while simultaneously procuring imported oil in a complex global economy and attempting to sustain world political alliances. Intangible geopolitics were overlaid with everyday needs. The State Department described a need to preserve "close ties" to Middle East "oil-producing monarchies" while also supporting democracies in the region. The US's choice to import oil required negotiating this risk, and the embargo made the potential failings immediately tangible:

> *Once the broader impact of these factors set in throughout the United States, it triggered new measures beyond the April and November 1973 efforts that focused on energy conservation and development of domestic energy sources. These measures included the creation of the Strategic Petroleum Reserve, a national 55-mile-per-hour speed limit*

on US highways, and later, President Gerald R. Ford's administration's imposition of fuel economy standards. It also prompted the creation of the International Energy Agency proposed by Kissinger.[1]

In this context, federal research on renewable energy emerges in earnest, often with remarkably direct concern and language. So too begins the tracking of production and consumption of renewable energy at a wide scale. Related scientific work accelerates dramatically, including mapping of the Sun and remote observation of the Earth and its climate by satellite. A series of ambitious but schematic new congressional laws applied to private property and markets merge the science of the atmosphere and space with attempt to influence the sustainability of settlement patterns and developments. The newly created Department of Housing and Urban Development, for example, finds itself involved with NASA, as renewable energy and its impact on new housing is imagined. A deeper understanding of the Sun's energy gives new insight into biodiversity and the delicate balance of life itself. The science of energy is framed in terms of blue-sky innovation and a real-time need for cleaner energy, accompanied by the hope to export, even, as a means to balance international trade.

The geopolitical shock of OPEC's embargo made energy shortages real, and we think it disguised the conflicted nature of how the federal government framed renewable energy's impact and purpose. Described as both inexhaustible and bound for markets, renewable energy emerges as both a denominator of economic arbitrage—a shared resource that can guarantee access to energy at a reasonable cost—and a fully new type of asset class defined in part by its abundance, which places it at odds with traditional markets that set prices based on limited availability, or scarcity. By the late 1980s, we believe the market logic of scarcity overwhelms the science of energy research and casts what eventually falls under the rubric of sustainability as fragile. Valuing innovation less than apportionment, market mechanisms ultimately failed to recognize renewable energy as, in the 1974 words of Federal Power Commission Chairman John Nassikas, *inexhaustible*.

All of these dimensions are evident in congressional documents on energy. They set up a situation in which renewables become a product of legislation that seeks to create new markets out of the scientific research but also must protect existing energy markets from government competition. There is a window in the 1970s during which renewable energy was being framed in ways that might have more deeply challenged scarcity and austerity, suggesting how it might have become a new as-yet-untitled *inexhaustible* asset and alleviate scarcity instead of shoring up the assets of another era.

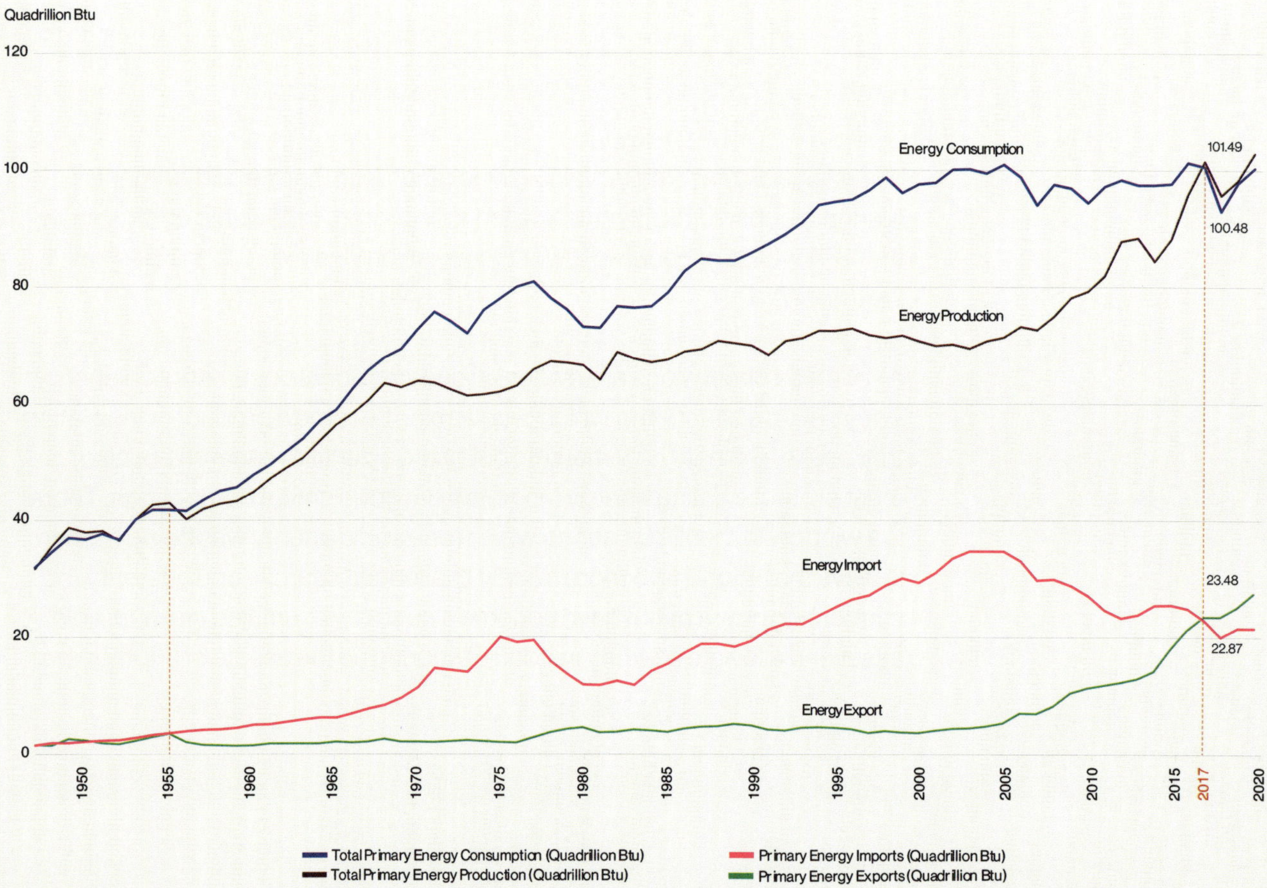

United States, Energy Information Administration, Primary Energy Overview 1949–2022 (Quadrillion Btu)[2]

The United States's primary energy production and consumption: "The United States has been an annual net total energy exporter since 2019. Up to the early 1950s, the United States produced most of the energy it consumed. US energy consumption was higher than US energy production in every year from 1958–2018. The difference between consumption and production was met by imports, particularly crude oil and petroleum products such as motor gasoline and distillate fuel oil. Total energy imports (based on heat content) peaked in 2007 and subsequently declined in nearly every year since then. Increases in US crude oil and natural gas production reduced the need for crude oil and natural gas imports and contributed to increases in crude oil and natural gas exports. The United States has been a net total energy exporter—total energy exports have been higher than total energy imports—since 2019."[3]

National Science Foundation

Twenty-Fourth Annual Report for Fiscal Year 1974

Letter of Transmittal

Washington, D.C.

DEAR MR. PRESIDENT:

I have the honor to transmit herewith the Annual Report for Fiscal Year 1974 of the National Science Foundation for submission to the Congress as required by the National Science Foundation Act of 1950.

Respectfully,

H. GUYFORD STEVER
Director, National Science Foundation.

The Honorable
The President of the United States.

National Science Foundation, Twenty-Fourth Annual Report for Fiscal Year 1974. Cover Page and Letter of Transmittal, H. Guyford Stever [4]

The Sun (Circa 1974)

In the early 1970s, congressional action on renewable energy provides groundwork for what would become the Department of Energy (DOE) and the National Renewable Energy Lab (NREL). When viewed from a historical lens, after the fact, the progression of research that leads to federal laws, federal research labs, and cabinet-level appointments seems direct, but the progress from law to action was far more circumspect, even if it was at times bold. Whether housing laws that impact property development and private developers or federal research on alternative energy, congressional acts often read as hedging a possible intrusion on private markets as opposed to a need to take on or backstop economic risks incurred by research and development that private enterprise might avoid.

In October of 1974, John Nassikas, then-chairman of the Federal Power Commission, made this case in simple terms in congressional testimony. But in conversation with industry and the press, the larger discussion of the nation's energy independence and environmental concerns were far more nuanced and reflected the realpolitik of energy production and market forces. Congressional testimony is not private, but in terms of calls for research, acknowledgement of needs, and market resistance or inability, it is often more candid.

In testimony to Congress on the Solar Energy Research, Development, and Demonstration Act of 1974, Nassikas stated:

> *An evaluation of necessary funding levels for solar R & D should include an assessment of the contribution that should be made by the private sector. In general, it is my belief that federal R & D expenditures should be concentrated in those areas where the amount of required investment is so large or the risks of commercial success are so speculative so as not to warrant substantial private investment as a matter of management responsibility.*[5]

Nassikas was discussing allocations of $600 million for the first six years' funding of the Solar Energy Research, Development, and Demonstration Act, the equivalent of more than $3.7 billion in 2023.

On October 31, 1974, the *New York Times* covered a speech Nassikas gave to the Aluminum Association at the Waldorf Astoria Hotel in New York. Nassikas asserted that the nation faced an energy crisis but also warned that the lens that defines this is not universally accepted. Energy conservation potentials are mixed with references and broad calls for creating federal policy and regulatory structures to allow research. His speech to the Aluminum Association was especially noteworthy; the article reminds that the secretary of commerce had recently pointed out that the aluminum industry had reduced its energy consumption by "62½ per cent over the last 30 years."[6] Nassikas described a need to create federal regulatory bodies around energy and to allow industry the freedom to innovate. Striking a broadly anti-regulatory stance, he described in other circumstances energy pricing that did not reflect actual reserves. Energy availability is also described as a matter of financial access: if energy is unaffordable it becomes scarce, in his estimation the same as a nonexistent.

The *Times* article did not list an author, but the timbre of writing is careful to characterize Nassikas's own tenor, noting he frequently put his written speech aside:

> *At a news conference after his talk, Mr. Nassikas said the energy crisis exists "not only because we are no longer assured of our supplies of fuel, but also because the ability of the people to pay for their energy supplies is seriously threatened." He added: "That's as real a crisis as the absolute physical shortage of supplies."*[7]

As the 1970s progresses, a call for energy innovation and use of nuclear and renewables is mixed with calls for energy conservation and, at times, austerity. The threat of energy scarcity even led to nearly unheard-of calls for changes in lifestyle and expectations of Americans. In his 1974 testimony to Congress regarding the Solar Energy Research, Development, and Demonstration Act, Nassikas's choice of words alternately offer an objective, scientific assessment about protocols for funding and a quiet, practically delirious view of solar energy:

> *Our current reliance on non-renewable fossil-fuel resources must be displaced by new, inexhaustible, environmentally acceptable energy forms and technologies. Solar energy is among the most promising of these new energy forms, and I support this legislation's emphasis on its expedited development and commercial utilization.*[8]

In one short passage, the term "inexhaustible" quickly leads to "commercial utilization," again returning us to the question, can one create a market for inexhaustible resources? In the realpolitik of markets, its price as a commodity would normally depend on having more demonstratively scarce characteristics such as having a limited means for delivery and transmission of power, a lack of industrial equipment needed to produce it, or there being inordinate governmental control over the resource. The delivery of power through utilities has never been such an open market. Utility companies act as quasi-governmental structure, delivering a service deemed essential to the public. The arrival of renewable production is essentially a threat to energy markets and has often been imagined so, as a form of radicality and a critique of markets. In the 1970s, these federal policies, new laws, congressional testimonies, and reports to the president reveal a generation of leadership taking on more than a new energy source: they are witnessing the birth of a perpetually renewable, inexhaustible resource.

Scarcity and its Opposite

Nassikas's 1974 comments acknowledge social division and difference of capacities: *a household that cannot afford energy would find itself unable to exist.* Scarce. That same year, Guyford Stever, director of the National Science Foundation, warned in the preface to its Twenty-Fourth Annual Report that the nation and its scientific community were facing profound questions about growth and the ability of technology to manifest a means to secure development. The discussion takes up the first eight paragraphs of his text, and one-and-half pages of a seven-page introduction. While the overall document offers a deeply detailed 141-page description of NSF-backed research, the opening is remarkably agile and poetic as it seeks to frame what Stever sees as a pivotal moment in industrialized society. Terms in the writing have become common in the intervening decades, but the tone and voice chosen seem precise and fragile when read today. The scope of his concern and the modalities and social implementation of science are today as in flux as then. His introductory paragraph concludes with a warning on uses of nonrenewable sources:

> *As our Nation approaches its third century and as Western Society approaches its third millennium, we enter an era that may be recognized as a turning point in human history. It is not difficult to realize why we have arrived at this point. The predominant reason is that through the marriage of science and technology, we have created an industrially based society that up to now has been able to sustain and advance a rapidly growing world population. The shift from an economy based on agricultural subsistence to one based on modern industry has been responsible for explosive growth, not only in population size but in a spectacular rise in mankind's activities—in mobility, speed of communication, range of knowledge, production of goods and services, and in the number of interfaces within his natural and social systems. Although much of this process is based on*

human innovation and industriousness, it is based also on humanity's exploitation of the natural world. It draws heavily on nature's capital, particularly on the store of nonrenewable resources, and it impacts heavily on her environment and living resources.[9]

The opening paragraph's focus on development and sustaining a century of growth offers concern that there are reasons to pause and reflect on our capability to sustain this path. He returns to technology as a means to avoid austerity or calamity, but his language is remarkably colloquial and personal. There is an aura of confidence mixed with concern. The changes in patterns of mobility, speed of communication, range of knowledge, production of goods and services, and interface within natural and social systems he enunciates have since only increased. The introduction can read like a primer written today in these variables, but its doubts about growth are based, reluctantly, it seems, on political concepts of scarcity that few would accept as a pivot point today. Stever argues against Malthusian predictions of growth outstripping resources, a positive enough goal, but also against the framing of growth from a negative, if not punitive position, which was historically used to marginalize populations and withhold resources. Stever writes:

While many have long warned that such growth could not continue indefinitely, their admonitions have usually been taken with a theoretical grain of salt. A combination of human ingenuity and nature's bounty has always seemed to disprove the Malthusians, or at least move the day of reckoning into the distant future. In the past, whenever scarcities conjured up the ghost of Malthus to predict impending doom, the ghost of Micawber seemed to appear beside him telling us that "Something will turn up." And fortunately, up to now it has. As we depleted one resource we were

> *able to find a replacement. As we overtaxed one region of the Earth environmentally, we found the means to move on. And as we reached the limits of one technological achievement, we were able to find another to exceed its performance.*[10]

Stever's text reads today as a time of discovery, an attempt to frame a threshold moment by a director of the NSF who is imagining how to coordinate billions of dollars in research. *The Limits to Growth*, the Club of Rome's 1972 assessment by a group of international scholars that unlimited growth was unsustainable and mankind was at a precipice, is not referenced directly, but its terms are present.

The focus on development in Stever's text continues in the opening pages and begins to be framed by concepts of "knowledge as developmental capital": science, technology, and research can in effect replace "the capital we have withdrawn from the Earth's supply of finite resources." This arrival at an equivalence of physical resources and intellectual or knowledge capital reads as startling, but is also backed up: Stever frames solar energy as capital that might replace "our use of the nonrenewable fossil and fission fuels."

Today we propose a more literal market and equivalency: solar energy as literally replacing income to turn housing into a downstream by-product of renewable energy, recalibrating how housing and its perpetual scarcity are arbitrated. Intellectual, knowledge capital here allows the production of new technologies, which in turn assure access to a not-scarce asset: inexhaustible—renewable—energy, available in ways that outflank any historical determinants of scarcity.

Stever's introduction makes intellectual leaps, but he also then carefully frames the narrower research goals presented in NSF work.

These include, for example, new spectroscopy of the Sun done apart from any overt goal of capitalizing on solar energy. The pure science of understanding the Sun in these decades, using techniques like remote sensing to measure infrared radiation emitted by gases in the Earth's atmosphere, is profound and precedes any known capitalizations, challenging the foundations of knowledge.

But where Stever's text truly startles is in a momentary philosophical framing of growth. He describes a need for "a more realistic appraisal of the human condition in relation to the physical world that supports it." Such an appraisal, he writes, raises "a host of questions not only over the possibility of feeding projected populations, but over the environmental, economic, and social consequences of the continued industrial development of the world along present lines."

The science is nationally funded but it is clearly geospatial, superseding any nation, creating a mandate for scientific research in relation to growth globally. This awareness and speculation is given urgency and "impetus by some new scarcities now appearing," he writes, and "has led to and intensified the debate over matters of growth… [bringing] forth more penetrating thought over the future role of science and technology." He concludes that the science and technology may inevitably spur growth, but implies that can be controlled and directed more wisely: "While there are some who fear that further advances in science and technology will only fire the engine of indiscriminate growth, there are others who feel there is a necessity for better and more wisely applied science and technology to enable better control and direction of growth and to allow us to continue to expand our physical frontiers."

Stever's text moves from verifying the value of intellectual capital to introducing a concern of millennial proportion—the dangers lurking behind an entire era of industrial society—and to invoking the social and environmental cost of scarcity. But like Nassikas, he also unlocks the term renewable as inexhaustible, while not quite venturing to see it as anything other than a prelude to the market logic of trading on controlled forms of scarcity. Renewable energy had and still has more capacity to vanquish what we imagine as scarcity in terms well beyond the powering of houses, mobility, and production.

Solar Energy Research Institute: The White House, NSF, HUD, FPC, NASA, and AEC

Fifty years have passed since the Solar Energy Research, Development, and Demonstration Act of 1974 was signed into law by the United States Congress. The eight-page document created the Solar Energy Research Institute (SERI), but the congressional document, in its spare form, allocated a substantial portion of its directive to an immediate call for SERI to launch an initial project. If the act is sprawling in its implications, it is also concise. It barely defines the research means, but highly defines the research team's leadership. This was a remarkable moment of imagining the team before the actual project.

In the 1974 legislation, the project's title was the Solar Energy Coordination and Management Project. It was to span six federal agencies, from the National Aeronautics and Space Administration (NASA) to the then nine-year-old Department of Housing and Urban Development (HUD). Its evolution from congressional act to institute to project formed the foundation for what soon became the National Renewable Energy Laboratory (NREL). The transition is rapid: NREL is formed in 1977, just three years later. The ramping up and scaling of these steps gives today's reader a sense of entrepreneurial imagination and follow-through. The language and initial project are immediate and tangible: Congress calling for focused work on solar energy and doing so with leadership of six federal agencies. The project was to be framed by its team.

While SERI was founded and titled as an institute, its initial focus and purpose seemed more precisely aimed at this singular initial project and the dynamics of the project's team. The project itself was not defined in the act, even as some of the team's goals were spelled out in schematic terms and in the makeup of the team itself. In reading the act in full, one senses the project quality of SERI was imagined as something larger than an experiment and smaller than an institute. The terms seem provisional.

President Carter Visits SERI 16

"No matter how good a job of conservation we do, the world's supply of oil and gas will dwindle, become more expensive and finally, run out."

"America's hope for energy to sustain economic growth beyond the year 2000 rests in large measure on the development of renewable and essentially inexhaustible sources of energy."

"We've been researching our energy needs in the last few months and I have just instructed the Department of Energy, through reprogramming, to provide an additional $100 million for expanded efforts in solar research, development, demonstration projects, and the development of commercial uses, such as windmills, in the next fiscal year."

"The question is no longer whether solar energy works. We know it works. The only question is how to cut costs so that solar power can be used more widely and so that it will set a cap on rising oil prices."

☆ U.S. GOVERNMENT PRINTING OFFICE: 1978—677-827.

SERI: The First Year shared research and goals of the Solar Energy Research Institute, founded in 1978. Director Paul Rappaport wrote: "The role of solar energy in meeting the future energy requirements of the United States and the world is not without controversy. There are those who envision solar energy as the ultimate energy alternative—a benign, democratic resource with enormous near-term potential. Others regard solar as something of an energy curiosity—a resource outside the mainstream of energy development with significant applications probable only in the next century."[11] Rappaport wrote that the future of solar energy was bound by "necessarily limited knowledge about our economic, social, and energy future, but there's no question in my mind that solar can emerge, in the next 15 or 20 years, as an important commercial energy resource." Fifty years later, we must do more to model a future of alternative energies, in particular where they challenge entire settlement patterns and their economies.

SERI and its initial project were intended to find the contours and outlines of what would be many experiments.

The defining momentum of SERI and the Solar Energy Coordination and Management Project is found in the collaboration it set forth between its founding leadership team. It reads today as an unstated prompt to employ the team's dynamics to create a parallel-path enquiry aimed at defining a worthy body of research with a yet-to-be-determined real potential. Its team membership was so divergent that the team itself seems like a design problem. Representing leadership from six diverse federal agencies, there was a necessity to bridge scientific aspects of solar-energy research with attributes and queries addressing urbanization, housing, and the economics of everyday life.

The Solar Energy Coordination and Management Project was to have one member designated by the President of the United States. Filling out five other seats were members addressing its scope and expertise. It is still today startling in its ambition. At its founding, the Solar Energy Coordination and Management Project was to include (in the order presented in the Act):

> *—the Assistant Director of the National Science Foundation;*
> *—an Assistant Secretary of Housing and Urban Development;*
> *—a member of the Federal Power Commission;*
> *—an Associate Administrator of the National Aeronautics and Space Administration;*
> *—and the General Manager Atomic Energy Commission [also newly formed in 1974].*

APPROVED
OCT 26 1974

EXECUTIVE OFFICE OF THE PRESIDENT
OFFICE OF MANAGEMENT AND BUDGET
WASHINGTON, D.C. 20503

OCT 23 1974

MEMORANDUM FOR THE PRESIDENT

Subject: Enrolled Bill S. 3234 - Solar Energy Research, Development and Demonstration
Sponsors - Sen. Humphrey (D) Minnesota and 11 others

Posted 10/28

Last Day for Action

October 29, 1974 - Tuesday

To Archives 10/29

Purpose

S. 3234 establishes a Solar Energy Coordination and Management Project to conduct research, and to demonstrate the commercial use of several solar energy technologies.

Agency Recommendations

Office of Management and Budget	Approval
Federal Power Commission	Approval
Atomic Energy Commission	Approval
Federal Energy Administration	Approval
National Science Foundation	No objection
Department of Housing and Urban Development	No objection
Department of the Interior	No objection
Department of Commerce	No objection
National Aeronautics and Space Administration	No objection

Discussion

Solar energy is broadly defined in the bill as energy recently originating from the sun including: direct and indirect solar radiation and intermediate forms of energy such as wind, sea thermal gradients (differentials in ocean temperatures), photosynthetic processes (converting light to other forms of

Memorandum for the President Subject: Enrolled Bill S. 3234 - Solar Energy Research, Development and Demonstration

Sponsors - Sen. Humphrey (D) Minnesota and 11 others Prepared by: Executive Office of the President, Office of Management and Budget, Washington, D.C. 20503, Oct. 23, 1974.[12]

Source: Gerald R. Ford Presidential Library

The Solar Energy Coordination and Management Project is the precursor to today's National Renewable Energy Laboratory, but in its first instance it was presumably far more fragile and subject to future renewals of congressional funding. It was a pilot project. The Solar Energy Research, Development, and Demonstration Act of 1974 stated overarching political and economic motives, including a need to reduce the nation's reliance on imported fossil fuels. It speculated on exporting solar technology and its potential beneficial impact on the country's balance of trade in doing so. While it describes the value of clean energy, it does not specify the impetus as climate change but instead describes a motivation to reduce disarray in the science and techniques of renewable-energy approaches in both government and industry. It speaks to disarray in varying degrees of research-readiness, especially regarding commercial development and incentives.

The act puts science in a central position, but it frequently refers to the role of economics and economic security. Solar energy was defined in the expansive global scope of the Earth and geospatial sciences, as well as an explicitly national and political concern. It called for a "national appraisal of all solar energy resources, including data on insolation, wind, sea thermal gradients, and potentials for photosynthetic conversion." Only the federal government could imagine taking on such an objective, but the act is also brief: We read it today as an immense challenge to deliver enough immediate scientific results to forge the reasons to renew and expand the act. There is also an unmistakable call to fuse the most ambitious and rarefied forms of state-funded science and technology with the everyday realpolitik of the markets, urban design, and housing. It gave HUD a seat at the table with the most advanced scientific realms of the federal government.

Public Law 93-473

AN ACT

To authorize a vigorous Federal program of research, development, and demonstration to assure the utilization of solar energy as a viable source for our national energy needs, and for other purposes. October 26, 1974 [S. 3234]

Be it enacted by the Senate and House of Representatives of the United States of America in Congress assembled, That this Act may be cited as the "Solar Energy Research, Development, and Demonstration Act of 1974". Solar Energy Research, Development, and Demonstration Act of 1974. 42 USC 5551 note.

DECLARATION OF FINDINGS AND POLICY

SEC. 2. (a) The Congress hereby finds that— 42 USC 5551.

(1) the needs of a viable society depend on an ample supply of energy;

(2) the current imbalance between domestic supply and demand for fuels and energy is likely to persist for some time;

(3) dependence on nonrenewable energy resources cannot be continued indefinitely, particularly at current rates of consumption;

(4) it is in the Nation's interest to expedite the long-term development of renewable and nonpolluting energy resources, such as solar energy;

(5) the various solar energy technologies are today at widely differing stages of development, with some already near the stage of commercial application and others still requiring basic research;

(6) the early development and export of viable equipment utilizing solar energy, consistent with the established preeminence of the United States in the field of high technology products, can make a valuable contribution to our balance of trade;

(7) the mass production and use of equipment utilizing solar energy will help to eliminate the dependence of the United States upon foreign energy sources and promote the national defense;

(8) to date, the national effort in research, development, and demonstration activities relating to the utilization of solar energy has been extremely limited; therefore

(9) the urgency of the Nation's critical energy shortages and the need to make clean and renewable energy alternatives commercially viable require that the Nation undertake an intensive research, development, and demonstration program with an estimated Federal investment which may reach or exceed $1,000,000,000.

(b) The Congress declares that it is the policy of the Federal Government to—

(1) pursue a vigorous and viable program of research and resource assessment of solar energy as a major source of energy for our national needs; and

(2) provide for the development and demonstration of practicable means to employ solar energy on a commercial scale.

DEFINITIONS

SEC. 3. For the purposes of this Act— 42 USC 5552.

(1) the term "solar energy" means energy which has recently originated in the Sun, including direct and indirect solar radiation and intermediate solar energy forms such as wind, sea thermal gradients, products of photosynthetic processes, organic wastes, and others;

The Solar Energy Coordination and Management Project as described within the Solar Energy Research, Development, and Demonstration Act:

To authorize a vigorous Federal program of research, development, and demonstration to assure the utilization of solar energy as a viable source for our national energy needs, and for other purposes.

Be it enacted by the Senate and House of Representatives of the United States of America in Congress assembled, That this Act may be cited as the "Solar Energy Research, Development, and Demonstration Act of 1974." [13]

The science seems to come first, but the act continually refers to potential commercialization by private industry. With solar energy, there is already an awareness of potential intrusion into private markets. The act includes a directive to "develop and carry out a general plan for inventorying all forms of solar-energy resources associated with Federal lands and (where consistent with property rights) non-Federal lands." The reality of property ownership is calibrated with its capacity to produce yet-un-realized and un-titled renewable energy, a federal imperative to use its aggregating capacity to generate it at a large scale with capabilities no private owner could mount.

Realpolitik / Real Science

The inclusion of a HUD assistant secretary as one of six members brought development, property, place, real estate, housing, and human need directly into the equation. The Solar Energy Coordination and Management Project sets up an ambitious creative conflict: between state-based science and its non-market research-and-development capacities and the state's interest in protecting markets and forms of property held by private citizens and companies. In bringing HUD's roles in distributing federal funds in an effort to improve equity and development of everyday building in cities, real estate, and housing into collaboration with Federal Power Commission (FPC), NSF, NASA, and the Atomic Energy Commission, the act asked if a new science of energy might reshape housing, its economy, and people's lives.

Has anything of this magnitude ever been enacted since within the federal government? In private industry? By the mid-1980s, federal funds for affordable housing were largely converted into LIHTC programs. HUD's housing goals were syndicated by way of the Treasury Department into tax credits. Immense federal funding was disaggregated and channeled into tranches to small-scale non-profit housing development corporations. R & D in this realm seems impossibly neutralized compared to what was imagined in 1974.

In the 1970s, HUD was still a very new entity, having been given Cabinet-level status only in 1965. HUD, however, preceded what would become the Department of Energy (DOE) as a Cabinet-level agency by 12 years. DOE was formed in 1977. The HUD secretary in 1974, James T. Lynn, held degrees in economics, political science, and law, and would have routinely found himself and HUD focused on major urban centers and cities in the aftermath of a massive rise of suburban development. In the decades immediately after World War II and leading up to the 1970s, vast portions of the US suburbs had exploded in growth. While HUD's focus is not exclusive to cities or urban centers, by the 1970s a major part of its focus was on disinvestment and urban renewal that often became a proxy for racial and social displacement. The Housing Acts of 1949 and 1954, while nearly twenty years earlier, had forged a deep distrust of the government's role in urban development and involvement in displacement through urban renewal, by then understood as a form of structural racism.

HUD would bring a deep and real-time experience of housing to SERI. Federal housing assistance dates back most prominently to the 1930s and a series of housing acts that created and administered the nation's entry into public housing. Today, fifty years after SERI, public housing developments are continually discussed as possible sites for solar energy installations. But housing as it is manifested in federal policy is always tied to questions of urbanism, urban planning, and design, and poverty today is growing more rapidly in non-urban areas. The demand for HUD's scope and reach, its mandate to define needs and depict the cartography of a constituency in need is accelerated.

The relationship between agencies instigated by SERI that fused HUD and the most technologically advanced work on renewable energy is essential today. A particular modus operandi is predominant today as it was in 1974: Real-estate interests are a driving factor in setting the limits and boundaries of how federal funds enter into otherwise market-driven aspects of development, from cities to suburbs to rural landscapes. The Solar Energy Research, Development, and Demonstration Act of 1974 offered what seemed like a window to imagine energy as a different form of public development: HUD could have presumably imagined other ways to address need and forge an alternate method of developing property in the context of the limitless potential of solar energy, a wealth from above Earth, not contained by land.

Existential Energy: Atomic Energy and Civilian Control

That same year, Congress enacted the Energy Reorganization Act of 1974, reorganizing leadership of large sectors of nation's energy research and production. The Atomic Energy Commission (AEC), formed in 1946 with the intention of moving research in atomic energy from military to civilian control, was in 1974 transformed into the newly created Nuclear Regulatory Commission (NRC). The NRC was identified in the act as having whistleblower protections; nuclear energy was far from resolved as an alternative source of power, and three decades after World War II, doubts about the safety of its management were widespread.

The Energy Reorganization Act of 1974 helps pave the way for what became the Department of Energy in 1977. It reads to a non-attorney as a second stage of establishing civilian leadership over the new scientific and industrial scale of the nation: the nuclear aspects of the law's scope create a degree of doubt that demands attention and a sharing of political negotiation with other renewables.[14] In reading these laws today, one senses that the attention and bandwidth of scientists and politicians alike was forced to mediate the seemingly benign and dangerous in energy, and if inclined, to attempt to convince a skeptical public and markets, or undermine further actions.

It reads as motivated to set the stage for appraising the use of nuclear energy in domestic settings, but it also marks a consolidation of renewable-energy research in the newly formed Energy Research and Development Administration. It transfers a range of technical research around energy from various other executive branch agencies; for example, it moves efforts within the "Office of Coal Research" from the Secretary of the Interior and transfers research on fossil fuels from the Bureau of Mines to a new executive agency, the Energy Research and Development Administration, whose director is appointed by the president. For renewables, it designated a transfer of research leadership from the National Science Foundation for developmental work related to "solar heating and cooling" and geothermal power. As a whole, the Energy Reorganization Act consolidates energy research across a wide scope of existing and future energy sources. Organizing work on energy less around its origins, physical sources, territories, and political denominations, it suggests a concern about the risk of nuclear energy and an effort to treat energy as a subject of its own. The legislation goes so far as to transfer research administered by the Environmental Protection Agency, noting work related to alternative "automobile power systems." In this act, one can see energy struggling to be seen as a category of its own destiny.

In retrospect, the Energy Reorganization Act of 1974 and the Solar Energy Research, Development, and Demonstration Act of 1974 seem to anticipate what would become a period of immense growth in the United States,

President Truman signs the Atomic Energy Act of 1946. On January 1, 1947, all atomic energy activities are transferred to the newly created Atomic Energy Commission in accordance with the act.

President Gerald Ford signs the Energy Reorganization Act of 1974 at the White House, October 11, 1974. Dixie Ray Lee, the Atomic Energy Commission's last chairman, watches at the far-right end of the table. Courtesy of the Department of Energy.

including in development and in housing markets. Our earlier chapters discussed the 1970s expansion of the suburbs, in particular the South and West regions of the census, as well as emerging uses of expanded household debt to fuel the purchase of single-family houses and private automobiles. The early 1970s were pivotal years in establishing federal directives on the future of energy in the US, reframing a national and global view of energy at aggregate scales. Explaining this in the context of immediate and real-time threats, for example, the oil shortages in the aftermath of import limits set by OPEC in 1973 make it more difficult for the federal government to act. While emerging from an immediate political and economic conflict, they nonetheless created a call for scientific innovation. Domestic urban development, mass production of housing, and manufacturing of automobiles and appliances were framed as unified under the framework of energy. This was done in ways that did not deny the real-estate goals of development but offered new frameworks that we have not fully embraced, in particular its multidisciplinary team formations, and processes of identifying problems.

If these legislative acts were occurring in an era that was beginning to acknowledge climate science and climate change, the terminology of the acts seemed far from conditioning federal action toward climate policy. Instead, the series of laws seemed to frame scientific inquiry against social needs, demand for clean energy, and the ultimate priorities of national security and trade. Yet in de facto ways, these concerns placed the scientific capacity that Congress might at least partially direct by funding research ahead of and even outside of commercial means.

Today, between the metrics of climate science suggesting a point of no return for global temperatures, and the new capacities for automation in design, production, engineering, and logistics generating the potential for transformation of energy and human habitation along a different pathway, we feel we are at a new crossroads even more urgent than the early 1970s. Recent research and publications increasingly outline pathways for decarbonizing our power grid and an entirely new cartography of energy production and distribution. The Andlinger Center for Energy and the Environment Center's research, in particular, points to a very different geographic origin of energy in a renewable era. It demands that we ask: will we move energy to us where we live now, or will we move to the energy? Given how rapidly we build housing, the emerging states of automation, and their potential impact on employment, we believe a significant percentage of the population could find itself facing an elective but critical relocation. To achieve this, we need a very different form of architectural practice that can produce the types of housing-as-energy product we believe will fuel housing as a form of universal income. This requires something far more fundamental than photovoltaics or batteries attached to existing housing. It demands an entirely new form of building product: an energy product that offers shelter.

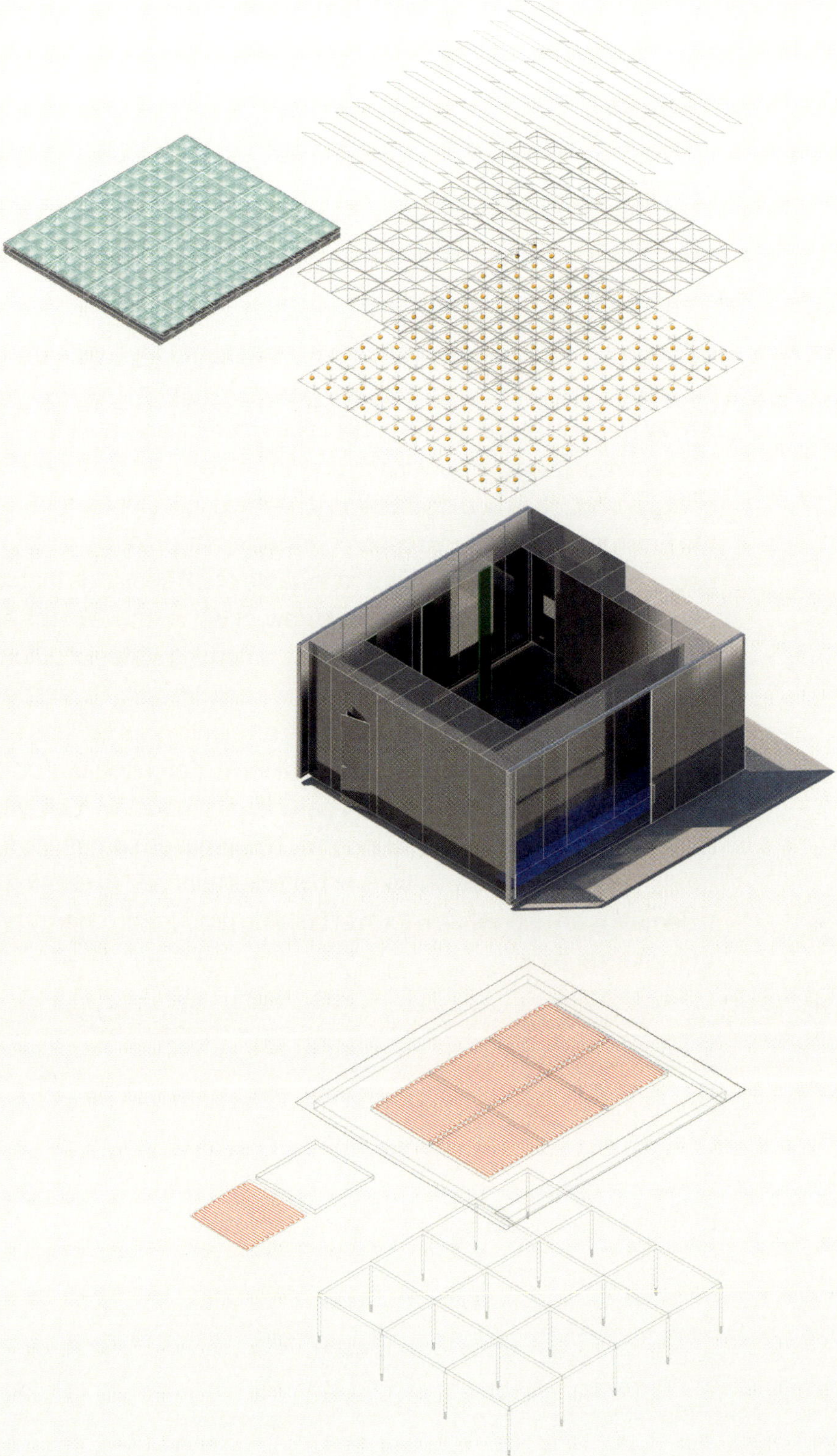

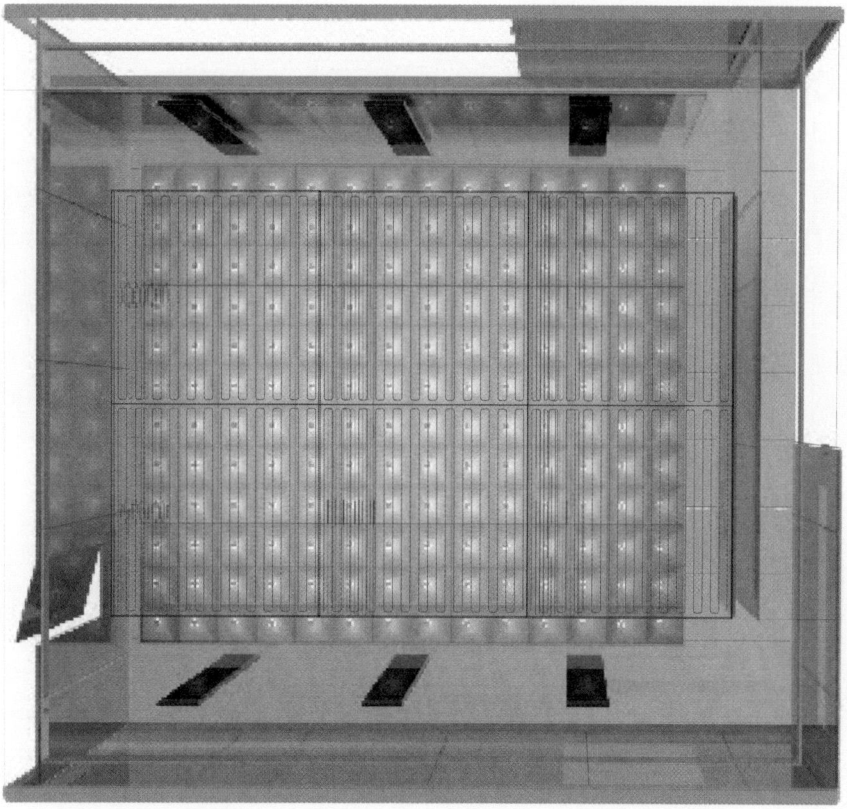

Model D, Micro-School
Layered view from above. A cassette-like box structure provides eyelet north-facing cells that distribute light evenly across entire interior. The cassette-like series of panels integrate south-facing photovoltaic cells. Heat gain and air exchange are integrated into wall systems, radiant heating and cooling integrated into floor panels. Prototype for a 600-square-foot micro-school.

Our Common Limits? Sustainable Development

Sustainability is a term that would be impossible to try to isolate, but one foundational source would have to be the United Nations' 1987 Report of the World Commission on Environment and Development titled Our Common Future. The UN document spanned more than 350 pages, indexing and outlining with incredible precision a global network of interlocking development goals, each of which were being reframed by a then-still newly global post-Bretton Woods economy and a growing awareness of climate change. At the core of the document are the terms sustainability and development, which continue to frame much of our discussion of climate today. The UN Commission on Environment described them as constituting the unavoidable human work of changing the planet, building upon and making use of the resources of the Earth and environment that precede us, which we have inherited and shall leave to a future generation.

Sustainability in this lexicon has an ethical, pragmatic, and measurable dimension. In Our Common Future, it means meeting one generation's needs should not inhibit the next generation from meeting theirs. As a UN document as well as a post-World War II and post-Bretton Woods-era study, development cannot be easily localized at national levels: it can be isolated provisionally but is inexorably interlocked with other economies and the destiny of world's peoples. The economic health of the world is interconnected, especially in an era in which climate and environmental externalities are often global and imposed inequitably by one nation on another. Global security is inextricably connected in, by, and through development in this equation, in part because poorer nations do not have the means to address climate when food security, for example, is more urgent, or industrial capacity and national wealth don't allow it, and when governmental or market mechanisms are not in place to adjudicate sustainable goals. Since 1987, these terms have all become common themes in how we frame sustainability. At their core, they point to a world where poverty and inequitable wealth distribution are a threat to climate itself. Addressing climate *is* addressing poverty. Inequity and the presence of poverty is by necessity a foundational start in addressing climate change.

Our Common Future often portrays resources as limited and directly relates their allocation to population growth, increasingly developed economies, more of the world living with an elevated level of consumption and access to higher-quality goods and services, and ultimately, to energy. Where Our Common Future might be reimagined today is how willing it might be to revise its projections in relation to a technological extension of what are presumed to be limited resources. Few pages are devoted exclusively to renewable energy, but the theme of renewables is found in several sections of the document. There are bold predictions that renewables might in theory meet current world power consumption but with caveats. It also points to economic realities such as the use of biomass such as wood for heat in developing countries. Biomass in this case is not sustainable because its use outstrips growth. Moreover, future energy consumption is understood as not static, especially if the uneven distribution of wealth and consumption among nations is made more equitable. This mixture of large-scale modeling, real-world circumstances, and the ability to capitalize innovations have become standard matrices by which we gauge the potential for sustainable development.

> *"The growth of energy demand in response to industrialization, urbanization, and societal affluence has led to an extremely uneven global distribution of primary energy consumption. The consumption of energy per person in industrial market economies, for example. is more than 80 times greater than in sub-Saharan Africa."*[15]

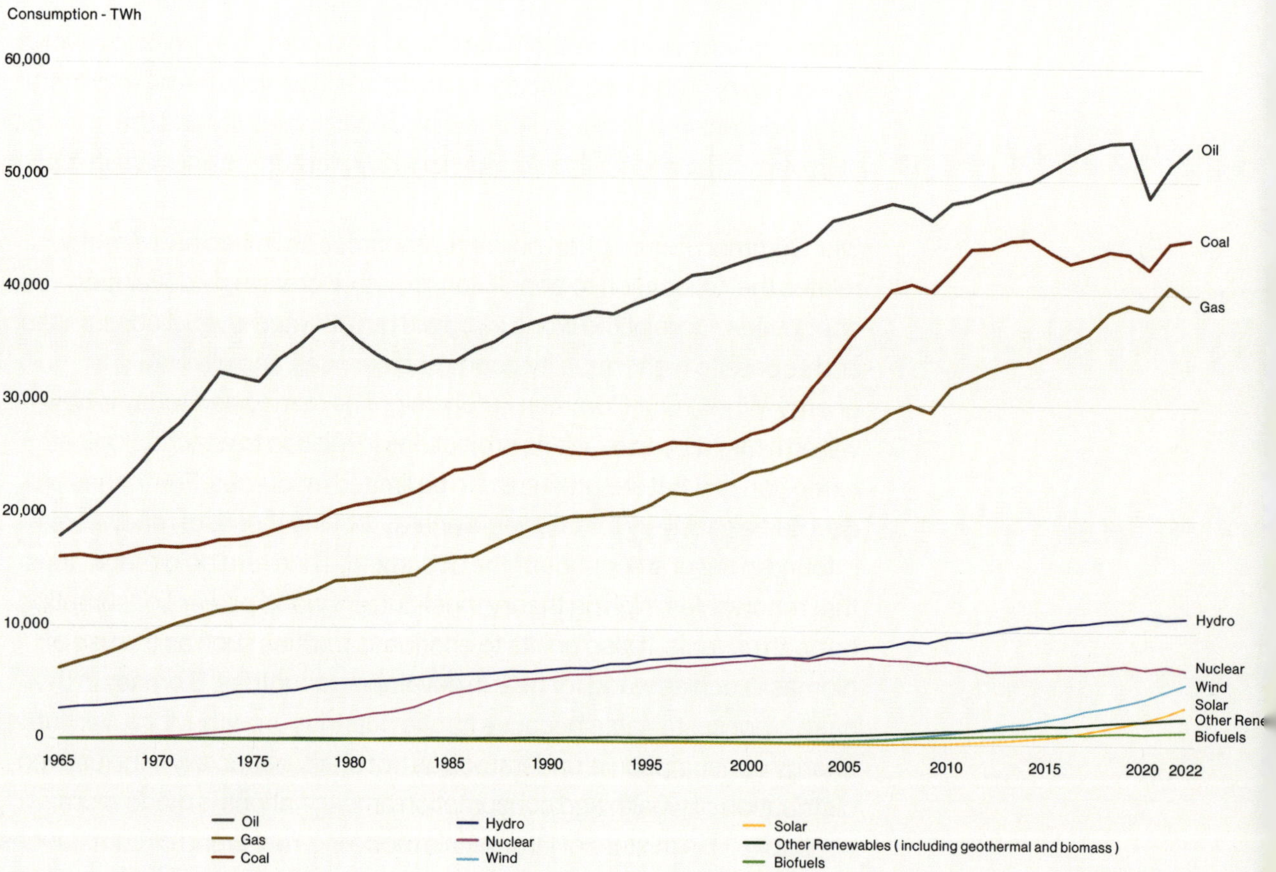

Primary Energy Consumption by Source, World
Graphic by authors

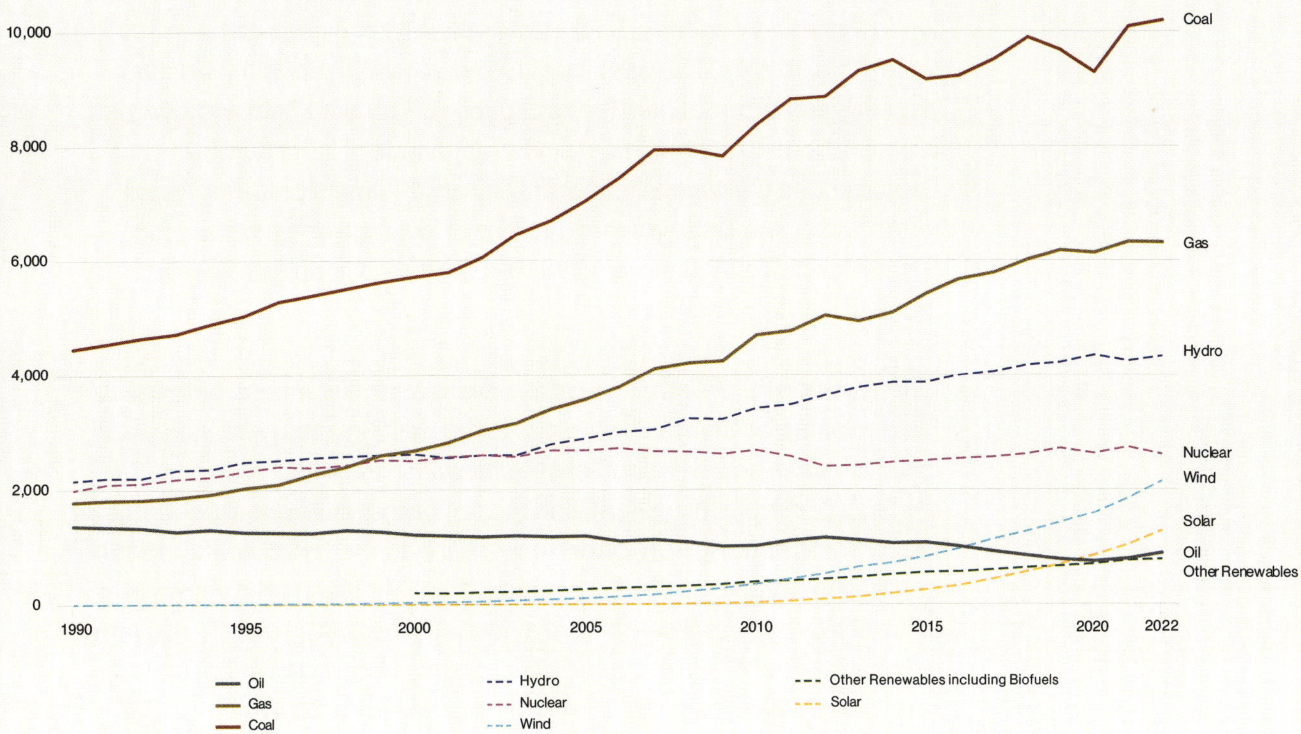

Electricity from Source, World[16]
Graphic by authors

Today, one can find a great deal of dedication on the part of governments, businesses, societies, and individuals to addressing the conditions described in Our Common Future; however, much of the developed world that it was conceived within has radically changed and been tested to extremes. The volatility of US housing markets in the last two decades and extraordinary levels of public and private debt and leverage will in the coming decade meet a new magnitude of labor automation, creating deep challenges to the stability of settlement patterns. As we noted earlier, the extraordinary degrees of leverage of the world's top ten central banks, shoring up what were assumed to be safe assets, is increasingly being questioned.

Our Common Future portrays renewables as a replacement for fossil fuels. Here we imagine them as disruptors to the existing energy economy and instigators of a new development regime within the wider economy. We want to accelerate this potential. In this lens, renewable energy becomes a precursor to housing as a form of universal income. This potential does not come from national treasuries or central banks. Instead of an incremental value achieved by renewable energy, we imagine it as an offset to poverty: a global source of energy not originating in any single nation, not titled, or prescribed within fossil fuel mining or other territorial licenses.

Human development in the industrial era has placed the burden of emissions on the poor and less economically fortunate, those who also did not partake in the wealth creation. Renewable energy is nothing if not a new potential to address inequity, but we need to also mind the scale of capital needed to achieve this technologically. Renewable energy is unfathomable in scale; the industrial mechanism to access it is not. It will only be achieved with a public and leaders who do not recoil from scale or fear the aggregation of capital needed to act.

UNITED
NATIONS

A

General Assembly

Distr.
GENERAL

A/42/427
4 August 1987
ENGLISH
ORIGINAL: ARABIC/CHINESE/ENGLISH/
FRENCH/RUSSIAN/SPANISH

Forty-second session
Item 83 (e) of the provisional agenda*

DEVELOPMENT AND INTERNATIONAL ECONOMIC CO-OPERATION: ENVIRONMENT

Report of the World Commission on Environment and Development

Note by the Secretary-General

1. The General Assembly, in its resolution 38/161 of 19 December 1983, *inter alia*, welcomed the establishment of a special commission that should make available a report on environment and the global *problématique* to the year 2000 and beyond, including proposed strategies for sustainable development. The commission later adopted the name World Commission on Environment and Development. In the same resolution, the Assembly decided that, on matters within the mandate and purview of the United Nations Environment Programme, the report of the special commission should in the first instance be considered by the Governing Council of the Programme, for transmission to the Assembly together with its comments, and for use as basic material in the preparation, for adoption by the Assembly, of the Environmental Perspective to the Year 2000 and Beyond.

2. At its fourteenth session, held at Nairobi from 8 to 19 June 1987, the Governing Council of the United Nations Environment Programme adopted decision 14/14 of 16 June 1987, entitled "Report of the World Commission on Environment and Development" and, *inter alia*, decided to transmit the Commission's report to the General Assembly together with a draft resolution annexed to the decision for consideration and adoption by the Assembly.

3. The report of the World Commission on Environment and Development, entitled "Our Common Future", is hereby transmitted to the General Assembly. Decision 14/14 of the Governing Council, the proposed draft resolution and the comments of the Governing Council on the report of the Commission can be found in the report of the Governing Council on the work of its fourteenth session. 1/

---

* A/42/150.

87-18467 2999h (E) /...

United Nations, General Assembly, Forty-Second Session, August 4, 1987. Item 83 (e) of the provisional agenda*

Development and International Cooperation: Environment Report of the World Commission on Environment and Development

The report of the World Commission on Environment and Development entitled "Our Common Future" is hereby transmitted to the General Assembly.

Stever's NSF report in 1974 enunciated a concern about the public reception of technological intervention and science's intersection with social goals. This is still a critical question today.

A Bloomberg News Energy Finance research group has estimated that the investment needed to be carbon neutral worldwide by 2050 could reach $196 trillion, or $7 trillion per year.[17] The International Monetary Fund estimates world GDP at $105 trillion in 2023. United States residential real estate has an estimated value of $41 trillion. Whatever equations are used to measure economic viability, the challenges we have already seen in the urban and architectural world ask us to refine what we are defending and what we imagine we are innovating. In some parts of the world, housing and shelter barely exist: it has to be created a new. In other parts of the world, its over-financialization and debt burden might thwart change. If energy were seen as the product to capitalize rather than shelter, we believe there is a clearer path to capitalizing a product that provides energy—and with it shelter—turning energy into a productive form of what has been called housing. It would bridge the agrarian world that our industrialized world superseded, in effect, harvesting the sky and relinquishing some of what we expect from the ground. A world that is increasingly automated, less employed at a distance from home, could reconnect aspects of life, restoring qualities our industrialized world severed.

Endnotes

1. "Oil Embargo, 1973–1974," Office of the Historian, US Department of State, https://history.state.gov/milestones/1969-1976/oil-embargo.

2. US Energy Information Administration, Monthly Energy Review, Table 1.4 c, Apr. 2023, https://www.eia.gov/totalenergy/data/monthly/pdf/sec1_3.pdf.

3. "US energy facts explained," Imports and Exports, US Energy Information Administration, https://www.eia.gov/energyexplained/us-energy-facts/imports-and-exports.php.

4. National Science Foundation Twenty-Fourth Annual Report for Fiscal Year 1974, National Science Foundation, Annual Reports, https://www.nsf.gov/pubs/1974/1974-NSF-Annual-Report.pdf.

5. "Statement of John N. Nassikas, Chairman, Federal Power Commission before the Subcommittee on Energy, Committee on Science and Astronautics, US House of Representatives, July 30, 1974," Digitized from Box 11, folder 1974/10/26 S3234, Solar Energy Research Development and Demonstration of the White House Records Office: Legislation Case Files at the Gerald R. Ford Presidential Library, 10, https://www.fordlibrarymuseum.gov/library/document/0055/1668753.pdf.

6. "Nassikas Backs Project Independence," *New York Times*, Oct. 31, 1974, https://www.nytimes.com/1974/10/31/archives/nassikas-backs-project-independence-no-consensus-found.html.

7. "Nassikas Backs Project Independence," Oct. 31, 1974.

8. "Statement of Nassikas."

9. National Science Foundation, vii.

10. National Science Foundation, vii.

11. SERI: The First Year, Solar Energy Research Institute, US Department of Energy, Dec. 1978, https://www.nrel.gov/docs/legosti/old/142.pdf.

12. "Memorandum for the President, October 23, 1974," Box 11, folder "1974/10/26 S3234 Solar Energy Research Development and Demonstration" of the White House Records Office, Legislation Case Files, Gerald R. Ford Presidential Library, https://www.fordlibrarymuseum.gov/library/document/0055/1668753.pdf.

13. Solar Energy Research, Development, and Demonstration Act of 1974, Public Law 93-473—Oct., 26, 1974, US Congress, https://www.govinfo.gov/content/pkg/STATUTE-88/pdf/STATUTE-88-Pg1431.pdf.

14. Energy Reorganization Act of 1974, Public Law 97-438, Nuclear Regulatory Commission, Oct. 11, 1974, https://www.nrc.gov/docs/ML0224/ML022410201.pdf.

15. Report of the World Commission on Environment and Development: Our Common Future, Official Records of the United Nations General Assembly, Forty-Second Session, Aug. 4, 1987, 171, https://digitallibrary.un.org/record/139811?ln=en.

16. Hannah Ritchie and Pablo Rosado, "Electricity Mix," OurWorldInData.org, 2020, https://ourworldindata.org/electricity-mi ; https://ourworldindata.org/grapher/primary-sub-energy-source.

17. Mark Gongloff, "$200 Trillion Is Needed to Stop Global Warming. That's a Bargain," Bloomberg, July 5, 2023, https://www.bloomberg.com/opinion/articles/2023-07-05/-200-trillion-is-needed-to-stop-global-warming-that-s-a-bargain.

Six

A Non-Denumerable Abundance: Post-Scarcity

Energy generated by nuclear fusion within the Sun reaches the surface of the Earth in ***8 minutes and 20 seconds.***

Massless photons transmit radiation at the speed of light—299,792,458 meters or ***186,000 miles per second.***

If the *speed of light* is difficult to imagine it becomes unfathomable when coupled with the duration of a day, or the persistence of days over weeks or a year. It becomes a light year. Or ***thousands and millions of light years.***

Energy reaches Earth in quantities we can't fathom.

It is ***not scarce.***

It is ***non-denumerable.***

Silent Machines Meet Infinite Resources

Energy at the scale of solar radiation is, by any measure, architecturally without scale. It is literally massless.

Architectural scale and purpose emerge in forms of material reciprocity. Solar energy is arrested and made into form as a building component. Le Corbusier's mid-20th century solar shading—what he titled a "brise soleil"—shaped a new plastic language of architectural space. Derived from the deep horizontal planes that formed the sun shading of the façade, his buildings became more porous, transparent, and continuous with the atmosphere. Today, energy correlated and interceptive in a photovoltaic panel creates plate-like forms, added to the building and creating a shell-like opacity. But these dimensions are incidental and manifested locally, given form inside an economy and semiology of buildings. They offer financial gains, beneficial yields in clean energy. Introduced as readymade components and products, we preclude a deeper perception and intuition of the energy before us. Photovoltaic panels designed to last 20 years, installed atop a house designed to last 50 years, are aimed at an agnostic energy source of such scale it precedes us and endures billions of years after us. The proposition embodies light-years of energy. There is no architectural capacity to offer a comparable scale to the energy created by the Sun—none.

A photovoltaic panel is a form of spectroscopy, an interaction of light penetrating matter. It is an electromagnetic and chemically enabled silent molecular machine. They form an optical panel, not a rationalized perspectival glass window for the human eye but one for the Sun's photons. They are today a window for a spectrum of light that the eye can witness, but they instigate an electro-chemical action; the physics of light activates a chemical exchange of electrons not visible to eye. They become a chemical machine, affixed as an aberration atop architectural form. We *imagine* we are seeing energy generation; instead, we see a geometric form added to an architectural form: a panel added to a house. It is a tectonic assembly, at a scale that reveals little to nothing of what is active and what is possible. A photovoltaic has a tautological presence, referring to something we assume to be self-evident that we rarely try to verify or interrogate. Research promises alternatives. Photovoltaic cells use other invisible spectra of light, furthering a reliance on what we can't architecturally see or verify.

Understood as additive to architecture, photovoltaic panels become *adjunct* to another structure. A PV adds its embodied energy to that of its host but brings a reverse flow to consumption. It adds to the life span of its host. The entire structure reacts to the climate: its materials degrade in relation to sunlight and natural elements. The engineering and materials science that a photovoltaic panel isolates as a commercial product could serve as a proxy for a deeper integration of materials science in building. The role of the semiotics of architectural history and design, if diminished, could allow a deeper focus on a building's thermodynamics rather than its form, the interaction of materials with energy guiding every decision and setting the terms of design. If we continue to see innovations in renewable energy as new sub-components of a mechanical system, for example, or even a new instrument—as a radio antenna would have been in the 20th century—we miss an opportunity to imagine a new architecture, a new way to imagine building.

Public discourse often reckons with scale in relation to cities and nations, wars and conflict, elections and representation, and vis-à-vis such diverse sublime, dramatic, and everyday phenomena as traffic, natural wonders, storms, extreme weather events, and the daily forecast. But climate change challenges the creative and public imagination, transposing our sense of the future beyond scale as we know it, beyond legislative and political territories. Creating ways to imagine the future requires a scientific dimension and expertise, and it also needs the intuition and imagination of the public to help supersede older, entrenched paradigms.

Scaleless but with Scale

Can we quantify solar energy within known figures or limits ascribed to other energy sources or other forms of renewable energy? A future that gives renewable energy adequate scale in the built world is a nascent and emerging question. But how do we imagine renewable energy outside of the built world? Tidal or wind energy, for example, offer observable laminar flows and mechanics, in which water and air travel smoothly in regular paths. California Institute of Technology Professor John Dabiri's research on the propulsion shared and amplified between fish within a school or in flocks of birds shows this.[1] The hydraulic action of water and the laminar flow of air are made measurable in Dabiri's research; the motion of fish traveling in a school is amplified, affording an increase in propulsion with less energy. Dabiri hypothesized about the potential of this if manifest in *schools* of wind turbines, amplifying energy generation in the atmosphere without the input of more energy. Scale is here startling, but measurable and observable. It follows the essential algebra of scale: output accelerates faster than compensatory input. Dabiri's findings offer profound potential if applied to development.

Immensity of scale can also be palpable, but in renewable energy, we often sell its scale short. In David Wallace-Wells's writing, natural systems and geospatial scales are made graspable without being diminished. He reminds us that oceans cover more than 70 percent of Earth's surface, something we are used to hearing even if we do not always fully grasp it. To this understanding, Wallace-Wells adds a new layer: oceans, he writes, are believed to have absorbed "more than a fourth of the carbon emitted by humans." Wallace-Wells's 2019 book *The Uninhabitable Earth: Life After Warming* offers a vantage point into the complexities of climate science with a literary skill. He reports that in our recent fifty years, oceans "have absorbed 90 percent of global warming's excess heat. Half of that heat has been absorbed since 1997, and today's seas carry at least 15 percent more heat energy than they did in the year 2000—absorbing three times as much additional energy, in just those two decades, as is contained in the entire planet's fossil fuel reserves."[2]

If the scale of oceans makes land, and thereby human life, seem limited, oceans have also imbibed our carbon and pollution, making them less safe or sustaining. Wallace-Wells is lucid: The oceans have a scalar territorial quality we learn as children, and data shows dangerous change in even recent observable time frames. Wallace-Wells also provides a dimensional vantage point on the atmosphere: "Already, climate change has depressed the velocity of the Gulf Stream by as much as 15 percent, a development that scientists call 'an unprecedented event in the past millennium,' believed to be one reason the sea-level rise along the East Coast of the United States is dramatically higher than elsewhere in the world." Understanding scale and political action go hand in hand in our current attempts to react to climate change. Wallace-Wells brings us close to known and complex variables. The arbitrage galvanizes concern and instigates a level of wonder and insight at the scale of life.

If we imagine renewable energy in the context of fossil fuels and the limits of their reserves, extraction, and refinement, renewables, especially solar, do not seem to break limits and extend dimensionally the way that SERI and other federal programs imagined. Instead, limits don't exist, or don't exist in any comparable way. Going forward one can ask, how do we bring scale to this debate without limiting the almost incalculable capacity of renewable energy? How can it be used in another manner, rather than to shore up a world that could more beneficially and dramatically change? It will take letting go of some denominators or traits that inhibit change. In our chapters on debt, density, scale, and empathy, we have tried to show these regimes are less stable and secure than they appear.

On the other hand, the mechanical and chemical means we create to interact with renewable energy, imbibe it, intersect with it, and temporally engage with its duration do have clear dimensions and limits. These are industrial enterprises and scaled products. They establish a scale in relation to architecture and the economy, one derived from machines and labs, and distributed through architecture and finance into real estate and its practices. If renewable energy emerges as an ancillary to these practices, its availability will be limited by how we capitalize industry. If so, we believe it will cede its capacity for abundance and be used to sustain practices that have produced inordinate scarcity. There is a reality of post-scarcity in renewables, but not as add-ons to established practices. An intuitive attempt to comprehend the shear abundance of renewable energy is often simply passed over. If mobilized as an ancillary to sustainability, renewable technologies can simply be hedged against other, older markets. They shore up a former hegemony. Even a provocative and challenging term such as "net-zero" identifies a house or building that withdraws from a market, but the market remains extant. These terms have reached a historical threshold: their use is diminished. They inhibit a more challenging and existentially daunting alternative that would follow if we witnessed renewable energy as a form of excess, not an unethical wasting of a scarce resource, but something that is not scarce and thus is difficult to capitalize on, that is hard to monetize because of its abundance and is not subject to markets that rely on scarcity to survive.

As we worked, we came to think of an alternate framing: "it is not *off-the-grid*; it was never on a grid."

Model 103: 1,000 square feet. Photovoltaic film interlayers in laminated glass shell. A transparent grid allows daylight inside. An excess of renewable energy provides shelter as a downstream by-product of distributed-energy production.

Technology Alters Limits

A warning and a tipping point: If renewable energy is seen as an add-on feature to real-estate markets as we know them, we will miss the deep potential before us. But given the levels of government support needed to sustain housing markets as we know them, especially through central bank interventions, are they worth saving, modifying, or slowly replacing? Instead, we ask, at what point does renewable energy join with other advanced technologies to instigate new markets around what are new assets? This may require arriving at a tipping point akin to what we are seeing in the conversion of internal-combustion engines to electric vehicles, spurred by the perception of climate change as an existential crisis, leading to a far deeper faith in stretching and imposing limits on former resources. Indeed, it may require a collapse of sorts, a falling forward that casts us past sustainability toward the kind of change in computation and micro-processors anticipated by Moore's law, which predicted the doubling of processing power of chips every 18 months.

Renewable energy, dramatically accelerated and measured on new terms, holds the potential to drown the regimes of austerity that most negatively impact the housing supply. There is a paradox: the basis of this disruption is embedded in the product itself. This is an industrial action and needs to be capitalized as such. It leads to renewable-energy production as a means to housing: the manufacturing techniques and what they produce become a new form of property, in effect, a proprietary or open-source code as a quantifiable step to energy capacities that we have not imagined. If it gains architectural scale, it would be in tandem with a flood of energy. Markets as we know them would be incapacitated by excess. We would not tolerate the scarcity we historically accept in either energy or housing markets, but the architectural-energy instrument needs to act to transact—or assign a title to—the energy on behalf of its owner.

We believe that the production of architecture as we know it today has rarely if ever come close to the levels of efficiency that are available to advanced manufacturing and to fields that operate as design for manufacturing. The disciplinary ways architecture and building are professionally contracted distances design from engineering, and often from the production of buildings, components, and the risk and potential wealth inherent in manufacturing.

Architects carry inordinate liability for outcomes, but this is often tied to the assembly of a given set of parts and materials. This is not how vertically integrated companies such as Tesla or Apple are organized, nor, historically, how comprehensive contractors such as Boeing, Airbus, or SEELE have leveraged the benefits of capital as a prompt for extensive R & D and a means to take on and control risk.

In other fields, electronics, electronic controls, and automation are coupled with machine learning, intersecting with new materials and capital to iterate design and production at scale. Software enables this, but so too do deeper-level parallel-path design processes. If we imagine an instrument that has an ancillary capacity to provide shelter, but shelter is not the basis for monetization, we are hinting at the transformative effects magnitudes of production achieve in logistics and tech-driven industries. Our question: who can produce such an invention? There is clearly nothing in the existing standards and practices of architecture pushing it to gain such expertise, but the legacy of architectural practice offers holistic insights into the assembly of such a team, an ability to coordinate materials in concerted interconnected capacities across specializations. Imagine reconvening SERI in 2025 with this as a horizon.

In an industrial setting, we usually look to labor—a job—to fund a housing mortgage. Yet we also often must acknowledge that wages from labor account for a diminishing percentage of the GDP in the United States. This has been true for 50 years and is a feature of our globalized economy. This diminishment has accelerated since 2000 and parallels the steep increase in computational capability in our economy and in the simultaneous steep decline in the cost of computation. If this is tempered by legislation and social action, we might of course see healthier housing markets and stable households. Government might protect wages and jobs, and thereby preserve housing markets. But if computational capability were to accelerate and its costs to further drop, how would we imagine a solution to housing costs? In an increasingly jobless world, what funds housing?

One model would be to embrace a higher level of automation in manufacturing, even if it were associated with diminished employment, if it came with the ability to transfer the wealth associated with renewable energy into what we have called housing, or what we imagine can be a form of supplemental or universal income. It is colloquial knowledge that labor seems a less a defining factor in wealth production of all kinds in the US and other advanced economies. Replaced in large part by housing appreciation, we have tolerated a diminished role for wages, but a further reduction will surely push society to a rupture. Moreover, wealth associated with homeownership has left many out.

Advanced manufacturing is not avoidable. It will recapitalize housing as we know it.

If scarcity prevails in framing the sure-to-increase implementation of renewable energy, it will stem from a limited ability to produce the mechanical, physical, and chemical research and means to harness the energy, not from the energy source itself. In this regard we are still reliant on the economics of industrial production and scale. The built architecture, engineering, and material world, however, has only begun to see a future of manufacturing advances that is already deeply enabling other industries. Manufacturing in other arenas dramatically increases efficiency and thereby productivity, but it also brings new levels of precision and control that in turn diminish risk. This is not just making things faster and cheaper but also lowering risk at every stage. Efficiency is a product of modelling risk, and risk is being increasingly diminished and even eliminated through computational modelling. Manufacturing that approaches new higher tolerances enables higher levels of risk forecasting and a refined arbitration of investment. Uses of stochastic modeling that exist in financial industries such as quantitative hedge funds or in medical research can here be applied to materials science and fabrication. One can look to real-world examples in Precision Castparts or VulcanForms, which advance casting and offer a new scale of metallic additive printing, all impossible without advanced computation. Seemingly mundane items, such as Tesla heat pumps, which simultaneously serve human and battery thermal demands, are more uniquely tailored and more precisely tuned to needs by advanced computation, while being nonetheless mass-produced at affordable costs.

In other words, emerging and already demonstrated fusions of computation and manufacturing are bending markets and dramatically breaking former limits. Fiber optics is an earlier example of this, compared to the transmission capacity of copper wire. Scarcity of natural resources is real: invocations for technologies to extend and remake scarcity are not new, but what are the limits if we imagine computation and advanced manufacturing remaking settlement patterns at the geospatial scale of renewable energy? We are calling this the non-denumerable, a scope of energy-production capacity that, when combined with advanced manufacturing and computation, theoretically has no limit.

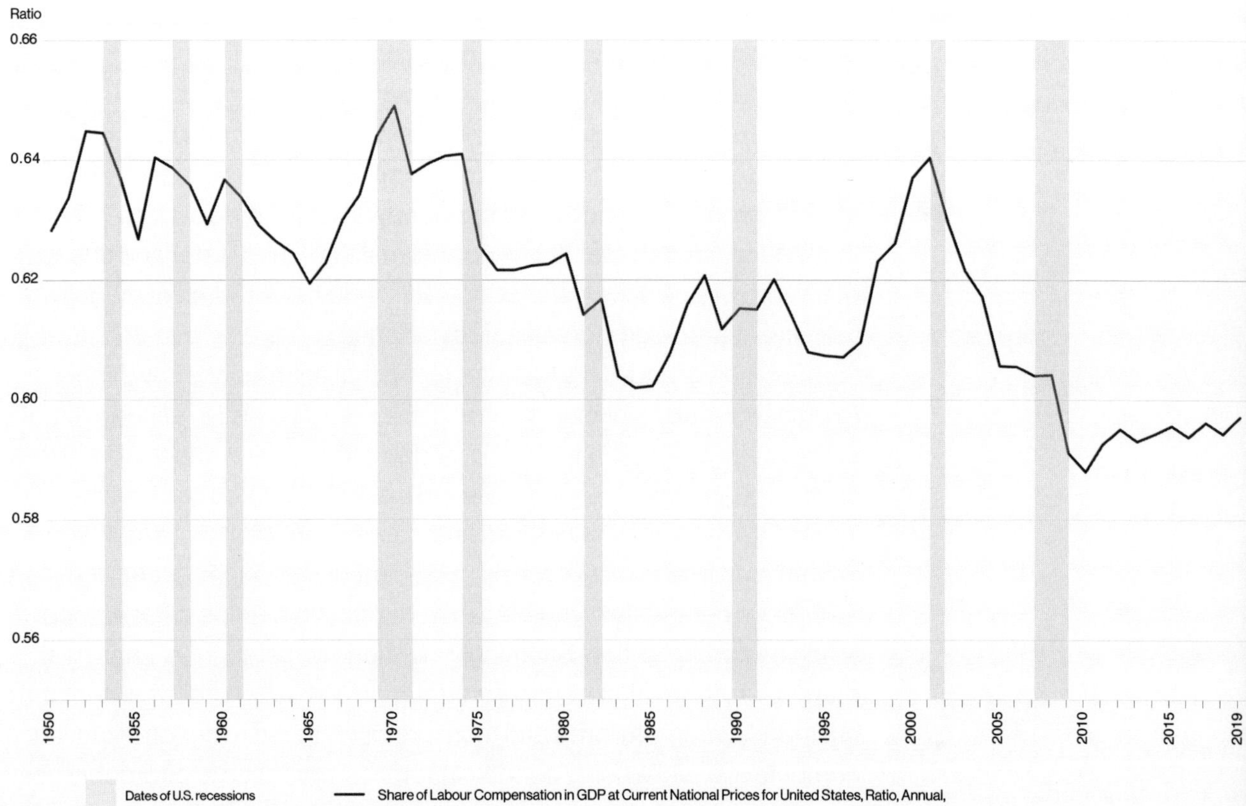

Share of Labor Compensation in GDP for United States at Current National Prices[3]
Graphic by authors. Source: Federal Reserve Economic Data

Apple's Invention Relates to Nano-Silica Fiber Coatings

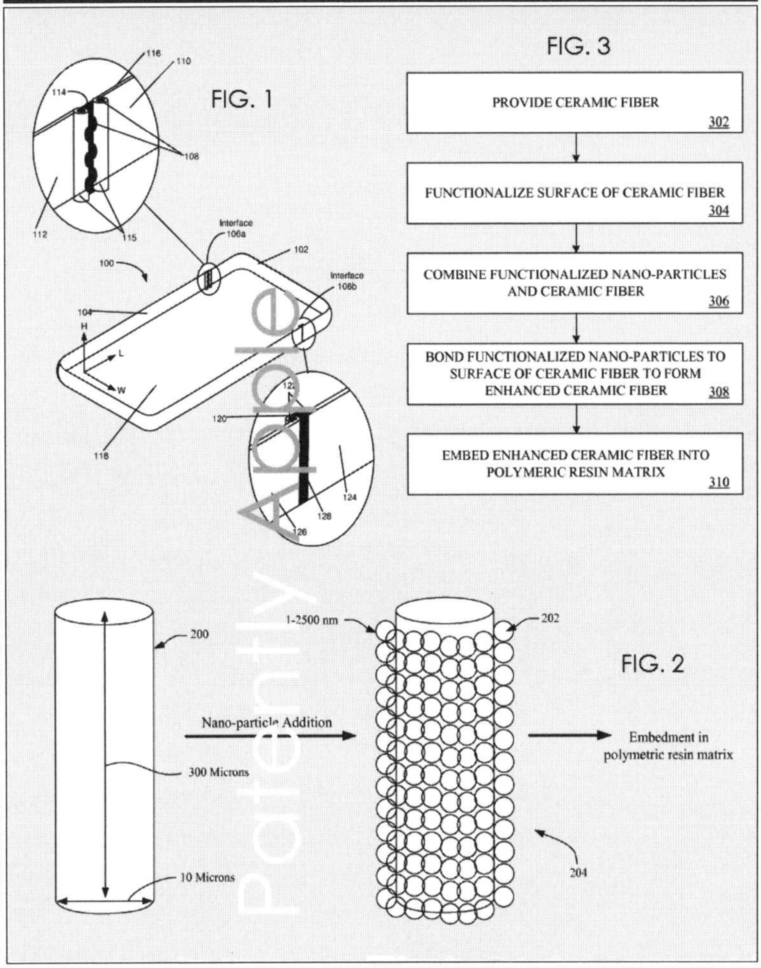

Advanced Manufacturing and Chemical Engineering, Apple patent submission. "Functionalized Nano-Silica Fiber Coating for use as an Adhesive Layer for Inorganic Fibers in Thermoplastic Composite" describes methods, an apparatus, and materials for forming frame components well-suited for use in consumer-electronic devices, such as laptops, cellphones, netbook computers, portable-media players, and tablet computers. Apple patent: Marta Giachino and Michael Pilliod.[4]

Source: United States Patent and Trademark Office and Patently Apple

The productive capacity of materials science and its invention of tools to engage materials and develop products derived from new materials is also immense in scope. Few companies create new means before there is a described need or use, but there is a covalence of means and needs that is evident in a company such as Apple. Some of this is well understood by reporting in the mainstream press on chip design and heat dissipation, for example. The extraordinary productive potential of materials science and invention is especially apparent in some of the public patents filed, made possible within research and development budgets that Apple shares in quarterly reports. They reveal the technology ingrained in materials, such as binding agents that become a project of chemical engineering. What has become possible in electronics and aeronautics could deeply alter what is mechanically and thereby economically possible in architecture and housing. This is not entirely absent in architecture: chemical engineering in adhesives and composites all spring from refinements to industrial silicone in the last century.

Micro-Processors: Singularity

In a wider lens, one must point out the dramatic increase in computational power and simultaneous drop in its cost. This occurs apart from manufacturing applications and is laced into every aspect of society today. It has simplified everyday tasks enabled by computing and is the harbinger of far-ranging discussions of steep devaluations of labor and human work. At the outer edges of this discussion, the concept of singularity, in which technology surpasses the capacity and control of humans, increasingly gains attention and appraisal. It involves a collapse in the role of human labor as a factor in production and in society at large, made possible by extreme levels of computational power becoming available at a lower cost. Singularity in the realm of Ray Kurzweil is imagined as a form of exponential growth and a change in conditions: The change in scale we have embraced in industrial realms becomes existential in nature when computational excess and recursive self-learning propagates itself as machine learning and artificial intelligence. In Kurzweil's 2005 book *The Singularity Is Near* he describes six epochs, beginning with human understanding of physics and chemistry. It leads to what he sees as our current and fourth epoch, a technological period that will forge future epochs, in which technology and the biology of human intelligence merge. The consequence: "When greater-than-human intelligence drives progress, that progress will be much more rapid."[5] Singularity is a concept that is increasingly a matter of political legislation; it is less and less seen as far-fetched and its consequences wholly unknown.

A broadly accepted aspect of singularity announces a diminished importance of humans as an economic entity and our role in production due to low-cost computational power. It's a seemingly arcane concept that has recently become far less marginal, discussed in a recent paper by economist William Nordhaus, whose earliest work evaluates the limits of materials and resources. In 2015, investigating the future of labor as a contributing factor of wealth production, Nordhaus asked whether the potential of singularity had become more real, using economic data on the power and cost of computation over the course of 50 years to analytically determine when it might become possible. The potential of its occurrence becomes quite imaginable, even if its implications remain arcane. He offers that his text may seem like science fiction:

> *For those with a background primarily in economics, the present section is likely to read like science fiction. It will explain the history and a modern view about how the rapid improvements in computation and artificial intelligence (AI) have the potential to increase its productivity and breadth to the extent that human labor and intelligence will become increasingly superfluous.*[6]

He frames the question in regard to growth and determines that he does not believe singularity is near. His rigor, however, leaves one startled at the directness of his enquiry.

> *The idea here is that rapid growth in computation and artificial intelligence will cross some boundary or Singularity after which economic growth will accelerate sharply as an ever-accelerating pace of improvements cascade through the economy. The paper develops a growth model that features Singularity and presents several tests of whether we are rapidly approaching Singularity. The key question for Singularity is the substitutability between information and conventional inputs. The tests suggest that the Singularity is not near.*

Nordhaus's research on growth and resource limits began in the 1970s, when he attempted to model the impacts of climate on economics and the inverse, the capacity to address climate change within economic thinking.

Forty-five years later, he asks if employment and labor are dramatically marginalized and reduced as a variable of economic production. He concludes that singularity is not upon us, but the fact that one might even ask the question so directly leaves concern. In the seven years since his essay first appeared, private development and the rise of AI derived from vast troves of human inputs harvested within social media has only increased a concern for the question. Everyday discussion of automation and labor are today deeply real and demand attention. They threaten to undermine the very foundations of housing and shelter.

There are inspiring facets of his research, despite the warning. In accepting the Nobel Prize in Economics in 2018, Nordhaus relates the context of his years as a PhD student. In the passage below, he recalls the intellectual context in the 1970s when the question of material limits on growth were particularly salient, as we discuss in chapter five. He mentions fiber optics as a breakthrough technology that transposed electricity distributed by copper wire to light transferred by fiber optics. The capacity of transmission is exponentially accelerated, resetting expectations and transcending limits. Nordhaus begins his career questioning the validity of accepted limits and returns to the question today as he queries the possibility of singularity. He writes in his Nobel biography:

> *Clearly there are limited resources of oil, gas, copper, and clean air. Just as clearly, technological change is finding substitute processes that replace scarce resources with superabundant resources. Perhaps the best example is fiber optics (light plus silicon) as a substitute for copper wire. The quadrillion-dollar question is whether technology will outpace depletion.*[7]

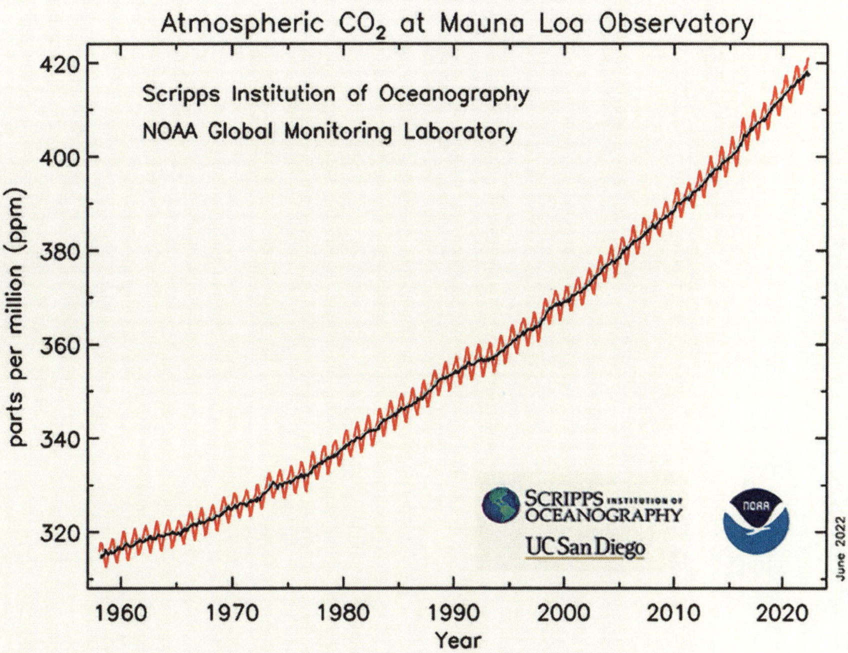

Atmospheric CO_2 measured at Mauna Loa Observatory, Hawaii. Scripps Institution of Oceanography, UC San Diego and the National Oceanic and Atmospheric Administration. The carbon-dioxide data and measurements recorded at Mauna Loa by Scripps Institution of Oceanography provide continuous direct measurements since 1958. According to the National Oceanic and Atmospheric Administration, the first measurements were taken by Charles David Keeling in March, 1958 at one of its facilities. NOAA started its own CO_2 measurements in 1974, continuing in parallel with those made by Scripps.

"NOAA's observatory, situated high on the slopes of the Mauna Loa volcano, is the global benchmark location for monitoring atmospheric CO_2. At an elevation of 11,141 feet above sea level, the observatory samples air undisturbed by the influence of local pollution or vegetation, and produces measurements that represent the average state of the atmosphere in the northern hemisphere."[8]

Source: NOAA Global Monitoring Laboratory, Scripps Institute of Oceanography at the University of California San Diego

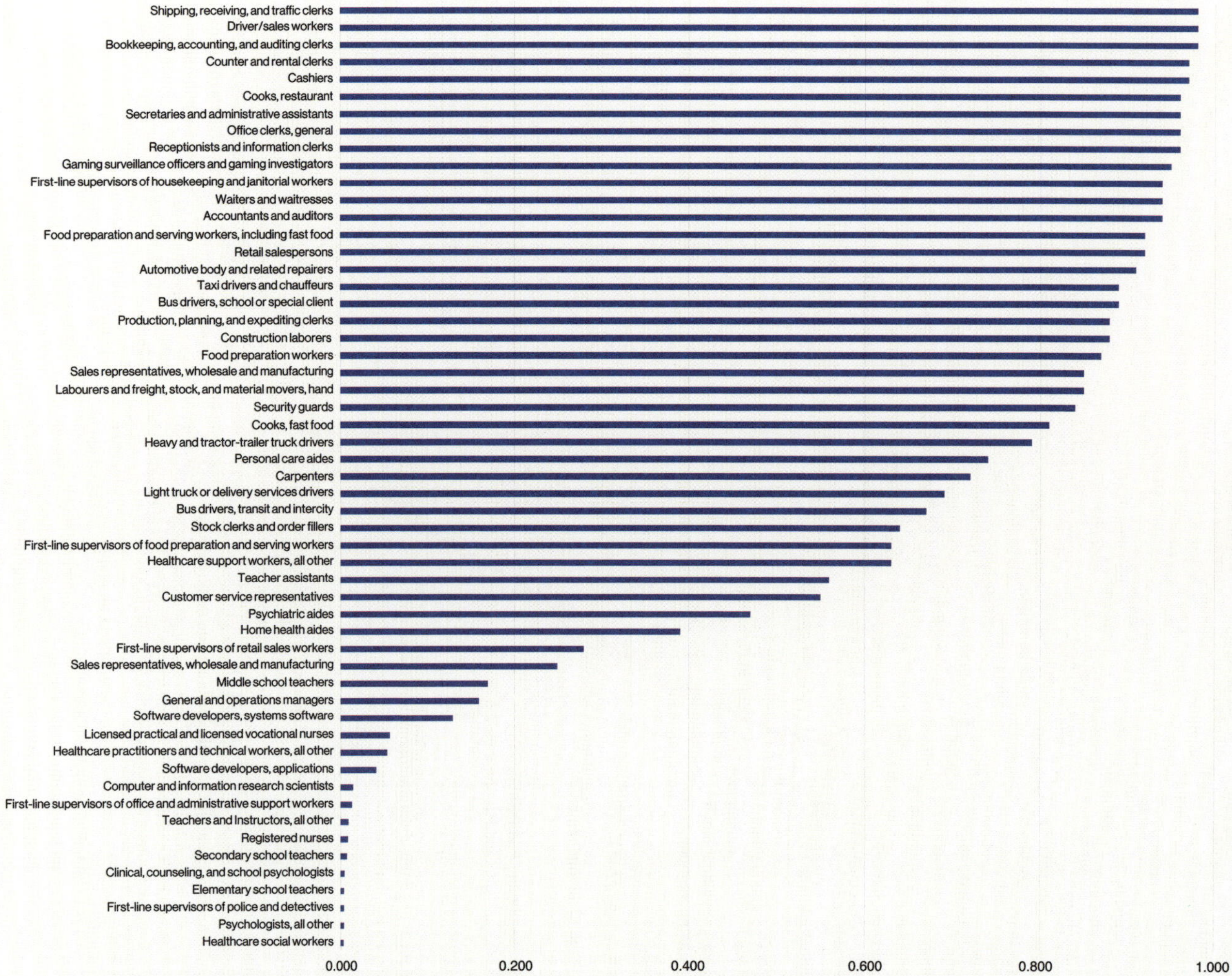

One critical form of labor highly susceptible to automation and displacement falls in the realm of "opportunity occupations." These are professions available to those without a college degree that allow one to live within the area median income. Projections about automation's impacts are speculative but urgent. Regional Federal Reserve Banks and private industry foresee vulnerability in lower-skilled and less-specialized professions. In Phoenix, Arizona, for example, opportunity employment accounts for 30.1 percent of the region's 2,116,640 jobs, according to the Federal Reserve Bank of Atlanta. In much of the nation "opportunity employment" accounts for 30 percent or more of jobs.[9]

Using data from a study by Carl Benedikt Frey and Michael A. Osborne on more than 700 occupations in the US labor market, we chart a selection that illustrate a range of professions that Frey and Osborne study as susceptible to computerization.[10]

Everyday Automation

Automotive assembly lines have for most of the last century been a foundation of measuring industrial productivity. Fordism is at the core of the mid-century, middle-class housing economy in the United States. Today, time estimates to manufacture and assemble an average automobile range from 18 to 35 hours.[11] Cars roll off assembly lines in less than a half hour. The estimates are difficult to quantify if one includes off-site work and sub-assemblies, but by any measure, the process of manufacturing a car in such a short time is remarkable. Stamping metal body parts occurs in under a second; welding entire monocoque structural body-shell assemblies is done in minutes. Paints are applied and cure in less than an hour. These are both refinements on historical assembly-line logistics and new potentials: combinations of mechanical engineering, materials science, and computation. The everyday quality of these thresholds distracts us from analysis of real change. For example, new forms of casting, aluminum alloys and injection allow the replacement of 79 parts with one singular element in a Tesla Model Y today.[12] The manufacturing is accelerated, but the now-monolithic part, should it be damaged, is more complex to repair, if at all.

We expect consumer computation devices to break limits each year, but this is occurring in our built world and in automotive industries that could transpose their means into housing. Housing needs are about to be exacerbated in unprecedented ways, as automation reduces work opportunities and diminishes the role of labor in building and construction. Any number of projections on automation and its impact on jobs could be realistic: If correlated to geographic territory, one can imagine change on the scale of the post-World War II creation of the suburbs, artifacts of middle-class jobs that funded their mortgages. In some regions of the United States, at least 40 percent of jobs will be lost or deeply altered by automation. In large sectors of the nation, post-war housing is now on average 80 years old. The specter of automation and extreme prognoses of singularity need not be fully realized to deeply undermine the stability of what is considered the norm.

On aggregate, the US housing industry already only serves a narrow percentage of the population, producing new housing only in markets that can sustain a high price point. Vast portions of the market are simply not served. An immense number of people in the US and worldwide occupy housing they cannot afford and will never be able to afford. Even as the markets leave so many underwater or unhoused, the US housing market routinely builds as many as one million units per year. More than 25 percent of the existing housing stock today was built since 1985. Yet the conditions are devastating for millions.

We must think past the urban matrices ascribed to sustainability if we are to open a new type of inquiry and allow a new perspective for the imagination of future housing. Sustainability, as broadly understood in contemporary practices, works within the known limits of materials, resources, and fuels or other forms of energy. In measuring resource availability, distribution, and access, models of sustainability address not only climate science, but critically and urgently, the social impacts and global inequities that constitute contributing factors to climate change. Increasingly, more options are available to challenge the known limits, invent new resources, and imagine new forms of settlement that break away from property-based laws that drove the political economies of the last two centuries.

Can development increasingly turn to the sky for energy and to the atmosphere? In doing so, is there a newly abundant form of energy before us not tied to the same forms of excavation and occupation of land that extant property valuations rely on? Advances in quantitative risk modeling make it possible to vet capacities of all kinds, including energy use, wealth outcomes, building mechanics, and operations. Given the way we fund housing, and increasing concerns about automation and the future of jobs and income, it is riskier not to change.

Imagination: Explosive Limits

I was on a par with the Creator of the Universe there in the dark in the cocktail lounge. I shrunk the Universe to a ball exactly one light-year in diameter. I had it explode. I had it disperse itself again.

Ask me a question, any question. How old is the Universe? It is one half-second old, but that half-second has lasted one quintillion years so far. Who created it? Nobody created it. It has always been here.

—Kurt Vonnegut, *Breakfast of Champions*

In the United States as a whole, only about thirty per cent of the rain fall gets into the ground; the rest is lost to surface runoff or evaporation, transpiration from leaves and similar interceptors. In the Pine Barrens, fully half of all precipitation makes its ways into the aquifer, for, as the government report put it, "the loose sandy soil can imbibe as much as six inches of water per hour." The Pine Barrens rank as one of the greatest natural recharging areas in the world. Thus, the City of New York, say, could take all its daily water requirements out of the pines without diminishing the basic supply.

—John McPhee, *The Pine Barrens*

It may appear to be an odd reference, but as we explored and assembled much of the work in *8 Minutes, 20 Seconds,* Kurt Vonnegut's 1973 *Breakfast of Champions* returned to us often. We also carefully reread John McPhee's essay, "The Pine Barrens." McPhee's essay, published in the *New Yorker* in 1967, was suggested to us as we tried to come to grips with what we were willing to imagine in seeking to reframe terms such as scarcity and excess with regard to housing and shelter, renewable energy, and in our understandings of foundational questions underlying the term sustainability.[13]

Vonnegut and McPhee each had an immediate yet cloaked way of bringing the reader closer to their subjects. They used narrative descriptions of experience and careful, unflinching detail in offering measurements, even when they are initially hard to grasp or fathom. They instigate a spatial imagination that makes excess palpable and realistic, even in the face of forms of power that would shut down critical spaces should they become too real or too liberating. We returned to this kind of novelistic writing often, seeking an antidote to the kind of formwork that often limits how one reads sustainability arguments, as well as an alternative to the UN Our Common Future's fusion of development and sustainability as a quasi-closed system.

The Anarchist Imagination

The character Kilgore Trout recurs in Vonnegut's novels, including those that precede and follow *Breakfast of Champions*. He has a literal-minded, engaged but also detached way of seeing the world, describing it back to himself in his utterances while transmitting what he sees to the reader. He tells a waitress to ask him "how old is the world," and before she can speak, he answers that it is "half second" old, but this half second has lasted a "quintillion years." Trout as written by Vonnegut might be dismissed as an absurdist or a reaction to a world that seems absurd to Vonnegut, but Trout is a lot like many of us, perhaps particularly in 1973 in the commercialized, mediatized US suburb Vonnegut is describing. Trout's seeming tautologies and self-motivated call-and-response throughout the book approaches an understanding of dimensions with a literalness exaggerated to the point of becoming comic. His *half second as quintillion years* uses a colloquial vernacular and mesmerizes as a burst of space-time physics. Trout repeats what he has heard, trying to make it his own experience, while remaking the experiences he is given. It resonates because humans are deeply gifted in this way: Vonnegut's Trout is not unusual. He is many of us.

John McPhee's "Pine Barrens" essay is a form of non-fiction, but when read today, it often feels like a work that put the world of the reader into a form of fiction. It makes the world in front of us seem other than what we assumed. In reading it, we feel like we've become a new kind of character. Rather than discover a character in the book, we rediscover what is in front of us. In this case, one is made aware of a form of excess and abundance that is right in front us but we didn't see: the water beneath the Pine Barrens, especially during the downtrodden oil-shortage days of the early 1970s. It was an era when discussions of climate change were emergent, and if addressed with covalent claims to shortages of all kinds, required instigating new austerity mandates, learning to do with less. McPhee and Vonnegut in differing ways offered a way to not so much disavow shortages as to sidestep them.

McPhee describes the alluvial flow of water into and then beneath the vast New Jersey Pine Barrens, giving intuitive dimension to the sandy soils' imbibing of water and the subsequent aquifer that meets the ocean beneath hundreds of thousands of acres of undeveloped landscape. All this is right between New York City and Philadelphia, untapped, secured by an unstated reverence. McPhee, without declaring climate change or preservation as a motive, seems to reveal in even the most modern and mercenary society an ability to be stopped in one's tracks. Obviously, legislation protects the Pine Barrens, but McPhee brings forth something far larger. A kind of human imagination grasps the immensity of the cartography beyond its acreage or number of square miles, seizing the alluvial flow and perpetuity of the movements that are the Pine Barrens. For us, McPhee was reminding about human imagination and the literalness of the real: it motivates a very deep reserve of human capital to act differently in the face of nature. The Pine Barrens, *a second but a quintillion year long* flow of water, right next to two cities that in 1973 were facing painful upheaval around shortages of all kinds.

In the years since these publications, the science of climate advanced in leaps. But in the design worlds, we wonder if the imagination of Vonnegut or McPhee needs to be remembered: a relinquishing of the creative thought to the non-denumerable aspects of renewable energy. The Sun, its five billion years of projected life span: the arrival of energy from the Sun to the surface of the Earth in eight minutes and twenty seconds. Its persistence. Are we instead often transporting the term renewable into an older world of shortage or austerity, and in doing so disallowing our collective imagination to create a different human experience, a different economy and arbitration of a renewable, post-scarcity form of energy and wealth?

Chapter five explored a moment in 1974 when the federal government began to calibrate its array of agencies—from NASA to the National Science Foundation to the Department of Housing and Urban Development—around renewable energies. Missing in this moment seems to be the Department of Commerce. Was that planned? Did we have a moment to imagine housing as a downstream product of renewable energy outside of accepted economic limits and miss it?

> *The water of the Pine Barrens is soft and pure, and there is so much of it that, like the forest above it, it is an incongruity in place and time. In the sand under the pines is a natural reservoir of pure water that, in volume, is the equivalent of a lake seventy-five feet deep with a surface of a thousand square miles. If all the impounding reservoirs, storage reservoirs, and distribution reservoirs in the New York City water system were filled to capacity—from Neversink and Schoharie to the Croton basin and Central Park—the Pine Barrens aquifer would still contain thirty times as much water. So little of this water is used that it can be said to be untapped. Its constant temperature is fifty-four degrees, and, in the language of a hydrological report on the Pine Barrens prepared in 1966 for the United States Geological Survey, "it can be expected to be bacterially sterile, odorless, clear; its chemical purity approaches that of uncontaminated rainwater or melted glacier ice."*[14]

Housing on Earth is in Space

The coupling between sun and climate is, in theory, so delicate that variation in solar brightness of only a few tenths of a percent can create flourishing biological productivity or freeze the earth in the grip of an ice age. Glaciers have advanced and retreated roughly every hundred thousand years in synchrony with the stretching of the earth's orbit. From circular to just slightly elliptical and back to circular.

—Herbert Friedman, *Sun and Earth*

After World War II, the use of newly refined rocket technology coupled with radio-based communications allowed humans to witness the relation of the Sun and Earth in ways never before possible.

In his 1986 book *Sun and Earth*, physicist Herbert Friedman unfolded observations about research on radiation in space culled from his forty years working with Naval Research Labs in Washington, D.C. In a language both scientific and colloquial, Friedman described a series of satellites that allowed quantifiable measurements verifying and contravening theories prior to satellite observations: a world newly seen from above the atmosphere and its clouds. Aware of the potential for climate change, Friedman was not, however, seeking to verify or prove its existence. Instead, either pure science drives the terms (how much energy is in a solar flare? how does radiation reach Earth?) or a pragmatic aspect of national security (why do radio signals become distorted in certain orbits of the Earth in relation to the Sun?). The inquiries lead to observations of climate change coupled with an emerging awareness of the conflation of solar wind and the Earth's magnetosphere, an elliptical orbital zone where slight change in make-up alters radiation meeting Earth and all of life. Deep change to biodiversity might follow. Friedman writes:

The earth itself nestles in the protective magnetic cocoon that carves a cavity out of the solar wind. On the Sunward side, the magnetic shield is blunted by the presence of solar wind. Downward, away from the sun, it is swept into a long tail, past the orbit of the moon, that reaches perhaps as far as 1,000 earth radii. The huge volume of electrified gas confined inside this magnetic bag is called the magnetosphere. It encompasses the Van Allen radiation belts, and is filled with charged particles of all energies. When the electrified wind blows across the magnetized polar caps, it creates a gigantic natural dynamo that generates power equal to all the kilowatts consumed in the United States. Sudden gusts of wind cause the magnetosphere to quiver like a mass of jelly, sending to the earth magnetic shivers that adversely affect transpolar radio transmissions and disturb the orbital stability of satellites.[15]

Sun and Earth reads as an attempt to speak to a broader audience after four decades of the rarefied realms of science in the form of classified research. Reading this today, you can see a discovery of potentials and understandings of space-time that may not be poetic in intention but that nonetheless alter anything we imagine of human understanding of Earth and the scale of human experience. Scarcity is the last term one could imagine in this context, and certainly not forms of sustainability filtered into the morphologies of real-estate patterns and land speculation much of the economy is leveraged with today, rooted in the same narrow markets and legislation that enable climate change in the first place. While not calling for a new plastic experience in architecture and the arts, Friedman is clearly turning to art and architecture as a vessel through which new experience occurs, alongside plant life, trees, and the human experience of life on Earth, natural and contrived.

Friedman traces out the ill effects of what he acknowledges as climate change—or at least a changing climate. While not declaring an ethical

Bristlecones, White Mountains, California. Friedman writes, “In live trees, the rings can be read for 5,000 years. Dead trees and wood on the ground carry the record back 9,000 years.”

dimension to climate change, Friedman chillingly gives spatial quality to a "magnetic cocoon" and solar winds that orbit the Earth. With a change in shape and temperature, entire life forms emerge or die. Friedman brings our attention to the White Mountains in California, describing bristlecone pines and their registry of thousands of years of carbon-14 evidence from photosynthesis. The bristlecone's tree rings show the evidence of changing radiation, and in Friedman's analysis, thousands of years of sunspot consistency or anomaly. Using similar scalar terms, he describes the heat sink around dense cities such as New York City—a climate-altering, anti-urban concern—and historical astronomical readings that sought to analyze sunspot activity using grain commodities markets. New York City, he writes, emits six times more heat than it absorbs; Moscow emits three times more than absorbed. McPhee comes to mind: The Pine Barrens, by contrast, imbibe water at hard-to-imagine levels with no damage to Earth. Friedman is already aware early in his career that sea-level rise will submerge many world cities, but his focus is on bringing forth another scale of imagination to understand this. Perhaps it's the nature of the Scientific American book's editorial goals, but he is coupling this to understanding the way radiation reaches Earth. The image of the bristlecone is starting after reading Friedman: Our feet on the ground, we are next to and adjacent to thousands of years of spent energy within something live.

How do we imagine an eight-minute architecture when the geological foundations of our work, from the materials we employ to the energy that fuels their production, are transported to a cosmic-scale imaginary? The work in Part Two, Encrypting the Sun will show some of our experiments.

Efficiency Advanced, Reversed, Accelerated

By 2009, housing in the United States is 40 percent more energy efficient on a per-square-foot basis then it was in 1980.[16] A tendency to build larger homes has concealed the innovations, negating the achievement. What made this possible is innovation in a myriad of building components, from Energy Star-rated mechanical equipment to insulation and enclosure materials. These savings have been captured in markets or by personal choices such as larger houses. Houses becoming energy positive could return billions of dollars to homeowners if the cost of the technology is less than the value of the energy over time and it is not captured by real-estate transactions.

Housing as an instrument that recedes into the economic future of its energy production—a house as an energy asset—is a switch from lack to abundance, in effect, potentially altering the national economy. Instead of seeking sustainability to enable the extension of a former lifestyle—the house as a hard asset to be paid for, heated and cooled—here housing is a downstream by-product of an electromagnetic-chemical action. Managed by simple computation, a pulse of photons instigates an autonomous process that sustains itself above us, unaware of our presence. The house does not know we are home.

Powerwall home batteries, glass photovoltaic shingles, and electric cars are upon us. While the nomenclatures persist—a house, siding, and a car—they are increasingly motivated by a chemical and physics-based discourse. They are a seed to a far more expansive transformation, one where electro-magnetic and chemical engineering takes a place at the table of architectural denominations, and where what seemed discontinuous and fragmented is now seen as having the potential of energy: renewable, sustainable, continuous for duration of the life of the Sun, inevitably productive, and ceaselessly persistent, regardless of humanity. Human life, a family, a group of workers, a retail experience, whatever exists beside the pulse of energy is on its own, free to move and perhaps alleviated of the fiscal demands to monetize or pay for settlement and shelter. Housing, a debt-laden capital investment for decades, a form of necessary hardware as home and shelter, here possibly migrates into something free of costs, and society instead labors not for shelter but for other concerns. Free from funding shelter with labor daily, life explodes with new potential.

A fiction? We take some heart in the ability to model futures in newly comprehensive ways, but we collectively have real anxiety about an overly controlled and centralized technological consolidation. Yet some of this is indeed happening, seen in projections of a steep decline in automobile production as electric vehicles are expected have far longer useful life spans and as transportation as a service (TaaS) diminishes the cost of mobility per mile. James Arbib and Tony Seba, in their RethinkX report on transportation, predict that as much as 95 percent of US passenger miles in 2030 could be travelled by TaaS in electric vehicles. If compared to private internal-combustion engine vehicles, the cost per mile could hypothetically fall by 93 percent.[17] This would occur in the midst of a need to repurpose entire automobile supply chains. Global personal communications have dropped to near zero for those who have digital access. How will these changes affect housing markets, real-estate mechanisms, and housing affordability and quality? At the heart of these questions is a demand to rethink how and why scarcity persists in housing, a goal to return to the blue-sky work imagined in the Solar Energy Research, Development, and Demonstration Act of 1974.

These projections offer a mixture of realistic innovation and imagined capacities that may seem extreme. But it would be a mistake to think that massive change will not occur in human settlements, and not to realize how briefly our life on Earth has been shaped by what we call real estate and governed by it through legislation. We need to encrypt the non-denumerable energy before us and transfer its wealth to the billions of people left out of the last two centuries of development, sharing it as sustenance with those excluded from the wealth of the last 50 years. The unsheltered—most of us.

Endnotes

1. Andrew Myers, "The movements of fish and birds inspire wind power generation improvement," Stanford Engineering, June 1, 2016, https://engineering.stanford.edu/news/movements-fish-and-birds-inspire-wind-power-generation-improvement.

2. David Wallace-Wells, *The Uninhabitable Earth* (Harlow, England: Penguin Books, 2019), 95.

3. Robert C. Feenstra, Robert Inklaar, and Marcel P. Timmer, "The Next Generation of the Penn World Table," *American Economic Review* 105, No. 10, 2015, 3150–3182, https://www.rug.nl/ggdc/productivity/pwt/related-research-papers/the_next_generation_of_the_penn_world_table.pdf?lang=nl., cited in "Share of Labour Compensation in GDP at Current National Prices for United States," Federal Reserve Economic Data (FRED), Federal Reserve Bank of St. Louis, Nov. 6, 2023, https://fred.stlouisfed.org/series/LABSHPUSA156NRUG.

4. "Apple Patents Reveal Nano Silica Fiber Coatings for Mac's iDevices and Future iPhone with Hearing Aid Detection," Patently Apple: Celebrating Apple's Spirit of Innovation, https://www.patentlyapple.com/patently-apple/2013/02/apple-patents-reveal-nano-silica-fiber-coatings-for-macs-idevices-and-future-iphone-with-hearing-aid-detection.html.

5. Ray Kurzweil, *The Singularity Is Near* (New York: Penguin Group, 2006).

6. William D. Nordhaus, "Are We Approaching an Economic Singularity? Information Technology and the Future of Economic Growth," *American Economic Journal: Macroeconomics* 13, No. 1, Jan. 2021, 299–332, https://williamnordhaus.com/files/williamdnordhaus/files/singularity-2021.pdf.

7. William D. Nordhaus, "Biographical [statement]," The Sveriges Riksbank Prize in Economic Sciences in Memory of Alfred Nobel 2018, The Nobel Prize, 2018, https://www.nobelprize.org/prizes/economic-sciences/2018/nordhaus/biographical/.

8. "Carbon dioxide now more than 50 percent higher than pre-industrial levels," press release, National Oceanic and Atmospheric Administration, June 3, 2022, https://www.noaa.gov/news-release/carbon-dioxide-now-more-than-50-higher-than-pre-industrial-levels.

9. "Opportunity Occupations Monitor," Federal Reserve Bank of Atlanta, May 18, 2023, https://www.atlantafed.org/cweo/data-tools/opportunity-occupations-monitor.

10. Carl Benedikt Frey and Michael A. Osborne, "The future of employment: How susceptible are jobs to computerisation?" *Technological Forecasting and Social Change* 114, Jan. 2017, 254–280, https://www.sciencedirect.com/science/article/abs/pii/S0040162516302244?via%3Dihub.

11. "How Long Does It Take to Build a Car These Days?" JVIS Blog, Oct. 17, 2022, https://jvis.us/2022/10/17/how-long-does-it-take-to-build-a-car-these-days/.

12. Iqtidar Ali, "Tesla Model Y Giga Casting and Structural Battery Innovations (Battery Day Part 1)," Sep. 23, 2020, https://www.teslaoracle.com/2020/09/23/model-y-giga-casting-structural-battery-innovations-battery-day-part-1/.

13. Kurt Vonnegut, *Breakfast of Champions* (New York: Delacorte Press, 1973); and John McPhee, "The Pine Barrens," *New Yorker*, Nov. 25, 1967, https://www.newyorker.com/magazine/1967/11/25/the-pine-barrens.

14. McPhee, 1967.

15. Herbert Friedman, *Sun and Earth* (New York: W H Freeman & Co, 1986).

16. Behjat Hojjati and Steven H. Wade, "US household energy consumption and intensity trends: A decomposition approach," *Energy Policy* 48, Sep. 2012, 304–314, https://www.sciencedirect.com/science/article/abs/pii/S0301421512004363; and "Drivers of US Household Energy Consumption, 1980–2009," US Energy Information Administration, https://www.eia.gov/analysis/studies/buildings/households/pdf/drivers_hhec.pdf.

17. James Arbib and Tony Seba, "ReThink X, Rethinking Transportation 2020–2030, The Disruption of Transportation and the Collapse of the Internal-Combustion Vehicle and Oil Industries," May 2017, https://www.rethinkx.com/publications/rethinkingtransportation2017.en.

In lieu of urban planning and an economics of fossil fuels, small-scale dwellings find bearing in relation to the Sun and the cartography of Earth. Levittown and a history of suburban development as real estate persists, but it is increasingly cast in a shadow of new technological instruments that enable daily life in the context of energy renewed every 8 minutes and 20 seconds. *Collage by authors*

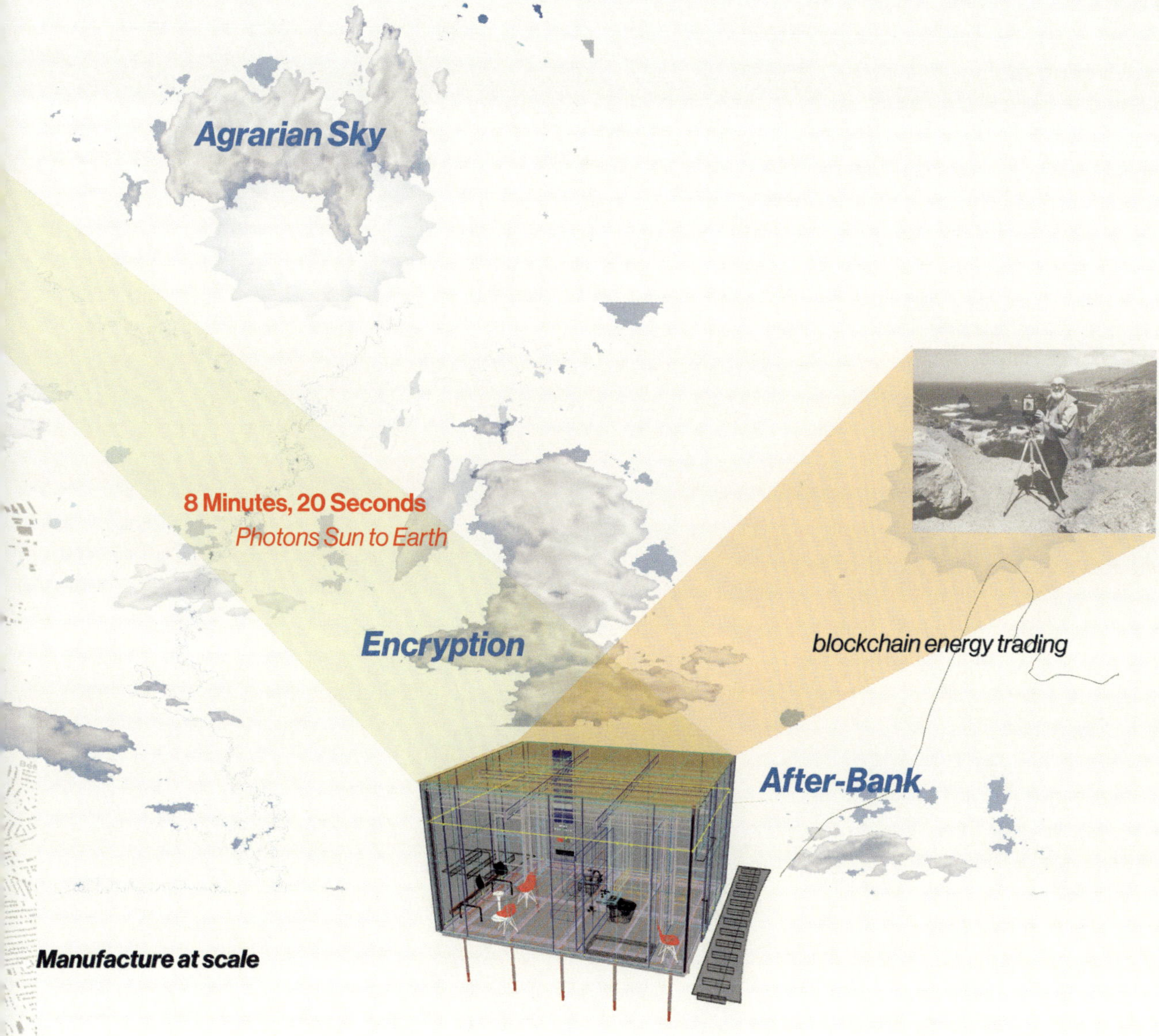

Agrarian Sky
8 Minutes, 20 Seconds
Photons Sun to Earth
Encryption
blockchain energy trading
After-Bank
Manufacture at scale

Part Two
Encrypting the Sun

About Bell-Seong Architecture and Visible Weather

Visible Weather was formed in 2010 as a parallel practice to **Bell-Seong Architecture**. The goal was to enhance real-time collaboration with partners in structural, mechanical, and environmental engineering, and materials, as well as housing development, economics, and real estate. In 2011, Bell-Seong was commissioned by the Museum of Modern Art to develop a proposal for their workshop and exhibition *Foreclosed: Rehousing the American Dream*. Our team included long-time partners from a wide range of disciplines including Rosanne Haggerty, founder and president of Community Solutions; Nadine Maleh, Community Solutions; Matthias Schuler, Transsolar; Zachary Kostura, structural engineer, Arup; as well as economics and housing specialist Eric Belsky of the Harvard Joint Center for Housing Studies; and real-estate, law, and climate specialist Jesse Keenan. The work produced for *Foreclosed* was developed in a constant dialogue with partners whose expertise and input ran parallel to the design work. We credited our team at that time as Bell-Seong and simultaneously as **Visible Weather**. The title refers to the first commodity markets hedging crops as futures contracts in the mid-19th century, a fusion of weather and economics. Here we imagined that the future of human settlement would ideally become a renewed balance with climate that also paid attention to the full spectrum of activities that produce the built environment. The work shared in this book has expanded from that and included frequent advice from colleagues.

The works presented are shown in chronological order, framed as bodies of work developed with shared goals and ideas. Design work was based in New York City and in Berkeley, California.

Lead Design: **Bell-Seong / Visible Weather:** Eunjeong Seong, Michael Bell

Bell-Seong Team: Eunkyoung (EK) Kim and Sunghoon (Sun) Lee

Materials and Advanced Manufacturing

Eunjeong Seong: Founder, Bell-Seong and Visible Weather: architecture, engineering, materials, energy, housing economics + policy analysis

Michael Bell: Founder, Bell-Seong and Visible Weather: architecture, engineering, materials, energy, housing economics + policy analysis

Michael Pilliod: advanced manufacturing, energy, materials science, ceramics, glass

Wills Sweney: advanced manufacturing, supply chain / bill of materials, energy, materials, glass,

Thomas Powers: architecture and project development advisor

Special thanks to:
Kenn Sparks: Head Emeritus, US Corporate Communications, BMW of North America. US National Spokesperson.

Zachary Kostura: structural engineering, materials, glass

Projects

Project One:
Reverse Engineering-Bill of Materials and Building Information Modeling

The Binocular House (Michael Bell Design), Bill of Materials
Developer Wood-Frame Spec House, Bill of Materials

Project Two:
Prototype Building and Structural-Energy Systems

Solar Roof 1
Solar Roof 2: Spectral – King Post (Horizonal)
Solar Roof 3: Spectral – King Post (Vertical)

Project Three:
Building/Energy Components & Manufacturing

Model 101 (X)
Model 102 (S)
Model 103

Project Four:
Accessory Dwelling Units / Micro Houses

Model A
Model B
Model C

Project Five:
Site and Context

ADU – Ensembles (Neighborhood Infill and Density)
Fort Ord, California

Encrypting the Sun

The extent, limits, and means of privacy are tested in every aspect of contemporary life. The terms of privacy are rarely not challenged by new and evolving tools. Development requires shared resources, transmitted between private and public agents. Our understandings of what constitutes private and public spheres have been shaped by social, political, and economic life over centuries, changing especially rapidly in the last century of industrialization and urbanization. Off-the-grid architecture and zero-emissions cars and homes are emerging aspirations, an embodiment of the desire for termination of energy dependence and a symbol of the occlusion or blockage of intrusive forces beyond our control into private life.

Encrypting the Sun imagines a house that was never on the grid, rather than one that is taken "off the grid." When communication can't be cut off because of the need for essential goods and services, encryption becomes necessary for communication, energy, and wealth accumulation.

A post-agrarian home is by its very nature an interface with the economic world and with development. The private space of housing is made by public policy and institutions, including regulations, debt, and development: housing thereby forms one of the margins and thresholds between public and private life. It encodes that relationship and manages our withdrawal into the private sphere, but it also brings us into proximity with public life and exchange.

For much of the 20th century, the public and private aims of housing are seen in objective terms. Its threshold is defined by an architectural edge, often by transparency of materials like glass, offering a highly defined or hidden relation between public and private life. It is inherent in much modern architecture: a controlled revealing of private life, privacy encoded but also revealed by new architectural means.

The transparency is made with a parallel participation and mirroring of industrial processes. Mass production of 20th century materials like modern concrete, steel, glass, and polymers are only possible through industrial processes, with substantial capital, and through development from laboratory-like origins. Each indeed is made liquid from geologically formed materials, reformed into shapes and spaces that then become private, if inextricably industrial in their nature. Industrialized components reveal the factory and capital behind the structure. Yet housing is different than, for example, offices or schools or hospitals in this way. It can't be manifest without immense risk and participation of others, but it also promises refuge, privacy, and security. Housing is a source of immense anxiety for many: its costs and the risk of markets hover over its provision of security.

Ciphering applied to language allows the encrypted transmission of a message to remain concealed, unreadable even to the messenger. The terms have a newly urgent contemporary meaning in the era of cloud-based digital communications, trading, sales, banking, and cryptocurrency, but their roots come from antiquity and emerge in ancient mathematics, language, and military communications. From simple transposition of letters to algorithmic coding, ciphering persists over centuries as a way to move content without interception. But it also takes on a more nuanced cultural posture, serving as a veil and to disguise, if not literally hiding the presence of something. It allows one to hide in plain sight. In architecture, there are often attempts to secure something in broad daylight: architecture is physically present and carried by material. The uses of architecture to veil a user and subject are many.

Encrypting the Sun here refers to the body of work we developed as a team that has included designers, architects, engineers, manufacturing experts, materials scientists, and real estate and housing professionals. Our own experience includes a wide range of these fields, but we routinely engage experts as well. As we progressed, we increasingly imagined renewable energy as a new asset whose persistence is defined by its transmission and flow. Encrypting the generation, transmission, and trade of renewable energy offers a means to enter a ciphered virtual grid—to balance the need for independence and connection. It is transitory and must be protected both in transmission and at rest. Solar energy is refreshed and made new on Earth by a constant flow from a distance of 8 minutes and 20 seconds away. How do we imagine this value locally retransmitted and encrypted, even as it is materialized as shelter and housing?

Themes of encryption are present throughout recent histories of architecture, particularly when the design of a building is understood as protection from intrusive or predatory forms of power. An existential aspect of architecture emerges throughout much of the 20th century as new forms of power shape human life. Ciphering in this era disguises one's presence, creating and enabling a mask of compliance while securing other forms of privacy, masking non-compliance. The work shared here seeks a greater explicit transparency of production and manufacturing in how it is made. Privacy is afforded in gradients of transparency provided by polymer interlayers in laminated glass. Thermal controls are precise and use heating-and-cooling sinks as interlayers. Solar energy is harnessed by internal and integrated photovoltaics, the entire structure a form of spectroscopy, light's penetration of matter. The value of energy harvested, secured, and owned by the inhabitant of the structure allows another form of privacy: economic independence. Shelter for more people in an entirely new and other market. The structure, an energy asset, effects the downstream provision of shelter. Renewable-energy values pay down the original debt. That originating cost of the structure, deeply undercut by advanced manufacturing, is arbitraged against an inexhaustible form of renewable energy from the Sun.

We imagine an entirely other form of temporality: a shelter manufactured and assembled in hours, not months, activated by photons and powered up indefinitely. Daily life happens amid and adjacent to a spectroscopic energy instrument you can live it. The instrument is easy to disassemble and recycle or upcycle, the occupant secure in broad daylight, the instrument trained to the sky, and the person's feet on the ground. The industry and capital required to build this are also immediately tangible. It requires little maintenance; indeed, it is a spare structure whose embodied energy is a fraction of that of the housing it replaces. But its wealth and thereby security are encrypted, ready to trade on a personal level. It's a precise, distributed-energy production that powers individuals.

Increasing Access to R & D

The home building industry is composed of relatively small, regional companies. As of July 2023, the top ten home builders have a combined capitalization of approximately $170 billion. This puts their collective value in the range of an individual company like Nike or a single bank such as Wells Fargo. The top five builders are collectively valued at approximately $144 billion. The next five companies are collectively valued at $26 billion, ranging from $3.8 to $8.4 billion. Only five of the publicly traded companies have a market capitalization greater than $10 billion. The valuations are, of course, relative, but their scale is small compared to automobile manufacturers, technology companies, and industrial conglomerates, and their value is often similar to their annual revenue. Tech companies can be worth as much as 35 times their revenue. The market capitalization of publicly traded homebuilders has risen as Covid19 instigated increased demand for single-family houses, instigating a new scope of growth and a wider awareness of what seems like a longer-term change in markets.

Home builders don't serve a consistent market. Land valuations and incomes vary, for example. New construction in the private sector is not obliged to serve all needs and in fact leaves a vast sector of needs unmet. Major suppliers such as window manufacturers, plumbing fittings, or raw materials are also relatively small compared to highly capitalized innovative companies. If one looks at base materials—steel, glass, aluminum, or an aggregate such as concrete—the scale might grow, but again, it's inconsistent even when there are clear dominant entities. There are small and large suppliers for most materials, and regional matrices of production and distribution: a national company such as Andersen Windows employs approximately 12,000 people but has countless small local competitors who provide lower-cost alternatives.

The potential for research-and-development funding varies with scale. Andersen has decades of improvements built into its manufacturing and supply chain, but it does not list an R & D budget in its stock profile. A company like Alcoa (aluminum) or Corning (glass) does show significant R & D expenditures in materials science to develop new materials, but Corning, for example, are themselves not manufacturers. Nike allocated approximately $353 million to research and development in 2022; an immense number but less than one percent of its revenue. Apple's annual report for 2022 shows a budget of $26 billion allocated to research and development, more than 6.5 percent of the company's revenue. Apple's revenue is more than 350 percent of the top ten homebuilders combined. Clearly there is a crisis of funding for research and development in housing and an opportunity to reimagine and revalue a more technologically advanced housing industry and one that serves a far broader social and human need.

Housing, as an aggregate concern, is assembled from thousands of components and their respective supply chains. It is on the whole an asperous end product, enabled and simultaneously hobbled by discontinuous innovation paths and a juxtaposition of divergent forms of research and development. Scale in housing is, however, in part enabled by these facts. Parts can be interchangeable; labor might be less specific or focused on precision; warranties are distributed among providers. But it is also broadly undermined: Designer and engineers rarely create a component for specific use; risk-taking in design and engineering is rendered tenuous by components not wholly designed for a narrow purpose, and the lack of precision in the end is a reason for slow construction times. In manufacturing, precision allows speed and reduces risk.

In 2022, the average new home price was $644,750, according to the National Association of Home Builders, with the average structure measuring 2,561 square feet on a 17,218-square-foot lot. Against this industry average, our work seeks to dramatically reimagine construction as manufacturing, transposing energy consumption into production. To do so requires a new type of company to develop would-be housing, and an entirely new form of hybridized design-and-engineering practice that can design for manufacturing.

A product of advanced research and development—design for manufacturing—that is only possible at scale. The Tesla heat pump provides heating and cooling to the automobile cabin and the battery pack from a small, efficient unit.

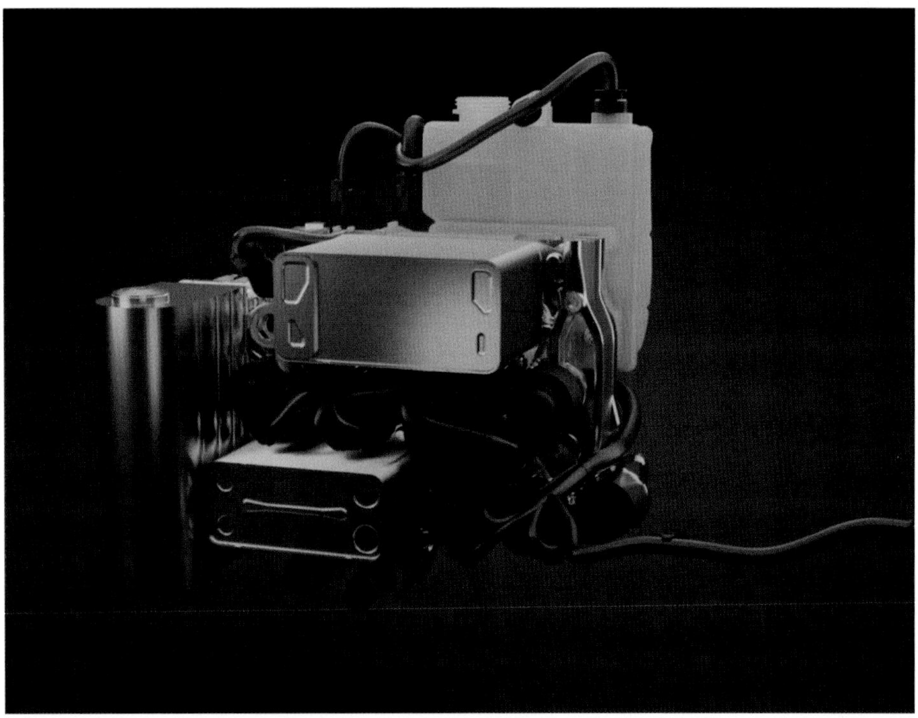

Working Terms

Parallel Path

As we initially developed *8 Minutes, 20 Seconds: Housing After Banking, Encrypting the Sun*, we relied on a matrix of current and former partners, and past and ongoing work and research. These range from materials science research on glass, concrete, metals, and polymers to political-economics work in housing. We avoided convergence on solutions and instead developed the work along multiple simultaneous paths, only converging where we saw meaningful crossovers.

Design for Manufacturing, or DFM

As we progressed, we moved away from construction and toward manufacturing, in particular adopting industry terms such as design for manufacturing (DFM), which recognize that the design of the manufacturing process and its machines and techniques needed to be scaled and accounted for as the generative basis of design and its limits. DFM enacts design as intended for manufacturing: it builds new means and methods into given manufacturing techniques. At the outer limits of DFM, one can imagine new processes and then imagine the capacity they may offer design, engineering, or any subsequent acts. As an example, a company may invest in new tooling processes or new materials before a need or purpose is defined or known. DFM requires a team, parallel investigations at many layers, from the user or imagined needs to the capacity of a factory and its sub-practices and processes. DFM can lead to the lowest common denominator, using what is easiest to access or the least expensive, but it can also redesign the original supposition, creating an opportunity for other paths, other design, and disruption of scale and outcome.

Bill of Materials, or BOM

A comprehensive accounting of each component or part in a manufacturing item, the bill of materials might be for assembly or engineering; an A-BOM or an E-BOM. The A-BOM describes each component and attributes such as unit count and the order of assembly. The E-BOM defines or reflects the designed or necessary interrelation of components by function or engineering demands. A bill of materials is here understood as far more exhaustive and comprehensive than the data provided by architectural software such as REVIT or building information management (BIM) software in general. Our BIM study begins with a retroactive and post-construction modelling of the Binocular House, built in the Hudson Valley between 2004 and 2007 by Michael Bell Design. We produced a bill of materials of the house and began a process of imagining how new means of industrialized manufacturing and materials science could cut that bill of materials and its associated labor dramatically. This lowers the cost of the house and allows one to imagine its renewable-energy production as the financial arbitrage that replaces debt, allowing clients normally ignored by the market to purchase the newly industrialized house.

Materials Science/Materials

Our design team was enhanced by Michael Pilliod, ceramics and material science engineer with a particular expertise in glass as lead of glass innovations on major technology products. Wills Sweney, an expert on new materials, supply chains, and design for manufacturing, aided in material and engineering. Our shared background in materials was based in part on our book *Engineered Transparency: The Technical, Visual, and Spatial Effects of Glass*, part of a series of books Michael Bell edited on architectural materials. The series derives from Bell's role as founding chair of the Columbia Conference on Architecture, Engineering and Materials, a collaboration between Columbia University's Graduate School of Architecture, Planning, and Preservation and the Fu Foundation School of Engineering and Applied Science, in addition to partnerships with industry materials-science labs, including glass manufacturers Oldcastle BuildingEnvelope and concrete manufacturers Lafarge Holcim. Pilliod and Sweney were familiar with the Binocular House, helping us to study it in a new frame of its materials and the potentials of advanced manufacturing.

Writing and Research

As our writing and research developed, it ran parallel to design and engineering work done in New York City and in a studio space we set up in Berkeley, California to collaborate with Bay Area and Los Angeles-based partners. This experience expanded our work and scope, and what was a book with an academic focus became more design-based. Bell also spent most of a year at Stanford as a visiting professor in 2016–17 with a mechanical engineering research group, the Center for Design Research (CDR), where he and Seong headed several colloquiums around design, creativity, and engineering with a small consortium of partners.

The book, which began as a plan to discuss a future of housing policy and energy, expanded in scope. We began to more fully imagine and expand on the term ecology we had worked with, and on what in earlier work we had called a "parallel path design process." The impact of the team, including expertise from economics and markets, materials and manufacturing processes, art and art history, all come to bear on and shape a new context for design, where R & D and scale reshape what is possible. This work became a form of forecasting, attempting to give shape to a future economy that would emerge around a new product.

Test Bed: The Binocular House formed a test bed.

The Binocular House as designed and built by Michael Bell formed an original test bed for new work presented here. Constructed between 2004 and 2007 on a site 100 miles north of Manhattan in the Hudson Valley, it's a steel-and-glass house comprising an enclosed area of 2,280 square feet with an 800-square-foot service basement for mechanical equipment. The total surface area of glazing is done with insulated glazing units that use three-eighths-inch-thick glass, low-e coating, and argon-filled interspace. The steel structure was constructed on site. All steel connections are welded full-moment connections. The house uses eight-inch-thick structural slabs with a two-inch-thick topping slab with integral radiant heat. The thermal mass is also dark gray for winter solar gain. A geothermal system was designed but not implemented. Summer tree shading reduces heat gain significantly. The floor plan is such that it creates a large linear envelope and thus has a significant scale for the building envelope, with a total area of glazing of approximately 2,253 square feet. The insulated glazing unit raw material cost approximately $40 per square foot prior to being assembled into frames on site. Costs included a quarter-mile-long driveway and power-supply line as well as a septic system and French drain. Weather, sequencing, site access, and labor were all complex factors due to the project duration and contractor cash flow. Total development costs in 2017 dollars amounted to approximately $653,762, excluding land acquisition.

New Building/Energy Products

At the outset we imagined a conflation of energy production, building, and manufacturing. This led to window systems that reduce their reliance on other structural systems and simultaneously incorporate energy production, using photovoltaics with optical transparency, and interlayers incorporated into laminated glass allow customized protection for IR, UV, and overall heat gain and privacy. We developed newly integrated architectural and thermal systems, using liquid heating and cooling as integral to the glass enclosures. The entire building proportions are designed to instigate low-energy air exchange. New forms of magnetic fastening systems are employed to lower the labor and mechanical assembly in the building, integrated with energy and thermal control, which also allow ease of disassembly.

New Scale, New Practice, New Asset

There are no protocols to produce or enable an expanded design team in the manner we propose. The proposal is to enact would-be housing as an energy product and a product of materials science, advanced manufacturing, and present and future forms of spectroscopy. The interchange of light and matter leads to a new type of asset class and a new type of practice that is closer to automobile manufacturing, while remaining reliant on financial and land-use speculation, as well as the analysis of populations, migration of people, climate change, automation of labor and jobs, and a deep expertise in economics and policy. Shelter is afforded by encrypting the value of privately tradable renewable energy, a post-real-estate form of shelter.

This is an experiment that in effect imagines that housing ceases to be a real-estate asset. Shelter becomes an agrarian action tuned to the sky.

Supply Chain is the Design Project

Supply-chain expertise and capital investment in supply chains are essential to developing a new type of housing. With the development of electric autonomous vehicles, industry experts project a longer life span for automobiles and a decrease in manufacturing economies of tributary products, materials, oil and gas fuels, and components for repairs and replacement. Combined with the increase in transportation as a service, entire regions of the automobile economy and supply chain are projected to decrease in scale, opening up a need to replace that economic activity and its associated jobs with new products. We imagine that product is the type of housing-as-energy we propose here. The production of this housing entails centralizing capital, but it also portends a wealth-generating and, ideally, lower-cost housing product.

Cap-Ex, Op-Ex

The work will integrate products that span architecture, mobility, and energy production and storage, seeking to reverse engineer the supply chain, capital expenditures, and operating expenses of entire development sectors. A new generation of design seeks to establish comparable advanced-manufacturing benchmarks to dramatically increase access to high-energy-performance sustainable architecture. This is achieved by advanced integration of solar energy and stationary storage of energy, as well as heating, cooling, plumbing, and electrical distribution. A low-consumption energy system in the house couples with bespoke machines on par with what one sees in electric automobiles, such as the Tesla heat pump that provides capacity in the car's cabin while heating and cooling the battery pack. The operating expenditures of the house would be decreased: the cost to buy a shelter would be dramatically cut by consolidating the capital expenditures to produce housing using advanced means. Our proposal also allows one to imagine an upgradable house whose parts can avoid becoming waste and be resold or repurposed. Imagine housing factories at the scale of a current Home Depot, their machining assembled and localized to reduce transportation costs and provide local manufacturing jobs.

Forecast a New Economy and Thereby Architecture

For a profession that is often forecasting the future, either in essential or philosophic terms, how we ascertain the state of the moment is also how we fortify our creative imagination, if not our political imaginary. The capital mechanisms that underlie much of the developed world have faced a series of severe stress tests already this century. In the US, their survival required immense and essentially artificial means of rejuvenation that did little to instigate innovation or new development processes. A future—any future, post-carbon, post-automobile, post-anything—might at this point in time assume large sectors of the past to be frail, if not outright impossible to continue. The past has shown clear evidence of its own failings: the posture of architectural and urban discourse today should imagine new reactions to what historically, at least since World War II, were omnipotent and pervasive conditions in housing and development. The roles of capital, central banks, debt, and leverage, as well as a wider imaginary of what constitutes a market are no longer what they were. We are in a pivotal moment, similarly conclusive and transformational to what occurred in development in 1945 following World War II, with the end of Bretton Woods in 1971, with the conflation of investment and commercial banking in the 1990s, and after the housing securities collapse in 2008.

Yet today, entire realms of scarcity that haunted development are now inverted, particularly with respect to energy. As solar and other renewable energy become ubiquitous, jobs and the calibration of housing, land, and mobility in relation to value are increasingly at risk, alongside a major reevaluation of labor as AI and machine learning displace workers. The components of development are changing dramatically in ways that will require entirely new ways to provide shelter.

Model C
Manufactured in one hour. Assembled on-site in hours.
Produce, store, and trade electricity.
Never on the grid.

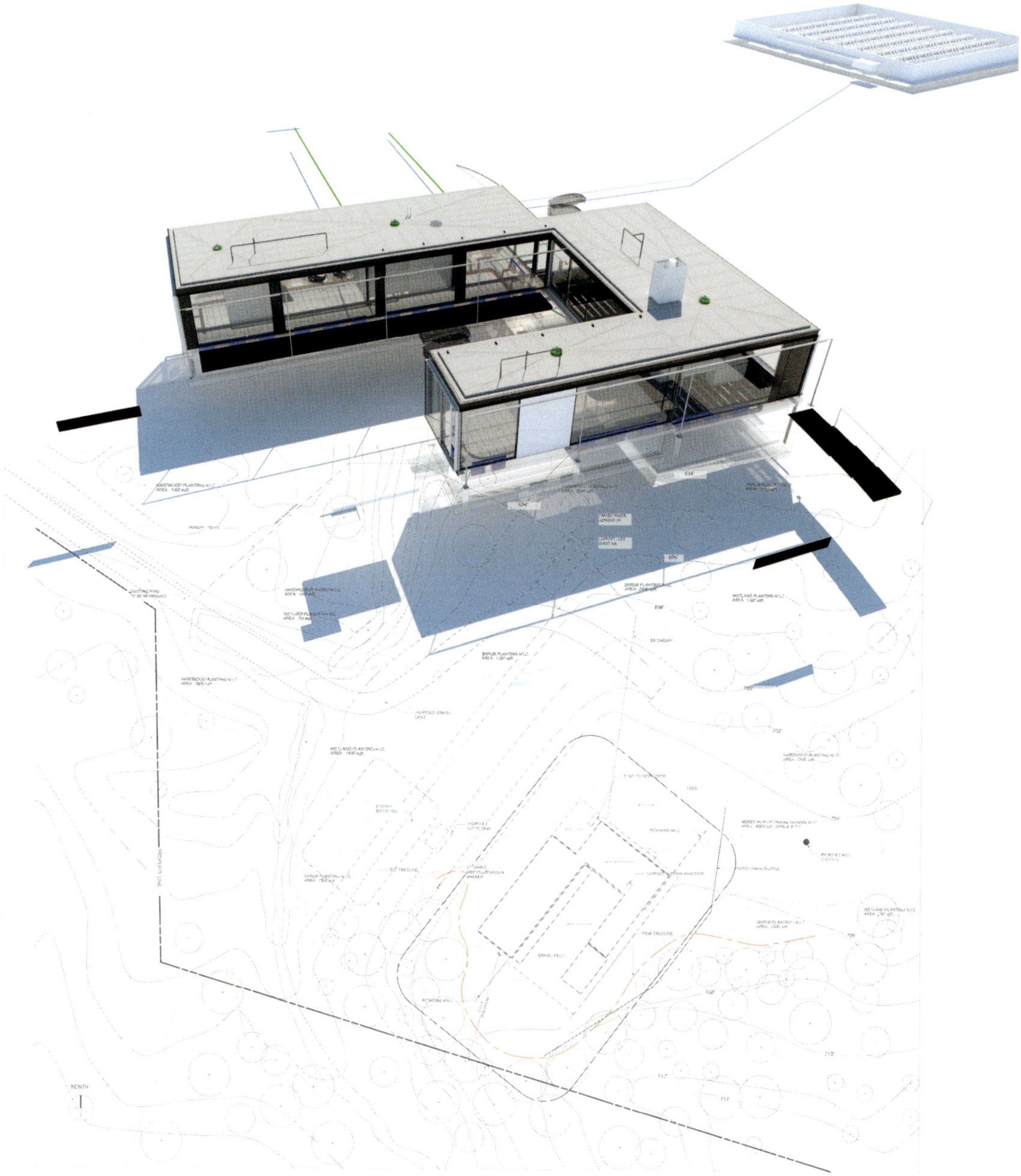

Binocular House, 2008
Test Bed: Bill of Materials (BOM)

The Binocular House, completed in 2008, formed a test bed and foundation from which to reverse engineer a new glass house.

Binocular House, 2008
Test Bed: Bill of Materials (BOM)

A comprehensive post-construction analysis was undertaken in 2017–18 modeling the building in Rhino and then Revit. The resulting building information and data provided a test bed and a preliminary manufacturing bill of materials. Photograph: Bilyana Dimitrova

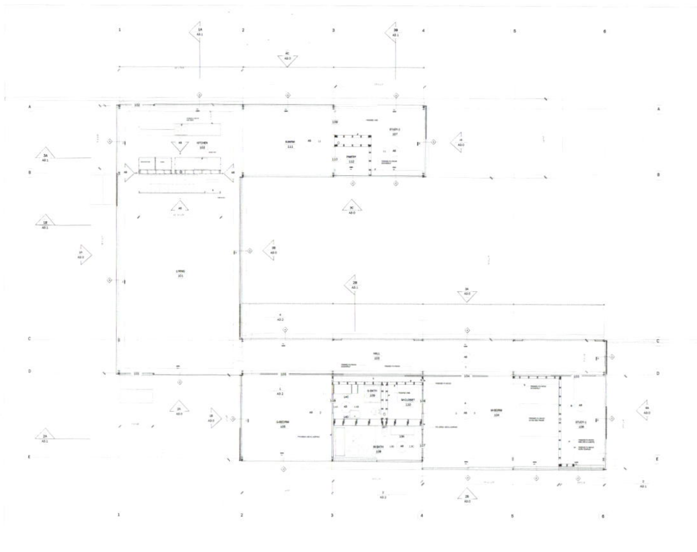

Binocular House, 2008
Test Bed: Bill of Materials (BOM)

Construction of the Binocular House included 9 x 14-foot insulated glazing units (IGUs).
The immense IGUs weigh as much as 1,300 pounds and are held in custom steel frames with structural silicone. When suspended outside the building structure, their thickness and weight become palpable.
Photographs: Bilyana Dimitrova

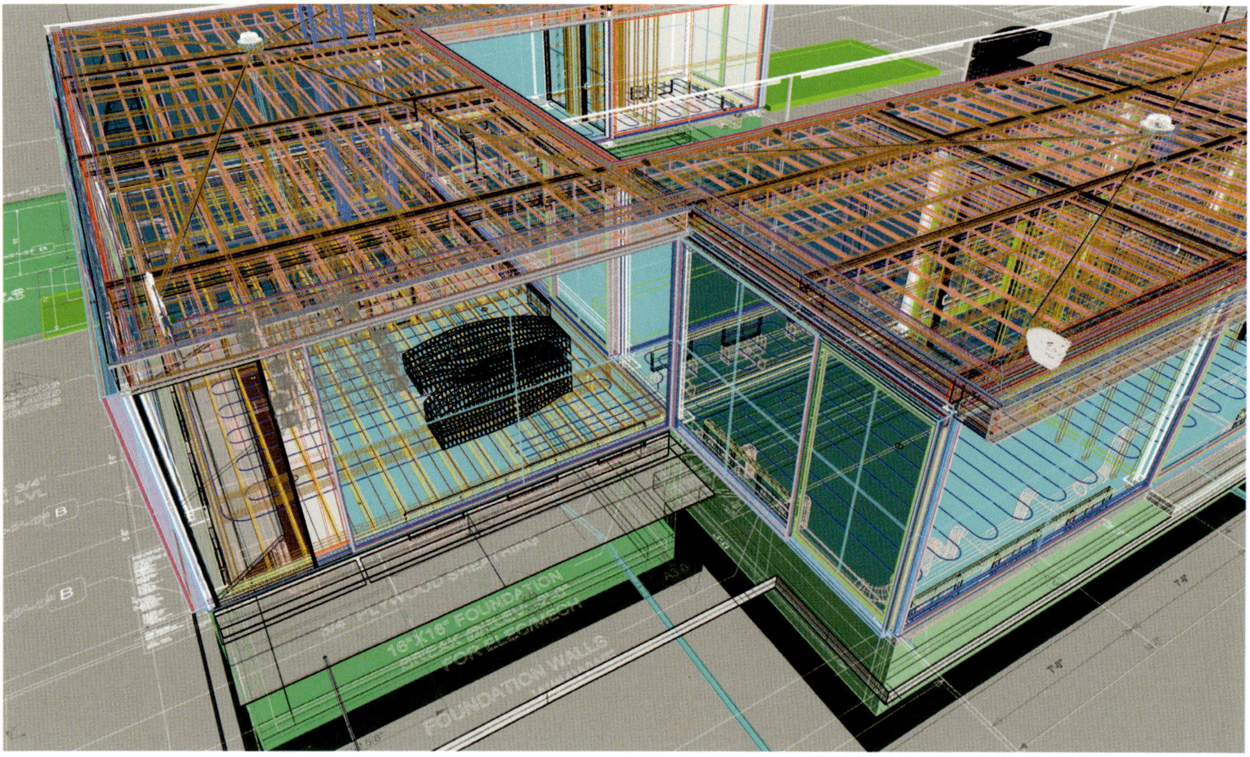

Binocular House, 2008
Test Bed: Bill of Materials (BOM)

The building perimeter measures 318 linear feet. Radiant heating is provided in a two-inch topping slab atop a six-inch structural floor slab. Air conditioning and supplemental heat are provided in 53 floor-based plenums that trace the perimeter and were integrated into the structural slab with custom steel vent outlets.

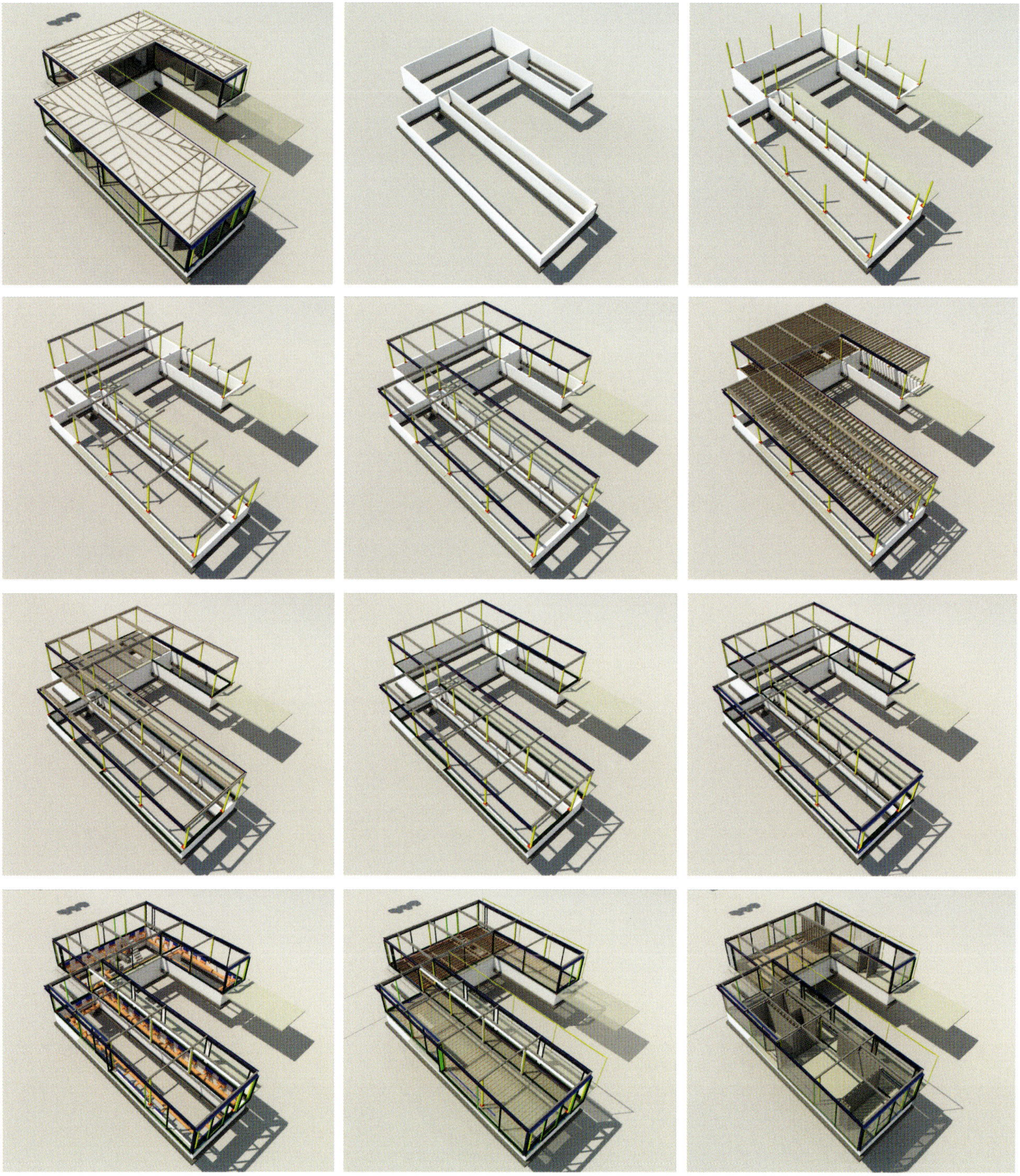

Binocular House, 2008
Test Bed: Bill of Materials (BOM)

Post-construction modelling reenacted the on-site sequence of construction for concrete foundation, steel moment frame, and mechanical systems.

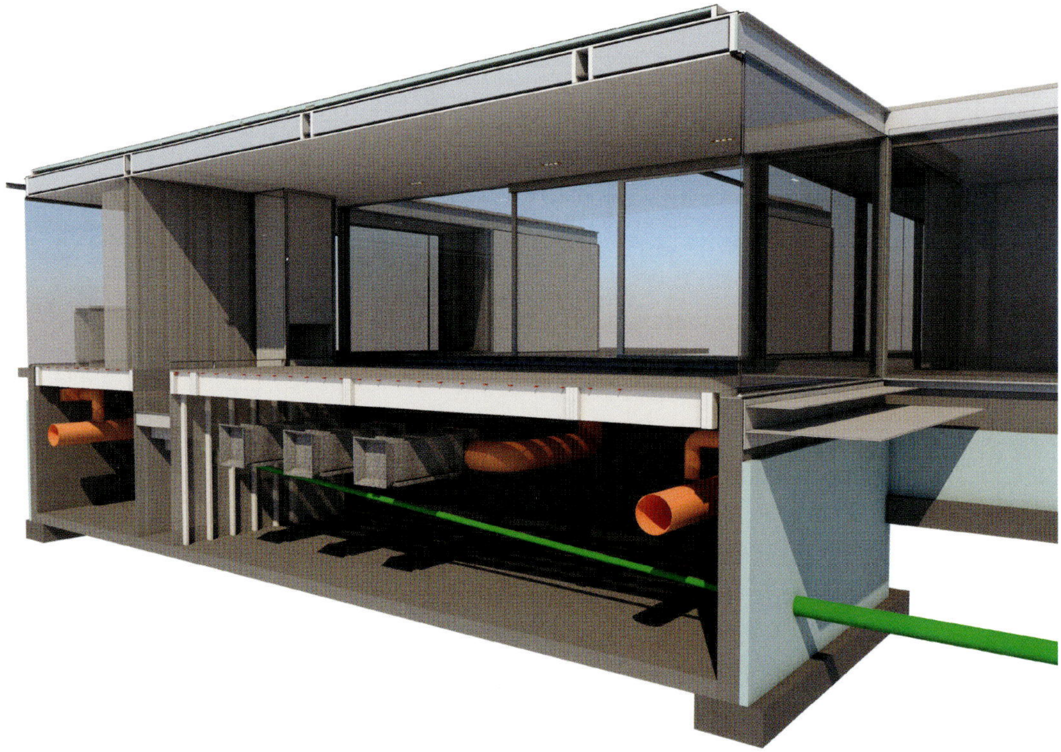

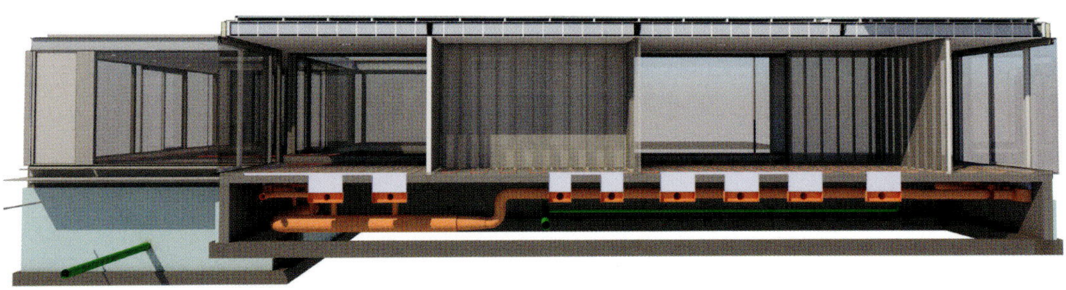

Binocular House, 2008
Test Bed: Bill of Materials (BOM)

Perspectival cross section shows 4 x 12-inch tube steel roof structure with lumber infill. The floor and roof wood structures are connected by anchor bolts to the side of the tube steel and concrete foundation walls. This leaves space for rigid insulation and a thermal break.
A front entry porch, fabricated of one-half-inch thick steel plates, is also anchored to the outside face of the foundation wall. The vertical planar organization of the structure is effectively parallel; it telescopes from the foundation.
Air conditioning and supplemental heat plenums and vents are coordinated with structural bays to allow the concrete floor to reach the foundation walls. A small wall-mounted boiler provides heated water to radiant-heat tubing.

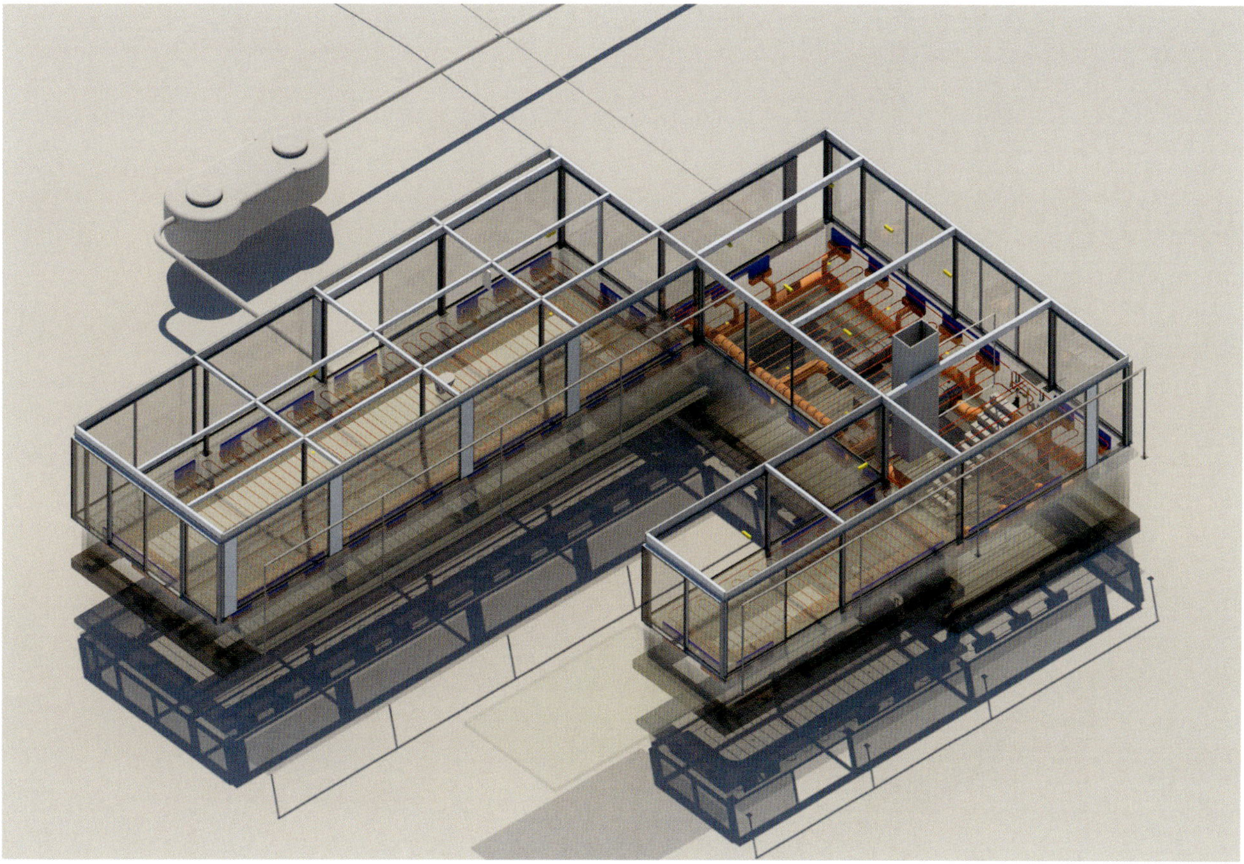

Binocular House, 2008
Test Bed: Bill of Materials (BOM)

The Hudson Valley climate required that we design for 120-degree annual temperature swings. Under most conditions, heat is provided by radiant heat: water/glycol in the thick concrete slabs is heated to ten degrees above the desired room temperature. A heat pump (forced air system) provides additional heating capacity (if temperatures go below ten degrees Fahrenheit). The heat pump also provides air conditioning and dehumidification.

A separate heat-recovery ventilator (HRV) completes an air exchange several times per hour. A small wall-mounted boiler provides heated water to radiant-heat tubing. Radiant-heat tubing is organized in three zones and coordinates with day-and night-time uses of the house, as well as the in-floor plenums. Four internal roof drains are contained in the building's sheer walls. Wastewater exits to a septic system.

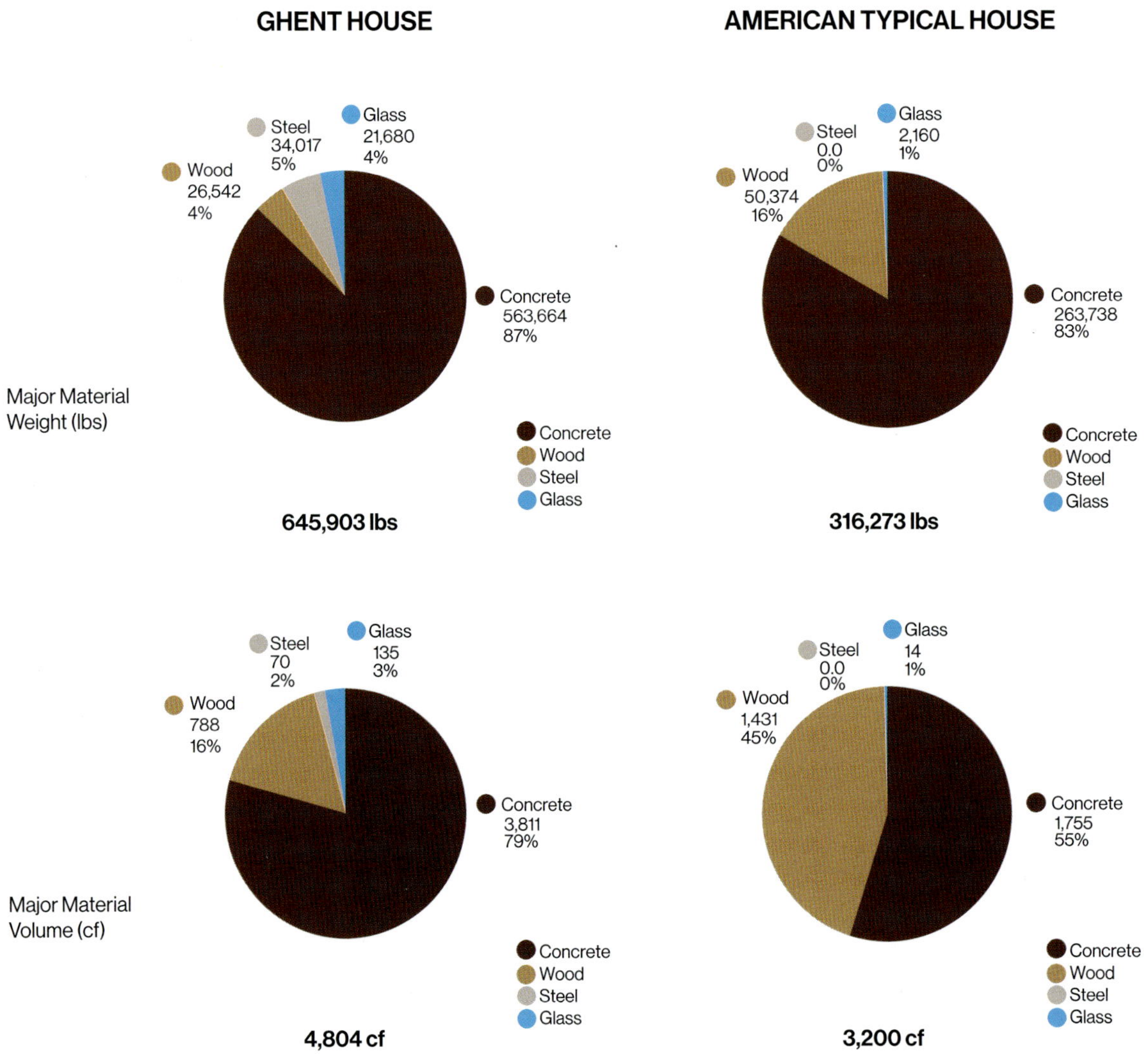

Binocular House, 2008
Test Bed: Bill of Materials (BOM)

The Binocular House was not originally constructed with the aid of Revit or building information management (BIM) software. In 2008, we had calculated the weight of glass, steel, and lumber but not concrete. A post-construction BIM model afforded a comprehensive measure of the immense volume and weight of the concrete necessary for both the light framing of the Binocular House and a standard speculative single-family house in the United States.

The spatial deployment of materials, their mass and volume, and the space they provide, are the essential physics of design. A reverse engineering and orchestration of the Binocular House materials, volumes, labor, and energy followed this analysis.

Material	Ghent				American House			
	Volume(cf)	Weight (lbs)	Volume(%)	Weight (%)	Volume(cf)	Weight (lbs)	Volume(%)	Weight (%)
Concrete	3,811.0	563,664.00	79	87	1,754.98	263,738.39	55	83
Wood	787.82	26,541.85	16	4	1,431.20	50,374.59	45	16
Steel	69.93	34,016.84	2	5	0	0	0	0
Glass	135.00	21,680.45	3	4	13.5	2,160.00	0	1
Total	**4,803.75**	**645,903.14**	**100**	**100**	**3,199.68**	**316,272.98**	**100**	**100**

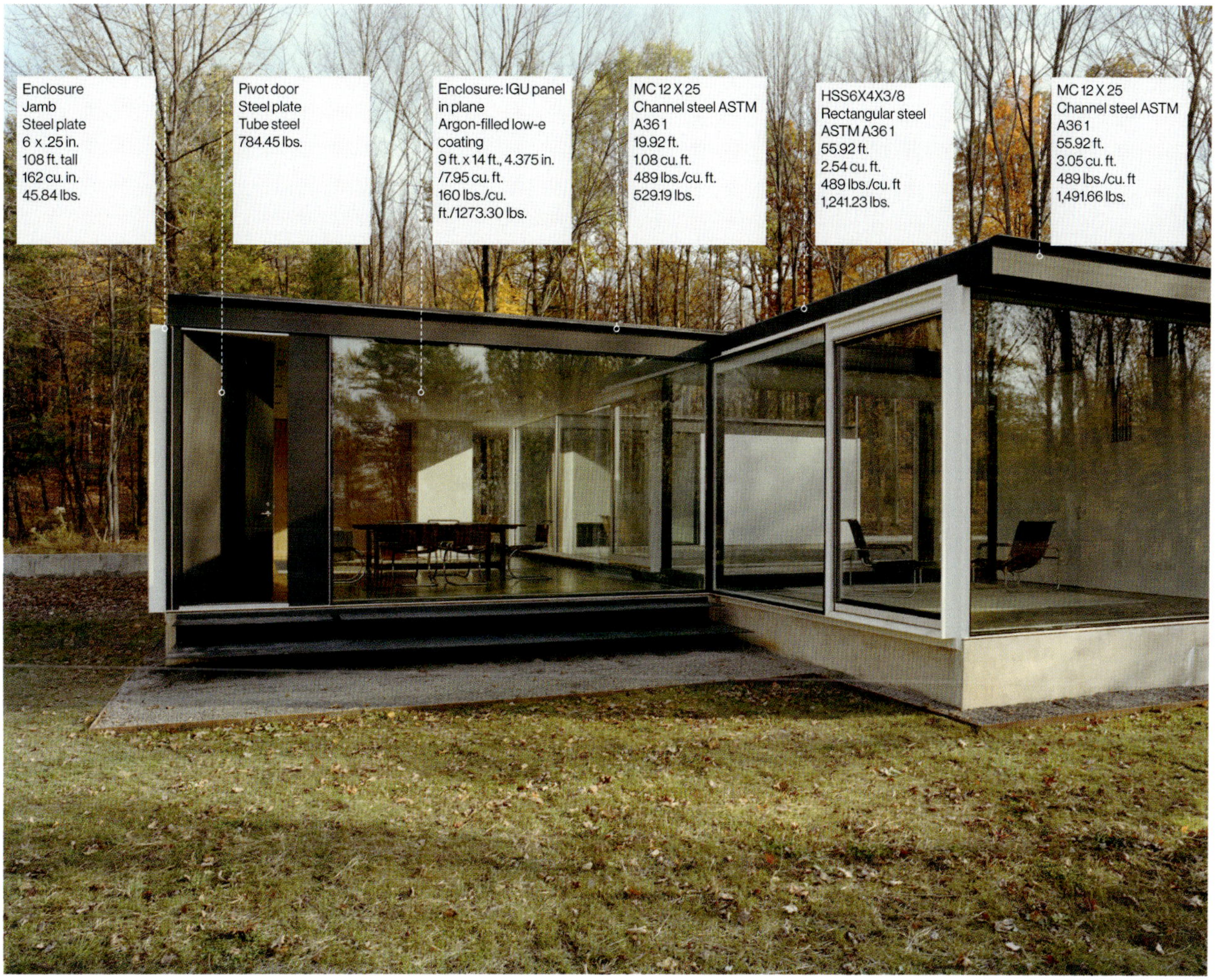

Division	Family	Count	Member	Length	Area	Volume	Weight	Area	Volume	Weight	
FLOOR								0	0.00	0.00	
	I_WF Plate-Rim Joist Total							0	14.59	526.99	
	I_WF Stud-Joist Total							0	92.14	3,328.10	
	Wood Joist 10" - Wood Finish Total							1602	267.00	9,200.82	
FLOOR Total								1602	373.73	13,055.91	Wood
FOUNDATION	Basic Wall		Foundation - 10" Concrete		24	16.81	2,526.21	24	16.81	2,526.21	
						20.00	3,005.60	24	20.00	3,005.60	
						20.40	3,065.71	24	20.40	3,065.71	
					39	27.12	4,075.59	39	27.12	4,075.59	
					147	120.01	18,035.10	147	120.01	18,035.10	
					231	192.78	28,970.98	231	192.78	28,970.98	
					236	196.67	29,555.57	472	393.34	59,111.14	
	Foundation Slab		6" Foundation Slab		637.08	318.54	47,870.19	637.08	318.54	47,870.19	
					817.68	408.84	61,440.48	817.68	408.84	61,440.48	
	Wall Foundation		Bearing Footing - 24" x 12"		12.18	2.68	402.75	12.18	2.68	402.75	
					14.51	3.17	476.39	14.51	3.17	476.39	
					22.67	6.12	919.71	22.67	6.12	919.71	
					28.8	8.16	1,226.28	28.8	8.16	1,226.28	
					116.36	37.18	5,587.41	116.36	37.18	5,587.41	
					177.5	57.83	8,690.69	177.5	57.83	8,690.69	
					181	59.00	8,866.52	181	59.00	8,866.52	
					193	63.00	9,467.64	193	63.00	9,467.64	
FOUNDA ION Total								3161.78	1,754.98	263,738.39	Concrete
Grand Total								4763.78	2,128.71	276,794.30	

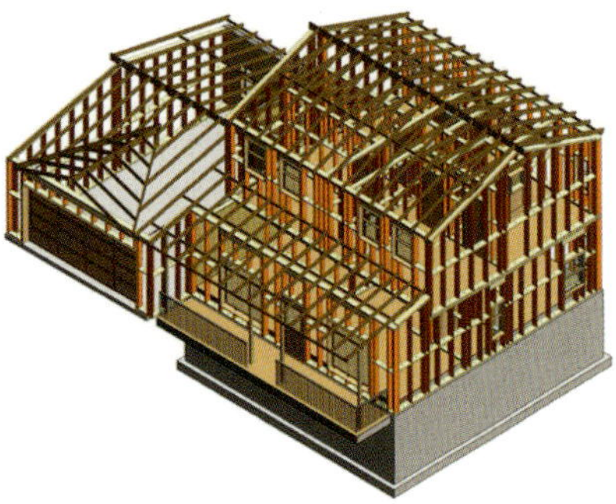

Division	Family	Framing Name	Length	Volume	Each Framing Weight	Count	Volume	Weight	
WALL	Dimension Lumber-Column Total					4	3.28	118.47	
	Exterior	Plywood, Sheathing	18' - 2 3/32"	428.38	12.43	0	12.43	428.38	
			2' - 6"	80.60	2.34	0	2.34	80.60	
			20' - 0"	318.50	9.24	0	9.24	318.50	
				631.28	18.32	0	18.32	631.28	
			24' - 0"	980.03	28.44	0	28.44	980.03	
				994.39	28.86	0	28.86	994.39	
			28' - 11"	772.48	22.42	0	22.42	772.48	
				784.56	22.77	0	22.77	784.56	
				916.13	26.59	0	26.59	916.13	
			29' - 6"	888.35	25.78	0	25.78	888.35	
			3' - 0"	67.84	1.97	0	1.97	67.84	
				73.55	2.13	0	2.13	73.55	
			31' - 0"	1,188.74	34.50	0	34.50	1,188.74	
			4' - 0"	84.12	2.44	0	2.44	84.12	
				129.23	3.75	0	3.75	129.23	
			5' - 6"	192.71	5.59	0	5.59	192.71	
	I_Wall_Frame Plate Total					481	171.29	6,186.99	
	I_Wall_Frame Stud Total					444	250.64	9,053.12	
	I_Wall_Frame Top Plate Support Total					54	15.60	563.47	
	Interior Total					0	159.09	5,482.28	Wood
WALL Total						983	847.46	29,935.23	
Windows	Double Hung Total					0	9.00	1,440.00	
	Fixed Total					0	4.50	720.00	
Windows Total						0	13.50	2,160.00	Glass
Grand Total						983	860.96	32,095.23	

Division	Family	Framing Name	Length	Count		Weight	Count	Volume	Weight	
ROOF	I_Rafter_Collar Beam			Total			0	0.00	0.00	
		Collar Beam	1.00	1		36.12	15	15.00	541.80	
	I_Rafter_Common Rafter			Total			0	0.00	0.00	
		Common Rafter	0.49	1		17.70	2	0.98	35.40	
			0.68	1		24.56	15	10.20	368.42	
			0.78	1		28.17	15	11.70	422.60	
			0.79	1		28.53	15	11.85	428.02	
			0.96	1		34.68	2	1.92	69.35	
			0.97	1		35.04	6	5.82	210.22	
						35.04	5	4.85	175.18	
		Valley Jack	0.02	1		0.72	2	0.04	1.44	
			0.10	1		3.61	2	0.20	7.22	
			0.18	1		6.50	2	0.36	13.00	
			0.26	1		9.39	2	0.52	18.78	
			0.28	1		10.11	1	0.28	10.11	
			0.34	1		12.28	2	0.68	24.56	
			0.37	1		13.36	1	0.37	13.36	
			0.42	1		15.17	2	0.84	30.34	
			0.45	1		16.25	1	0.45	16.25	
			0.55	1		19.87	1	0.55	19.87	
			0.63	1		22.76	1	0.63	22.76	
			0.73	1		26.37	1	0.73	26.37	
			0.81	1		29.26	1	0.81	29.26	
			0.90	1		32.51	1	0.90	32.51	
	I_Rafter_Girder Beam			Total			0	0.00	0.00	
		Girder	0.73	1		26.37	2	1.46	52.74	
			1.03	1		37.20	4	4.12	148.81	
			1.10	1		39.73	4	4.40	158.93	
	I_Rafter_Ridge Beam			Total			0	0.00	0.00	
		Ridge Board	1.30	1		46.96	1	1.30	46.96	
			2.03	1		73.32	1	2.03	73.32	
			2.99	1		108.00	1	2.99	108.00	
	I_Rafter_Valley Rafter			Total			0	0.00	0.00	
		Valley Rafter	1.17	1		42.26	2	2.34	84.52	
ROOF Total							110	83.32	3,190.12	
ROOF_surface	Plywood surface	Plywood, sheathing grade	0.96	Total			0	0.96	33.08	
			52.96	Total			0	52.96	1,824.83	
			67.77	Total			0	67.77	2,335.42	
ROOF_surface Total							0	121.69	4,193.33	
Grand Total							110	210.01	7,383.45	Wood

United States speculative single-family house, 2017–18. Test Bed: Bill of Materials (BOM), 2017–18 Revit (BIM) Model

A standard speculative house in the United States was modelled in Revit and compared to the Binocular House. Both houses are more than 80% concrete by weight, but the speculative house relies almost entirely on lumber and fasteners, and loose tolerances.

Roof Structure

Type	Material Name	Count	Length f	Volume cf	Unit weight lbs/ft³	Weight lbs
HSS6X4X3/8	Steel ASTM A36	1	10.35	0.48	489.00 lb/ft³	232.72
HSS6X4X3/8	Steel ASTM A36	1	19.84	0.89	489.00 lb/ft³	435.59
HSS6X4X3/8	Steel ASTM A36	1	19.84	0.89	489.00 lb/ft³	435.59
HSS6X4X3/8	Steel ASTM A36	1	19.44	0.88	489.00 lb/ft³	430.06
HSS6X4X3/8	Steel ASTM A36	1	19.44	0.88	489.00 lb/ft³	430.06
HSS6X4X3/8	Steel ASTM A36	1	22.24	0.88	489.00 lb/ft³	430.06
HSS6X4X3/8	Steel ASTM A36	1	55.92	2.54	489.00 lb/ft³	1,241.23
HSS6X4X3/8	Steel ASTM A36	1	73	2.54	489.00 lb/ft³	1,241.26
HSS6X4X3/8	Steel ASTM A36	1	19.84	0.89	489.00 lb/ft³	435.59
HSS12X4X5/8	Steel ASTM A36	1	19.44	2.34	489.00 lb/ft³	1,145.57
HSS12X4X5/8	Steel ASTM A36	1	54.51	6.61	489.00 lb/ft³	3,230.65
HSS12X4X5/8	Steel ASTM A36	1	39.93	4.88	489.00 lb/ft³	2,385.38
HSS12X4X5/8	Steel ASTM A36	1	9.97	1.26	489.00 lb/ft³	616.95
HSS12X4X5/8	Steel ASTM A36	1	27.6	3.34	489.00 lb/ft³	1,634.00
MC12X25	Steel ASTM A36	1	55.92	3.07	489.00 lb/ft³	1,500.42
MC12X25	Steel ASTM A36	1	55.92	3.05	489.00 lb/ft³	1,491.66
MC12X25	Steel ASTM A36	1	47.75	2.62	489.00 lb/ft³	1,282.36
MC12X25	Steel ASTM A36	1	27.91	1.52	489.00 lb/ft³	744.31
MC12X25	Steel ASTM A36	1	19.92	1.08	489.00 lb/ft³	529.19
Total Steam Beam			618.78	40.64		19,872.66

Type	Material Name	Count	Length f	Volume cf	Unit weight lbs/ft³	Weight lbs
Unit Area of 2x12: .1172 sf						
Dimension Lumber 2x12	Softwood, Lumber	1	40.21	5.33	36.12	192.633
Dimension Lumber	Softwood, Lumber	1	19.13	2.55	36.12	92.239
Dimension Lumber	Softwood, Lumber	1	19.23	2.57	36.12	92.959
Dimension Lumber	Softwood, Lumber	1	39.42	5.35	36.12	193.353
Dimension Lumber	Softwood, Lumber	1	18.24	2.51	36.12	90.799
Dimension Lumber	Softwood, Lumber	1	40.21	5.31	36.12	191.913
Dimension Lumber	Softwood, Lumber	1	17.94	2.51	36.12	90.799
Dimension Lumber	Softwood, Lumber	1	38.69	5.29	36.12	191.192
Dimension Lumber	Softwood, Lumber	1	18.24	2.51	36.12	90.799
Dimension Lumber	Softwood, Lumber	1	18.24	2.51	36.12	90.799
Dimension Lumber	Softwood, Lumber	1	18.24	2.51	36.12	90.799
Dimension Lumber	Softwood, Lumber	1	18.24	2.51	36.12	90.799
Dimension Lumber	Softwood, Lumber	1	18.24	2.51	36.12	90.799
Dimension Lumber	Softwood, Lumber	1	18.24	2.51	36.12	90.799
Dimension Lumber	Softwood, Lumber	1	18.24	2.51	36.12	90.799
Dimension Lumber	Softwood, Lumber	1	18.24	2.51	36.12	90.799
Dimension Lumber	Softwood, Lumber	1	18.24	2.51	36.12	90.799
Dimension Lumber	Softwood, Lumber	1	18.24	2.51	36.12	90.799
Dimension Lumber	Softwood, Lumber	1	18.24	2.51	36.12	90.799
Dimension Lumber	Softwood, Lumber	1	18.24	2.51	36.12	90.799
Dimension Lumber	Softwood, Lumber	1	2.82	0.42	36.12	15.226
Dimension Lumber	Softwood, Lumber	1	2.82	0.42	36.12	15.226
		22	457.59	62.38		2,255.9
Total Lumber		22	457.59	62.38		2,256

Envelope

Type	Material Name	Count	Length f	Volume cf	Unit weight lbs/ft³	Weight lbs
Glass, Clear Glazing	1	8'-4"	10'-0"	8769.15	160.00 lb/ft³	811.96
Glass, Clear Glazing	1	8'-4"	10'-0"	8768.81	160.00 lb/ft³	811.92
Silicon	1	8'-4"	10'-0"	274.70	78.04 lb/ft³	12.41
Silicon	1	8'-4"	10'-0"	274.70	78.04 lb/ft³	12.41
Steel Plate_Base_6x1/4	1	8'-4"	10'-0"	180.01	489.00 lb/ft³	50.94
Steel Plate_Base_6x1/4	1	8'-4"	10'-0"	180.00	489.00 lb/ft³	50.94
Steel_Plate Top 1 3/4 x1/4	1	8'-4"	10'-0"	52.50	384.00 lb/ft³	11.67
Steel_Plate Top 1 3/4 x1/4	1	8'-4"	10'-0"	52.50	384.00 lb/ft³	11.67
Steel_Plate_Bottom 1 3/4 x1/4	1	8'-4"	10'-0"	52.50	384.00 lb/ft³	11.67
Steel_Plate_Bottom 1 3/4 x1/4	1	8'-4"	10'-0"	52.50	384.00 lb/ft³	11.67
Total Enclosure IGU Panel				18,657.37		1,797.24
Steel_Plate_Top 1 3/4 x1/4	1	9'-0"	14'-4 3/8"	75.41	384.00 lb/ft³	16.757164
Steel_Plate_Top 1 3/4 x1/4	1	8'-6"	14'-1 5/8"	74.23	384.00 lb/ft³	16.494667
Steel_Plate_Top 1 3/4 x1/4	1	8'-6"	14'-0 1/8"	73.56	384.00 lb/ft³	16.34602
Steel_Plate_Top 1 3/4 x1/4	1	8'-6"	10'-11 3/4"	57.64	384.00 lb/ft³	12.809377
Steel_Plate_Top 1 3/4 x1/4	1	8'-6"	13'-11 3/4"	73.39	384.00 lb/ft³	16.309364
Steel_Plate_Top 1 3/4 x1/4	1	8'-6"	10'-11 3/4"	57.64	384.00 lb/ft³	12.809377
Steel_Plate_Top 1 3/4 x1/4	1	8'-6"	6'-9 5/8"	35.73	384.00 lb/ft³	7.939229
Steel_Plate_Top 1 3/4 x1/4	1	9'-0"	14'-8 1/4"	77.1	384.00 lb/ft³	17.134042
Steel_Plate_Top 1 3/4 x1/4	1	8'-6"	14'-0 1/8"	73.56	384.00 lb/ft³	16.34602
Steel_Plate_Top 1 3/4 x1/4	1	9'-0"	1'-0 1/4"	5.36	384.00 lb/ft³	1.190968
Steel_Plate_Top 1 3/4 x1/4	1	9'-0"	13'-10 7/8"	73	384.00 lb/ft³	16.221309
Steel_Plate_Top 1 3/4 x1/4	1	9'-0"	6'-10 1/8"	35.92	384.00 lb/ft³	7.981612
Steel_Plate_Top 1 3/4 x1/4	1	9'-0"	14'-0 5/8"	73.75	384.00 lb/ft³	16.388769
Total Enclosure_IGU_Panel_In_Plane				786.29		174.73

Steel Column

Type	Material Name	Count	Length f	Volume cf	Unit weight lbs/ft³	Weight lbs
W4X13	0.026	1	9'-0"	0.24	489	119.87
W4X13	0.026	1	9'-0"	0.24	489	119.87
W4X13	0.026	1	9'-0"	0.24	489	119.87
W4X13	0.026	1	9'-0"	0.24	489	119.87
W4X13	0.026	1	9'-0"	0.24	489	119.87
W4X13	0.026	1	9'-0"	0.24	489	119.87
W4X13	0.026	1	9'-0"	0.24	489	119.87
W4X13	0.026	1	9'-0"	0.24	489	119.87
W4X13	0.026	1	9'-0"	0.24	489	119.87
W4X13	0.026	1	9'-0"	0.24	489	119.87
W4X13	0.026	1	9'-0"	0.24	489	119.87
W4X13	0.026	1	9'-0"	0.24	489	119.87
W4X13	0.026	1	9'-0"	0.24	489	119.87
W4X13	0.026	1	9'-0"	0.24	489	119.87
W4X13	0.026	1	9'-0"	0.24	489	119.87
W4X13	0.026	1	9'-6"	0.26	489	119.87
		21				
Total Steel Column		21.00	189.00	5.06		2,517.00

Foundation

Type	Material Name	Count	Length f	Volume cf	Unit weight lbs/ft³	Weight lbs
6" Foundation Slab	Concrete, Cast-in-Place gray	1	24.2	12.1	150.28	1,818.33
6" Foundation Slab	Concrete, Cast-in-Place gray	1.14	48.34	24.17	150.28	3,631.97
6" Foundation Slab	Concrete, Cast-in-Place gray	1.17	32.94	16.47	150.28	2,474.97
6" Foundation Slab	Concrete, Cast-in-Place gray	1.17	23.13	11.57	150.28	1,738.33
6" Foundation Slab	Concrete, Cast-in-Place gray	4.5	245.43	122.72	150.28	18,442.15
6" Foundation Slab	Concrete, Cast-in-Place gray	4.93	277.45	138.73	150.28	20,848.09
6" Foundation Slab	Concrete, Cast-in-Place gray	10.93	308.6	154.3	150.28	23,188.76
6" Foundation Slab	Concrete, Cast-in-Place gray	12.01	240.1	120.05	150.28	18,041.79
6" Foundation Slab	Concrete, Cast-in-Place gray	18.67	1,050.26	525.13	150.28	78,918.03
6" Foundation Slab	Concrete, Cast-in-Place gray	39.54	758.09	379.05	150.28	56,964.07
Total Foundation Slab		95	3,009	1,504		226,066
Bearing Footing - 24" x 12"	Concrete, Cast-in-Place gray	2.77	2	5.53	150.28	831.00
Bearing Footing - 24" x 12"	Concrete, Cast-in-Place gray	10.93		24.52	150.28	3,684.82
Bearing Footing - 24" x 12"	Concrete, Cast-in-Place gray	12.39		23.45	150.28	3,524.74
Bearing Footing - 24" x 12"	Concrete, Cast-in-Place gray	13.4		29.47	150.28	4,428.91
Bearing Footing - 24" x 12"	Concrete, Cast-in-Place gray	19.84		38.34	150.28	5,762.12
Bearing Footing - 24" x 12"	Concrete, Cast-in-Place gray	20.51		42.35	150.28	6,363.79
Bearing Footing - 24" x 12"	Concrete, Cast-in-Place gray	26.91		52.49	150.28	7,888.05
Bearing Footing - 24" x 12"	Concrete, Cast-in-Place gray	26.91		52.49	150.28	7,888.05
Bearing Footing - 24" x 12"	Concrete, Cast-in-Place gray	38.53		75.73	150.28	11,381.51
Bearing Footing - 24" x 12"	Concrete, Cast-in-Place gray	40.21		81.75	150.28	12,285.74
Bearing Footing - 24" x 12"	Concrete, Cast-in-Place gray	54.93		112.52	150.28	16,910.34
Bearing Footing - 24" x 12"	Concrete, Cast-in-Place gray	54.93		109.52	150.28	16,459.49
Bearing Footing - 24" x 12"	Concrete, Cast-in-Place gray	56.26		111.19	150.28	16,710.63
Total Foundation Footing		379		759		114,119

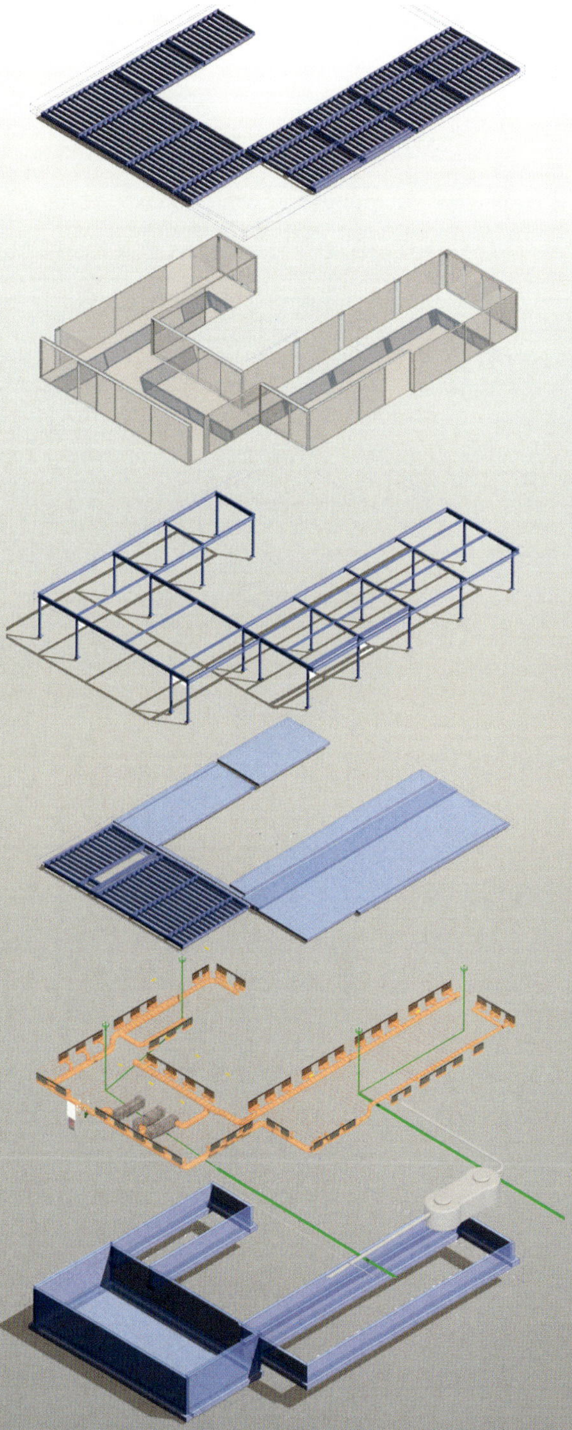

Binocular House, 2008
Test Bed: Bill of Materials (BOM), 2017–18 Revit (BIM) Model

The layering of structural and enclosure systems required intricate coordination. They are essential to each other. The concrete foundations are unified and effectively overbuilt to afford a continuously stable J-shaped base for the linear steel and planar-glass enclosure.

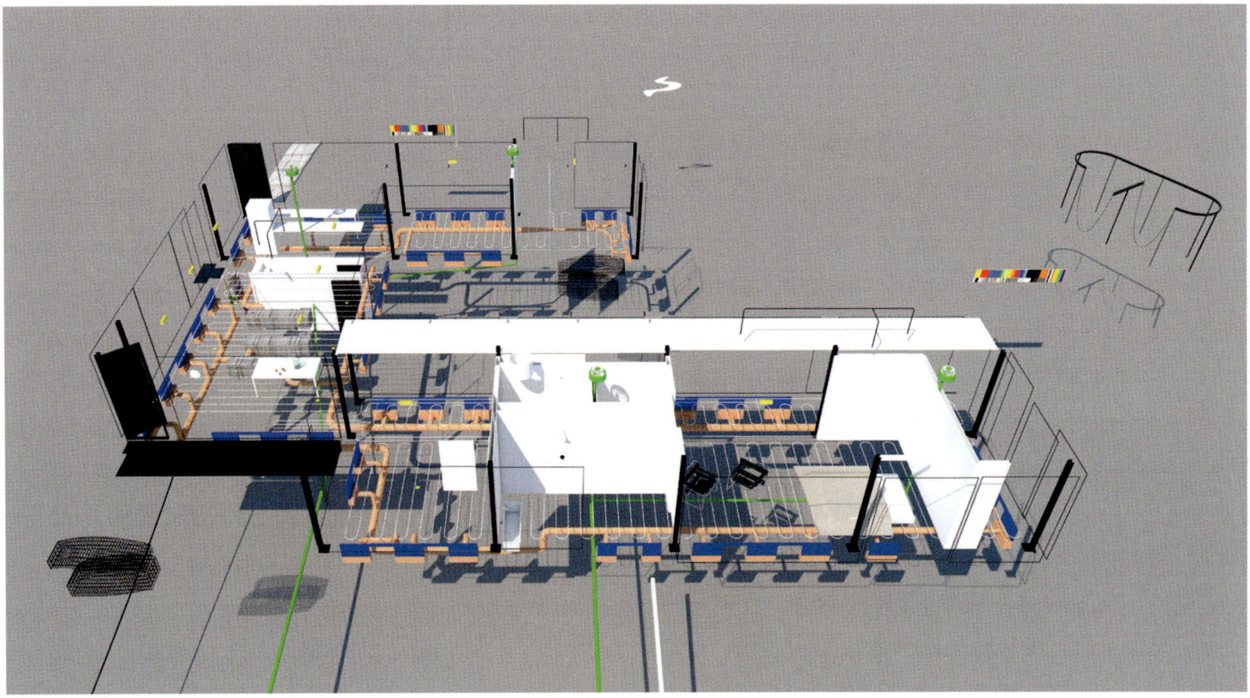

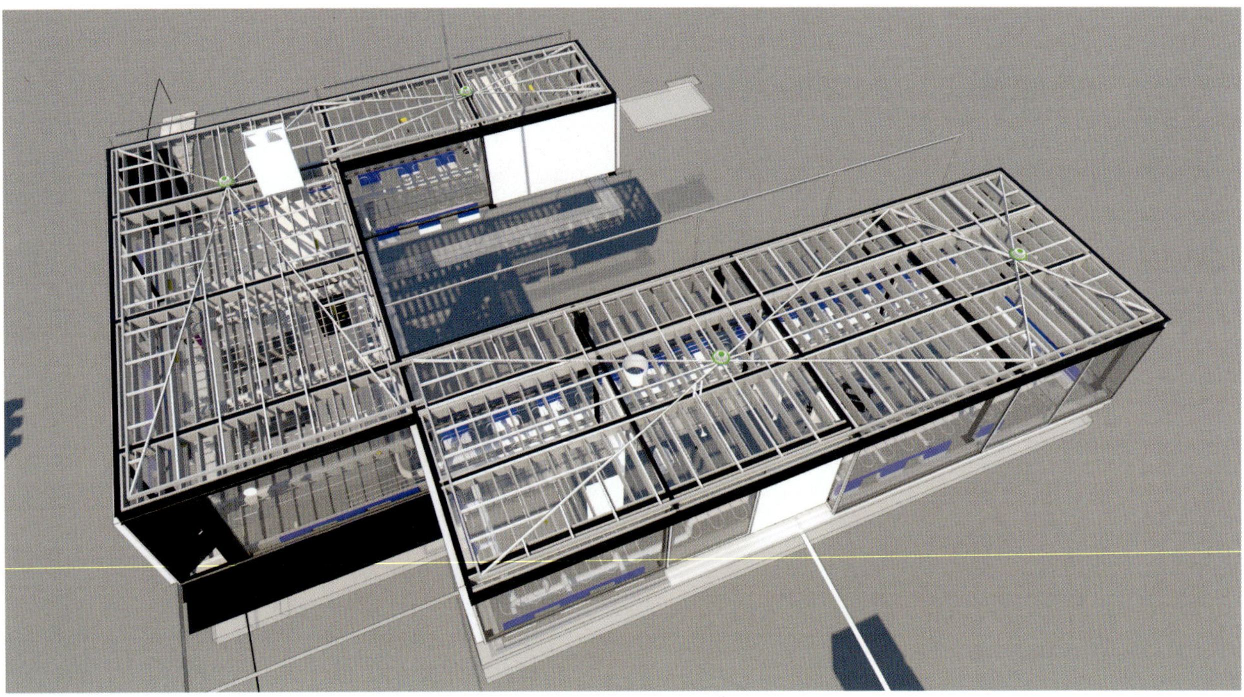

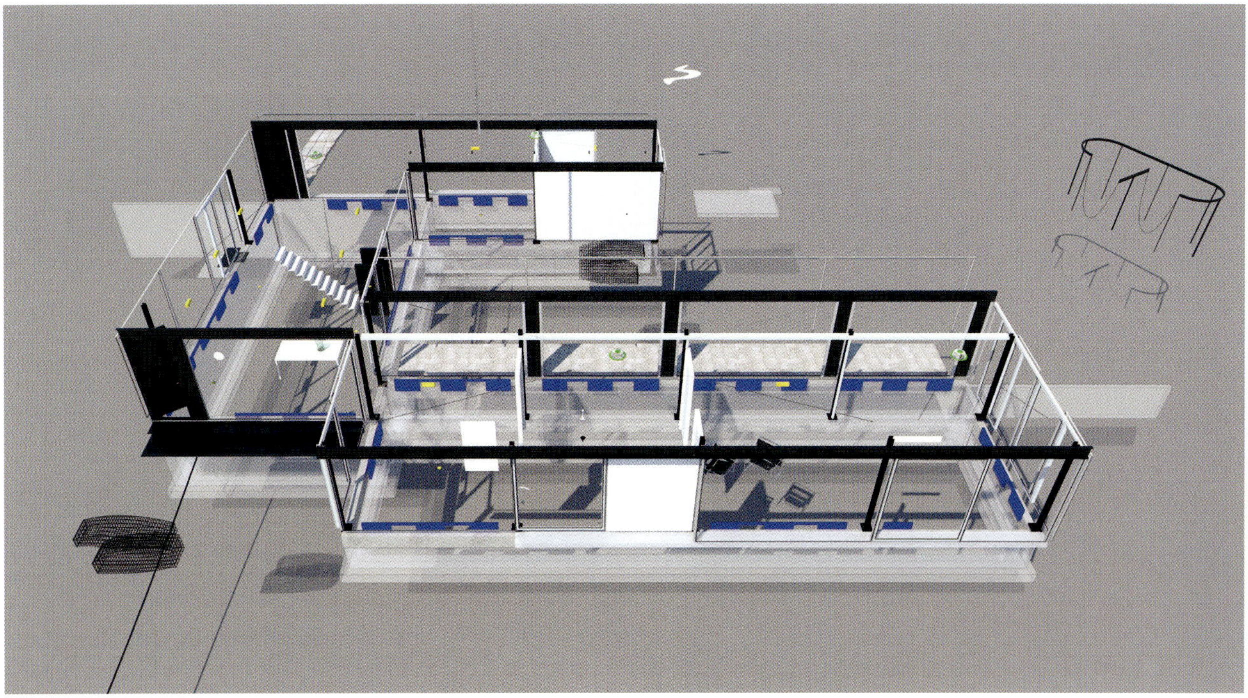

Binocular House, 2008
Test Bed: Bill of Materials (BOM), 2017–18 Revit (BIM) Model

The coordination of thermal controls (heating, cooling, air exchange/dehumidification) with enclosure (glass, IGUs, steel framing, and structural silicone) shape the building's thermodynamics. Modelling all components reveals their necessary integration and codependence, and ability to react to thermal expansion and contraction.

The handmade nature of construction required immense care to place every component. On-site construction was a challenge given the annual weather changes in the Hudson Valley.

Welded steel framing was constructed in days with specialized labor but few components.

The steel was cut on-site from a stock of oversize members. The use of lumber increased the part count but allowed on-site verification and measurement and simple labor. On-site fabrication was a rare potential afforded by a large and remote construction site.

Internal roof drains allowed a minimal roof-edge detail that revealed the structural channel.

Glazing was standardized during the design process, but construction tolerances required on-site measurements. The resulting 31 IGUs were each modified to address tolerances in steel framing. Assuring tolerances for the silicone glazing bite was essential.

Solar Roof 1
An initial attempt to reverse engineer the Binocular House was done quickly but with foundational goals. We sought to use glass as the singular element—for structural and enclosure—and to remove as much concrete and steel as possible, integrating photovoltaic film in the roof and building envelope. We imagined a liquid-heated-and-cooled glazing system with polymer interlayers that did not require an IGU or insulation. Batteries are used as the underside of newly engineered distributed-cooling panels that form a distributed ballast, providing the weight that stabilizes the entire structure and equilibrium in the structure and environment.

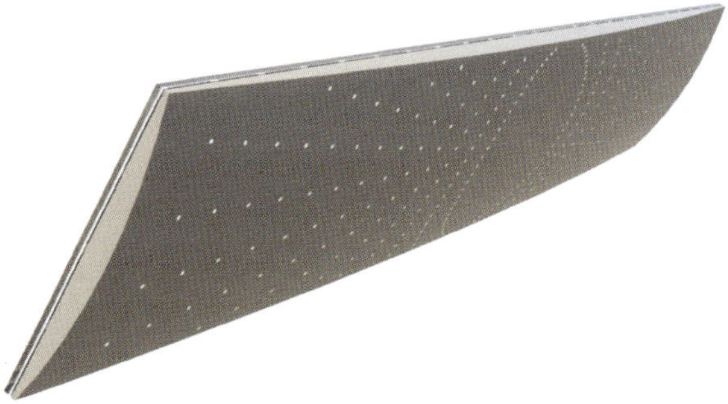

Solar Roof 2:
Spectral—King Post (horizonal)

Building-and-Energy Products: All systems induce deflection, and their weight is manifested as structural capacity in the roof structure. All equipment can easily be upgraded and switched out. Liquid heated-and-cooled glazing is seen in the subtle "stripes" in the glass panels.

The shallow depth of the steel wide-flange roof structure instigates deflection, in turn causing tension in king-post cabling below.

Two layers of solar photovoltaic panels are placed beneath low-iron laminated glass roof. All systems induce deflection and their weight is manifested as structural capacity in the roof structure. The photovoltaic panels include a bottom layer hosting a proposed "Wafer AC" and battery. The panels provide solar shading. Beams or AC panels can be fitted with an air exchanger. The extensive and persistent low-pressure-heat exchange requires little energy.

Steel Wide Flange / Shallow depth deflects to cause tension in king-post. Two layers of solar PV panels are placed beneath low-iron laminted glass roof. A lower layer of "Wafer AC" and Battery panels provide solar shading. All systems induce deflection and their weight is manifest as structural capacity in roof structure. Beams or AC panels can be fitted with air exchange for persistent and low pressure but extensive heat exchange.

Solar Roof 3:
Spectral—King Post (vertical)

An all-glass structure: walls, roof, and floors. Deep overhangs provide an expansive roof to host photovoltaic cells and shade the south elevation of the structure. The central span opens to the sky but provides UV, IR, and structural protection via interlayers.

Steel Wide Flange / Shallow depth deflects to cause tension in king-post. Vertical Battery and "Wafer AC" induce deflection and their weight is manifest as structural capacity in roof structure. PV's are laced into glass structural panel roof . 2 x 5 meter Panels and Beams can be fitted with air exchange for persistent and low pressure but extensive heat exchange.
Long Over Hang provided by structural glass roof panels provides solar shading. Clear glass center section parallles Model S or X roof solar capacity.
Laminated Glass: Liquid cooled capillary veins (see products PDF) uses glycol / Novec in gravity or temperarture induced movement. Low volume persistent heat/cool exchange replaces IGU insulating capacity. Here the capillary glass is used as a structural insulated panel of approx. 8" thickness.
Geo-thermal concrete floor with capillary glass over concrete for double heat/cool sink capability.

Building-and-Energy Products

Mechanical equipment is "laminated" into a glazing-and-structural panel. Electrical harnesses link photovoltaic film to electronic controls, batteries, and mechanical equipment. Each element has the capacity to be easily exchanged and upgraded.

Cable connectors tighten the components into a unified diaphragm structure but can also be easily dismounted. Beams act as plenums. Integrated electrical is carried in wiring harnesses.

A proposal for a laminated-glass panel with integrated glass veins to provide liquid heating and cooling. The thin laminated-glass panel creates a heat-and-cool sink. It would replace an insulated glazing unit and separate mechanical systems for heating and cooling. One advanced-energy product replaces many parts and often under-engineered systems. We later decreased the length and orientation of the internal veins to better control the consistency of the liquid temperature.

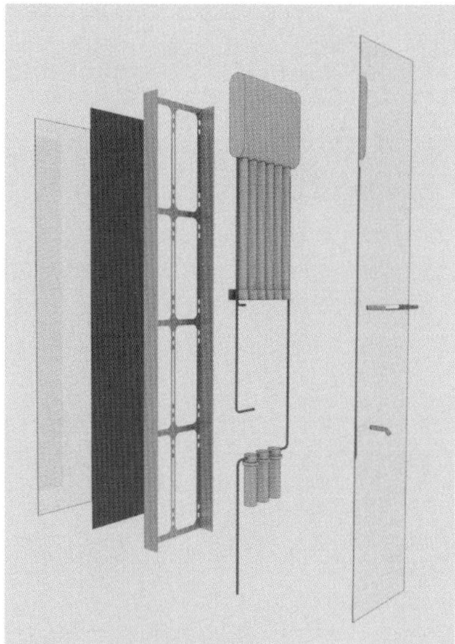

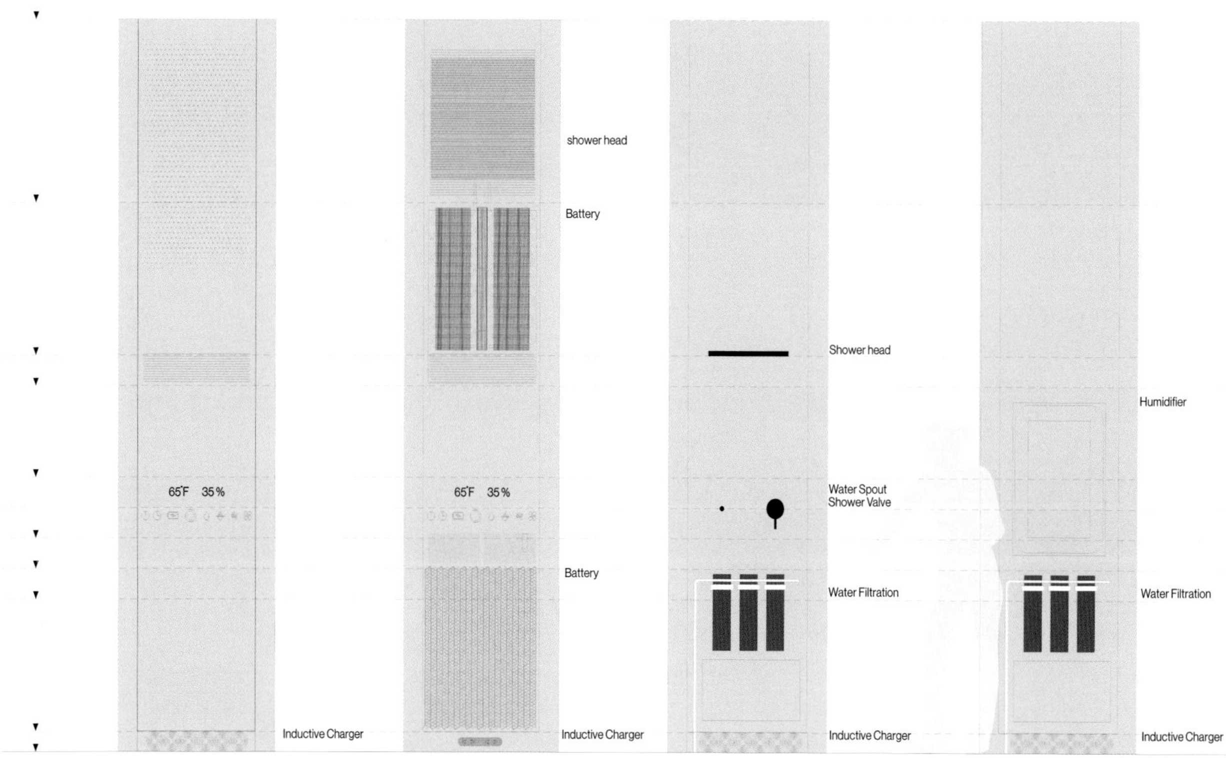

Building-and-Energy Products

Pressurized air energy storage. A user-friendly interface forms the column fascia. It allows easy control and monitoring of energy systems.

The tall proportion of the column is a by-product of allowing heat to rise before being evacuated by low-pressure and low-energy air exchangers.

Building-and-Energy Products

Eyes in the Heat: Optical Comfort. Building equipment for heating and cooling and energy storage is laminated and integrated with the columnar structures.

Renewable energy integrated into building products transforms housing into an energy asset rather than a real-estate asset, creating a new form of economy and scale for housing, and reinventing would-be housing markets.

We developed six proposals that range in size from a large house to a smaller self-contained accessory dwelling unit.

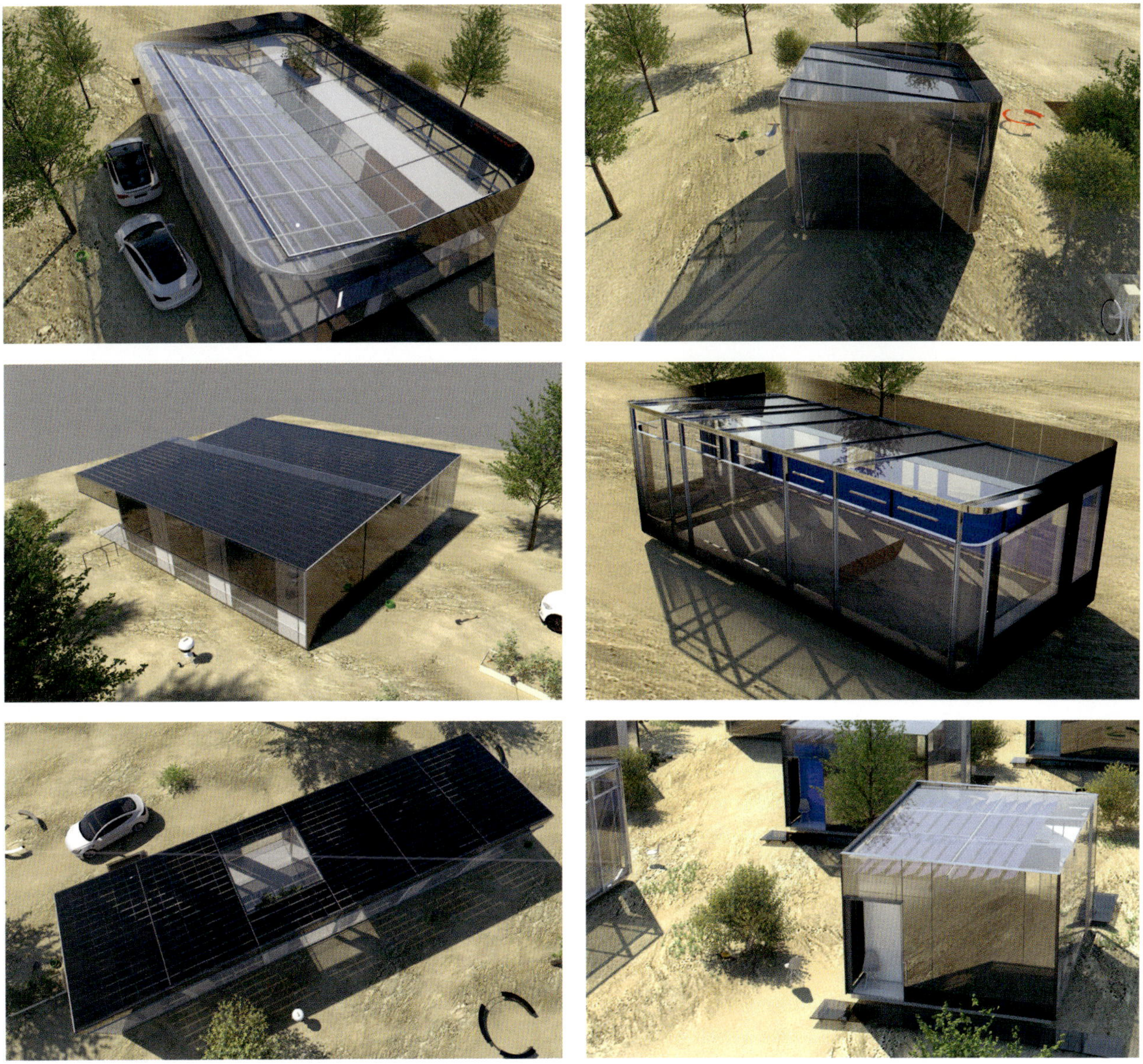

Model 101 (X) — 1,800 square feet
Model 102 (S) — 1,500 square feet
Model 103 — 1,000 square feet

Model A — 340 square feet (ADU)
Model B — 540 square feet (house)
Model C — 400 square feet (ADU)

Model 101 (X)

The radial aspects of Model 101 (X) were designed to give lateral support to the overall structure, but they also respond to the rotation of the solar orientation.

The interlayers that control IR, UV, and the structure in the glazing panels also fades and darkens due to solar exposure. The tint fades to the north, revealing the internal solar panels, batteries, and air conditioning systems.

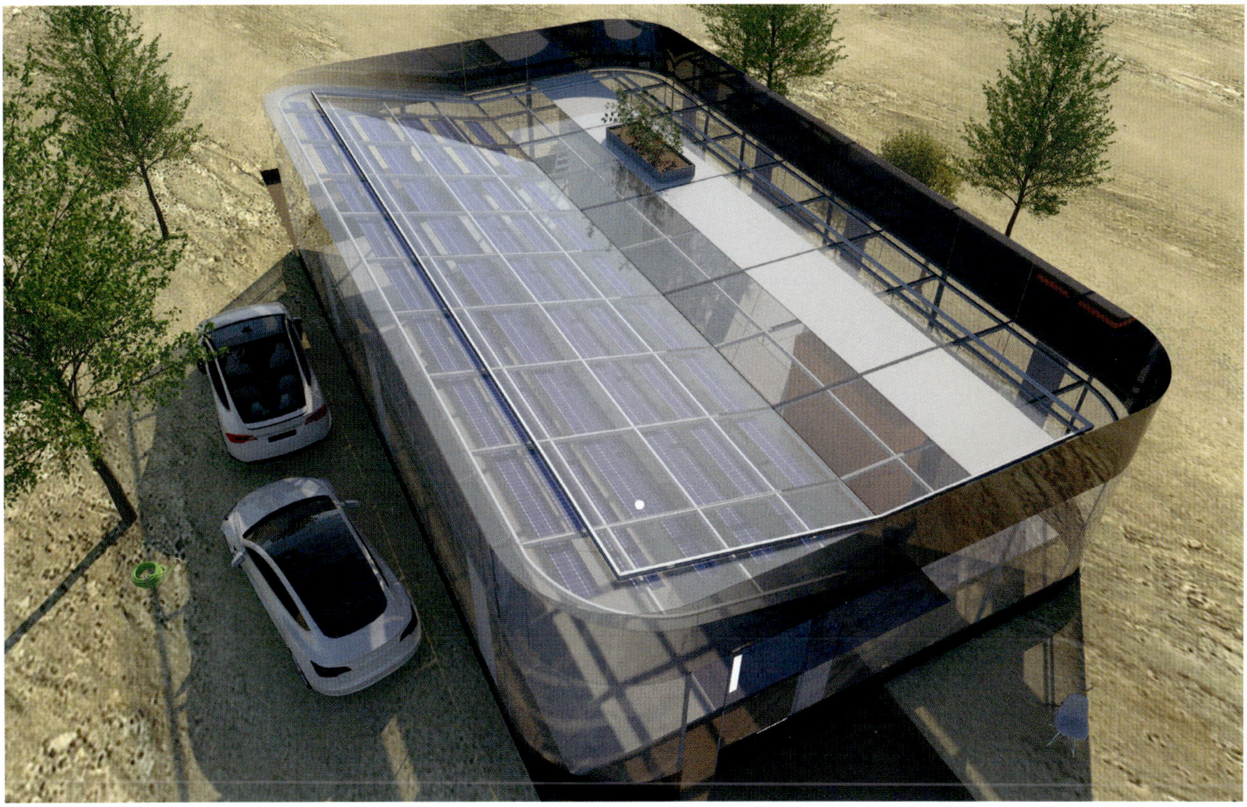

The building's primary façade is to the sky. Its reference and economy are geospatial, and, while situated on Earth, it is a type of geospatial infrastructure.

Model 101 (X) includes:
1. Renewable solar energy integrated below the roof glazing system.
2. Battery energy storage laminated beneath and to PV panels.
3. Liquid heating and cooling integrated into vertical glazing.
4. Laminated, tinted, and shaded glass.
5. Maglev panel door and window openings.

Model 101 (X)

An interior view shows the horizontally oriented liquid heating-and-cooling capillaries within the glazing. Use of engineered fluids avoids the potential of freezing.

The two-meter run of each tube allows each of the fluids to be recharged at the window system's hybrid frame and heat sinks. Propulsion of fluids is abetted by their own volumetric expansion as they are heated by the Sun and climate during the day.

We imagined the curvature of the glass structure and its radius, and the larger curvature of the Sun's movement, as a kind of eccentric chiaroscuro and sfumato.
An inspiration for this comes from the painter Frank Stella and his 1986 book *Working Space*.

"What Leonardo does, as no one else could do, is to spin off the shadows of modeling, creating a sense of atmospheric softness that gives way in turn to a kind of magical sculptural impressionism. The result is a pictorial 'rounding' of space that paves the way for Caravaggio and becomes, at the same time, part of our basic spatial vocabulary for judging great painting."

Judith Beheading Holofernes, Caravaggio, 1602

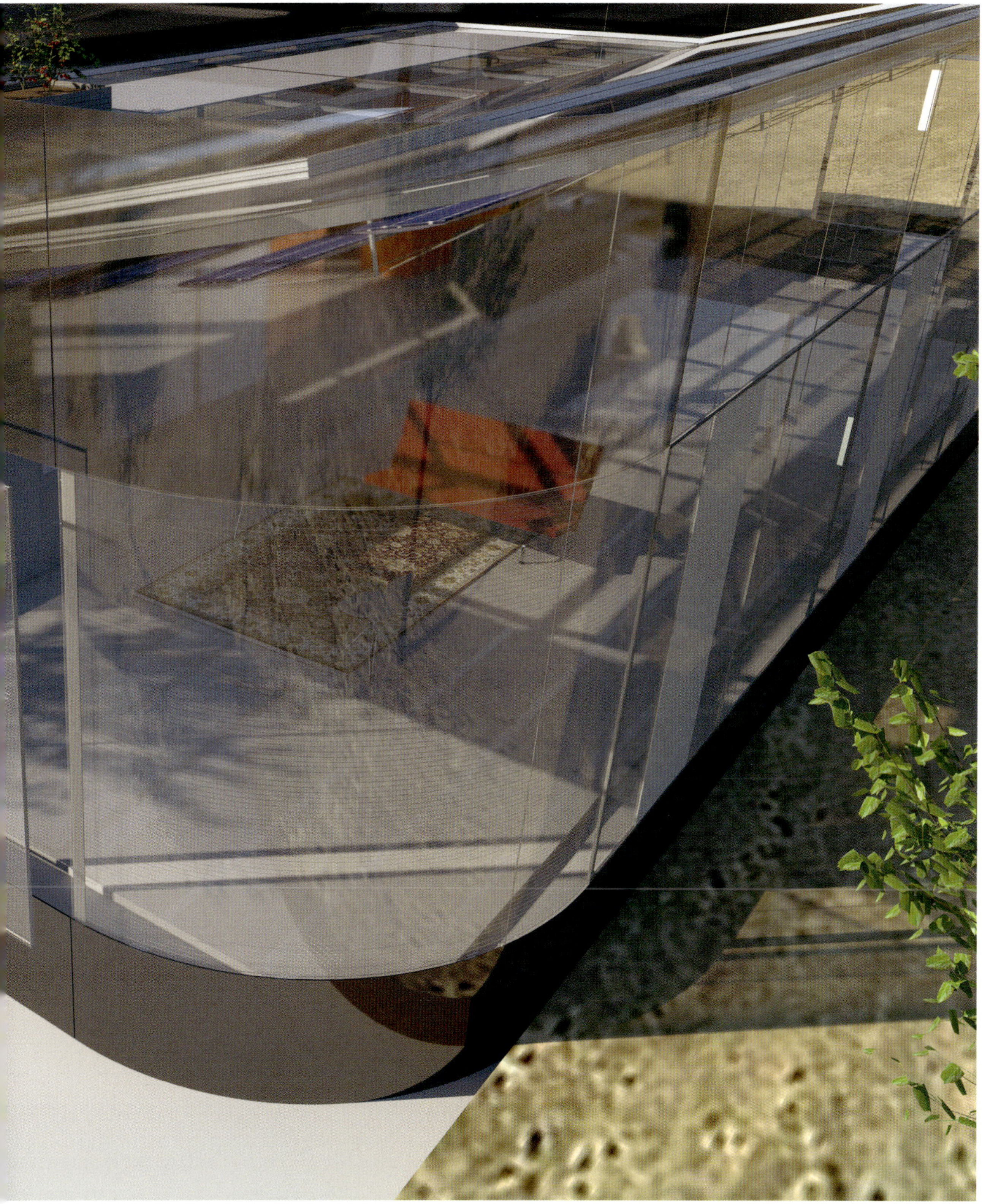

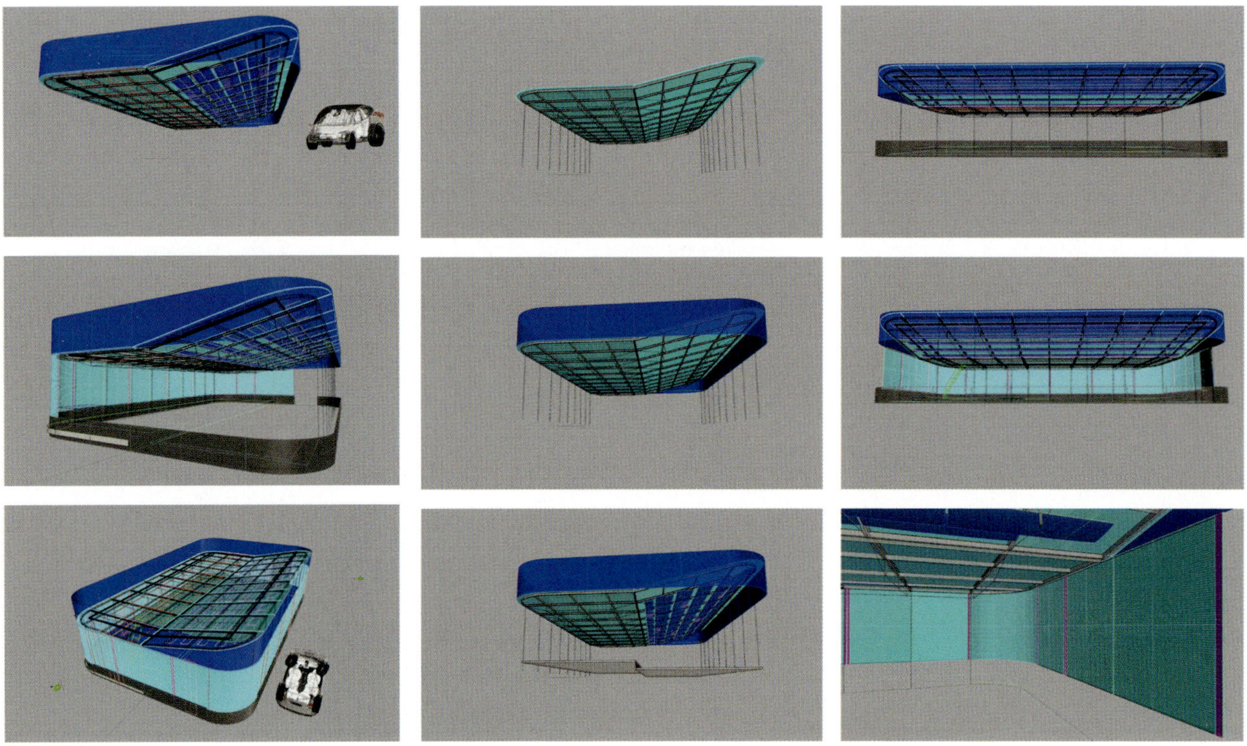

Model 101 (X)

A screen capture shows components and the integration of components in the assembly process of the Model 101 (X).

Model 101 (X)

The use of interlayers in the laminated glazing allows a progression of opacity and coordination with climate demands.

The building-energy systems are revealed as one progresses to the north, revealing the conflation of shelter and renewable-energy production.

Making use of fewer components requires larger, heavier glazing panels. Their weight is used as a ballast that once in place stabilizes the entire structure as a rigid diaphragm. Assembly would require a crane but also far less time.

Model 102 (S)

Model 102 (S) uses large, shell-like, laminated-glass panels to both enclose the house and create structural support. Fourteen wall panels supply heating and cooling, and twelve roof panels enable solar-energy generation, all precision-made for rapid assembly. A shallow roof slope allows for doubling of the photovoltaic film oriented to the Sun and adds an iconographic house form.

Model 102 (S)

Photovoltaic film and solar shading form interlayers in structural-glass roof panels. The panels are immense but used as the building structure. The "veil"-like shade on the south façade lowers the center of gravity of the material mass in the building.

The interlayers allow more transparency in the north-facing clerestory section of the otherwise continuous laminated-glass roof. Northern light available over the full horizon at ground and sky creates a feeling of being outdoors. The horizon curves, creating a topology with the house's interior.

Model 102 (S)

A cast-aluminum column inspired by Eames Aluminum Chair: the casting allows a tapering of materials and unique anchors.

Above: Building Process: The weight of the laminated-glass roof ties the structural columns and beams together in a diaphragm structure.

Below: A screen capture shows a planar column and roof beam composed of laminated glass.

On Earth and in space: The Sun is indifferent to its witness.

A small human-scaled structure on Earth produces an abundance of solar energy. The climate impact registered as one-time embodied energy—fabricating the components—is offset by the structure's persistent and durable encrypting of the Sun's photons. An entirely other form, scale, and density of settlement follows.

My house communicates with the sun every "8 Minutes, 20 Seconds." It is not in need of my presence; my house does not know I am home.

Model 103 A "veil."

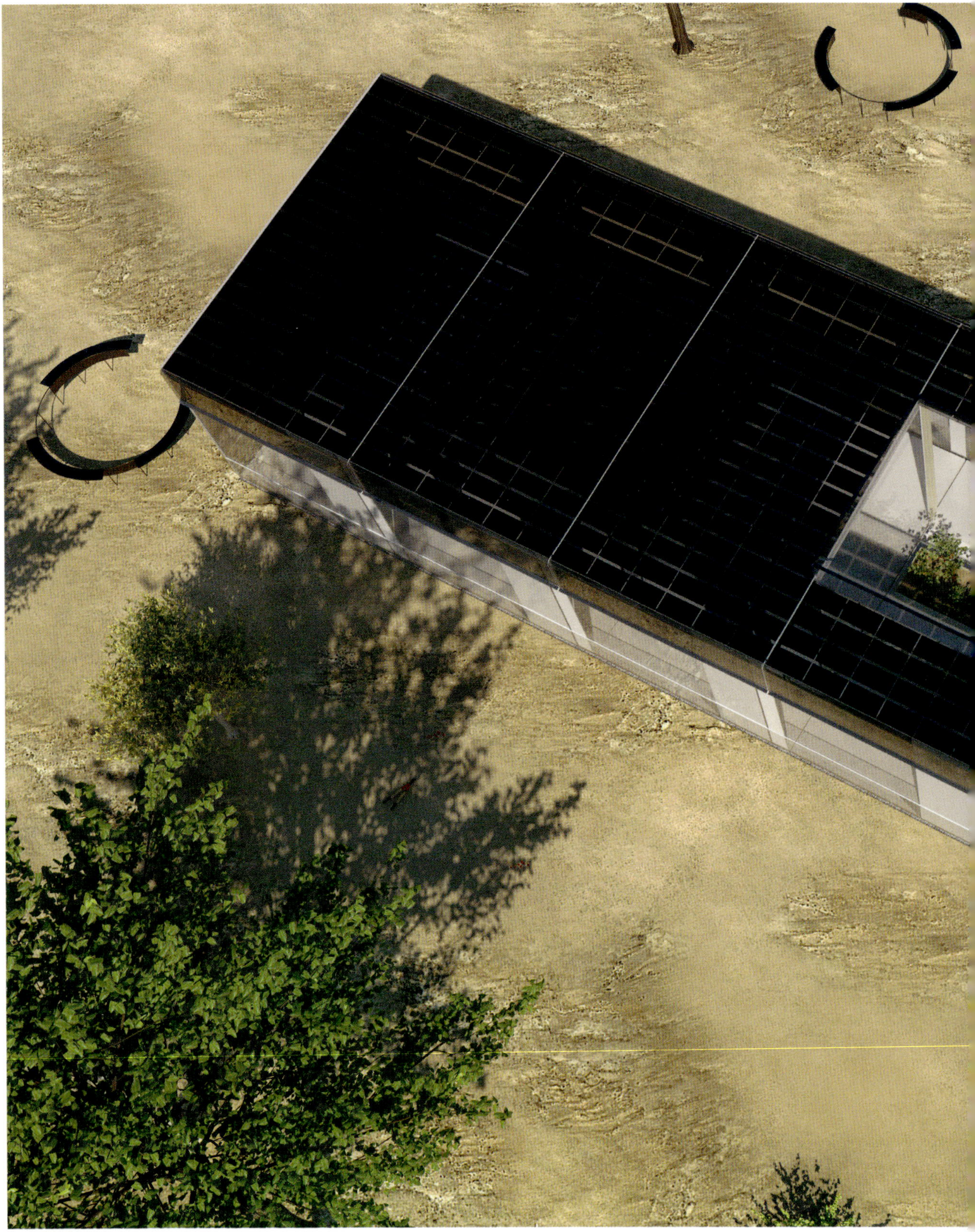

Model 103

Eighteen wall panels supply heating and cooling, and six roof panels enable solar-energy generation, all precision-made for rapid assembly. Photovoltaic and solar shading form an interlayer in structural-glass roof panels.

Laminated glass with an interlayer provides owners the option to choose a color. A site-specific "solar veil" and an opaque mag-lev-track-enabled operable door and interior window panels allow for privacy and offer color and material options.

Veterans seeking homes are often unable to find stable, high-quality housing. To assist in addressing this issue, we have often sought advice from Community Solutions (CS) whose founder, Rosanne Haggerty, and principal of housing systems, Nadine Maleh, have been our former partners in practice and teaching.

Community Solutions acquires, rehabilitates, and leases multifamily properties in select markets, using a first-of-its-kind social-impact-investment model. We propose that CS launch pilot projects that use renewable energy as a tool of housing stability, using advanced manufacturing to lower the cost of production and renewable energy to offset financing costs. Housing becomes a downstream by-product of renewable energy. Housing stability and universal income are provided by the Sun.

Across the country, thousands of veterans have housing benefits that go unused.

ADU—Ensembles (neighborhood infill and density). Sand City and Fort Ord, California

Sand City, California is adjacent to the decommissioned United States military base at Fort Ord. It offers critical solar capacity and sites where CS and other organizations could address veterans' homelessness. ADU and mixed-scale housing and services form ensembles, constituting a new type of solar-choreographed density. CS has explored similar needs in the Denver region. Other former military sites such as the Concord Naval Weapons Station would be candidates to test projects.

Model A provides 340 square feet of interior space. It weighs only 13,000 pounds and is composed entirely of laminated glass. Interlayers provide thermal and privacy controls and are optimized for your site.

Automatically generate your housing costs with tradeable energy. Integrated photovoltaic cells provide power to run your home and to trade as universal income.

It was never on the grid

Model A

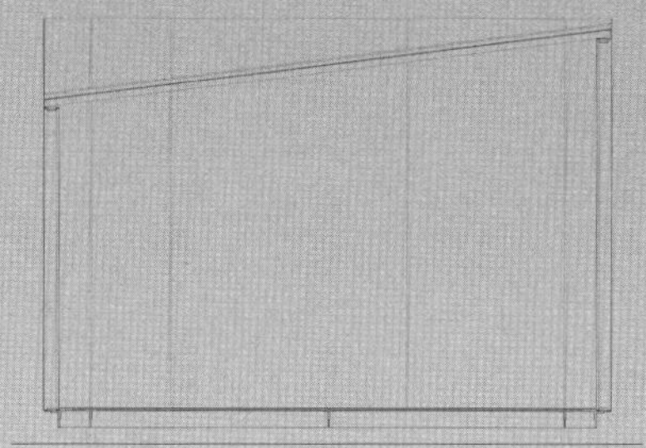

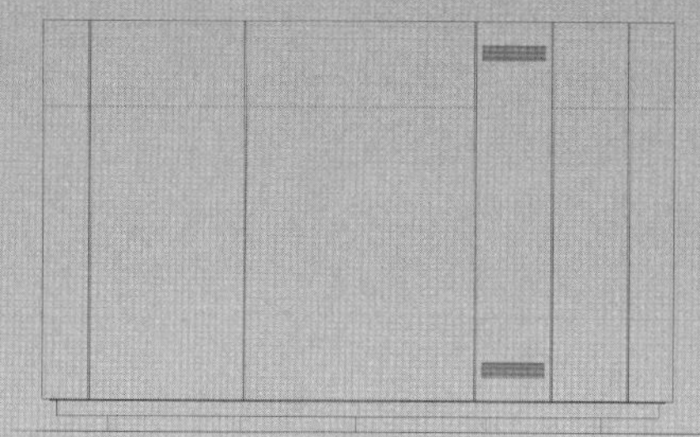

Model A as ADU or Medical Clinic

Glass offers the opportunity for antimicrobial surfaces and allows medical levels of cleanliness.

Medical levels of air filtration and persistent exchange are all powered by renewable energy.

Category	Types	Dimensions (WxHxD)	Counts
Wall Panel	L2.5'	2.5'x12'x6"	4
	L5'	5'x12'x6"	4
	L7.5'	7.5'x12'x6"	4
	L2.5' Mech	2.5'x12'x6"	1
	L2.5' Door	2.5' x12'x6"	1
	Corner	R1.5'x12'x6"	4
Floor Panel	A	R1.5'x 2'3"x1'6"	4
	B	4'0"x1'6"	8
	C	2'3"x7'6"	4
	D	4'0"x7'6"	8
Roof	A	R1.5'x18'0"x1'6"	2
	B	18'0"x5'0"	2
	C	18'0"x7'6"	1
Base	A		4
	B		8
	C		4
	D		8
Foundation			10

Construction	Manufacturing
3,000 Components	100 Components
8 Months	8 Hours
19 Tons of Concrete	0 Tons
13,837 Board-feet of Lumber	0 Board-feet of Lumber
3,061 sq/ft of Insulation	0 sq/ft of Insulation
11-39 Sub-Contractors	0 Sub-Contractors
1 Years Warranty	10 Years Warranty
Insurance- $6,000 / Year	Included

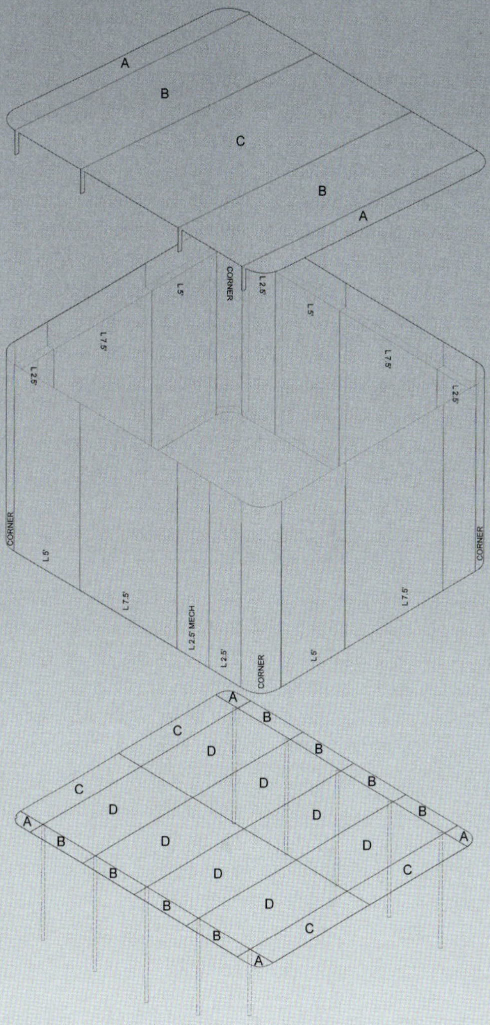

11% of the mass
10% of the time
10 % of the energy

81 components, 13,000 pounds. Fewer parts means less transit energy.

Bill of Material (BOM)

75–90% less mass while maintaining durability and other performance criteria is critical.
Less embodied / manufacturing and shipping energy.

Less mass = faster installation
Mass per house (kg per m^2).
Fewer parts / components and assemblies.

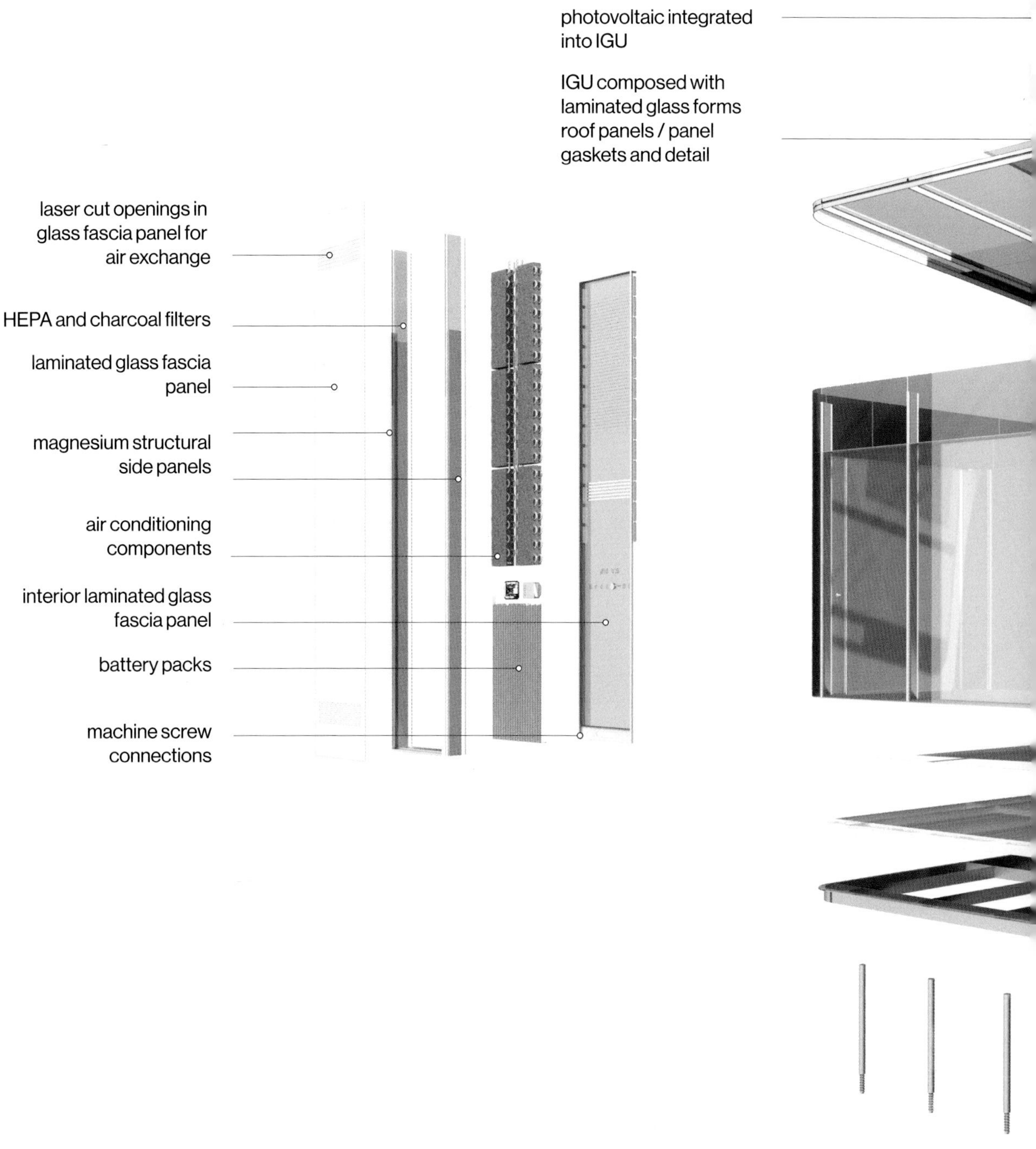
photovoltaic integrated into IGU
IGU composed with laminated glass forms roof panels / panel gaskets and detail
laser cut openings in glass fascia panel for air exchange
HEPA and charcoal filters
laminated glass fascia panel
magnesium structural side panels
air conditioning components
interior laminated glass fascia panel
battery packs
machine screw connections

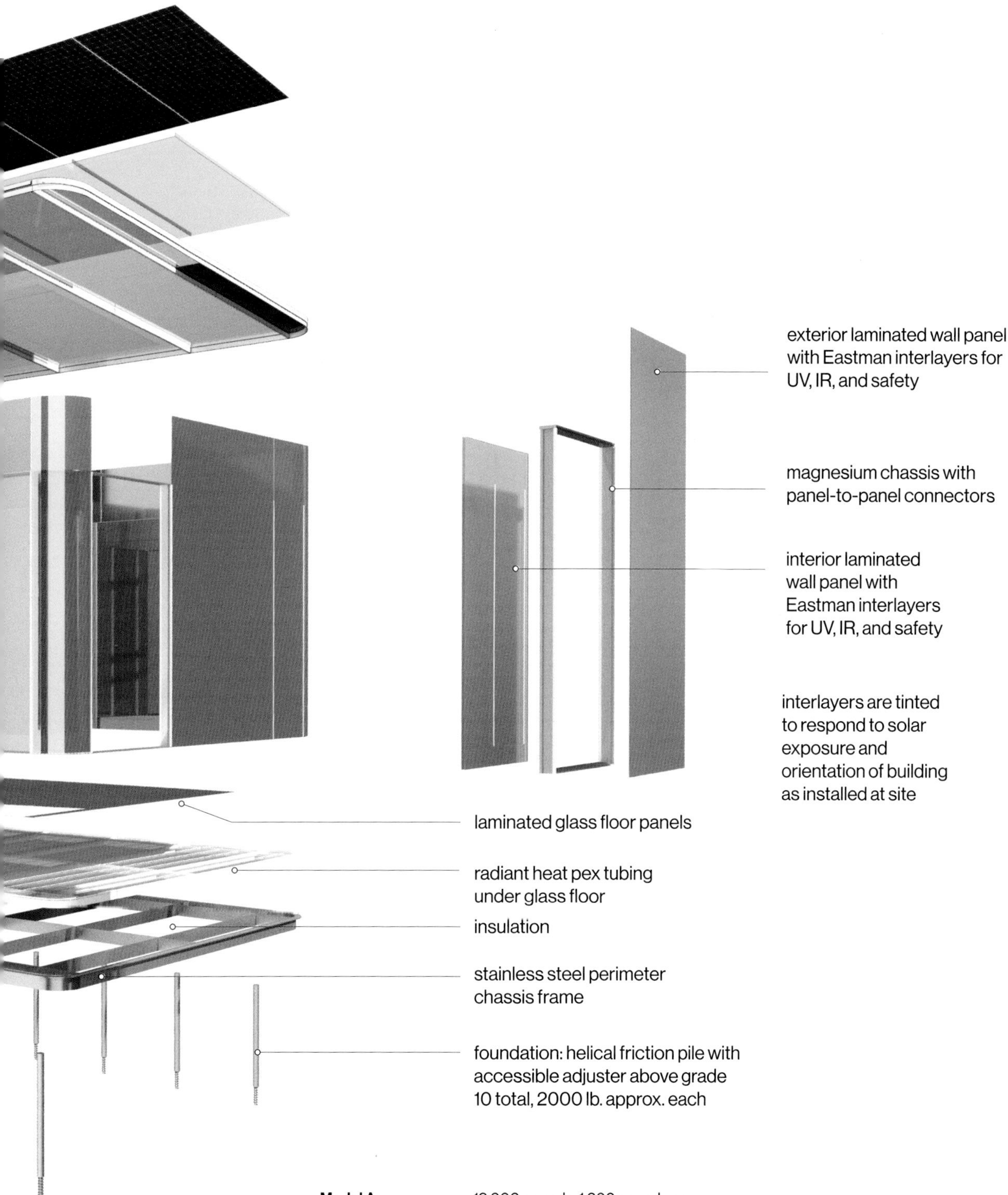

Model A 13,000 pounds, 1,300 pounds per foundation mini-pile.

Model B

Six-inch-deep structurally insulated glass panels.

Separate interior and exterior laminated-glass lites allow distinct interlayers providing unique color gradations.

Customized shading and coloration can be calibrated to unique locations and environments.

High levels of transparency on north-facing elevations fuses the interior with nature.

Manufacturing with high levels of precision is afforded by the most advanced materials.

Dramatic new benchmarks are achieved in housing production and provision of shelter.

Precision allows speed and a new level of affordability, opening entirely new markets.

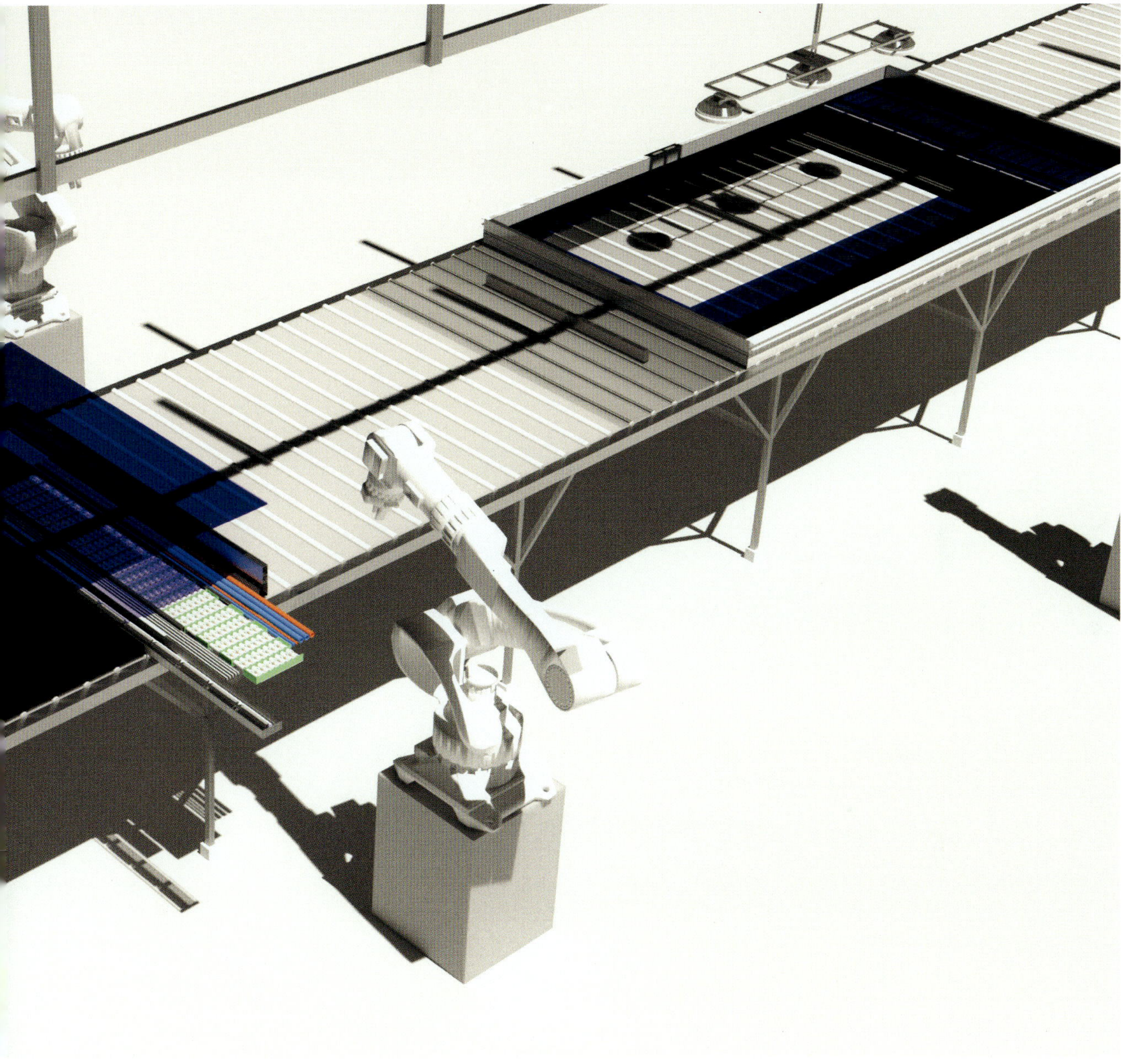

Model B: Structurally Insulated Glass Panel: Design for Manufacturing, or DFM

We curate existing materials and technologies from automobile and electronics industries and integrate them into residential products. We develop new materials with higher durability and lower masses, enabling a larger scale and faster production. Cassette packaging allows easy installation and upgrading of power, battery storage, and plumbing, combining building and energy products. Key innovations: Thin laminated glass that does not require traditional strengthening and embedded energy. Shelter and housing gain an entirely new and more advanced supply chain with a seamless flow from manufacturing to transit to end-use.

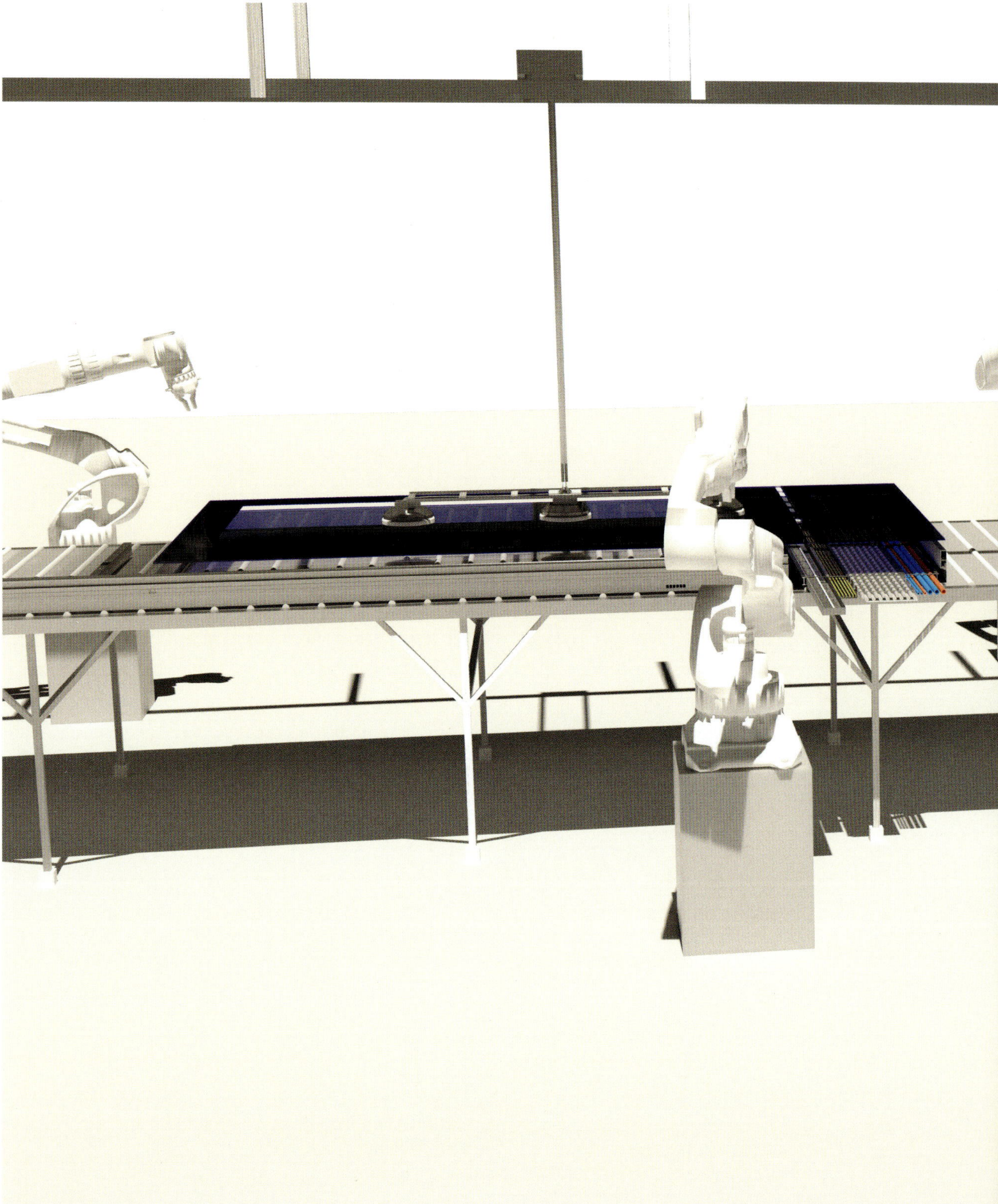

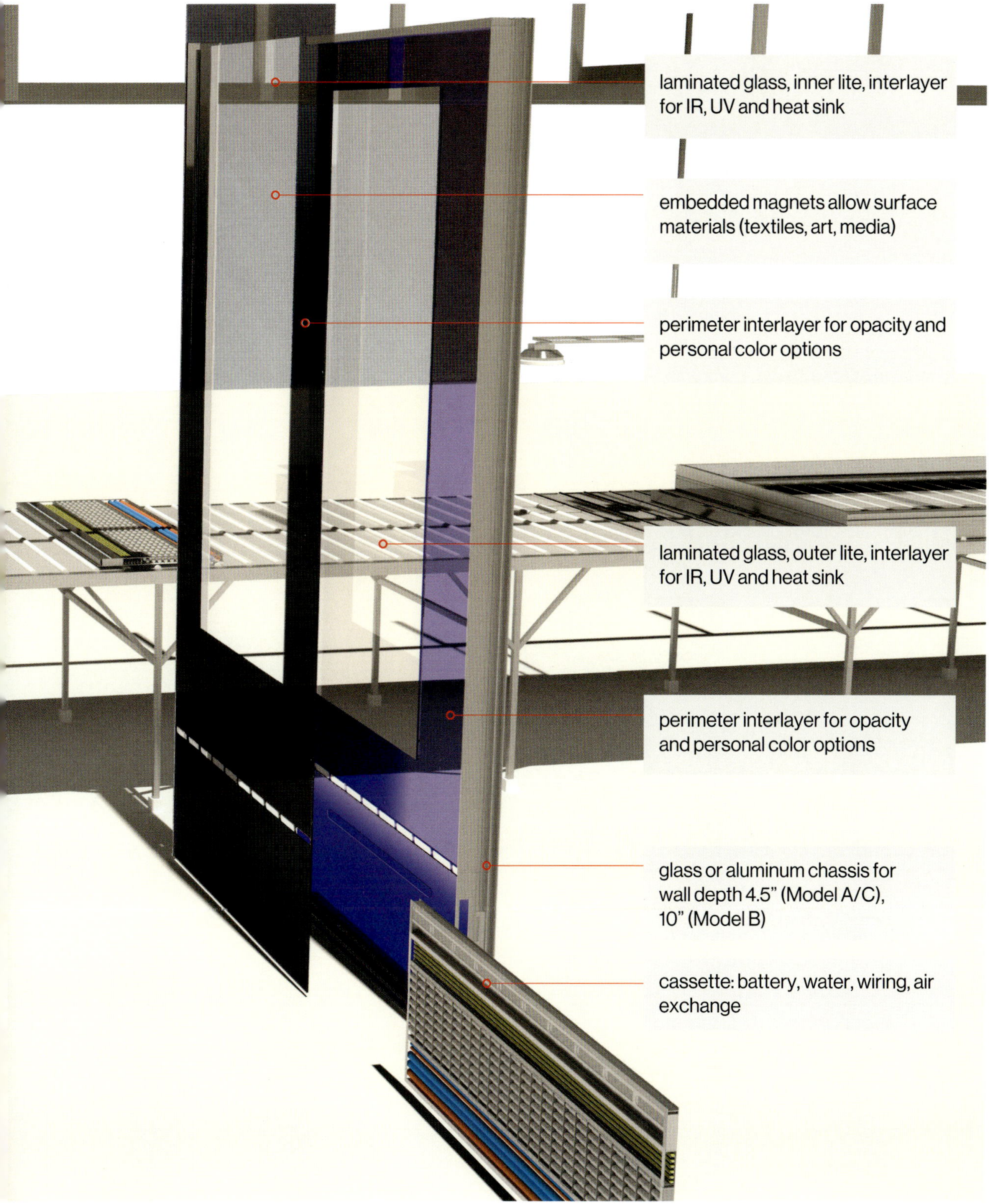
laminated glass, inner lite, interlayer for IR, UV and heat sink
embedded magnets allow surface materials (textiles, art, media)
perimeter interlayer for opacity and personal color options
laminated glass, outer lite, interlayer for IR, UV and heat sink
perimeter interlayer for opacity and personal color options
glass or aluminum chassis for wall depth 4.5" (Model A/C), 10" (Model B)
cassette: battery, water, wiring, air exchange

Model B and Model A

There were never on the grid. They are transparent, invisible to nature.

Model B and Model A

Monthly Cost *Sales Price/ Mortgage*	Solar Bank *Solar Income in Lieu of Interest*	Energy Sale *Export encrypted solar energy*		Reach *How many households can afford?*
$800 $121,650 / 15 yrs / 2.3%	$22,304 Interest / 15 Years	$124 Amortized Interest - Solar Income	15.0%	101,000,000
$900 $137,000 / 15 yrs / 2.3%	$25,119 Interest / 15 Years	$140 Amortized Interest - Solar Income	15.5%	96,885,000 total I - $12.56 b (100K units / 5 yrs)
$1,000 $152,000 / 15 yrs / 2.3%	$27,869 Interest / 15 Years	$156 Amortized Interest - Solar Income	15.6%	91,183,000
$1,300 $197,800 / 15 yrs / 2.3%	$36,266 Interest / 15 Years	$201 Amortized Interest - Solar Income	15.5%	80,834,000
$1,500 $228,800 / 15 yrs / 2.3%	$41,840 Interest / 15 Years	$232 Amortized Interest - Solar Income	15.5%	71,585,000 total I - $2.092 b (10K units / 5 yrs)
$1,644 $250,000 / 15 yrs / 2.3%	$45,837 Interest / 15 Years	$255 Amortized Interest - Solar Income	15.5%	67,054,000

Model C — 400 square feet (ADU) is an evolution of Model A.

The radial corners of Model A were replaced by a magnesium corner gasket that provides an integrated roof drainage gutter and also serves to anchor the building's tie-rod tension connections.

The building is composed of fewer parts than Model A and effectively bound together by tension. Its assembly and disassembly is a result of few mechanical connections that are visible and accessible, with specialty tools for safety.

Model C

The solar array is inboard of the building envelope and visible through the gradient of the building's laminated-glass structure and enclosure.

Glass beams are anchored in the enclosing glass panels and seated in nylon saddles. They integrate to form a diaphragm structure composed entirely of glass.

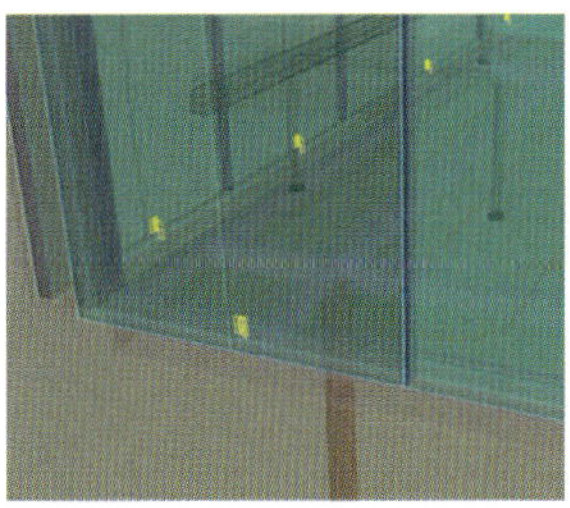

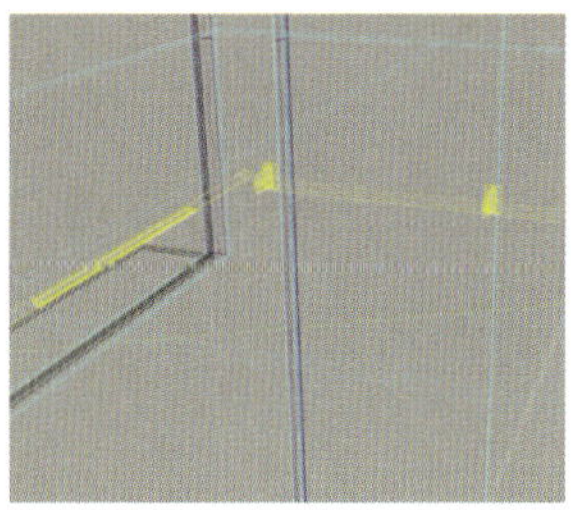

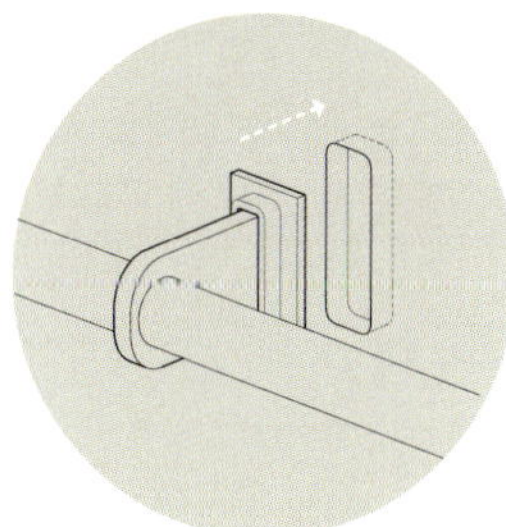

Model C

Tie rods connect to precisely set anchors at the midpoint of each glass panel. Similar anchors seat the panel in relation to the roof and floor.

The assembly is a process of integers, each precisely coordinated by factory-set anchors.

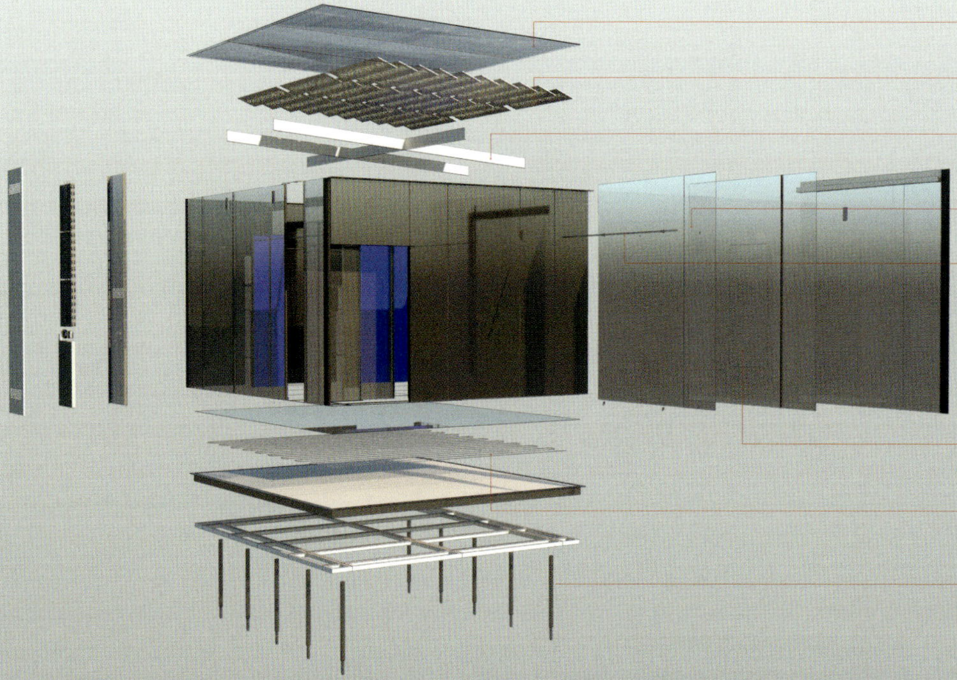

A proprietary manufacturing that cannot be replicated. We design the factory and its machines.

Laminated glass beams and magnesium tension rods form diaphragm structure.
Glass panels are not mechanically connected at perimeter but suspended from center.

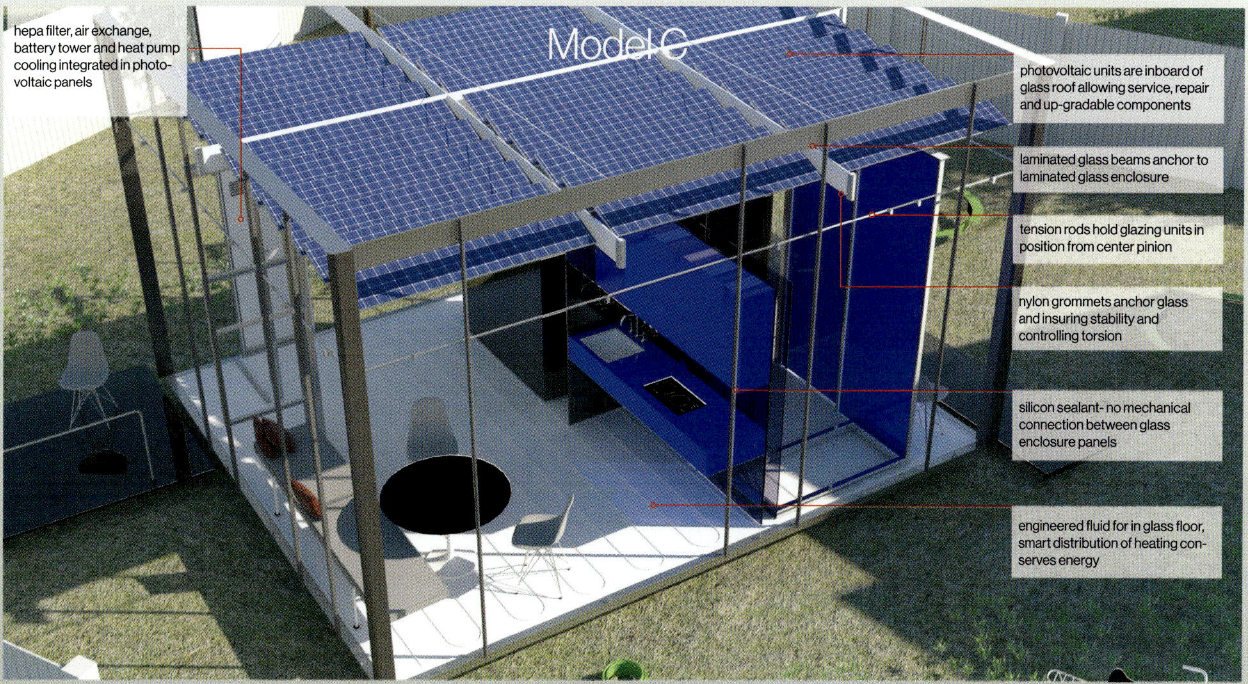
Model C
hepa filter, air exchange, battery tower and heat pump cooling integrated in photo-voltaic panels
photovoltaic units are inboard of glass roof allowing service, repair and up-gradable components
laminated glass beams anchor to laminated glass enclosure
tension rods hold glazing units in position from center pinion
nylon grommets anchor glass and insuring stability and controlling torsion
silicon sealant- no mechanical connection between glass enclosure panels
engineered fluid for in glass floor, smart distribution of heating con-serves energy

Model C

Model C

A chance to resettle close to your former home and maintain connections to people and places.

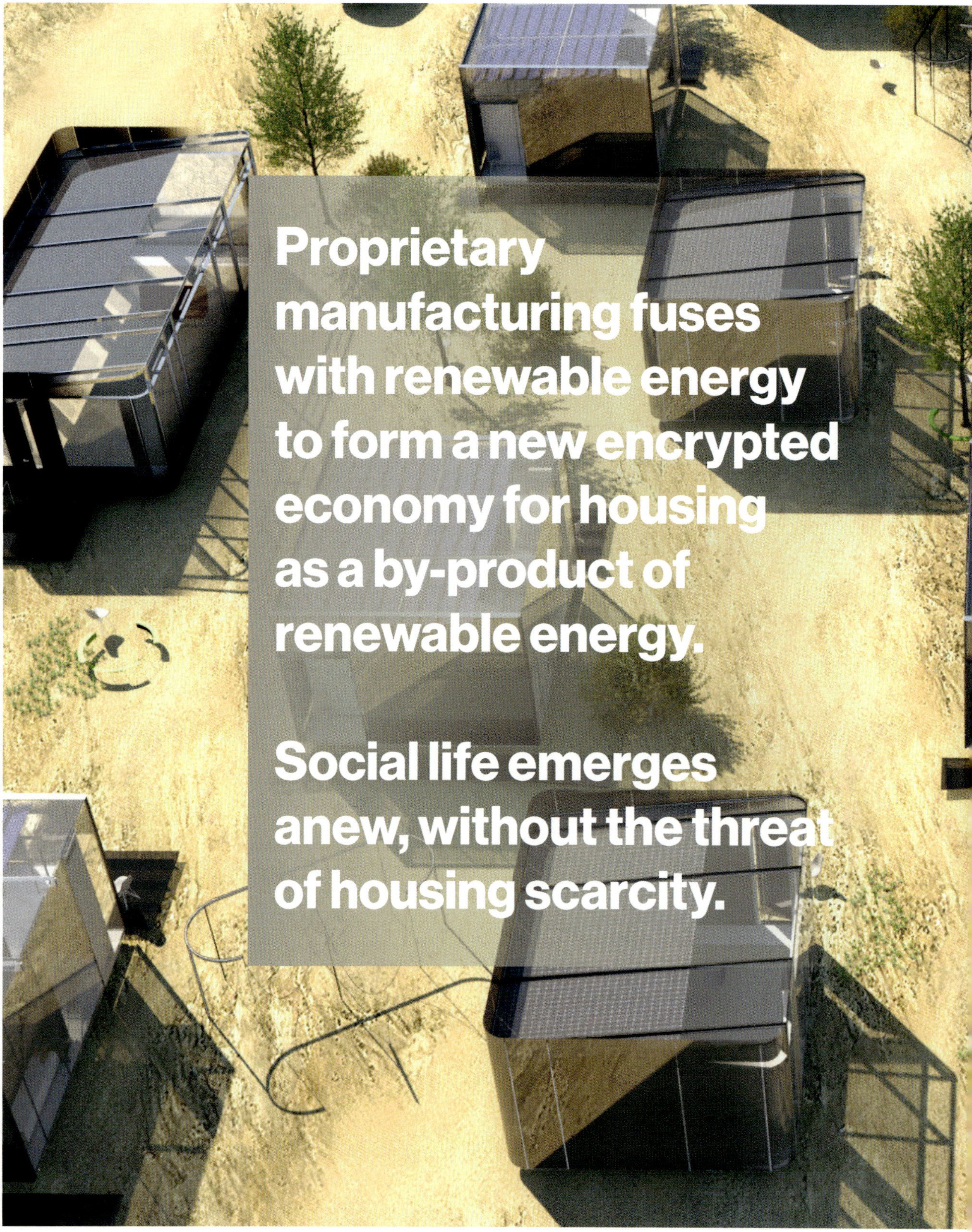

Proprietary manufacturing fuses with renewable energy to form a new encrypted economy for housing as a by-product of renewable energy.

Social life emerges anew, without the threat of housing scarcity.

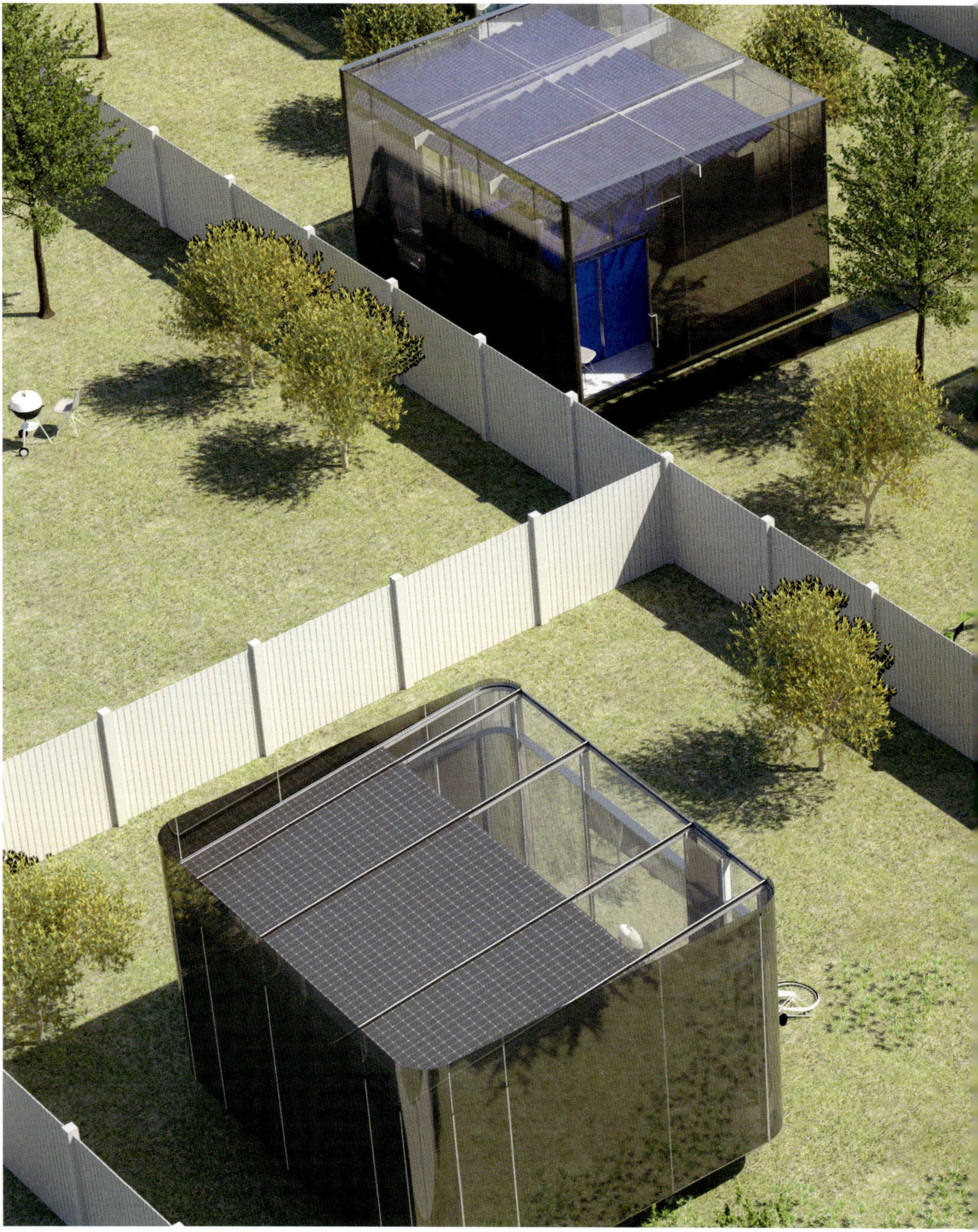

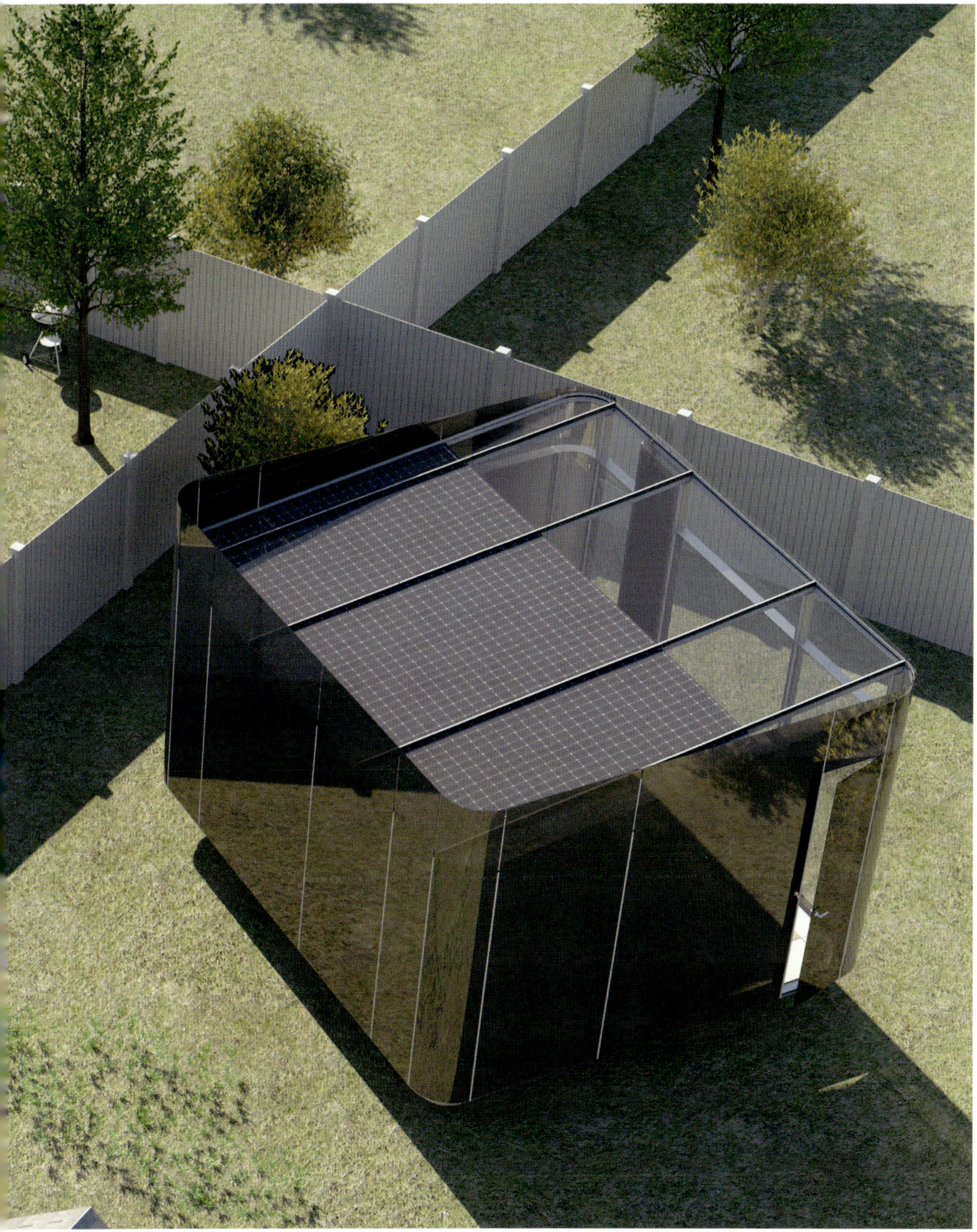

Biographies

Eunjeong Seong is a registered architect in New York and co-founder of Bell-Seong Architecture and of Visible Weather, a research and design collaboration founded to work with partners in advanced manufacturing, materials, energy, engineering, and housing finance/economics.

Seong's architectural and urban design work has been commissioned by the Museum of Modern Art, the Westbund Biennale, Shanghai, and Columbia University Graduate School of Architecture, Planning and Preservation / Studio X, Beijing. Seong's writing and design has been published by the Museum of Modern Art, *Architectural Design* (AD, London), *Technology, Architecture, Design* (TAD) and *Log*. Her firm's work has also been featured on MSNBC, Fox Business News and Reuters.

Seong is a member of faculty at Pratt Institute where she is an Adjunct Associate Professor of Architecture, CCE. Seong is Coordinator for the Fourth Year Design Studios and teaches studio courses as well as seminars in housing, housing policy and economics and architectural tectonics. Seong has taught at Cornell University, Rensselaer Polytechnic Institute, Parsons School of Design, and Rhode Island School of Design.

Seong's experience in practice includes design roles at SHoP and Dean/Wolf Architects. She also opened and directed a New York City satellite office for Yamasaki Associates where she led a team to develop design work for the firm with New York based engineers and consultants. Seong was a designer at SPACE GROUP in Seoul, Korea and New York contributing editor and writer for the firm's long running journal *SPACE*. Seong holds a Master of Architecture Degree from Columbia University Graduate School of Architecture, Planning and Preservation, and an undergraduate degree in Architectural Engineering from Inha University, Incheon, Korea.

Michael Bell, Professor at Columbia University Graduate School of Architecture, Planning and Preservation(GSAPP) is founding Chair of the Columbia Conference on Architecture, Engineering and Materials, a research program in coordination with Columbia's Fu Foundation School of Engineering and Applied Science and the Institute for Lightweight Structures and Conceptual Design (ILEK), the University of Stuttgart. Bell served as a Director of the Master of Architecture Studios, GSAPP (1999-2015) and Coordinator of the GSAPP Housing Studios (1999 -2011).

Bell's architectural design has been commissioned by the Museum of Modern Art, New York and is included in the permanent collection of the San Francisco Museum of Modern Art. His Binocular House is included in *American Masterwork Houses of the 20th and 21st Century* by Kenneth Frampton. Books by Michael Bell include: *Engineered Transparency, The Technical, Visual, and Spatial Effects of Glass; Solid States, Concrete in Transition; Post-Ductility, Metals in Architecture and Engineering; Permanent Change, Plastics in Architecture and Engineering; 16 Houses: Owning a House in the City; Michael Bell: Space Replaces Us*; and *Slow Space*. Bell founded 16 Houses: Owning a House in the City—a collaboration with the Fifth Ward Community Redevelopment Corporation and DiverseWorks in Houston—as an attempt to bridge innovative architecture in ways that expanded access to housing.

Bell has taught at the University of California, Berkeley and Rice University School of Architecture. He served as the Saarinen Visiting Professor of Architecture at the University of Michigan; the Friedman Professor in Architecture at Berkeley; and was a Fellow at the Joint Center for Housing Studies, Harvard. In 2016 Bell was Visiting Professor at the Stanford University, School of Engineering, Center for Design Research. Michael Bell received a Master of Architecture degree from the University of California, Berkeley and a Bachelor of Science degree, the Catholic University of America, Washington DC.

Acknowledgements

This book benefits from a long-term engagement with housing, housing economics, and policy, as well as engineering, building physics, materials, and more recently, design for manufacturing. The role of renewable energy binds this together. Our enthusiasm would not have been possible without Michael Pilliod and Wills Sweney. Their expertise is embedded in the proposals shared in Part Two, Encrypting the Sun. Thomas Powers has been a foundational figure. His reading of our earliest outlines, critiquing and suggesting its architectural design and goals, and helping shape and guide the entire team, has been invaluable and irreplaceable.

At the Columbia University Graduate School of Architecture, Planning and Preservation (GSAPP) we thank Amale Andraos, dean emeritus, and Andrés Jaque, dean, for their encouragement and support.

At Pratt Institute School of Architecture we thank Harriet Harriss, dean emeritus, for her insight and encouragement.

At the Stanford University School of Engineering, Larry Leifer, founder and director of the Center for Design Research (CDR), provided the opportunity to be in residence as a visiting professor. At the CDR we expanded our ideas through colloquiums and lectures. We thank Chris Ford (CDR) for his role as a critic and as an editor at *Technology | Architecture + Design* (TAD).

Michael Shanks, professor of classics and archeology at Stanford University, lent his insight to every part of this project, joining CDR colloquiums we ran, and hosting us in his courses and at the Ng House, Stanford. Michael critiqued the design work and goals as well as joining design studio reviews at Columbia and hosting our students at Stanford.

Critical opportunities to present work in progress were created by Jonathan Massey and Marc Norman at the California College of the Arts (CCA) in San Francisco and the University of Michigan. Yung Ho Chang, Zheng Tan, and Xiangning Li provided lecture and symposium opportunities at Tongji University, Shanghai. Cynthia Davidson and Elisa Iturbe invited us to publish an early version of "Encrypting the Sun" in *Log*. Hina Jamelle's University of Pennsylvania conference and book titled *Under Pressure* provided an early opportunity to frame our work.

Work we began with Barry Bergdoll and Reinhold Martin as participants in the Museum of Modern Art workshop and exhibition *Foreclosed: Rehousing the American Dream* is still central here. Our long-time collaborators from *Foreclosed* critiqued and engaged this new work: Jesse Keenan's research in climate change and real estate; Zachary Kostura's building physics; and Rosanne Haggerty's and Nadine Maleh's work in homelessness and housing systems. Mohsen Mostafavi and Eric Belsky offered the opportunity to serve as a fellow at the Harvard University Joint Center for Housing Studies.

Richard Plunz and Gwendolyn Wright—as mentors and friends—have given long standing and essential support. Thom Mayne, Sanford Kwinter, Steven Holl, Jonathan Crary, Stanley Saitowitz, John Parman, Catherine Ingraham, Elliott Sclar, and Kenneth Frampton have inspired us and offered critiques of this work as it developed. At Berkeley we are grateful to Jennifer Wolch, dean emeritus, and Carol Galante for feedback and engaging us in a Terner Center for Housing Innovation and Fisher Center for Real Estate + Urban Economics conference and retreat. Patricia McShane and Erik Adigard (MADxs) as early advisors helped us visualize the book's economic information graphically.

At Pratt we thank Architecture Chairs Erika Hinrichs, David Erdman, and Stephen Slaughter for opportunities to take on focused work on housing, and Frederick Biehle for his collaboration on three IDC Foundation design studios focused on mass timber and housing. Lawrence Blough and John Szot generously responded during a symposium focused on an early version of this research. Deborah Gans' work as an architect and educator is an inspiration. Thanks to Thomas Hanrahan, dean emeritus, and to Quilian Riano, dean, who have shaped housing as a central concern at Pratt.

Young Sohn, Mark Armenante, and Evan Sharp offered insight into their experience creating and scaling technology companies. Young and Mark, current owners of the Binocular House, gave our team access to the renewed house, which we originally built for Philip Gefter and Richard Press. Philip and Richard helped forge this project with their vision for glass and architecture.

In our office, Sunghoon Lee and Eunkyoung Kim were invaluable and essential: their energy and talent show in this work.

Kenn Sparks, emeritus head, US corporate communications and national spokesperson, BMW of North America, has helped our team shape and imagine the design at the scale of manufacturing.

David Nieh engaged this project and our wider team during its entire evolution. We benefited from David's vision for development in an era of climate change, gaining opportunities for formal and casual discussions. David's optimism and generosity allowed us to gain insight from Marc Porat, Charlotte Pera, and Arun Majumdar.

Rosanne Haggerty, founder and president of Community Solutions, was the first person we shared the idea for this book with. We believe that the future-oriented forecasting of need that drives Community Solutions is essential in an era of rapid change.

Richard Bender, dean emeritus, UC Berkeley College of Environmental Design, was a frequent and important reader and critic. Richard's empathy as a teacher with real-world experience was invaluable.

Special thanks to Stephen Zacks whose own career in housing, urbanism, and architecture enhanced our writing as text editor. Stephen had written about the Binocular House at its completion in 2008 for *Metropolis*.

Ramon Prat's insight from a career of fostering and enabling architectural and urban discourse as the founder of Actar spurred us on. We were honored that he accepted to take on our project.

Published by:
Actar Publishers
New York_Barcelona

440 Park Avenue South, 17th Floor
New York, New York 10016, US

Roca i Batlle 2-4
Barcelona, ES

Library of Congress Catalog-in-Publication-Data

First Edition. Actar Publishers, 2025
Printed in Europe

ISBN I978-1-63840-183-4

Book Designers: Ramon Prat
Schematic Design: Eunjeong Seong, Michael Bell

Editor: Ramon Prat
Text Editor: Stephen Zacks